THE GALESIA TRILOGY
and
SELECTED MANUSCRIPT POE[...]

OF

Jane Bark[...]

WOMEN WRITERS IN ENGLISH
1350–1850

GENERAL EDITORS

Susanne Woods and Elizabeth H. Hageman

MANAGING EDITOR

Elizabeth Terzakis

SECTION EDITORS

Carol Barash

Stuart Curran

Margaret J. M. Ezell

Elizabeth H. Hageman

Sara Jayne Steen

WOMEN WRITERS PROJECT

Brown University

THE GALESIA TRILOGY

AND

SELECTED MANUSCRIPT

POEMS

OF

Jane Barker

EDITED BY

Carol Shiner Wilson

New York   Oxford

OXFORD UNIVERSITY PRESS

1997

Oxford University Press

Oxford   New York

Athens   Auckland   Bangkok   Bogota   Bombay   Buenos Aires
Calcutta   Cape Town   Dar es Salaam   Delhi   Florence   Hong Kong
Istanbul   Karachi   Kuala Lumpur   Madras   Madrid   Melbourne
Mexico City   Nairobi   Paris   Singapore   Taipei   Tokyo   Toronto

and associated companies in
Berlin   Ibadan

Published by Oxford University Press, Inc.,
198 Madison Avenue, New York, New York 10016

Oxford is a registered trademark of Oxford University Press

Library of Congress Cataloging-in-Publication Data
Barker, Jane.
The Galesia trilogy and selected poems of Jane Barker / edited by
Carol Shiner Wilson.
p.   cm. — (Women writers in English 1350–1850)
ISBN 0-19-508650-3; ISBN 0-19-508651-1 (pbk.)
I. Wilson, Carol Shiner, 1946-   .   II. Title.   III. Series.
PR3316.B28A6   1997
828'.409—dc20   96-12314

This volume was supported in part by the National Endowment
for the Humanities, an independent federal agency.

1 3 5 7 9 8 6 4 2
Printed in the United States of America
on acid-free paper

This volume is dedicated to
the Memory of my Mother, Nelda Shiner
and to Daniel, my dearest friend

CONTENTS

FOREWORD

Women Writers in English 1350–1850 presents texts of cultural and literary interest in the English-speaking tradition, often for the first time since their original publication. Most of the writers represented in the series were well known and highly regarded until the professionalization of English studies in the later nineteenth century coincided with their excision from canonical status and from the majority of literary histories.

The purpose of this series is to make available a wide range of unfamiliar texts by women, thus challenging the common assumption that women wrote little of real value before the Victorian period. While no one can doubt the relative difficulty women experienced in writing for an audience before that time, or indeed have encountered since, this series shows that women nonetheless had been writing from early on and in a variety of genres, that they maintained a clear eye to readers, and that they experimented with an interesting array of literary strategies for claiming their authorial voices. Despite the tendency to treat the powerful fictions of Virginia Woolf's *A Room of One's Own* (1928) as if they were fact, we now know, against her suggestion to the contrary, that there were many "Judith Shakespeares," and that not all of them died lamentable deaths before fulfilling their literary ambitions.

This series is unique in at least two ways. It offers, for the first time, concrete evidence of a rich and lively heritage of women writing in English before the mid-nineteenth century, and it is based on one of the most sophisticated and forward-looking electronic resources in the world: the Brown University Women Writers Project textbase (full text database) of works by early women writers. The Brown University Women Writers Project (WWP) was established in 1988 with a grant from the National Endowment for the Humanities, which continues to assist in its development.

Women Writers in English 1350–1850 is a print publication project derived from the WWP. It offers lightly annotated versions based on single good copies or, in some cases, collated versions of texts with more complex editorial histories, normally in their original spelling. The editions are aimed at a wide audience, from the informed undergraduate through professional students of literature, and they attempt to include the general reader who is interested in exploring a fuller tradition of early texts in English than has been available through the almost exclusively male canonical tradition.

SUSANNE WOODS
ELIZABETH H. HAGEMAN
General Editors

ACKNOWLEDGMENTS

The collaborative effort that is the Women Writers Project thrives on the contributions of all its members. Ongoing thanks are due to Brown University and its administrators, especially President Vartan Gregorian, Provost Frank Rothman, Dean of the Faculty Bryan Shepp, and Vice President Brian Hawkins. Members of the Brown English Department, particularly Elizabeth Kirk, Stephen Foley, and William Keach, have provided indispensable advice; many thanks to Marilyn Netter for her help in finding the WWP a new director. Gratitude is also owed to Don Wolfe, of Brown's Computing and Information Services. At Brown's Scholarly Technology Group, Geoffrey Bilder and Elli Mylonas are unfailingly resourceful and obliging in all matters, and Allen Renear is a rare source of energy and inspiration.

Working with Oxford University Press is always a pleasure; many thanks to Elizabeth Maguire for making the Series possible and to Claude Conyers for his unlimited patience, his unfailing sense of humor, and the laugh that goes with both.

A more committed set of colleagues than the WWP staff is hard to imagine. Project Coordinator Maria Fish facilitates all contacts with the outside world with her unerring knowledge of protocol and her considerable diplomatic skills. The computer textbase from which this volume was drawn approaches perfection largely through the efforts of Carole Mah and Syd Bauman. I thank Julia Flanders for defining the position of managing editor and easing me into the very big shoes she left behind. New Director Carol DeBoer-Langworthy deserves thanks for bringing a hearty serving of Midwestern pragmatism into the office. Others who have made this series possible include Elizabeth Adams, Anthony Arnove, Rebecca Bailey, Kim Bordner, Susie Castellanos, Paul Caton, Nick Daly, Cathleen Drake, Faye Halpern, Loren Noveck, Anastasia Porter, Kasturi Ray, Caleb Rounds, and Kristen Whissel.

ELIZABETH TERZAKIS
Managing Editor

ACKNOWLEDGMENTS

All scholarly texts are a collaboration in the broadest sense. I would like to thank many splendid collaborators for their contributions to this volume.

This project grew out of a 1990 National Endowment for the Humanities summer seminar on women writers, led by Stuart Curran at the University of Pennsylvania. I am grateful to Professor Curran for his continued support and encouragement. Much of the European archival work was accomplished during the summer of 1994. The NEH summer seminar on Biography and Biographical Methods, led by Paula R. Backscheider and held at the Public Record Office in London, was an important part of that summer. My thanks to Professor Backscheider for her support of this project. I also appreciate the support of a grant from the American Philosophical Society for research in France and England and for a grant from Muhlenberg College to support the transcription of *Love Intrigues*.

The entire Muhlenberg College library staff has been encouraging throughout this process. I am grateful for the patience and persistence of Scherelene Schatz, Interlibrary Loan, and Kris Heintzelman, and to Barbara Eastland and Linda Bowers. I am also indebted to librarians Daniel Traister, University of Pennsylvania; Christine Ferdinand, Magdalen College, Oxford; Georgianna Ziegler, the Folger Shakespeare Library; Frances Harris, the British Library; Neville Thompson, the Winterthur Library; Lisa Browar, the New York Public Library; Diane Shaw and Rani Sinha, Lafayette College; Philip Metzger and Marie Boltz, Lehigh University; and to archivists Margaret Connor and Ruth Paley, Public Record Office; Jacques Louet, Archives municipales de Saint-Germain-en-Laye; Rachel Watson, Northamptonshire Record Office; and Lady Sheila de Bellaigue, the Royal Archives. My thanks as well to staff members at the Houghton Library, Bodleian Library, Public Record Office, Lincolnshire Record Office, Northamptonshire Record Office, Corporation of London Records Office, Victoria and Albert Museum, the Royal Commission on Historical Manuscripts at Quality House, and the Archives Nationales, Paris.

I am particularly grateful to my Feminist Research Group for their thoughtful responses to early drafts of the Introduction and for the spirit of warmth and encouragement, personal and professional, that has permeated our community of scholars for the past decade. I also thank Kathryn R. King for her patience and generosity during and after our London research on Barker, and I thank Jeslyn Medoff for her enthusiasm and keen editorial eye. These scholars responded to early drafts of the Introduction to this volume, and I benefitted from an early reading of a manuscript on their archival research on Barker's life and family history. I also appreciate the generosity of Edward T. Corp, who is working on a history of the Jacobites in Saint-Germain-en-Laye; William J. Tighe; Howard Marblestone; Darrell Jodock; and Carl Oplinger. Eveline Cruickshanks, Natalie Genet-Rouffiac, Toni Bowers, and Carol Barash were also most helpful. Alan Mittleman, James Bloom, Cecilia del Castillo, and Didier Jungo have contributed uniquely to the spirit of this work. Others who have advanced this project are Peter Beal, Terry Belander, Peter-John Byrnes, Vinton Dearing, Patrice DiQuinzio, Jane Flood, David L. Gants, Jay Hartman, Jack Kolb, Margarete Lamb-Faffelberger, Janet Loengard, Linda Merians, Elaine Petkus, Martha Reid, Judy Schlegel, Larry E. Shiner, Laura Snodgrass, Alan Tjeltveit, Lynn Van Dyke, Virginia Wiles, Robert Wind, James Winn, James Woolley, and Steven Zwicker. Student readers who provided helpful responses to early drafts of the novels and notes were Navtika Desai, Johanna Hollway, Anthony Kennedy, Corinne Orts, Nancy Siefert, Tiana Shekari, Christopher Simar, and Kristine Wilton.

The colleagues whom I have come to know through the Women Writers Project are patient, professional, and impressively committed to the celebration of women writers. I could always depend upon Margaret J. M. Ezell's wit and generosity in her readings of the Introduction and apparatus, as well as her tact and diplomacy whenever needed. I could also depend upon Elizabeth H. Hageman's fine editorial suggestions and her commitment to textual integrity. My thanks go also to Julia Flanders, Elizabeth Terzakis, Carol DeBoer-Langworthy, and Susanne Woods.

At Muhlenberg College, I have been most fortunate in the encouragement, support, and goodwill of Arthur Taylor, president, and Kathryn Taylor; Deans Richard Hatch and Curtis Dretsch; and Thomas Cartelli, head of the Department of English. At the Lehigh Valley Association of Independent Colleges, I appreciate the encouragement of Galen Godbey, executive director, and members of the Women's Studies Coalition. I wish I could thank by name other supportive colleagues at lunch and academic functions, neighbors, and other friends in the United States, Europe, and Asia who have listened indulgently to tales of Jane Barker and of editing joys and woes.

I can never adequately thank my extraordinary family: Larry, Kay, Richard, Mary P., and, most of all, Daniel. I am, moreover, particularly grateful to my parents, educators Nelda and Ernest Shiner, and my grandmother, Lula P. Wetz, whose lifetime love of learning was perhaps their greatest gift.

CAROL SHINER WILSON

INTRODUCTION

The eighty years from Jane Barker's birth in Northamptonshire in 1652 to her death in France in 1732 mark one of the most turbulent, perilous, and anxious periods in English history. Endless wars at home and abroad, virulent religious intolerance, and the very real fear of dying from plague were just a few of the crises that affected how women and men conducted their lives. Those politically complicated and dangerous years were also marked by an energy and vitality in the literary landscape that rivals any age. A publishing explosion of both imaginative literature and non-fiction accompanied a growth in the literacy rate and an increase in the number of writers, women and men, who wrote for a living rather than pursued aesthetic and intellectual ends in genteel circles. The life and literary oeuvre of Jane Barker provide rich insights into the multifaceted, complicated, shifting intersections of public and private history in this tumultuous period. Her fiction, much of it written for popular appeal, and her poetry, much of it privately circulated, illuminate important issues of her age from the perspective of a person several times marginalized: woman unmarried by choice, learned lady, Jacobite, convert to Roman Catholicism, and published author.

Scholars such as Margaret J. M. Ezell in *Writing Women's Literary History* have focused on women writers in the 1600s and 1700s in order to expand, challenge, and reconfigure theories about a female tradition that have grown out of feminist studies of women's literature and lives in the nineteenth and twentieth centuries.[1] In her ground-breaking 1983 article on Barker, Jane Spencer acknowledged that Barker's poems and fiction were intensely autobiographical. Spencer's enterprise was not to verify actual links to Barker's life but to investigate those parts of the texts that portrayed Barker's mythic self-definition "as a woman and a writer, and [her creation of] a self-image that would be acceptable to

---

1. See Margaret J. M. Ezell, *Writing Women's Literary History* (Baltimore: Johns Hopkins, 1993).

herself and to her public."[1] That self-representation—shaped primarily through Barker's semi-autobiographical protagonist and narrator Galesia—included identities as a committed literary artist, energetic spinster (the legal term for an unmarried woman at the time), student of the healing arts, devoted sister, manager of agricultural property, and fervent political partisan. Barker shaped, reshaped, and foregrounded those identities, singly or in combination, as she constructed a very particular narrative about her life as an independently thinking woman devoted to high ideals—whether in politics, art, or religion—and engaged in meaningful action in community. That identity does not ignore the practical side, since economic survival, particularly problematic for women dependent upon men, informs much of her literary oeuvre. Although Galesia is the persona who speaks most often, Fidelia is Barker's reflective poetic alter ego in the unpublished verse of the late 1600s. Barker's self-conscious presentation of her numerous identities has led scholars to list those identities in order to capture and communicate the variety of her life.[2] Some conclusions about the links between the lists and Barker's actual life have proven accurate, but often, too, her recasting of material and her selective silences have misled scholars. Most scholars, for example, have assumed that Barker had only one brother since she mentions only Edward in her poetry and fiction. The discovery of a virtually disinherited brother Henry in extra-literary sources forces us to consider Barker's reticence regarding his existence and the possibility of other selective silences.[3]

---

1. Jane Spencer, "Creating the Woman Writer: The Autobiographical Works of Jane Barker," *Tulsa Studies in Women's Literature* 2 (Fall, 1983): 166. For an early full-length study relying primarily on the imaginative literature, see Karl Stanglmaier, *Mrs. Jane Barker: Ein Beitrag zur Englishchen Literaturgeschichte*, doctoral dissertation, K.B. Ludwig-Maximilians-Universitat zu Munchen (Berlin: 1906); microfilm: New Haven, Connecticut: Research Publications, 1977.

2. See, for example, Spencer, 167, and Kathryn R. King and Jeslyn Medoff, "Jane Barker (1652–1732) and Her Life: The Documentary Record," note 1, p. xvii.

3. Northamptonshire Record Office (hereafter cited as NRO), Blatherwycke Parish Register, 1621–89, 34 P/1. The existence of Henry Barker had been overlooked until research for this study.

How does this extra-literary evidence help us avoid biographical reductionism and appreciate other dimensions of her texts? The question is central to scholars' inquiry into many women writers of the period, especially writers of so-called noncanonical literature who are being rediscovered and studied seriously. Because personal evidence such as letters or journals rarely exists for these women, literary scholars must examine kinds of documents more commonly used by social historians like Lawrence Stone in *The Family, Sex and Marriage in England, 1500–1800* (1977), Natalie Zemon Davis in *The Return of Martin Guerre* (1983), and N. J. G. Pounds in *The Culture of the English People* (1994). Moreover, evidence for their lives must often be traced through the records of male members of the family since, if married, a woman had no independent legal standing. Her name might appear within a document such as a will or, in this highly litigious era, in lawsuits over inheritance rights or property. For this study of Barker's life, literary works, and times, I drew on documents in France as varied as registers of baptisms, burials, and marriages in parish records; city maps; housing records; and convent and other ecclesiastical records. In England, I consulted parish records, wills, a complaint and answer at law, property leases, Papist (Catholic) oath records and oaths of allegiance to the Church of England, Coronation and Funeral rolls, and records of payments and pensions from the royal household. Scholars Kathryn R. King and Jeslyn Medoff are completing an analysis of important documents, many of which they have recently recovered, in a biographical essay on Barker.[1] Although much has been found, much remains to be found—or, as historians have long known, never to be found.

What, then, emerges from the ensemble of legal and ecclesiastical records, Barker's fiction, her poetry, and four extant letters? Parish records note her baptism on 17 May 1652 in Blatherwycke, Northamp-

---

1. King and Medoff, "Jane Barker (1652–1732) and Her Life: The Documentary Record," provide a fuller analysis of documentary sources than appropriate for this Introduction. See also Medoff's headnote on Barker in *Kissing the Rod: An Anthology of Seventeenth-Century Women's Verse*, ed. Germaine Greer, Susan Hastings, Jeslyn Medoff, and Melinda Sansone (London: Virago Press, 1988; New York: Farrar Straus Giroux, 1989). King is now completing a book on Barker's texts and contexts that focuses on her imagined communities.

tonshire.[1] Her father was Thomas Barker, a Royalist who once served in the court of Charles I,[2] and whose will shows his family bore a coat of arms.[3] His court position is noted as "Secretaire du grand sceau d'Angleterre" in Jane's burial notice, which I located in France.[4] The title, translated "Secretary to the Great Seal of England," suggests that he worked for the Lord Chancellor, Keeper of the Great Seal. The title is consistent with Barker's claim, in her incarnation as narrator Galesia, that her father held an important post before the devastations of the English Civil Wars (1642–49). Jane's mother Anne, from Cornwall, was of the respectable Connock family that could trace its ancestry to the era of William the Conqueror. Many Connocks were noted for their distinguished military service for the Stuart monarchs. Barker was proud of her royalist heritage, and an important dimension of her self-representation is as a member of two families who lost lives, property, and place—but never dignity and a sense of commitment to a moral cause—in service to the rightful heirs to the English throne. As she once wrote to the Prince of Wales, she gained "a secret satisfaction to have suffered something for such a cause."[5] Barker found important resonances in the works of other writers committed to the Stuarts, among them Katherine Philips, Aphra Behn, Anne Finch, and John Dryden.

---

1. NRO, Blatherwycke Parish Register, 1621–89, 34 P/1.

2. The sequence of English rule is important for this discussion: Charles I (1625–49), beheaded by Oliver Cromwell and Parliamentary forces; the Commonwealth (1649–60), led primarily by Oliver Cromwell; Charles II (1660–85); James II (1685–88), deposed in the Revolution of 1688; and William III (1689–1702, with Mary II until her death in 1694). James Francis Edward Stuart (b. 1688), son and heir of James II, was called James III by supporters but was never recognized as rightful King of England.

3. Public Record Office (Cited hereafter as PRO), PROB 11/367. My thanks to William J. Tighe and Kathryn R. King for their recovery of the probate record and actual will of Thomas Barker.

4. Archives Municipales de Saint-Germain-en-Laye, Registre GG 99, 45r. (Cited hereafter as Archives municipales.)

5. Dedication, "Poems on several occasions," Magdalen MS 343.

Barker's family, like many in seventeenth-century England, was caught in the bitter political and religious struggles of the Civil Wars. Those wars culminated in the beheading of the Stuart king, Charles I, and eleven years of unstable, repressive Puritan rule, much of it under the authoritarian Lord Protector, Oliver Cromwell. Barker's powerful accounts, in published and unpublished sources, of the painful losses to both her mother's and father's side echo the stories of thousands of Royalists: "in Battel slain . . . in Prison dy'd . . . ruin'd in their Estates . . . [and] Persons."[1]

The restoration of Charles II in 1660 overturned much of the sobriety and austerity created by Puritan laws against worldly pleasure.[2] A bon vivant and libertine, Charles set the standard of a witty, merry court life that provided rich material for Restoration literature. Two catastrophes were a sobering counterpoint to his reign: the Great Plague (1665), in which one quarter of the residents of London perished, and the Great Fire (1666), which destroyed more than four hundred acres of buildings within the city walls. In fiercely anti-Catholic England, many believed that Papists, as Catholics were then called, had set the fire. Anti-Catholic hysteria also lay behind the "Popish Plot" concocted in 1678 by Titus Oates and Israel Tonge. According to Oates, the Duke of York (the future James II) had conspired with the Pope, Jesuit priests, and even the Queen, Catherine of Braganza, to murder Charles II and members of Parliament so James could come to the throne and launch a campaign to exterminate Protestantism. Barker, Dryden, and many others wrote passionately against the villainous Oates.

Several members of Barker's family were university trained. One relative, John Connock, matriculated at Christ Church, Oxford, in December 1670, and would have overlapped with Barker's brother, Edward, who entered St. John's College in 1668 and completed his M.A. at Christ Church in 1674–75.[3] Probably the most distinguished of Anne

---

1. *Love Intrigues*, page 8 in this volume.

2. For an introduction to the political, social, and economic history of the period following the Restoration, see Geoffrey Holmes, *The Making of a Great Power: Late Stuart and Early Georgian Britain, 1660–1722* (London: Longman, 1993), which includes helpful chronologies of major events and an extensive compendium of factual data.

3. Joseph Foster, comp., *Alumni Oxonienses: The Members of the University of Oxford, 1500–1714* (1891–92; reprint Nendeln, Lichtenstein: Kraus Reprint, 1968).

Connock's academic relations was Richard Lower, prominent London physician in the 1670s and co-founder of the Royal Society.[1]

According to Northamptonshire parish records, Anne Connock Barker gave birth to four children: George, who died at five months of age, in 1648; Edward in 1650; Jane in 1652; and Henry in 1655.[2] Only Edward is mentioned in Barker's poems and fiction. She portrays him with admiration and affection, in part for his fine character and promise for a medical career and in part because he is her educator, sharing with her knowledge he has gained at Oxford, a realm prohibited to females. He instructed her in Latin, herbal medicine ("simpling"), and anatomy. She was devastated by his early death in the fall of 1675. Barker's emphasis on Edward's tutelage tempts us to ignore her own level of education which is signaled, for example, by her skillful allusions to classical literature in her poems and fiction. We may read the epigraph to *A Patch-Work Screen for the Ladies*, drawn from Dryden's *Love Triumphant* (1694), as Barker's dedication of the work to Edward's memory. In Dryden's play, the heroine Victoria calls Alphonso, whom all believe to be her brother, the "Star of Day" and herself "Sister of the Night, / Eclips'd" when he is absent. Praising to all his fine public virtues of noble love and courage in battle, Victoria privately struggles to extinguish her sexual passion for Alphonso. They are, it is revealed later, cousins. Barker, in choosing the epigraph, may have sought to honor her own brother's character and accomplishments and to articulate her love that, while probably not incestuous, was unusually deep.[3]

Henry Barker, on the other hand, is absent from Barker's pages as her brother but may be fashioned in some way in her fiction. He is also absent from Thomas Barker's revised lease on the Lincolnshire property discussed below, presumably written soon after Edward's death, which names Jane as heir to leasehold rights in the land.[4] Henry is not absent

---

1. *Dictionary of National Biography*, s.v. "Lower, Richard."

2. NRO, 34 P/1.

3. John Dryden, *Love Triumphant; or, Nature Will Prevail*, 2.1.14-17 (London: Jacob Tonson, 1694). See page 49 in this volume.

4. NRO, S(T) 674.

from all legal records, however. Thomas Barker's 1681 will identifies his son Henry as living in London, and leaves him only £10.[1] All other property, real and personal, is left to Thomas Barker's wife Anne and daughter Jane, who serve as joint executrixes of his will. It may be that a family rift had occurred, possibly over differing views on politics typical of the times, or that Barker senior felt his son already had an adequate income.

The Barker property lay in Wilsthorp, Lincolnshire, and Kings Cliffe, near Blatherwyckes, Northamptonshire. The family had moved to Lincolnshire by 1662, the year that Thomas Barker signed a lease agreement with John Cecil, fourth earl of Exeter, on sizeable agricultural property that included fields for cultivation of crops, pasture for livestock, an orchard, outbuildings such as barns and stables, and a manor house.[2] According to Barker's fiction, it was about this time that she ended her education at a girls school in Putney, near London, and returned to her family. She was to visit an aunt in London some five years later, probably to acquire the polish considered necessary for a country gentlewoman to become marriageable.[3] Another part of Jane's education—this less usual for a woman—was learning to manage farmland. Farming has always been challenging and hard work, combining careful reading of weather patterns, assessment of quality of grain or livestock, business acumen, patience, and stoicism. To judge from Galesia's reaction, Barker probably enjoyed the challenges and responsibilities. We do wonder, however, about her management practices—probably typical of her day—as she describes her power over the farm hands as that of a "Great Turk." Nonetheless, her praise of the skill and knowledge of the laborers reflects her respect of their work.[4] Her firsthand observation of farm work complements the pastoral conventions that romanticize the rural setting in Barker's poetry and fiction. In these passages, she draws on Virgil's *Eclogues* (37 B.C.), Sir Philip Sidney's *Arcadia* (1590), and others, contrasting the presumed morality, sense of propor-

---

1. PRO, PROB 11/367.

2. Burghley House, Ex. 62/74, cited in King and Medoff. The earl of Exeter is identified as the earl of Essex in the headnote to Barker in *Kissing the Rod* and in several subsequent publications.

3. *Love Intrigues*, pages 8–9 in this volume.

4. *Love Intrigues*, page 35 in this volume.

tion, and opportunity for reflection tied to rural life with the immorality, bustle, and thoughtlessness of the city.

Barker engaged in an active intellectual and literary life during her years in Lincolnshire. Her early poetry suggests that she had already begun her first fiction, a royalist allegory and heroic romance published three decades later as *Exilius; or, The Banish'd Roman*. Moreover, typical of a gentlewoman of her day, she exchanged learned verse and prose—witty, playful, serious, richly allusive—with friends and family. Particularly important were Cambridge students, introduced by "a Kinsman" studying there, who visited Barker's home and with whom she corresponded. According to her fiction, they provided friendship and solace after the death of her brother. The group's poems appeared in the two-part collection *Poetical Recreations* (1688).[1] It was in this publication that Galesia, Barker's semi-autobiographical literary persona, first appeared in print.

By 1685, Barker and her mother, apparently troubled by bad luck in farming and beseiged by "debters, creditors, and lawyers," left their rural home for London.[2] That year also marked the accession of James II to the throne, following the death of his brother Charles II. Charles's illegitimate son James, duke of Monmouth, attempted to wrest the throne from James II and was defeated in the savage battle of Sedgemore. In her poetic persona of Fidelia, Barker powerfully recounts the horrors of a noncombatant fearing the worst for relatives on the battlefield: "methinks I hear the bullets fly; / I see a cousin wounded, brother dy / . . . hear my aged Uncles dying groans / . . . [and] see his grandson's shattered bones."[3]

---

1. *A Patch-Work Screen*, pages 92–93 in this volume. For further discussion of the Cambridge circle, see Kathryn R. King, "Jane Barker, Poetical Recreations, and the Sociable Text," ELH 61 (Fall, 1964): 551–72. The full title of the volume is *Poetical Recreations: Consisting of Original Poems, Songs, Odes, &c. With Several New Translations. In Two Parts. Part I. Occasionally Written by Mrs. Jane Barker. Part II. By Several Gentlemen of the Universities, and Others.* Part One is prefaced by six poems praising Barker's verse. One of the contributors to Part Two is volume publisher Benjamin Crayle.

2. "A dialogue between Fidelia and her little nephew, Martius," lines 97–98, page 317 in this volume.

3. "Fidelia alone lamenting her parents lately dead, and her relations gone into the west against Monmoth," Magdalen MS 343, Part 1, page 1, lines 7–10.

Whereas Charles had converted to Roman Catholicism only on his deathbed, James had openly converted in 1669. The new monarch sought to make England secure for his co-religionists, by then reduced to less than two percent of the population. He granted freedom of private worship to Catholics and Quakers, placed Catholics in positions of responsibility at the Anglican-dominated universities, and allowed Catholics to serve in government—all rights forbidden until his reign. He also installed Benedictines in the new Royal Chapel at the Palace of St. James in order to encourage conversions to Catholicism. His Papist agenda, already viewed with suspicion by many Protestants, unfortunately coincided with the expulsion of thousands of Protestants from France after Louis XIV revoked the Edict of Nantes, which had guaranteed Protestants freedom of worship in the predominantly Catholic country. Yet the powerful Protestant leadership in England, hostile to the Catholic James, was reluctant to take measures to overthrow him as long as there was no male heir to the throne.

Once in London, it is likely that Barker found a circle of royalist sympathizers and that she was one of many, including Poet Laureate John Dryden, who converted to Roman Catholicism through Benedictines installed by the new monarch at the Palace of St. James. With literature, religion, and at least one friend in common, Barker and Dryden may have known one another.[1] As Fidelia recounts, the Benedictine convent was a "terrestial Paradice / where man, man's follys can despise, / . . . his thoughts above ambition rise / . . . vertue takes the place of noble birth / . . . and wisdome's valu'd more than shining earth."[2] The conversion was a profound commitment for Barker, and she was wounded when she and others were later reviled as chameleons who had changed their religious color out of convenience rather than

---

1. My thanks to Steven Zwicker for his insights regarding the possibility of a Barker-Dryden acquaintance. See also Jeslyn Medoff, "Dryden, Jane Barker, and the 'Fire-Works' on the Night of the Battle of Sedgemore, 1685," *Notes and Queries* 33 (June, 1988): 175–76, for the observation that phrases in poems by Dryden and Barker indicate that the two described the same phenomenon.

2. "Fidelia having seen the Convent at St. James's," Magdalen MS 343, Part 1, page 12, lines 1–5.

conscience. She valued Dryden's response to charges of opportunism in *The Hind and the Panther* (1687), regretting that its author—and by inference herself—was "so raild at, and ridicul'd . . . when he took up Religion, and Holy life."[1]

The London years were also active years for Barker's literary life and, to some extent, practice in the healing arts. Calling herself, in mock heroic playfulness, a "fam'd Physician," Barker boasts of preparing a treatment for "Sturdy Gout," a painful circulatory disease, that was sold through apothecary shops.[2] Kathryn R. King discovered support for Barker's claims of its sales in a 1685 advertisement indicating that *"Dr. Barkers Famous Gout Plaister"* was available at publisher Benjamin Crayle's shop.[3] Although it was common for seventeenth-century women to be knowledgeable about herbal medicine, it was rare for women to have the knowledge of current medical theories such as Harvey's circulation of blood. Barker incorporates her learned medical knowledge in "Anatomy" and the apothecaries poem, two of over fifty Barker contributions to *Poetical Recreations*. One early nineteenth-century reader, Poet Laureate Robert Southey, commented that he was puzzled by Barker's "odd anatomical verses" and her apparent desire to practice medicine.[4]

Poetical Recreations (which Barker later claimed had been published "without her consent"[5]) was not reprinted, but in one of his poems in Part Two, publisher Benjamin Crayle—the same Crayle who advertised the gout plaster—suggested that he intended to publish a heroic romance Barker had been writing; Edmund Curll, not Crayle, was to publish that revised romance as *Exilius* in 1715. Although three of Barker's poems from *Poetical Recreations* were printed in 1690 with music by Johann Wolfgang Franck in *Remedium Melancholiæ; or, The Remedy of Melancholy*, few of her poems have been anthologized until recently.

---

1. Dedication, Magdalen MS 343.

2. "On the Apothecaries Filing my Bills," page 116 in this volume.

3. King, "Sociable Text," 569 n. 25.

4. Robert Southey, *Southey's Common-Place Book*, ed. John Wood Warter (London: Longman, Brown, Green, Longmans, 1850), 4:296-97.

5. Headnote, Magdalen MS 343, Part 3.

Barker's life was to change dramatically with the shifting fortunes of James II. Alarmed by the birth and Catholic baptism in 1688 of a male heir to the English throne, important political leaders intensified negotiations with the Dutch William of Orange, who was reassuringly Protestant. Had James and his heir died, William could have rightfully claimed the throne: he was James's nephew and had married Mary, the monarch's Protestant daughter by his first wife Anne Hyde. Late in 1688, William's troops invaded England. Mistakenly believing that William was close to London and on the verge of deposing him, James II fled the city. Assuming that James would have popular support and shortly regain the throne, the royal family set up their court-in-exile in France. Anti-Catholic riots erupted in London. Dreams of toleration for Catholics and a nation at peace were shattered. As Fidelia, Barker agonizes over the unhappy day, wishing "Iscariot's fate" on the usurpers and describing a mob in "mock procession carrying before them / a cat crucified" and singing the praises of the traitors.[1] The king's departure from London and William's subsequent replacement of him became contested and ambiguous territory. Did James abdicate the throne by his hasty departure? Did William usurp the rightful monarch through opportunistic collaboration with treasonous English leaders? Williamites went to great efforts to assure appearances of a legitimate transition of power, but few were fooled by this fiction.

Barker was one of almost 40,000 supporters of James—soon to be called Jacobites—to follow their king into exile in France.[2] The king and Mary of Modena resided in St. Germain-en-Laye, near Paris, in a palace lent them by Louis XIV.[3] Parish records in St. Germain, taken with Barker's poetry from the period, assist us in tracing her activities.

---

1. "Fidelia weeping for the Kings departure at the Revolution," Magdalen MS 343, Part 1, page 31, lines 7, 20–21.

2. For a discussion of Jacobitism that combines political, social, and cultural history, see Paul Kléber Monod, *Jacobitism and the English People, 1688–1788* (Cambridge: Cambridge University Press, 1989).

3. For collections of essays describing the court-in-exile, including the royal residence and etiquette, see *L'autre exil: Les Jacobites en France au début du XVIIIè siècle*, ed. Edward T. Corp (Presses du Languedoc, 1993), and *The Stuart Court in Exile and the Jacobites*, ed. Eveline Cruickshanks and Edward Corp (London: The Hambledon Press, 1995).

Moreover, these records help us establish other members of her circle and to suggest her social standing. She settled in St. Germain-en-Laye with her Connock relatives, probably in the Chancellerie, a house just two blocks from the royal palace and the domicile recorded on the burial notices of Barker and her cousin Colonel William Connock. Both as a member of the Connock household and as a woman with royalist and Jacobite credentials of her own, Barker would have been a respected part of the community. Honors included in William's burial notice are his military service in the European campaigns, governorships, and knightages.[1] Connock also became Knight and Baronet under James III in 1732.[2] His son Timon would serve as Aide-de-Camp to the King of Spain and be named to the Jacobite peerage. Timon's wife was a daughter of Sir Ignatius White, Secretary of State to James II, and former Maid of Honor to Queen Mary of Modena.[3] The 22 August 1702 marriage notice of William's daughter Agnes to Jean [John] O'Hanlon includes as witnesses three gentleman in attendance upon the king or queen.[4] Another mark of William's prestige appears in his burial notice in 1738: the signatures of numerous prominent members of the surviving Jacobite community that included John Middleton, son of the second earl of Middleton who had served as Secretary of State to James II.[5]

Barker's poetry, convent records, and secondary sources suggest the importance of the English Benedictine convent of Pontoise to the Jacobites. One of her poems suggests that she witnessed the "moving sight" of Arabella FitzJames, illegitimate daughter of James II by Arabella Churchill, as the "bless'd maid" gave up the world to take sacred vows

---

1. Archives Municipales, Registre GG 106, 81r.

2. Melville Henry Massue, Marquis de Ruvigny & Raineval, *The Jacobite Peerage: Baronetage, Knightage, and Grants of Honour* (1904; reprint, Edinburgh and London: Skilton, 1974), 37.

3. Marquis de Ruvigny & Raineval, 38.

4. Archives Municipales, Registre GG 69, 89r.

5. My thanks to Edward Corp for providing, in a 6 June 1994 letter to this editor, information regarding the signators to Connock's burial notice. Corp is currently working on a historical account of the Jacobites who remained in St. Germain after the departure in 1716 of James III and the Stuart court to Italy.

on 30 April 1690 at Pontoise.[1] Another Barker poem suggests that she spent time at the convent of Pontoise, perhaps for reflection and spiritual retreat, during the Irish campaigns.[2] Pontoise convent records also show that her relative Agnes Connock, probably William's granddaughter, entered the convent in 1729, at age 9, not to prepare for holy orders, but for an education suitable for a young lady.[3]

St. Germain parish records indicate that on 29 January 1691 Barker stood witness as godmother for the baptism of Christine Winiffe, the daughter of a London attorney, then in exile.[4] The godfather was Robert Brent, "Conseiller du Roy d'Angleterre" or close advisor and counsel to James II.[5] We return to her poetry to find that in 1696, Barker was near-blind from cataracts and therefore unable to bid the king good fortune as he departed St. Germain for military operations against England. Those cataracts, she notes, were "couched" (removed surgically by a needle).[6] Yet another poem indicates Barker's presence as one of the mourners viewing the body of James II, "Hero, saint, and King," as it lay in state at the Church of the English Benedictines in Paris in 1701.[7] In a letter almost thirty years later, Barker added her voice to others seeking canonization for James II because of the putative curative powers of two hundred bits of cloth dipped in the dying sovereign's blood. The touch of this miraculous cloth, Barker claimed, cured her niece's diseased eye and what Barker called "a deaths head," a cancerous

---

1. "To Madame Fitz James, on the day of her profession, at Pontoise, she taking the name of St. Ignace," lines 10, 26, pages 297–98 in this volume. Her profession of faith is catalogued in Edward T. Corp, *La Cour des Stuarts à Saint Germain-en-Laye au Temps de Louis XIV* (Paris: Réunion des Musées nationaux, 1992), 173–74.

2. "To My dear cosen Coll—," page 300 in this volume.

3. Archives of the English Benedictine Nuns at Pontoise, cited in a letter to the editor from Edward T. Corp, 5 October 1994.

4. Archives Municipales, Registre GG 56, 146v.

5. Archives Municipales, Registre GG 62, 32v.

6. "To Her Majesty the Queen, on the Kings going to Callis this carnival 1696," page 295 in this volume.

7. "At the sight of the body of Our late gracious sovereign Lord King James 2d As it lys at the English Monks," line 3, page 310 in this volume.

tumor, about the size of a "grain of oatmeal," on her own breast.[1] Efforts to canonize James—as much a tribute to his martyred father Charles I as to James himself—were abandoned by the 1750s.[2]

Barker's literary oeuvre and official records suggest that she was known at court but not necessarily an intimate there. Extant records of James II and Mary of Modena consulted for this study indicate no pension awarded or promised her. She did, however, write several poems in honor of the royal family and, in 1700, presented a manuscript book of her poems to the Prince of Wales. That volume found its way into the library of the Duc d'Aiguillon, a descendent by marriage of the illustrious Cardinal Richelieu, and eventually to the British Library.[3] There was frequent intercourse—political, religious, social, and artistic—between Jacobites at St. Germain—"les Anglais," as they were known to the French—and many Parisians, both French and British. Discussions when the two nationalities met might well have been in French since James II, brought up in France during the Commonwealth, spoke French—badly, some claimed—and many others read and spoke French, as well.[4] It is likely, therefore, that Barker met others sharing her literary and religious interests. It is also likely that while she was in France Barker continued to work on her poetry; a revision of her heroic romance, later published as *Exilius*; and her romance *Love Intrigues*.

Life was often arduous and discouraging at St. Germain, as Barker records powerfully in many of the poems from the Magdalen manuscript appearing at the end of this volume. Soldiers continued to die in the endless European wars, leaving widows and children without support; the king and queen, dependent upon an allowance from Louis XIV, had little money for themselves or others; famine and pestilence

---

1. Stuart Papers, 208:129.

2. See Bernard and Monique Cottret, "La sainteté de Jacques II, ou les miracles d'un roi défunt (vers 1702)," in Corp, *L'autre exil*, 79-106, and Monod, *Jacobitism and the English People*.

3. "A Collection of Poems Refering to the times, since the Kings accession to the Crown," British Library (hereafter BL), Add. MS 21,621.

4. Interview with Natalie Genet-Rouffiac, Ministère de Culture, Paris, 16 June 1994. See her 1991 unpublished dissertation *Les Jacobites à Paris et à Saint-Germain-en-Laye*.

struck the community.[1] Despite private doubts and clear evidence in succeeding years that the Stuarts would not be restored to the throne, devoted followers such as Barker never openly abandoned that cause.

Barker's return to England in 1704, information long unknown, emerges from a complaint by Barker in 1717 and the subsequent answer at law by her niece Mary Staton and the latter's second husband John. These documents give voice to numerous silences in the Galesia narrations. According to the answer at law, Barker, "having been abroad beyond the Seas a considerable time," returned to England "to live upon her ffarm at Willsthorp." Mary Barker, Henry's daughter, left London to work for her aunt on the Lincolnshire property. By 1710, Mary had married her first husband, given birth to two daughters, and was widowed. She and her children then lived with her aunt. Barker took care of the little girls and continued to do so after Mary eloped with John Staton, a shoemaker, in 1714. Three years later, Barker posed a bill of complaint against the Statons to discourage a lawsuit in which the couple might claim rights to the children and to "upwards of fforty pounds" that Mary insisted she had lent, not given, Barker. An oblique accusation leveled against Barker by the Statons was that, as a Roman Catholic, she could not provide proper religious principles for the girls. We do not yet have evidence about the outcome of the case, which may even have been settled out of court.[2] Barker's Catholicism occasioned other indignities, including double taxation on her leasehold property and registration of the land so the government could monitor the movements of a religious minority they feared would plot to restore a Stuart to the throne.[3]

Probably already amidst family squabbles and, as Jane Spencer and others suggest, in economic straits, Barker published *Love Intrigues* in 1713. The most reprinted of her novels, its dedications to various edi-

---

1. "The Miseries of St. Germains," page 302 in this volume.

2. PRO, C11/237/28. Information in this section is based on the answer at law. I am grateful to Kathryn R. King for sharing her recovery of Barker's bill of complaint with me and for providing information essential in my recovery of the answer at law. See King and Medoff for a full discussion of this and other legal material relating to Barker's life.

3. Lincolnshire Record Office, Kestevan Quarter Sessions: Papists' Estates Rolls, 1717.

tions honored a pastoral peace that must have seemed long past for her. Barker articulated, in particular, her admiration for Elizabeth, countess of Exeter, from whose family the Barkers had leased property for over fifty years and whose great Burghley House and vast estate had provided a model of rural excellence.[1] In 1718, Barker dedicated *The Christian Pilgrimage,* her translation of Bishop Fénelon's Lenten meditations, to Anne, countess of Nottingham, a distinguished Anglican. Barker claimed her fervent desire to have Catholicism reach more hearts by having its sentiments "speak in the Dialect of the Church of England."[2] Although dedications in this period honored patrons who helped finance authors, Barker's esteem for the countess of Exeter and her religious purposes in the Nottingham dedication were probably as strong, if not stronger, than any desire for financial gain.

A review of four letters and a burial notice bring the story of Jane Barker's life to a close. In 1718, Barker apparently wrote to the noted Jacobite James Butler, second duke of Ormonde, indicating in code that England was ready for an invasion, under his leadership, to restore the Stuart monarchy under James III.[3] The letter is a copy, not in Barker's hand, and has no corroborating evidence to indicate that Barker was a Jacobite spy. Dated the same year as *The Christian Pilgrimage,* the letter may also call into question the sincerity of her overture of conciliation between Catholicism and Protestantism. Yet her desires to have Catholicism better understood and accepted need not be contradictory to her desire for a Stuart restoration. Moreover, judging from William Connock's letter of 11 February 1726 to his son Timon in Spain, many Jacobites had lost any hope of a restoration and, in fact, favored it only in principle because James III was foolish and undiscerning: "In short, the King's Restauration is impossible unless somebody can find out a way to restore King James, without King James."[4]

---

1. Dedication, page 2 in this volume.

2. Dedication to Salignac de la Mothe Fénelon, *The Christian Pilgrimage; or A Companion for the Holy Season of Lent,* trans. Jane Barker (London: Printed for E. Curll, 1718), i–vi.

3. BL, Stowe MS 232, f. 93.

4. BL, Add. MS 21,896, f. 3.

In a 17 January 1726 letter to Timon, Connock recounts that "cosin Barker" had been ill and received the last rites.[1] Clearly she survived the ordeal, for Connock's 26 May 1727 letter to Timon indicates that Barker was expected in France at any moment.[2] Barker's letter praising the miraculous cure of her tumor also dates from this period. The last evidence we note is the record of Jane Barker's death on 29 March 1732, in the parish register of St. Germain-en-Laye. She was almost eighty years old. Signed only by two priests, Barker's burial notice seems strangely quiet—unlike the earlier Christine Winiffe baptism and Agnes Connock marriage and the later William Connock burial notices. The stillness of Barker's simple burial notice also contrasts with the political chaos of her times and the exuberance of the literary scene in which she participated.

❦

As a reader, author, and London playgoer, Barker was stimulated and nourished by the rapid expansion of literary output from the Restoration through the early eighteenth century: religious tracts, political pamphlets, devotional poems, philosophical and scientific essays, chatty magazine articles, almanacs, romances of various types and lengths, high-minded heroic drama, witty and even bawdy plays, epic poems, imitations of classical forms, translations of ancient authors, translations of contemporary French and Spanish pieces, literature explicating proverbs, privately circulated poetry of all tones and topics, rogue fiction, moral tales, and more. It was, moreover, the period in which the "novel" emerged by that name and, manipulated by Barker, Aphra Behn, Delarivier Manley, Daniel Defoe, and others, made itself up as it went along, shaping an identity that remains today, elastic, vibrant, and subversive.[3]

Barker's literary career exemplifies the shift from the genteel tradition of literary production to a market-driven literary scene, where writ-

---

1. BL, Add. MS 21,896, f. 1.

2. BL, Add. MS 21,896, f. 11.

3. For further discussions of women novelists in this period, including Jane Barker, see Jane Spencer, *The Rise of the Woman Novelist: From Aphra Behn to Jane Austen* (Oxford: Basil Blackwell, 1986), and Janet Todd, *The Sign of Angellica: Women, Writing and Fiction, 1660–1800* (New York: Columbia University Press, 1989).

ers increasingly sought to please popular tastes to earn a living by their pens. In *Poetical Recreations*, Barker was still working within the tradition of coterie authorship, in which writing for private, if extended, circulation among women and men of shared intellectual interests and education was far more common and respectable than writing for pay.[1] In her works, Barker pays tribute to several writers in the previous generation, especially Katherine Philips, the "Matchless Orinda," greatly admired for her image of female virtue and for verse that celebrated friendship and moral excellence. In Barker's poetry and fiction, Philips is the model of excellence in the inspired realm of Parnassus, something that she can never quite attain. Barker also incorporates Sir Philip Sidney, particularly his pastoral romance, *Arcadia* (1590), and Abraham Cowley, known for his pastoral poetry, royalist satire and drama, and, in particular, his much-admired love poems in *The Mistress* (1647). Barker also cites *Cooper's Hill* (1642), the celebrated topographical poem by Sir John Denham, and poems by John Wilmot, second earl of Rochester, libertine and wit at the court of Charles II. Later authors, like John Dryden, manifest the erudition of the tradition while writing for pay. Barker and others keenly admired Dryden's heroic dramas, thoughtful religious and political poems, and translations of classical authors that remain respected today. Barker, like all of these writers, expected those who read her poetry to be familiar with literary traditions such as the Pindaric ode or pastoral and with allusions to authors like Ovid, Virgil, and Horace.

To accommodate a wider audience, Barker, especially after her heroic romance *Exilius*, increasingly incorporated a wide range of authors and genres popular in her time. Like other authors of the day, she drew on Restoration comedies such as Shadwell's *Epsom Wells* (1672), Etheredge's *Man of Mode* (1676), and Wycherly's *Country Wife* (1675), peopled by

---

1. For further discussions of the coterie tradition, see Margaret J. M. Ezell, *The Patriarch's Wife: Literary Evidence and the History of the Family* (Chapel Hill: University of North Carolina Press, 1987); Harold Love, *Scribal Publication in Seventeenth-Century England* (Oxford: Clarendon Press, 1993); and Arthur F. Marotti, *Manuscript, Print, and the English Renaissance Lyric* (Ithaca: Cornell University Press, 1995).

libertines, controlling husbands, fops, country bumpkins, lustful older women, and virtuous heroines engaged in complex games of power revolving around love and seduction. Barker also drew on immensely popular compilations of ancient and modern proverbs and fables, including Sir Roger L'Estrange's translation and interpretation of *The Fables of Aesop* (1692) and Oswald Dyke's *Moral Reflections upon Select English Proverbs* (1708). Of the contemporary authors Barker cites, Daniel Defoe was among the most prolific in the emerging tradition of writing for an audience that would not bring a fine education to the texts: political pamphlets and essays, poetry, rogue fiction, histories, travel adventures, and novels.

Barker also incorporates material from Aphra Behn, known as "Astrea" and reputed to be the first woman to earn her living by her pen. By her death in 1689, Behn had produced numerous poems, at least nineteen plays, and more than a dozen novels, including *Oroonoko; or, The Royal Slave* (1688). Although recognized as a genius, she constantly contended with accusations of lewdness—in her literary works and her person—and plagiarism. As part of their identities as women writers, Barker and others had to negotiate Behn's reputation long after her death, especially in contrast with the genteel model of Katherine Philips. Marilyn L. Williamson, in *Raising their Voices*, organizes her discussion of women writers around the descendants of Philips, the "Matchless Orinda," and Aphra Behn. Williamson notes Barker's and her Cambridge scholars' placing of her in the tradition of the chaste Orinda.[1] Barker had even exclaimed, ambiguously perhaps, in *A Patch-Work Screen for the Ladies* that it was unthinkable to mention Behn's name and Philips's together. Behn and Barker borrowed from the *Lettres Portugaises* (1669; trans. 1678), the popular tale, published anonymously in France, that told in the erotic immediacy of letters, the story of a seduced nun trying to rid her heart of passion and guilt. Barker and

---

1. Marilyn L. Williamson, *Raising their Voices: British Women Writers, 1650–1750* (Detroit: Wayne State University Press, 1990), 102–4. Williamson's interpretation of the Barker voice is solid, although she repeats some factual errors about Barker's life and income from earlier scholars.

her negotiation of the Behn legacy have been figured prominently in recent scholarship by Jeslyn Medoff and Jacqueline Pearson.[1]

Barker, who in *Poetical Recreations* complained about literary commercialism as prostitution, claims her place in that very literary marketplace in *A Patch-Work Screen for the Ladies* (1723). Considered by Josephine Donovan as "one of the most important . . . works in women's literary history,"[2] it was published by Edmund Curll, who had also published Barker's *Love Intrigues* and *The Christian Pilgrimage*. The enterprising Curll was savvy about book formats and content that would generate sales, and it was possibly he who suggested marketing her last two fictions as "novels" and including some of the popular material. Although Curll's list included around 170 standard works, he was also tried and convicted for publishing obscene books (1725), twice called up before the House of Lords for writing unfavorably about some of its members, and sued by John Locke for allegedly pirating his personal letters for publication.[3]

In the advertisement "To the Reader" in *A Patch-Work Screen*, Barker directly addresses the potential buyers of her novel, "Your Ladyships," urging them to "buy these Patches up quickly." Moreover, Barker cleverly places herself among popular writers, in particular Daniel Defoe, by playfully and audaciously claiming her "novel" equal to his fiction and other important writings of their day. It was, in fact, Barker's novelistic fictions that were the most reprinted of her works, especially *Love Intrigues* and *Exilius*, which were reprinted as the *Entertaining Novels of Mrs. Jane Barker* well into the middle of the eighteenth century.

Literary critics have argued interminably about the "origins" and "rise" of the novel, its connections with shifting social and political

---

1. See Jeslyn Medoff, "The daughters of Behn and the problem of reputation," *Women, Writing, History 1640–1740*, ed. Isobel Grundy and Susan Wiseman (Athens: University of Georgia Press, 1992), 33-54, and Jacqueline Pearson, "The History of *The History of the Nun*," *Rereading Aphra Behn*, ed. Heidi Hutner (Charlottesville: University of Virginia Press, 1993), 234-52.

2. Josephine Donovan, "Women and the Rise of the Novel: A Feminist-Marxist Theory," *Signs* 16 (Spring, 1991): 442.

3. *Cambridge Biographical Dictionary*, s.v. "Edmund Curll," and David Foxon, *Pope and the Early Eighteenth-Century Book Trade* (Oxford: Clarendon Press, 1991), 5, 29.

contexts, and the meaning of that generic designation when it first appeared in the age of Jane Barker. Barker has figured prominently in this debate. In 1969, for example, John Richetti included her in his examination of the landscape of popular fiction, 1700–1739. Although his analysis of her centers on the work as a "pious polemic," thereby overlooking the ambiguities, wit, and fun in Barker, his study remains an important starting point for analysis of the novel and women's roles as writers of fiction.[1] Another valuable resource that allows us to see Barker in the context of the emerging novel is Charlotte E. Morgan's *The Rise of the Novel of Manners*, which includes a lengthy list of prose fiction publications between 1600 and 1740.[2] Reading the conflicting debates and contemporary sources, we realize that prose fiction—including the slippery, shifting, and elastic categories of "novel," "nouvelle," "romance," and "history"—could mean virtually anything, depending upon the context. For example, as Ros Ballaster argues, the term "romance" underwent numerous reconfigurations, neither clean nor linear, from the combination of actual historical events and idealized love in Madeleine de Scudéry's immensely popular and influential French romances of the 1640s, 50s, and 60s, to the erotic Portuguese letters noted above, and, I would add, the anti-romances, suspicious of either idealized or erotic love, of Jane Barker.[3] In this discussion of terminology, we cannot ignore, as scholars of French and English romance argue, that amatory fiction was often territory for examining complex political issues. Toni Bowers, for example, finds the obsession of broken vows in amatory fiction linked to ambiguities over James II's flight from London and the easy transition to William III. Ultimately, Bow-

---

1. John J. Richetti, *Popular Fiction before Richardson: Narrative Patterns, 1700–1739* (Oxford: Clarendon Press, 1969), 230–39. See also J. Paul Hunter, *Before Novels: Cultural Contexts of Eighteenth-Century English Fiction* (New York: Norton, 1990).

2. Charlotte E. Morgan, *The Rise of the Novel of Manners: A Study of English Prose Fiction between 1600 and 1740* (New York: Columbia University Press, 1911).

3. Ros Ballaster, *Seductive Forms: Women's Amatory Fiction, 1684 to 1740* (Oxford: Clarendon Press, 1992), 42–66. For other discussions of the romance, see Toni Bowers, "Sex, Lies, and Invisibility: Amatory Fiction from Restoration to Mid-Century," *The Columbia History of the British Novel*, ed. John Richetti (New York: Columbia University Press, 1994), 50–65, and Margaret Anne Doody, *The True Story of the Novel* (New Brunswick: Rutgers University Press, 1996).

ers argues, the sexualized and feminized "representation of agency . . .
as complex and shifting, never finally assignable" participated impor-
tantly "in the central political issues of its day."[1]

Clearly, as the "Note to the Author" for *Love Intrigues* suggests, the
term "romance" had come into disfavor. In the commendatory verse
comprising that Note, George Sewell, a hack writer for Curll, feigns
relief at finding truth to the complexities of human experience and love
in Barker's narrative instead of "Nymphs and Knights / . . . all the Trifles
of a Love-Tale Scheme; / Poor dry *Romances*," suggested by the conventional title. Indeed, authors of prose fiction claimed that "truth" was a
powerful new—hence "novel"—dimension of their narratives. The
English term is also entwined with the emerging prose fiction "nouvelle" in France and the concept of "vraisemblance" or verisimilitude,
probability, and truthfulness to experience. Rather than feel distant
from aristocratic figures, heroic actions, idealized love, and unlikely
coincidences in romance, readers should be able to identify with the
experiences of supposedly ordinary figures in prose fiction.

Aware of the market, Barker remarks in her preface to *A Patch-Work
Screen* that "Histories"—that is, fictional accounts of figures like Robinson Crusoe, Moll Flanders, and Sally Salisbury—were immensely
"Fashionable" in her day. The claim that the story recounted was
"true"—a very slippery claim, indeed—became, in fact, a standard
claim of authors for over a century. Those claims could ward off accusations of the novel as subversive and dangerous. In fact, novel-reading,
especially the reading of romance, was deemed particularly dangerous
for young female readers. The story of Dorinda in *The Lining of the
Patch Work Screen* is a cautionary tale of the disruption of power relations in class and gender that can occur when a young woman confuses
romance and real life: Dorinda marries her servant, who sells their son
and strips her of her property and dignity. Claims that truthfulness was
also tied to a high moral purpose enabled Barker and later authors like
Samuel Richardson in *Clarissa* (1747–48) to have it both ways: examples of lewd behavior that would titillate readers—rakes with venereal

---

1. Toni Bowers, "Sex, Lies, and Invisibility," 51.

disease, seduced nuns, and so forth—combined with material that would ostensibly show the salutary effects of decent behavior. The more concrete truthfulness might be manifest in excruciating detail of time and place, as in Defoe's *Robinson Crusoe* (1719); the epistolary style of narration, as in adaptations of the *Lettres Portugaises;* or, in the case of Jane Barker, the psychological realism of *Love Intrigues* or the clever manipulation of a narrative structure that simulates actual conversation in *A Patch-Work Screen* and *The Lining of the Patch Work Screen.* Actual historical contexts—the court of Henri II in Mme de Lafayette's *Princesse de Clèves* (1678), the seduction by Lord Grey of his sister-in-law in Behn's *Love Letters between a Nobleman and his Sister* (1684–87), or the Rebellion of 1688 and its consequences in Barker's *Lining of the Patch Work Screen*—have persisted as important dimensions of romance or novel. Whatever the particular manifestation of form or content of their fiction, Barker and others followed the classical impulse to "instruct" and "please" articulated in Horace's *Ars Poetica* (A.D. 19) and reiterated in French neoclassicism and Augustan literature in England—with a more commercial spin than Horace might ever have imagined.

❧

Love Intrigues; or, The History of the Amours of Bosvil and Galesia (1713), revised and reprinted in 1719 in *The Entertaining Novels of Mrs. Jane Barker,* is the first novel in the Galesia trilogy. The author of the first edition was designated "A Young Lady," although Barker was in 1713 over sixty, and the story is narrated by a mature Galesia looking back on her days as a young lady amorously pursued by her cousin Bosvil. "Galesia," first in print as "Galaesia" in *Poetical Recreations,* follows in the tradition of coterie writers adopting pseudo-classical literary names such as Orinda, Strephon, and Lucasia. Barker's chosen pseudonym recalls the female form of the Latin name "Galaesus," a son of Apollo, god of poetry. It is also the name of the Numidian princess briefly portrayed in *Exilius.* Both sources articulate Barker's bold sense of self, actual and desired, as an assertive woman who vigorously pursues the intellectual and the athletic lives, both male-dominated domains during her lifetime. The Numidian princess is a masculinized huntress of jungle beasts and a student of philosophy and law. The Greek figure was both poet and prophet.

Walking with a friend in the garden at St. Germain, a mature Galesia in *Love Intrigues* relates the story of her youth in England. Although the title suggests conventional romance, Barker challenges and subverts the conventions of earlier romance by communicating a cynical view of love and a dread of a woman's surrender to a man's power, sexual and otherwise. Moreover, despite the title and the focus on her failed romance, Galesia sets out themes more important to shaping her identity, in particular the merits and difficulties of choosing to be an unmarried, independent, educated woman and her aspirations to literary and personal excellence modeled by Katherine Philips. She also details the importance of her brother's tutelage and her family's sacrifices in the cause of the Stuarts.

Love Intrigues is exceptional, first of all, because of its keen psychological realism and narrative mode. Rather than see action through a clear-sighted omniscient narrator, we interpret the young Galesia from the perspective of her older self, still unsure of what to make of the early courtship with Bosvil. The narrator creates most immediately the confusion, anxiety, and fear of the inexperienced girl. Both Galesias perceive a Bosvil who seems by turns passionate, attentive, respectful, uninterested, and cruelly manipulative. Galesia is, by frequent and sudden turns, madly in love, angry, and, above all, fearful of this suitor, whom she suspects to be a libertine and heartbreaker.

Galesia's cynical view may be manifest in the name "Bosvil." It suggests "bossive," or deformed, and "vile."[1] Strephon, his name in her early poetry, is a conventional figure in pastoral poetry and a name applied to many male writers. Barker may have had in mind a particular libertine known as Strephon: the licentious court wit John Wilmot, second earl of Rochester. At one point, in her fevered imagination, Galesia takes a rapier and thrusts it into Bosvil's body. At another point she is anguished because she learns he has fallen ill. Despite the interior turbulence, Galesia conceals her passion and pretends that she

---

1. Margaret Anne Doody, "Jane Barker," *British Novelists, 1660–1800*, Part 1: *A-L*, ed. Martin C. Battestin, vol. 39 of *Dictionary of Literary Biography* (Detroit: Gale Research Company, 1985), 27, suggests that "the name—*bos* is Latin for *ox*—may indicate an Oxford connection."

is indifferent to Bosvil. Having protected herself, Galesia seeks a life of meaningful rural activity through farm management, acts of charity, friendships, and literary pursuits. Most of Barker's female characters in the later narratives fail to withdraw from Bosvils or other dangerous men, thereby sacrificing their reputations, happiness, and, if moneyed, their fortunes. Barker, ever keen and audacious, has the last witty barb in *Love Intrigues*. As Bosvil is about to marry, Galesia sends him, anonymously, the horns that everyone in her age knew symbolized the cuckold, that is, the husband whose wife deceives him by making love to other men.

A Patch-Work Screen for the Ladies; or, Love and Virtue Recommended: In a Collection of Instructive Novels. Related After a Manner intirely New, and interspersed with Rural Poems, describing the Innocence of a Country-Life (1723) and *The Lining of the Patch Work Screen: Design'd for the Farther Entertainment of the Ladies* (1726) reiterate some of the themes found in *Love Intrigues* but are structured in a far more imaginative way. Reconfiguring tale-telling reminiscent of Boccaccio and Chaucer, the works have the freshness of friends and neighbors sharing stories with one another. *A Patch-Work Screen*, in particular, is a lively hybrid genre—romance, bourgeois fiction, poems, hymns, odes, recipes, philosophical reflections, and more—woven together by multiple narrators, pulled together by principal narrator Galesia, with the whole introduced by the self-conscious narrator as author, Jane Barker. Central to the excellence and ingenuity of these narratives is Barker's manipulation of the female quotidian, women's sewn work, as an artistic and political vehicle worthy to explore the complexities of human experience.[1]

A typical patch-work screen of the day—manifest in several ways in Barker's narrative—was a large decorative piece of several panels, each

---

1. This discussion of Barker's use of sewing as a female quotidian grows out of a paper I presented to the 1990 NEH seminar, University of Pennsylvania, and a conference paper, "Material Culture, Gender and Art: Jane Barker's *A Patch-Work Screen for the Ladies* and *The Lining of the Patch Work Screen*," Northeast Modern Language Association, April 1992. One of many important studies of needlework is Rozsika Parker, *The Subversive Stitch: Embroidery and the Making of the Feminine* (New York: Routledge, 1989). For another view of Barker's use of the female topos of sewing, see Kathryn R. King, "Needles and Pens and Women's Work," *Tulsa Studies in Women's Literature* 14 (Spring, 1995): 77–94.

measuring perhaps 9 x 2 feet. Smaller screens had practical functions, such as shielding one from the intense heat of a fireplace. Screens often displayed the skill of the needleworker and the status of her family, and could take years to finish. The patches or cloth pieces for the screen were appliquéd to the surface first, not sewn together first and then applied to a background, as some commonly think of patchwork quilts today.

The screen—as structure, metaphor and female work—is intensely political as well as artistic. Through this vehicle, Barker asserts that political differences; obsessions with legal, economic and sexual control; and pursuit of riches and finery fragment the world, with disastrous results for women, children, and men: women duped by suitors' smooth words and abandoned, or stripped of their own property and personal identities once married; children sold by their fathers; women and men cheated in shady financial schemes; men maimed or killed in senseless wars, often bloody civil wars; women and men ruined by the pursuit of pleasure, especially lewd encounters, in the city. The women in Barker's preface are more reasonable than men. Rather than creating conflict, they try to create communities that strive for harmony, taking the disparate patches of bitterly oppositional politics and religion of the day—Whigs, Tories, Jacobites, Williamites, and so forth—and sewing them together to "compose this glorious Fabrick of the UNIVERSE."[1] The screen depicts domestic as well as public life: a work in progress, composed of fragments of experience, light and dark, of all different sizes and shapes.

Barker cleverly asserts equality of her work, with its political content and ability to please and instruct, to the histories of the popular Defoe and the works of other men, whom she domesticates as "Male Patch-workers." The screen as trope also enables Barker to articulate her belief that women will accept the female artist, who has rejected marriage and pursues her art and an independent life. In an idealized scene in *A Patch-Work Screen*, a group of gentlewomen invite Galesia to add patches to

---

1. *A Patch-Work Screen*, page 52 in this volume.

the screen they are stitching. Looking in her trunks, she discovers only scraps of her poetry and other writings. Without hesitation, they encourage her to add those patches to the screen.

Of the last two novels, *A Patch-Work Screen* contains more autobiographical elements. Reviewing and continuing her semi-autobiographical narrative of *Love Intrigues*, Barker includes her own revised poems from *Poetical Recreations* as by the narrator-heroine Galesia. "Anatomy," "A Poem on her Brother's Death," "An Invitation of my learned Friends at Cambridge," "A Virgin Life," and others stand beside popular tales about adulterers, murderers, wrong-headed maidens, and a wife who is unaccountably more loyal to her husband's mistress than she is to him. Near the beginning, Barker playfully dumps her alter ego Galesia into a river when a coach overturns. The tone can also be serious, as in sincere religious reflections in two poems at the end of this work.

As Barker notes in *The Lining of the Patch Work Screen*, the patches she uses to "line" the patch-work screen in the previous narrative are really "panes," large pieces of fabric used to decorate the back—not the front—of the screen. Many of Barker's "panes" are fabric cut from popular themes, plays, and fictional narratives that would appear in any checklist of publications in the period. Here, for example, are "The Story of the Portugueze Nun" and "The Cause of the Moors Overrunning Spain." "Philinda's Story out of the Book," strongly resembling Aphra Behn's *History of the Nun* (1689), tells of a woman who believes she is a widow, marries another man, and subsequently murders the first husband when he returns. Discarded women again play prominent roles, as in the aptly named "Mrs. Castoff." Yet the optimistic centerpiece of *The Lining of the Patch Work Screen* is the vigorous and independent Mrs. Goodwife. Reduced to poverty because of her Stuart sympathies, this resilient and resourceful woman slowly builds a successful business that supports her family and renders her a happy, productive member of society. Wiser and more practical than the Numidian princess of *Exilius*, Mrs. Goodwife is the model of heroism that seems appropriate for Galesia and Barker at the end of their lives. There is, in fact, a twilight feeling about Barker's last novelistic venture, published when she was in her seventies. The work also ends abruptly, perhaps because of Barker's ill health, loss of spirit, or something else altogether.

Selected poems from part 2 of the Magdalen manuscript, previously unpublished, appear at the end of this volume. Most of the poems were written in France. Barker speaks in several voices in the poems, and the range of tones and topics is impressive: from the homely talk of "slabbering bibs" in one poem to the anguish of "mothers . . . who with pitty dy" in yet another. Biblical allusions permeate the poems to or about James II and Queen Mary of Modena, thereby recasting and elevating their political woes and religious convictions to the heroic and divine. Even the Prince of Wales is granted special status as Barker compares him to Jesus, sought out to be killed by Herod. Barker, as the unnamed speaker in "To My dear cosen Coll—" and as Fidelia in the dialogue with Martius, recounts the personal grief brought on by politics, including wars in which one fears loved ones will be killed. Of the poems, "The Miseries of St. Germains" most powerfully portrays the anguish that comes to the noncombatants, helpless to save the lives of loved ones in battle or to find enough bread to eat in the hell of a 1694–95 famine, compounded by plague, in which almost a million in France perished. In this and other poems, Barker portrays the king and queen as compassionate but unable to help their subjects. Dependent upon Louis XIV for much of their own income, the royal couple could not even provide adequate support for their loyal followers. Many, like Timon Connock's bride, were promised pensions "upon the Restauration." The Queen was particularly saddened when she could not keep up the payments she had promised to the convent of the Visitation of Chaillot for its support.

Barker intended these poems for private circulation among sympathetic associates, in part to reinforce shared commitments among loyal Jacobites. It was also important, particularly in the 1690s, that no pessimistic account of St. Germain become public to be used against James II by William's propagandists. For readers today, poems such as "The Miseries at St. Germains" engender new ways of reading Barker's fictional narratives, such as those of Mrs. Goodwife and Captain Manly, which only allude in passing to the ordeals at St. Germain. Barker, aware of politics and of her reading public, carefully gauged how much and how little to say in her later fiction.

🌿

Reflective, audacious, intellectual, resourceful, devout, playful, and generous. The resilient Jane Barker and her richly varied oeuvre have become important in the expansion, challenge, and reconfiguration of theories of women's writing which have been, until the past decade, heavily grounded in studies of nineteenth- and twentieth-century writers. Through her poems and fiction, and through extra-literary sources, scholars will continue to explore Barker to illuminate categories such as gender, genre, social class, political identity, sexuality, the literary marketplace, and the nature of authorship as we rethink literary history, only to rethink, rewrite, and rethink it again.

Selected Bibliography

Backscheider, Paula R. "Women Writers and the Chains of Identification." *Studies in the Novel* 19 (Fall, 1987): 245–62.

Barash, Carol. *English Women's Poetry 1649–1714: Politics, Community and Linguistic Authority.* Oxford: Clarendon Press, 1996.

Doody, Margaret Anne. "Jane Barker." In *British Novelists, 1660-1800*, Part 1: *A-L.* Vol. 39 of *Dictionary of Literary Biography*. Edited by Martin C. Battestin. Detroit: Gale Research Company, 1985.

Greer, Germaine, Susan Hastings, Jeslyn Medoff, and Melinda Sansone, eds. *Kissing the Rod: An Anthology of Seventeenth-Century Women's Verse.* London: Virago Press, 1988, and New York: Farrar Straus Giroux, 1989.

Hunter, J. Paul. *Before Novels: Cultural Contexts of Eighteenth-Century English Fiction.* New York: Norton, 1990.

King, Kathryn R. "Jane Barker, *Poetical Recreations*, and the Sociable Text." ELH 61 (Fall, 1994): 551–70.

———. "The Unaccountable Wife and other Tales of Female Desire in Jane Barker's *A Patch-Work Screen for the Ladies.*" *The Eighteenth Century* 35 (Spring, 1994): 155–72.

King, Kathryn R. and Jeslyn Medoff. "Jane Barker (1652–1732) and Her Life: The Documentary Record." Unpublished essay.

McBurney, William H. "Edmund Curll, Mrs. Jane Barker, and the English Novel." *Philological Quarterly* 37 (October, 1958): 385–99.

Morgan, Charlotte E. *The Rise of the Novel of Manners: A Study of English Prose Fiction between 1600 and 1740.* New York: Columbia University Press, 1911.

Pearson, Jacqueline. "The History of *The History of the Nun.*" In *Rereading Aphra Behn: History, Theory, and Criticism.* Edited by Heidi Hutner. Charlottesville: University Press of Virginia, 1993.

Richetti, John J. *Popular Fiction before Richardson: Narrative Patterns, 1700–1739.* Oxford: Clarendon Press, 1969.

Spencer, Jane. "Creating the Woman Writer: The Autobiographical Works of Jane Barker." *Tulsa Studies in Women's Literature* 2 (Fall, 1983): 165–81.

———. *The Rise of the Woman Novelist.* Oxford: Basil Blackwell, 1986.

Todd, Janet. *The Sign of Angellica: Women, Writing and Fiction, 1660–1800.* New York: Columbia University Press, 1989.

Notes on the Text

The texts for this volume are drawn from the last editions of each work over which Barker could have had editorial control. *Love Intrigues; or, The History of the Amours of Bosvil and Galesia, As Related to Lucasia, in St. Germains Garden* (1713), originally authored by "A Young Lady," is taken from volume 2 of *The Entertaining Novels of Mrs. Jane Barker* (London: Printed for A. Bettesworth and E. Curll, 1719),[1] in which it appears as *The Amours of Bosvil and Galesia, As related to Lucasia in St. Germain's Garden.* The first volume of this collection comprises *Exilius; or, The Banish'd Roman: A New Romance: In Two Parts, Written after the Manner of Telemachus,* originally printed separately in 1715. The 1719 version of *Love Intrigues* is reprinted by permission of the Van Pelt-Dietrich Library Center, University of Pennsylvania: Classmark PR3316 B28 A6 1719, v. 2.

A Patch-Work Screen for the Ladies; or, Love and Virtue Recommended: In a Collection of Instructive Novels. Related After a Manner intirely New,

---

1. Four editions of *The Entertaining Novels of Mrs. Jane Barker* appeared: 1719, 1733, 1736, and 1743. The work was translated into German as *Der ins Eiend verjagte Exilius* in 1721.

and interspersed with Rural Poems, describing the Innocence of a Country-Life (London: Printed for E. Curll and T. Payne, 1723) was transcribed by permission from the copy held in the Folger Shakespeare Library: Acq. 228697. The present edition incorporates the changes listed on the errata sheet in the 1723 edition. *The Lining of the Patch Work Screen; Design'd for the Farther Entertainment of the Ladies* (London: Printed for A. Bettesworth, 1726) is taken by permission from the copy at the Houghton Library: shelfmark 15492.33.25. The poems at the end of this volume are taken by permission from part two of "Poems on several occasions in three parts: The first refering to the times. The second, are poems writ since the author was in France, or at least most of them. The third, are taken out of a miscellany heretofore printed, and writ by the same author" (ca. 1701), housed at the Magdalen College Library, Oxford: MS 343.[1]

Obvious errors in the printed texts have been silently emended, but eighteenth-century variants in orthography have been retained. Author's or publisher's notes have been incorporated into the footnotes with bracketed markers indicating their provenance. When glosses are required for notes, this editor's remarks appear after these brackets. In some cases, Barker placed the markers for her footnotes before the word or phrase to which the note refers; these have been moved to follow modern convention and conform to current guidelines for the Women Writers in English series. Multiple layers of emphasis in the headings have been reduced, and original line breaks in the headings of the printed texts have not been preserved. The first letter of each line of poetry has been regularized to upper case.

---

1. Part one of Magdalen MS 343 is virtually identical to "A Collection of Poems Refering to the times, since the Kings accession to the Crown," dedicated to the Prince of Wales in 1700, a volume of manuscript poems now held in the British Library: BL, Add. MS 21,621. No poems from this volume are reprinted in their entirety in this edition; however, some poems are cited in the Introduction. Part three of the Magdalen manuscript contains Barker's revised versions of her poems in *Poetical Recreations* (1688), hereafter cited as PR.

LOVE INTRIGUES:

OR, THE

HISTORY

OF THE

AMOURS

OF

BOSVIL and *GALESIA*,

As related to

LUCASIA, in St. *Germain's* Garden

A

NOVEL.

Written by a Young LADY.

Omne tulit punctum qui miscuit utile dulci.

LONDON,
Printed for E. Curll, at the *Dial* and *Bible*
against St. *Dunstan's* Church in *Fleetstreet;*
and C. Crownfield, at *Cambridge.*
MDCXIII.

This page is an approximation of the title page of the 1713 edition of *Love Intrigues; or, The Amours of Bosvil and Galesia.* The text that follows is from the 1719 edition; see Notes on the Text, pages xliv–xlv. Epigraph: **Omne tulit punctum qui miscuit utile dulci.** Horace (65–8 B.C.), *Ars Poetica,* line 343: The poet winning every vote blends the useful and the sweet.

To the Right Honourable the Countess of *Exeter*

Madam,[1]

As I was extreamly confus'd to find my little Novel presenting itself to your Ladyship without your Leave or Knowledge,[2] so I am as much delighted in having Permission to lay this large Composure at your Ladyship's Feet, by which Means I have the Opportunity to beg Pardon for the Offences committed by the other (which I do with all Humility) tho' I was not guilty, nor can conceive by what Concurrence of Mistakes it so happen'd, unless design'd by Fate to render your Ladyship's Goodness the more conspicuous, in pardoning those Indecorums and Breaches of Respect always due to Persons of your Quality and Merit, but especially on such Occasions.

Madam, it was this profound Respect which has long oppos'd my addressing to you in this Kind; and which, I believe, would have wholly suppress'd all such Thoughts in me as too arrogant, but that I was encourag'd by casting an Eye on that great Wit, worthy of his Time, Sir PHILIP SIDNEY,[3] whose Steps with awful[4] Distance, I now take Leave to trace; and beg this may find the same Acceptance thro' your Goodness, as his found thro' its own Merit; and then I am sure my *Roman* Heroes[5] will be as safe in the Protection of the Countess of *Exeter*, as his

---

1. Dedication to *The Entertaining Novels of Mrs. Jane Barker* (1719), in which a revised version of *Love Intrigues* (1713) followed *Exilius; or, the Banish'd Roman* (1715). The Countess of Exeter was Elizabeth Brownlow (1681–1723), wife of John Cecil (1674–1721), sixth earl of Exeter.

2. **Knowledge**: Barker suggests that the dedication to the 1713 edition of *Love Intrigues* was not authorized by the countess.

3. **Sir Philip Sidney**: statesman and influential writer (1554–86), known for his pastoral romance, *Arcadia* (1590), and vindication of literature, *A Defence of Poesie* (1595).

4. **awful**: full of awe, respectful.

5. **Roman Heroes**: the principal characters in *Exilius*.

Arcadians were in that of the Countess of *Pembroke*.[1] Your Ladyship's Virtue and Prudence having gain'd so absolute an Empire over the Hearts of the World, that none can reject what you are pleas'd to approve, nor slight what you are pleas'd to encourage. So that one gracious Look from your Ladyship will raise my EXILIUS from his Dust, and make him live; live in the Hearts of all the Fair, and in the Esteem of all his own Sex, 'till they make his unfashionable Constancy become the newest Mode, by their wearing it, in practising what they have so long exploded and ridiculed.

Thus it is in your Ladyship's Power to reform the World, and restore heroic Love to its ancient Jurisdiction. It is in your Power, Madam, to dissipate all those Clouds of Tribulation which encircled these my *Roman* Lovers, from the Time of their Separation at *Rome*, 'till their Return to their Father's House in the Country.

And now, Madam, give me Leave to pause a little—Was it not *Burleigh-house*[2] with its Park, Shades, and Walks, that form'd in me the first idea of my SCIPIO's[3] Country Retreat? Most sure it was; for when I compos'd my *Romance*, I knew nothing farther from Home than *Burleigh* and *Worthorp*.[4] And 'tis as true, that those bright Heroines I have endeavour'd to characterize, are but some faint Resemblances of the noble Ladies, who inhabited those stately Palaces; amongst whom none has been a greater Ornament to this noble Family than your Ladyship. I dare not enter upon the Particulars of those Perfections which charm all that know you, lest I should lessen what I most desire to commend, they being above my Capacity; and tho' this be the common Excuse of all defective Writers, yet, I rather chuse that beaten Tract, than deviate into Complements, which my Education renders me uncapable to

---

1. **Countess of Pembroke:** Mary Herbert (1561–1621), younger sister of Sir Philip Sidney, for whom the first version of *Arcadia* was written, and who oversaw the publication of his works after his death.

2. **Burleigh-House:** Burghley House, the Cecil family great house in Northamptonshire.

3. **Scipio:** noble Roman, uncle of Clelia in *Exilius*.

4. **Worthorp:** Wothorp, a Cecil family lodge one mile from Burghley House.

perform; therefore shall conclude with the Words of that great Sage; *Many Daughters have done virtuously, But thou excellest them all:*[1] Chiefly in Humility and Condescention, in raising me from my Obscurity to the Honour of subscribing myself, with profound Respect,

MADAM,
Your Ladyship's most humble,
And most obedient Servant,
JANE BARKER.

---

1. **Sage...all**: Solomon; Prov. 31:29.

To Mrs. *Jane Barker*

Condemn me not, *Galesia,*[1] Fair unknown,
If I, to praise Thee, first my Error own;
A partial View and Prejudice of Fame
Slighted thy Pages for the *Novel's*[2] Name:
Methought I scorn'd of Nymphs and Knights to dream,

And all the Trifles of a *Love-Tale* Scheme;
Poor dry *Romances*[3] of a tortur'd Brain,
Where we see none but the Composer's Pain.
Thus I, by former Rules of Judgment led,
But soon my Fault recanted as I read.

So by false *Seers* misdoubting Men, betray'd,
Are often of the real Guide afraid;
But when by Proof convinc'd they lend an Ear,
Their Truths *Diviner* from their Foils appear.
Who now can bear their stiff affected Vein,

Their *Loves,* their *Cupids,*[4] and the idle Train,
Which Fools are pleas'd with, and which Mad men feign?
When here he may with juster Wonder view
The Charms of Nature, and those painted true;
By what strange Springs our real Passions move,

---

1. **Galesia:** Barker's semi-autobiographical persona, first in print in *Poetical Recreations,* Part 1 (hereafter cited as *PR1*). Also the Numidian princess, huntress, and student of philosophy and law in *Exilius.* The name recalls the feminine form of Galaesus, prophet and son of Apollo, Greek god of poetry.

2. **Novel:** from the term for "new," a fictional prose narrative intended to be more truthful to actual experience than romances.

3. **Romances:** fictional narratives, often with abstract figures, unlikely coincidences, and plots turning on idealized love. Mlle de Scudéry (1607–1701) wrote popular French romances that influenced the English genre.

4. **Cupid:** Greek god of love.

How vain are all Disguises when we love;
What Wiles and Stratagems the Men secure,
And what the tortur'd *Female Hearts* endure;
Compell'd to stifle what they feign would tell,
While Truth commands, but Honour must rebel.

All this, so well, so naturally dress'd,
At once with Wit and Innocence express'd,
So true appears, so just, and yet so plain,
We mourn thy Sorrows and we feel thy Pain.
None here is like thy false Dissembler found,
All pity Thee, but He who gave the Wound.

And yet the perjur'd Swain,[1] *Galesia,* spare,
Nor urge on Vengeance with a hasty Pray'r;
Tho' much He merits it, since all agree
Enough He's punish'd in his losing Thee.

G. Sewell.[2]

---

1. **Swain:** sweetheart, lover.

2. **Sewell:** George Sewell (d. 1726), pamphleteer, satirist, translator, and hack writer for Barker's publisher, Edmund Curll.

The *Amours* of *Bosvil* and *Galesia* as related to *Lucasia* in St. *Germains* Garden.[1]

It was in the Heat of Summer, when News is daily coming and hourly expected from the Campaigns;[2] which, as it employs the Heads of the Politicians, and Arms of the Heroes, so it fills the Hearts of the Fair with a thousand Apprehensions, in Consideration of their respective Friends and Relations therein concern'd. This induc'd *Galesia* to an early Walk in St. *Germains* Garden, where meeting with her Friend *Lucasia*, they took a Turn or two by the little Wood, entertaining themselves on the Adventures of the present and foregoing War and what they had to hope or fear from the Success or Overthrow of either or both Parties; their dearest and nearest Relations being equally engag'd on both Sides. King *James's* Affairs having so turn'd Things in *Europe,* that the War between *France* and the Allies[3] was almost like a Civil War, Friend against Friend, Brother against Brother, Father against Son, and so on. After divers Disquisitions and Turns of Discourse on these Occurrences, *Lucasia,* being willing to quit this melancholy Theme, desir'd *Galesia* to recount to her the Adventures of her early Years, of which she had already heard some Part, and therefore believ'd the whole to be a diverting Novel. Wherefore seating themselves, *Galesia* related as follows.

The *History* of *Galesia.*

My Father (said *Galesia*) and all his Family being of the Loyal Party,[4] in the Time of King *Charles* the First, is a sufficient Demonstration of the

---

1. **The Amours of Bosvil and Galesia**: author-corrected version of *Love Intrigues* (1713), written by "a Young Lady." Her name appears on the 1719 edition. **Bosvil:** the name suggests a combination of "bossive," physical deformity, and "vile." **Lucasia:** probably the literary name for an actual friend of Barker; after the literary name for Anne Owen, a friend addressed in the poetry of Katherine Philips, much admired by Barker. **St. Germains Garden:** garden adjacent to the palace of exiled James II (1633–1701) and Mary of Modena (1658–1718) at Saint Germain-en-Laye, near Paris. James was deposed by William of Orange and others, December 1688.

2. **Campaigns:** military battles in the 1690s European wars, in particular the campaigns in Ireland to restore James to the throne.

3. **Allies:** primarily the English and the Dutch.

4. **Loyal Party:** Royalists, supporters of Charles I (1600–49), rather than supporters of Oliver Cromwell (1599–1658) and Parliamentary forces in the English Civil Wars (1642–49).

Non-existence of Riches amongst them; for some were in Battel slain, and some in Prison dy'd; some ruin'd in their Estates, some in their Persons, and so (like most of the Adherents to the Royal Cause) were unhappy. My Father, in particular, lost a very honourable and profitable Place at Court;[1] after which he retir'd into the Country,[2] leading a very private, or rather obscure Life,[3] just above the Contempt of Poverty, and below that Envy which attends Riches, of which he laid aside all Hopes, contenting himself to give his Children such Education as might fit them for a more plentiful Condition of Life, if Fortune shou'd ever make them her Favourites: Thus he made a Vertue of Necessity, and, as I have worded it in some Poem, elsewhere,

> *Where Fortune wou'd not with his Wish comply,*
> *He made his Wish bear Fortune Company.*[4]

I was about ten or eleven Years old, when my Mother took me from *Putney*-School,[5] finding those Places the Academies of Vanity and Expence, no Way instructive in the Rudiments of a Country Gentlewoman's Life, for which, in all Probability, I was destin'd; therefore reasonably judg'd her own House fitter Class to prepare me for that Station.

Here I had not been long, e'er there came to our House a young Gentleman of our Neighbourhood, one Mr. *Brafort,* a School-fellow and particular Companion of my Brother's. This Gentleman took such a liking to Miss,[6] (for I was not yet past that Title) that he resolv'd to have no other Wife, tho' he was already a Man, and I but a Child;

---

1. **Father…Court:** according to Barker's death notice, her father Thomas Barker (?–1681) served the Lord Chancellor of England as "Secretaire du Grand Sceau" (Secretary of the Great Seal).

2. **retir'd into the Country:** in 1662 Thomas Barker signed a long-term lease to manage property owned by John Cecil, fourth earl of Exeter (1628–77), near Wilsthorpe, Lincolnshire.

3. **obscure Life:** humble, undistinguished.

4. **Where…Company:** See "A dialogue between Fidelia and her little nephew Martius," lines 40–41, page 315 and *Patch-Work Screen*, page 122.

5. **Putney-School:** girls' boarding school near London, where students were taught genteel subjects such as music and needlework.

6. **Miss:** still an adolescent and unmarried. An older married or single woman would have been called "Mrs.," an abbreviated form of "Mistress."

which he not only said but demonstrated, in refusing all Proposals of that Kind, always alledging, that he would stay for *Galesia;* and accordingly frequented our House, dispens'd with my Follies and Humours, making himself my Companion even in my childish Recreations.

I cannot but reflect on this Part of Life as the happiest Time we are born to know, when Youth and Innocence tune all Things, and render them harmonious; our Days in Play and Health, and our Nights in sound Sleep; our Pillows are not stuff'd with Cares, nor our waking Hours incumber'd with Passions: We reflect not on what is past, nor take a Prospect of what is to come: We toss our Shittlecock while weary, and at our Tutor's Beck we chearfully go to our Lectures. Thus we pass our happy Days, 'till Reason begins to bud in our Actions; then we no sooner know that we have a Being, and rejoice that we are the noblest Part of the Creation, but Passion takes Root in our Hearts, and very often out-grows and smothers our rational Faculties. This I experienc'd; for I was scarce arriv'd to those Years in which we begin to distinguish between Friendship and Affection, but I became sensible of the latter towards a Kinsman of ours, one Mr. *Bosvil,* who came to our House; and notwithstanding that I had arm'd my Thoughts with a thousand Resolutions against Love, yet the first Moment I saw this Man I lov'd him, tho' he had nothing extraordinary in Person or Parts to excite such an Affection; nevertheless, the Moment that his Eyes met mine, my Heart was sensible of an Emotion it had never felt before.

I was now about the Age of Fifteen, at which Time my Mother thought fit to send me to *London,* to remain under the Government of my Aunt, my Lady *Martial,*[1] a vertuous Matron, under whose prudent Conduct I might learn a little of the Town Politeness, its Civilities without its Vanities, its Diversions without its Vices, &c. This Journey was extreamly pleasing to me, as is usual to any young Country Creature: *London,* the Idol of the World, might naturally create Longings in a young female Heart. It was also pleasing to Mr. *Brafort,* my reputed Lover; he supposing this Voyage would ripen my Understanding and Knowledge of the World, which was yet very green, wanting Experience

---

1. **my Lady Martial:** probably a relative of Barker's mother.

and Conversation to bring Maturity to those Parts wherewith Nature
had endued me. In the mean Time declaring to his Relations, that he
intended to marry me at my Return; not doubting (I suppose) my Parents Consent whenever he shou'd ask it, his Estate rendering the
Demand too advantageous to be refus'd; His Person not disagreeable;
therefore concluded he had no Opposition to fear, having always found
a kind Reception at our House, not only as a Neighbour, but my
Brother's Friend and Particular Acquaintance.

The Satisfaction I took, was not only that I should enjoy a little
Ramble and Diversion of the Town, always agreeable to Youth, but
knew I should there see my Cousin *Bosvil,* who was then a Student at
the Inns of Court.[1] But, alas! how was I non-plus'd,[2] when at the first
Visit he made me, he let me know, that he was inform'd that this my
coming to *London* was to buy me Cloaths in order to be married to Mr.
Brafort. This he affirm'd with such an Air, as left no Room to suppose it
Jest or Banter, withal letting me know his Author, which was Mr.
Brafort's Man; insomuch, that I really began to fear that it was so in the
Bottom, and that such an Affair might have been transacted between
him and my Parents: However, I assuring him that I knew nothing of
any such Intention, he believ'd me with great Pleasure and Satisfaction;
and from Time to Time made me understand, by his Looks and Gestures, that his Visits proceeded rather from Passion than Friendship,
and that he was drawn to my Aunt's House by other Cords than those
of Consanguinity[3] or Respect to her Ladyship, which my vigilant Aunt
soon perceiv'd; but (as the Proverb is) look'd thro' her Fingers,[4] and
under the Cloak of Kinsman, gave the Lover just so much Opportunity
as serv'd to blow up his Flame, without too far my engaging my young
and unexperienc'd Heart; she knowing, that besides his Pretensions[5] to
the Law, his Estate render'd him an advantageous Party.

---

1. **Inns of Court:** Lincoln's, Gray's, Inner Temple, and Middle Temple, the four London law
societies; site of education in English common law, which was not taught at the universities.

2. **non-plus'd:** perplexed, embarrassed.

3. **Consanguinity:** blood relationship.

4. **look'd thro' her Fingers:** winked at, overlooked.

5. **Pretensions:** aspirations.

By this discreet Proceeding of my Aunt he had very little Opportunity to testify his Affection; nevertheless, he found some Moments to assure me of his everlasting Love, and to sue for the same of me. I, young and unexperienc'd as I was, had the Cunning to conceal my Passion, and to pretend not to believe his. The Truth is, I had heard so ill a Character of the Town Amours, as being all Libertinism,[1] and more especially the Inns of Court, that I dreaded to launch on so dangerous a Sea; thinking each Sigh a Storm to overset ones Reputation, which too often proves true in Fact, especially if the Amour be secret, or without Parents' Consent, that good Pilot which conducts young Lovers to the safe Harbour of Matrimony, without which we can hope for little but Shipwreck of our Fortunes and Quiet. This Consideration made me pretend to take all he said for Banter, or youthful Gallantry: In fine, I put him off with one little Shuffle or other, which he pretended to believe was only the Effect of Modesty, 'till such Time as we should come into the Country, and there be authoriz'd by our Parents to make him happy: In the interim, he resolv'd to demean himself so as to merit their Consent. All which pleas'd not only my amorous but my haughty Inclination; for I disdain'd to be courted thus in hugger-mugger.[2] Thus Crimes and Folly mix themselves with our Vertues, Pride with Honour, Dissimulation with Modesty, &c. However, as the World now rolls, we are under a Kind of Constraint to follow its Byass.[3]

Now as Pride agitated my Thoughts in regard of *Bosvil,* so did Revenge a little in regard of *Brafort;* for I pleas'd my self to think how he would be balk'd, who I thought had been very remiss in his Devoirs[4] towards such a Goddess, as the World's Flatterers had made of me.

Seven or eight Months being pass'd in this Manner, my Mother sent for me into the Country; and my Brother,[5] who was to be my Convoy, carry'd me by *Oxford,* to shew me the Glory of the University; at the Time of the Act,[6] when it shines with greatest Splendor.

---

1. **Libertinism:** dissolute living.

2. **hugger-mugger:** secretly.

3. **Byass:** term at bowling to describe the path of the ball.

4. **Devoirs:** duties.

5. **Brother:** Edward Barker (1650–75?).

6. **Act:** the annual conferral of degrees at Oxford.

The Complements and Civilities I there receiv'd from the Students of all Ranks, were so many, and so much above my Merit, that it would look like a Fiction for me to repeat: Therefore, with Friar *Bacon's* Speaking Head,[1] I will only say *Time is past,* and for ever keep Silence on that Subject; for the very naming of those bright Encomiums,[2] then given up to my Youth, would now be like dressing up a Death's Head in Lace, Curls and Ribands: However, all this Vanity did not sequester my Thoughts one Moment from my belov'd *Bosvil;* but I return'd Home into the Country, full of Longings for his Arrival.

In the mean Time our Neighbour, Mr. *Brafort,* had got some little Hints of this Amour, so resolv'd speedily to accomplish his intended Marriage with me: But Almighty Providence order'd it otherwise; for soon after my Arrival into the Country, he fell sick of a continu'd Fever, which in the space of ten Days carry'd him into his Grave, instead of his Nuptial Bed, to the great Grief of all his Relations. Thus we see that human Projects are meer Vapours, carry'd about with every Blast of cross Accidents; and the Projectors[3] themselves, push'd by the Hand of Death, into the Abyss of Oblivion; or, according to the Proverb *Man purposes, God disposes.*

This unlook'd for Death of *Brafort* was no Way afflicting to me, more than as a Friend or Neighbour; for all my tender Thoughts were bound up in *Bosvil,* whose Absence made my Life tedious, and every Minute seem'd a Year 'till his Arrival. But, ah my *Lucasia!* what are our Hopes when founded on any Thing but Heaven? My long'd for *Bosvil* came, and instead of bringing with him the Caresses of an overjoy'd Lover, or at least the Addresses of a fond Admirer, nothing accompany'd his Conversation, but a certain cold Respect, scarce surmounting common Civility. Instead of engaging my Parents to intercede on his Behalf with me their darling Child, he, in my Presence, consulted my Father about

---

1. **Friar Bacon's speaking Head:** Roger Bacon (ca. 1210–ca. 1292), Franciscan monk and philosopher, said to have fabricated an artificial head of brass to learn Nature's secrets. It said only "Time is. Time was. Time is past." and figured in the often-reprinted Robert Greene, *The Honourable History of Friar Bacon and Friar Bungay* (1594).

2. **Encomiums:** high praises.

3. **Projectors:** planners.

a certain Neighbouring Gentlewoman, who was propos'd to him in Marriage. This Discourse I heard with seeming Tranquility, and prais'd the young Lady, wishing she might be so sensible of his Merit as to make him speedily happy. Here, my *Lucasia,* Truth and Sincerity were supplanted by a Tincture[1] of Modesty and Pride; for no Mouth spake more directly against the Sentiments of a Heart than mine did at that Time: But this is one of the finest-spun Snares wherewith the Devil intraps us, when he makes us abandon one Vertue to idolize another: As when the learned Casuists[2] contend for the Faith to the Breach of Charity; and the Enthusiasticks,[3] in their fantastick Raptures, neglect the common Duties of human Life. Thus I, silly Maid, set up a pretended Indifferency, to which false Idol I sacrific'd all my Satisfaction.

Now, tho' in *Bosvil's* Presence I made a shift to keep up this seeming Insensibility, yet interiorly I was tormented with a thousand Anxieties, which made me seek Solitude, where I might, without Witness or Controul, disburden my over-charg'd Heart of Sighs and Tears. This Solitude I sought was not hard to be found, our Habitation being situate in a remote Country Village where one has full Opportunity to sooth and cajole[4] Melancholy, 'till it becomes rampant, and hardly to be restrain'd. Sometimes I endeavour'd to divert my Chagrin,[5] by contemplating, in these shady Walks, the wonderful Works of the Creation. In the Spring methought the Earth was dress'd in new Apparel, the soft Meadow Grass was as a Robe of green Velvet imbroider'd with Pearls and Diamonds, compos'd of the Evening Dew, which the Sun's Morning Rays made bright and sparkling; all the Borders curiously lac'd with chequer'd Work of Sun and Shade, caus'd by the Trees and Hedges. It was in one of these solitary Walks that my rolling Thoughts turn'd themselves into these Verses.[6]

---

1. **Tincture:** coloring.
2. **Casuists:** those who give plausible but false arguments.
3. **Enthusiasticks:** religionists known for emotional outbursts.
4. **cajole:** flatter.
5. **Chagrin:** acute anxiety, vexations.
6. **Verses:** See "The lovers Elesium," lines 85–102, page 324.

Methinks these Shades strange Thoughts suggest,
Which heat my Head, and cool my Breast,
And mind me of a Lawrel Crest.[1]

Methinks I hear the Muses sing,
And see 'em all dance in a Ring,
And call upon me to take Wing.

We will (say they) assist thy Flight,
Till thou reach fair Orinda's *Height,*[2]
If thou can'st this World's Folly slight.

We'll bring thee to our bright Abodes,
Amongst the Heroes and the Gods,
If thou and Wealth can be at Odds.

Then, gentle Maid, cast off thy Chain,
Which links thee to thy faithless Swain;
And vow a Virgin to remain.

Write, write thy Vow upon this Tree,[3]
By us it shall recorded be,
And thou fam'd to Eternity.

Looking behind me, I saw a very smooth-bark'd Ash, under which I sate, and in the midst of melancholy Whimsies, I writ these Lines on the Body of the Tree, having commonly a little Pen and Ink in my Pocket. This Fancy, joyn'd with what I had lately read in a little Book of my Lord *Bacon's*,[4] that a wise Man ought to have two Designs on Foot at a Time, or, according to the Proverb, *two Strings to his Bow;* so I, finding my self abandon'd by *Bosvil,* and thinking it impossible ever to love any

---

1. **Lawrel Crest:** crown of laurel, symbol of poetry, awarded for victory and excellence.

2. **Orinda:** pen name for Katherine Philips (1632–64), among the most celebrated poets in the seventeenth century, model of personal and literary excellence.

3. **Tree:** "the bark of a Shady ash tree"; see "The lovers Elesium," page 324.

4. **Lord Bacon:** Francis Bacon (1561–1626), writer on science, metaphysics and affairs of state.

Mortal more, resolv'd to espouse a Book, and spend my Days in Study. This Fancy having once taken Root, grew apace, and branch'd it self forth into a thousand vain Conceits.[1] I imagin'd my self the *Orinda* or *Sapho*[2] of my Time, and amongst my little Reading, the Character of the faithful Shepherdess in the Play[3] pleas'd me extreamly. I resolv'd to imitate her, not only in perpetual Chastity, but in learning the Use of Simples[4] for the Good of my Country-Neighbours. Thus I thought to become *Apollo's*[5] darling Daughter, and Maid of Honour to the Muses. In Order to this, I got my Brother, who was not yet return'd to *Oxford*, to set me in the Way to learn my Grammar, which he readily did, thinking it only a Vapour of Fancy, to be blown away with the first Puff of Vanity, or new Mode; or a Freak without Foundation, to be overthrown by the first Difficulty I shou'd meet with in the *Syntax*, knowing it to be less easy to make Substantive and Adjective agree, than to place a Patch,[6] Curl,[7] or any other additional Agreement, on a young Face, so as to render it (if not more charming) more gallant. He, not knowing the Foundation of my Enterprize, laugh'd at my Project, tho' he humour'd me out of Complaisance; for I had not let him know any thing of this Amour, supposing an Affront of this Kind might produce some fatal Accident; besides, my Pride would not permit me to let this Contempt of my Youth and Beauty be known to any. These Considerations made me keep this a Secret even from my Brother, tho' otherwise he was the Confident of all my poor Heart was able to conceive; for he was dear to me, not only as a Brother, but as a Friend; fraternal Love and Friendship were united in him, and those Bonds drawn streight by

---

1. **Conceit:** idea, notion.

2. **Sapho:** Sappho (b. ca. 650 B.C.); celebrated Greek poet, called the "Tenth Muse," whose lyrics were a model of excellence. Barker's Cambridge University friends compared her to Orinda and Sappho in *PR* 1.

3. **faithful Shepherdess in the Play:** See John Fletcher (1579–1625), *The Faithful Shepherdess* (1609?).

4. **Simples:** herbal medicines.

5. **Apollo:** Greek god of poetry.

6. **Patch:** artificial beauty mark, fashionable at the time.

7. **Curl:** artificial curl.

Choice and Inclination, and all united by Reason; for never was Man fitter for an Election of this Kind, where Reason might have the casting Voice, which indeed ought to be in all our Actions. But to return to where I digress'd.

I follow'd my Study close, betook my self to a plain Kind of Habit, quitted all Point-Lace,[1] and Ribands, and fine Cloaths, partly (I suppose) out of Melancholy, not caring to adorn that Person slighted by him I lov'd, and partly out of Pride, vainly imagining that the World applauded me, and admir'd that a Person in the Bloom of Youth should so perfectly abdicate the World, with all those Allurements which seldom fail to please our Sex, in all the Stations of our Life, but much more in the juvenile Part of our Time. But thus it was, I sought vain Glory through differing Paths, and seem'd to scorn what I really courted, popular Applause, and hid a proud Heart under a humble Habit. The Consideration of this makes me see how difficult it is to draw a Scheme of vertuous Politicks, whereby to govern this little Microcosm, but by that Model of all Perfection, *Deny thy self*, &c.[2] and that not only in Deeds, but in the most secret Intentions; for while I strove to cast out the Devil of Love, I made Room for Pride, with all its vile Adherents.

However, I thought I had set my self in a good and convenient Road to pass my Life's Pilgrimage; but this my design'd Tranquility was disturb'd by the frequent Visits of *Bosvil*, who, as a Kinsman and a Friend, had free Access to our House; and tho' he made no formal or direct Address to me, yet his Eyes darted Love, his Lips smil'd Love, his Heart sigh'd Love, his Tongue was the only Part silent in the Declaration of violent Passion; that between his cold Silence and his Sun-shine Looks, I was like the traveller in the Fable;[3] the warm Rays of his Eyes made me cast away that Garment of firm Resolution, which the Coldness of his

---

1. **Point-Lace:** from the French for stitch, thread lace made wholly with the needle.

2. **Deny thy self, &c:** commonplace of Diogenes (ca. 400–ca. 325 B.C.) and other Greek philosophers who advocated austere living as the path to understanding.

3. **Traveller in the Fable:** "The Travelers and the Plane Tree," *The Fables of Aesop.* Aesop (sixth century B.C.) was a legendary compiler of moral tales. Roger L'Estrange published a much-imitated translation and interpretation of the *Fables* (1692).

Silence had made me to wrap close about my Heart.

> *Thus were my Resolutions cross'd,*
> *'Twixt Hope, Despair, and Love were toss'd;*
> *His Looks were Sun-shine, Words were Frost.*[1]

But why, *Galesia,* (said *Lucasia*) did you not consult your Parents, and in particular your Mother, whose Care and Prudence might have adjusted the Business to all your Satisfactions? I consider'd much upon that Point, reply'd *Galesia,* but I concluded if I discover'd it to my Mother, she would discourse him about it, and he, perhaps, might put it off with a Laugh, and say he only rally'd with his young Cousin, during her residence in *London,* to try how her Heart was fortify'd against such like Assaults: So by this Means I should have pass'd for an ignorant Country Girl, not capable of distinguishing between Jest and Earnest, which would have grated hard upon my proud Humour: Wherefore I resolv'd (that as long as he remain'd silent towards my Parents) to take all he said or did for Banter, or little Efforts of Gallantry. Thus, Fool as I was, I conceal'd from my dear Mother the Thing in which I had greatest Need of her Counsel and Conduct; and as most young People have too great an Opinion of their own Wisdom, so I, no doubt, thought my self as capable to make or use a Conquest, as any Town-Lady, arm'd *Cap-a-pee*[2] with all Sorts of Embellishments, who had serv'd divers Campaigns under the Banner of *Venus;*[3] but too late I found my Folly and Weakness in this my opinionated Wisdom.

Bosvil frequently came to our House; where he made the outward Grimaces[4] of a Lover with an indifferent Heart, while I bore up the Outside of Indifferency with a Heart full of Passion. Thus a Mask is put on sometimes to conceal an ill Face, and sometimes to conserve a good one; and the most Part of Mankind are in Reality different from what they seem: Youth affects to be thought older, and they of riper Years

---

1. **Thus...Frost:** Unless otherwise noted, Poem fragments are presumed to be Barker's.

2. **Cap-a-pee:** in military dress, covered from head to foot.

3. **Venus:** goddess of love.

4. **Grimaces:** affected or sham gestures.

younger; the sober young Gentleman affects to talk like a Rake,[1] and the Town Miss to pretend to Modesty; therefore I wonder not that I, silly Country Girl, assum'd to my self a Discretion which Time and want of Experience had deny'd me. But Things were on this Footing, when Mr. *Brafort,* Cousin to my dead Lover *Brafort,* cast his Eyes upon me with greater Esteem than I merited; and as if he had been destin'd to chuse the Devil for his Confessor, he chose my Cousin *Bosvil* for his Confident, desiring him to introduce him to me, and make his Proposals to my Parents. *Brafort* knowing nothing of *Bosvil's* pretended Inclinations for me (though otherwise his trusty Confident) address'd to him as my near Relation and intimate Friend. To this Proposal *Bosvil* frankly reply'd, that he could not serve him, saying, that he design'd his Cousin *Galesia* for himself, and was so far from introducing any Body on that score, that on the contrary he should be careful to keep off all Pretenders. Hereupon Mr. *Brafort* remain'd satisfy'd, laying all Thoughts of me aside.

> *Now to what Meaning could this Falshood tend,*
> *Thus to deceive his Mistress and his Friend.*

This Transaction, tho' coming to me by a third Hand, gave me a strong Belief of *Bosvil's* Sincerity, and made me interpret every little dubious Word, which he sometimes mix'd with his fond Actions, to be Demonstrations of a real Passion; not doubting but a little Time would ripen the same into an open Declaration to my Parents, as well as formerly to me, and now lastly to young *Brafort.* In the mean Time attributing this Delay to his Prudence, in acquainting himself with my Humour and Inclinations, before he gave himself irrevocably to me, it oblig'd me to regulate my Behaviour with the discreetest Precautions my poor unexperienc'd Thoughts could dictate. My Grammar Rules now become harsh Impertinencies; for I thought I had learnt *Amo* and *Amor*[2] by a shorter and surer Method; and the only *Syntax* I study'd, was how to make suitable Answers to my Father and him, when the long'd-for Question

---

1. **Rake:** Rakehell or libertine; man of loose moral habits.
2. **Amo...Amor:** Latin for "I love" and "love."

should be propos'd, that I might not betray my Weakness in too ready a Complyance, nor ruin my Satisfaction in too rigid an Opposition.

In the mean Time, a Friend of mine, that had marry'd a Sister of my dead Lover, *Brafort,* and for that Reason he and his Wife always call'd me Sister; this Gentleman, whether out of Kindness or Curiosity, (or because his Cousin the young *Brafort* had discover'd his Inclinations for me) I know not, but he had a great Desire to inform himself of the Secret between me and *Bosvil;* for he and his Wife being much in our Company, could not but remark something in his Carriage towards me; and being very intimate with *Bosvil,* told him, that he wonder'd that he, being an only Child, and Heir to a considerable Estate, besides his growing Practice in the Law, did not fix on a Wife, thereby to establish his Family, and make his aged Parents happy. That Affair is not undone, reply'd *Bosvil,* I am fixed on my Neighbour *Lowland's* Daughter, and hope shortly to enjoy your good Company, with the rest of my Friends and Relations, at the Celebration of our Marriage. This Answer my Friend little expected to receive; however, believing it concern'd me nearly, took the first Opportunity to tell me, which he did in a frank jocose[1] Manner, not seeming to suspect how great my Concern was, which indeed was the greatest in the World. The Notes of a stuttering Cuckoo are not half so disagreeable, tho' they sing the Obsequies of the Spring, and proclaim Silence to the whole Quire[2] of chirping Musicians. The Edifice I had so lately built on the Foundation of that Discourse between *Bosvil* and young *Brafort,* prov'd a meer airy nothing, serving only to make my Fall the greater, by how much I had rais'd my Hopes on its Battlements. I spent my Days in Sighs, and my Nights in Tears; my Sleep forsook me, and I relish'd not my Food; nor had I made any Friend or Confident, into whose Bosom I might discharge my Griefs, or receive Consolation. My dear Brother was then at *Paris,* to improve his Studies in that University; where, complaining of his Absence, I also hinted this other Original of my Sorrows.

---

1. **jocose:** playfully, in a joking manner.
2. **Quire:** choir.

Nothing at present wonted Pleasure yields,
The Birds, nor Bushes, nor the gaudy Fields;
Nor Oiser *Holts, nor flow'ry Banks of* Glenn,[1]
For the soft Meadow Grass seem plush; as when
We used to walk together kindly here,
And think each Blade of Corn a Jem[2] *did bear:*
Instead of this, and thy Philosophy,
Nought but my own false Latin *now I see,*
False Verse, or Lover falsest of the three.[3]

Thus I walk'd on in Sorrow and Desolation, without reflecting that my Vanity deserv'd greater Punishments: For in our Youth we commonly dress our Thoughts in the Mirrour of Self-Flattery, and expect that Heaven, Fortune, and the World, should cajole our Follies, as we do our own, and lay all Faults on others, and all Praise on our selves. How far I was guilty of this I know not; but whatever I deserv'd from the Hand of Heaven, I am sure I deserv'd nothing but well from *Bosvil,* whose Scorn (the Cause of my Afflictions) I endeavour'd to conceal; yet, spite of all my Industry, this Melancholy, together with my plain Dress, was taken Notice of, and it was believ'd I mourn'd for *Brafort.* My Parents fearing this might prove a Hindrance to my Fortune, commanded me to quit that plain Dress, and endeavour to forget *Brafort.* This their Fancy of my Affection for *Brafort* I did not much contradict, it being a proper *Cur-feu*[4] to that Flame I had for *Bosvil.* Thus we see how easily we are deceiv'd by outward appearances, and what Care we ought to take of censuring, judging, or condemning Things or Persons, without knowing the true and genuine Cause of Contingencies, which are often very hard to be understood; for, according to the Fable, the Ass seems valiant in the Lions Skin, and the Crow glorious in her borrow'd

---

1. **Oiser:** osier, a kind of willow. **Holts:** plantings, wooded areas. **Glenn:** river in Lincolnshire, near Barker's home.

2. **Jem:** gem; new leaf bud.

3. **Nothing...three:** This poem is a slightly revised version of "To my Brother, whilst he was in France," *PR* 1 lines 7-16.

4. **Cur-feu:** from the French "to cover the fire," extinguishing.

plumes.[1] We often give undeserv'd Applause, where Fortune makes a Fool her Favourite; and on the other Side, as often condemn the wisest Designs when not attended with Success. We are Fortunes Machines, and the Alarum[2] of popular Applause must run off, as she is pleas'd to turn the Key of our Affairs:

> *For very few will praise the good Intent,*
> *But every one condemns the bad Event.*

But Pardon (Madam) this Digression, and give me Leave to return.

After my aforesaid Discourse with my Friend, that he told me of *Bosvil's* intended Marriage with Mrs. *Lowland*, there pass'd many Weeks that I neither saw nor heard from him, he keeping close at his Father's House, (which was about twenty Miles from us) where I thought he pass'd his Time at the Feet of his Fair Mrs. *Lowland*, who liv'd in his Father's Neighbourhood: But the Truth prov'd, that he was detain'd by a light but lingring Sickness, in which Time I gain'd much upon my distemper'd Mind, and thought my self so perfectly cur'd, as never more to relapse by the Infection of any Lover, how contagious soever Youth, Gallantry, or Riches might render him: But, alas! I had not yet pass'd the Dog-days[3] of *Bosvil's* hot Pursuits; but at his Return he treated me in another Manner than ever: If before he admir'd, honour'd, or esteem'd me, he now doted, ador'd, and dy'd for me; vow'd a thousand Times that he could not live without me; that his Passion had been the Cause of his late Indisposition, and wou'd be of his Death, if the salutary Remedy of *Hymen's*[4] Rites were not speedily apply'd; in order to which he had brought a License with him, and therewith took it out of his Pocket, and shew'd it me: All which so astonish'd, pleas'd, and confounded me, that I know not what to reply; but with Tears in my Eyes told him that I was wholly non-plus'd, and knew not what Interpretation to make of all that had pass'd between him and me. 'Tis true, reply'd he, I have

---

1. **Fable...Plumes:** referring to the "Asse in the Lyon's Skin" and the "Daw and the Borrow'd Feathers" in *The Fables of Aesop* (1692). A daw is a jackdaw or crow.

2. **Alarum:** alarm, warning sound.

3. **Dog-days:** hottest days of the year.

4. **Hymen:** Greek god of marriage.

been extreamly remiss in my Devoirs[1] towards you, for which I deserve
the utmost Punishment your Scorn can inflict; nor should I dare to ask
Pardon of a Goodness less perfect. Be not cruel then to your Penitent,[2]
but forgive him who now asks it with all Submission; him, who vows
never to offend you; him, who swears to suffer any Thing, rather than
deserve your Anger; him, who dedicates every Action of his Life to love,
please, and serve you. Cease (said I) these Asseverations;[3] I never pretended to be displeas'd with you; and as you have done nothing to
offend me, so I have done nothing to deserve your Love, beyond that of
a Kinswoman or Friend, which I hope I shall never forfeit, but as such I
shall for ever love you. If you love me as a Kinsman or a Friend, reply'd
he, testify the same in saving my Life; which, as a wretched Criminal I
beg, and as a faithful Lover hope to receive from your Goodness, in
consenting to a speedy Marriage; for without that, you cannot pretend
to either Friendship, Love, or Charity it self, my Life and Love being
now inseparable. Sure, dear Cousin, said I, you forget in whose Company you are, and believe your self with fair Mrs. *Lowland:* If such an
amorous Slumber has cast you into this *Delirium,* pray awake, and
behold before you your Cousin *Galesia.* I need no Monitor (reply'd he)
to tell me, that it is my Cousin *Galesia* with whom I converse at present:
The reserv'd Behaviour with which she treats me, her faithful Lover,
shews, that it is the prudent, vertuous, chast *Galesia.* It is this reserv'd
Mein,[4] Madam, which has often deter'd me, and commanded my
Tongue to a respectful Silence; whilst my poor Heart, over-charg'd with
Passion, only eas'd it self with Sighs, and my Looks were the only Language whereby to express my interior Thoughts. How far your Silence
has been guilty of your Sufferings, (reply'd I) it is not easy for me to
penetrate; but I believe the Insincerity of this Declaration might prove
very obnoxious to my Quiet, if my pre-ingaged Resolution of a single
Life did not secure me from those Dangers, to which my Youth and

---

1. **Devoirs:** obligations, respects.

2. **Penitent:** one who feels remorse and does penance under the counsel of a confessor.

3. **Asseverations:** opinions.

4. **Mein:** mien; manner.

your Merit might betray me. Ah, Madam! reply'd he, and is it possible that you should doubt the Sincerity of what I now assert? The Great God of Heaven that created us knows what I say is true, when I say I love you above all Things in this World; that I will never marry any Woman but your self; that I never did, can, or will, place any Beauty or Interest in Competition with you; that I have thought of nothing but you since I first beheld you; that I deny'd all the Diversions of the Town for your sake; and when I tugg'd the Oar of *Cook upon Littleton,*[1] and other harsh studies, it was to arrive safe to the Harbour of your Embrace. This Heaven knows to be true; and not Heaven only, but there is not a Person on Earth with whom I have convers'd, that has not been entertain'd with *Galesia's* Perfections and my Passion: There is not one of my Acquaintance but has heard that I love *Galesia.* Ah, Madam! this is true, Heaven that inspir'd me with this vertuous Affection, knows it to be true; Earth which adores you, knows it to be true, and you your self know it to be true: Look into your own Conscience, and it will bear Witness to this Truth, that I have lov'd you since the first Moment that I saw you. Remember (Madam) how after the first Salutations, I sate and gaz'd on you with such a deep Surprize, that there was little Difference between me and a Statue, except sometimes a stoln Sigh, which call'd the Blood into your Cheeks, and made me know, (that, young as you were) you understood that Language. Moreover, Madam, that when I sate at Table, I could not eat for looking on you; insomuch, that your charitable Mother thinking me indispos'd, sent to her Closet[2] for Cordial.[3] Then it was I gaz'd away that Life you now refuse to save, and have ever since labour'd under deadly Pangs; and after thus suffering Martyrdom, to have the Truth of what I profess call'd in Question, is downright Tyranny. Those (reply'd I) who have once swerv'd from the Faith they profess, ought always to be suspected; you have offer'd your

---

1. **Oar of Cook upon Littleton:** referring to dull legal studies. Sir Edward Coke (1552–1634), barrister of the Inner Temple, legal scholar, and chief justice, wrote numerous volumes of commentary on law reports, including those of Sir Thomas Littleton (1422–81), which served as the principal law textbook during the Restoration and early eighteenth century.

2. **Closet:** small, private room.

3. **Cordial:** beverage that stimulates the heart.

Vows to Mrs. *Lowland*——and so stopt with a stoln Sigh. With that, he call'd to Mind what he had said to my Friend, and told me, that all he had then said, was only to put a Stop to his Curiosity, not thinking it proper to name me as the Object of his design'd Espousals,[1] without my Leave; and then again and again call'd Heaven to witness that he lov'd me above all terrestrial Beings: And if you believe me not, (continued he) I hope you will believe my Father, who intends to be here next Week, to bear witness of this Truth: He will tell you how often I have avow'd it to him, when he has propos'd Matches to me, telling him that nothing but my fair Cousin, the vertuous *Galesia,* could make me happy. My fond Mother also, when she hears me sigh, knows it is for you and then blames your Cruelty. If you persist in this Rigour, you will not only cause my Death, but theirs also, whose Lives are bound up in mine. When my Father comes, I hope you will compassionate his Years, when he courts you for his only Child; think how much your tender Mother loves you, and then consider mine; and as your Tenderness extends to them, 'tis hoped you shall have little Beauties of your own to do the same, one Day, for you.

In this Kind of Discourse, my *Lucasia,* we pass'd some Hours; and it was with great Difficulty that I restrain'd my foolish Tongue from telling the Fondness of my Heart, but the Restraint was with such broken Words, stoln Sighs, suppress'd Tears, that the meerest Fresh-man in Love's Academy could not but read and understand that Language, much more he that had pass'd Graduate amongst the Town-Amours. What Interpretation he made I know not; but I thought myself safe landed on Love's Shore, where no cross Wind, or unseen Accident, could oppose my Passage at *Hymen's* Palace, or wreck me in this Harbour of true Satisfaction: For since he assur'd me of his Parents Consent, I knew his Fortune to be too advantageous to be refus'd by mine; that now my Thoughts swam in a Sea of Joy, which meeting with the Torrent of the aforesaid Vexations, made a Kind of dangerous Eddy, ready to overset my Reason. I pass'd some Nights without Sleep, and Days without Food, by Reason of this secret Satisfaction; at last, being over-

---

1. **design'd Espousals:** intended marriage.

come with a little Drousiness, I fell asleep in a Corner of our Garden, and there dream'd that an angry Power on a sudden carry'd me away, and made me climb a high Mountain, where I met *Bosvil,* who endeavoured to tumble me down; but I thought the aforesaid Power snatch'd me away, and brought me to that Shade, where I had writ those Verses heretofore on the Bark of an Ash, as I told you; in which Verses I had seem'd to prefer the Muses, and a studious Life, before that of Business and Marriage: Whereupon,

> ———*my uncouth Guardian said,*
> ———*unlucky Maid,*
> *Since, since thou hast the Muses chose,*
> Hymen *and Fortune are thy Foes;*
> *Thou shalt have* Cassandra's *Fate,*[1]
> *In all thou sayst, unfortunate.*
> *The God of Wit sent her that Curse,*[2]
> *And Fortune sends thee this, and worse:*
> *In all thou dost, tho' ne'er so good,*
> *By all the World misunderstood:*
> *In best of Actions be despis'd,*
> *And Fools and Knaves above thee priz'd:*
> *Foes, like Serpents, hiss and bite thee,*
> *All thy Friends agree to slight thee:*
> *Love, and Lovers, give thee Pain,*
> *For they, and thou, shalt love in vain.*
> *Either Death shall from thee take 'em,*
> *Or they thee, or thou forsake 'em:*
> *Thy Youth and Fortune vainly spend,*
> *And in thy Age have not a Friend:*
> *Thy whole Life pass in Discontent,*
> *In Want, and Woe, and Banishment:*
> *Be broken under Fortune's Wheel,*

1. **Cassandra's Fate:** in classical mythology, Cassandra was given the gift of prophecy by Apollo but doomed never to be believed.
2. **God of Wit:** Apollo.

Direct thy Actions ne'er so well.
A thousand other Ills beside,
Fortune does for them provide,
Who to the Muses are ally'd.
At this Harangue my Grief was so extream,
That I awak'd, and glad it prov'd a Dream.[1]

But it has prov'd so true in the Event, that I think one can hardly call it so, but a real Vision, as will appear by the Sequel of my Story, to which I return.

Many Days and Weeks pass'd, and several Visits he made with repeated Assurances of his Passion, still expecting the Coming of his Father. How far my Looks or Gestures might betray my Thoughts, but I kept my Words close Prisoners, till they should be set at Liberty by the Desire of his Father, or the Command of mine; or at least convey'd into the Mouth of my prudent Mother. Thus I thought I planted my Actions, in a good Soil, on the Ground of Vertue, and water'd them with the Stream of Discretion, but the Worm of Pride and Self-esteem was at the Bottom, and gnaw'd the Root: I did not enough reflect on the Author of all Good, but thought perhaps I trod the Path of Vertue by the Clue of my own Wisdom, without due Reflection or Thanks to the Donor: Which is, as if one should wind up a Watch, and keep it clean, but never set it to the Hour; by which Means the little Machin is useless, tho' it goes never so well: So if we perform all moral Vertues, without directing them to Heaven, they prove very little available to our Happiness.

Whether *Bosvil* knew or was inform'd that his Father would not come, or was impatient of his Delay, I know not; but he dispos'd himself to go to his Father, who liv'd twenty Miles from us, (as before remark'd) tho' my Lover had establish'd himself in our Neighbourhood, both for his Health (as being a more serene Air) and more convenient for his Practice nearer London. When he took his Leave of me, he begg'd me a thousand times to remember him when absent. How is it possible (said he) that I shall pass this tedious Time without you? Every

---

1. The poem is from "The lovers Elesium," lines 104–29, pages 324–25 in this volume.

Minute I am from you seems an Age. Nothing is gratful, nothing satisfactory. When absent, my Senses take Pleasure in nothing but you; even Reason loses her Regency,[1] and I rave on nothing but my absent *Galesia.* Ah! that I might call you truly mine: However, let me flatter my self that I am so far yours, that you will not quite forget me when absent, but pity my Banishment. Pity and promise to think on me; promise but that, and I shall consolate my self with that Thought. Our Souls have subtile Ways of corresponding, they converse when these terrestrial Organs know nothing of the Matter: Then breathe a Sigh, and bid it go to your *Bosvil,* it will meet whole Legions of mine, which will surround it, and bring it safe to my Heart unmix'd with other Air; and when you are in your solitary Walks, whisper that you want your *Bosvil's* Company; and some little waiting Spirit, appointed by my good Genius to attend you, shall quickly bring it to his Master, and I shall in a Moment, by a secret Inspiration, know my *Galesia's* Desires, and so be happy at a Distance! Then promise me, my sweet, my fair, my bright Charmer, this small Consolation: This is the Way by which Souls converse, independant of these heavy Tenements in which they are imprison'd: Promise this, and your *Bosvil* shall not be quite unhappy in these three Weeks Absence; which otherwise would be a *Tædium.* In this manner he took his Leave of me, all which I answer'd with alternate Smiles, Sighs, and broken Words, scarce containing common Sense.

When he was gone I thought on him perpetually, I sigh'd every Moment, I counted the Hours of his Absence as no Part of my Life, wish'd these tedious three Weeks cut out of the Records of Time, often repeating to my self his Vows and Assurances of everlasting Love, resolving to be no longer cruel to my self and him, but let him know what mighty Sums of Love I had been hoarding up for him since the Moment of our first Interview. O my *Bosvil,* (said I to my self) I will let thee know how true a Master thou hast been of my Affections; I will beg thy Pardon for all the Pains I have made thee feel by my seeming indifference, and kindly reproach thee for thy feign'd Negligence; and then repair all with infinite Testimonies of everlasting Fidelity, tye my self to the nuptial Bands, and ratify all by a constant Obedience. Thus a

---

1. **Regency:** rule.

thousand rambling Thoughts, a thousand fond Fancies, agitated my poor young Head and Heart. Sometimes I busied my self with thinking what I should say to his Father, whom I concluded he would bring along with him: I said and unsaid a thousand Things; this speech I fear'd betray'd too much Fondness, that, too little Kindness; this seem'd too submissive to the Son, that not respectful enough to the Father; now I study'd what Excuse to make to my Mother, for having so long conceal'd from her a Matter of such Importance; then, what to say to my Father, for being so ready to leave him for an Husband: Thus I pass'd my Hours in perpetual Agitation of Mind, Part of which was, what Cloaths, what Friends, what Ceremonies should be at this my approaching Marriage.

The tedious three Weeks being elaps'd, *Bosvil* came, but not my Lover: He came with greater Coldness and Indifferency than ever! No Ray of Love darted from his Eyes, no Sigh from his Heart, no Smile towards me, nothing but a dusky cold Indifferency, as if Love had never shin'd in his Hemisphere. The Truth is, I took it for Disguise, but could not imagine what should make him put it on; I thought the *Mumming*[1] went too far, when the Masqueraders[2] murder'd those they pretended to divert: But to convince me that this was no feign'd Indifference, he stay'd several Days at our House, acting this Scene of Inconstancy to Perfection. Much I study'd, but could think of nothing that could have disoblig'd him; I examin'd my Words, to find if I had said anything that might have been affronting at his Arrival. I consulted my Glass,[3] to see if my Person was chang'd in those fatal three Weeks; I reflected on all Things, from the Beginning to the End, but could find nothing whereof to accuse myself: Sometimes in my Thoughts I confronted his past Kindness with his present Coldness; his passionate Speeches, Looks, and Gestures, with his Neglect, Coldness, and Indifferency; one rais'd my Hopes above *Ela*,[4] the other cast

---

1. **Mumming:** pretending, performing.
2. **Masqueraders:** actors in masks.
3. **Glass:** mirror.
4. **Ela:** in music, the upper E in the treble.

my Despair below *Gamut*.[1] Thus I ran Divisions in my Fancy, which made but harsh Musick to my Interiour. Methought I resembled the Sisters in Hell, whom the Poets feign to catch Water in a Sieve.

Now, whether this Affliction was laid on me by the immediate Hand of Heaven, or that Fate, or my unhappy Constellations, produc'd it by secondary Causes, I knew not, but Innocence was my Consolation; for I had nothing wherewith to reproach myself; I had acted justly and honourably towards him: He could not upbraid me with Coyness nor Kindness; for tho' I had squar'd my Actions by the exact Rules of Vertue and Modesty, yet I did not exclude Civility and Good-nature; for I always stay'd in his Company, heard him, laugh'd, fool'd, and jested with him; yet not so freely as to transgress good Manners, or break Respect on either Side all which might assure a Person, less judicious than himself, that neither his Person nor Proposals were disagreeable. All these Considerations serv'd to render his Coldness the more surprizing; but it pleas'd God to have it thus. *Bosvil,* perhaps, was my Idol, and rival'd Heaven in my Affections: That I might say to him as *Cowley*[2] to his Mistress,

> *Thou ev'n my Prayers dost steal from me;*
> *For I with wild Idolatry,*
> *Begin to God, and end 'em all in thee.*[3]

This Vicissitude in my Affairs made me reflect on those Verses in my Dream, or rather Vision, which said, *Hymen and Fortune are thy Foes:* In which I endeavour'd to be resign'd, and bring my Thoughts and Inclinations to a true Submission to the Will of Heaven; tho' it is a Grief extreamly hard to bear, to find ones self thus abandoned, in the Flower of Youth, and that by my own Relation, who ought to have sustain'd me against any false Pretender, according to the Song then in Vogue;

---

1. **Gamut:** in music, the lowest G of the bass stave.

2. **Cowley:** Abraham Cowley (1618–67), playwright and lyric poet.

3. **Thou…thee:** a close paraphrase of *The Mistress* (1647), "The Thief," stanza 1, Lines 5–7.

> *You, of all Men, had least Reason,*
> *Thus to abuse my poor Heart;*
> *For if another had done it,*
> *You ought to have taken my Part, &c.*[1]

But Things going thus, I endeavour'd to detach my Thoughts from him; or, if I must needs think on him, I resolv'd it should be on his Crimes, Falshood, and cruel Usage; which I put in Practice; so that by Degrees his Company began to grow troublesome, and his Presence ungrateful. Yet could I not avoid either; for I had no Reason to quarrel with him, unless for not courting me as formerly; and that was turning the Tables, and making myself the Lover, instead of the Belov'd; which was not only contradictory to my haughty Humour, but seem'd, in a Manner, to invert Nature. Nevertheless, I forc'd myself to bear it, with a seeming Equality of Mind, 'till a fit Occasion should offer for my Revenge; like the Quaker,[2] that is smitten on the one Cheek, turns the other also; but after that having, as he thinks, fulfill'd the Law, can beat his Adversary as well as any carnal[3] Man: So I waited but for a Left-cheek Blow, that might give (at least a seeming) just Cause to quarrel, so as to take Occasion to banish him, his Presence being almost as disagreeable to me as a Spectre; for 'tis natural enough, that the Cause of Grief should be the Object of Aversion.

I remain'd full of this Wish many Months; at last, Fortune was a little propitious to my Desire, at least, I wrested an Occasion to my Caprice,[4] which was this:

Bosvil and another young Gentleman met my Father at a certain Place over a Bottle; here *Bosvil* proposed his Friend to my Father as an Husband for me. All Conditions of Portion and Jointure[5] were there

---

1. **you . . . &c.:** The source of this popular song has not yet been identified.

2. **Quaker:** member of the Society of Friends, a religious group that believed in non-violence, even turning one's cheek to be struck again rather than retaliating to a blow.

3. **carnal:** from the Latin for meat, pertaining to humanity's weakness, including the propensity for anger and violence.

4. **Caprice:** whim, sudden change of mind.

5. **Portion:** used as provision of land or income for wife's dowry, money or property established for a daughter by her parents' marriage settlement.   **Jointure:** support if she were widowed.

propos'd and approv'd on both Sides, and the Day appointed on which the Gentleman should come to visit me, which was to be the Week following. This my Father told me with Satisfaction, also minding me how much I was oblig'd to my Cousin *Bosvil.* To which my Answers were few, dubious, and obscure; which pass'd with my Father for a little Virgin Surprize, which Discourses of this Kind raise in the Hearts of young Creatures. But oh! my *Lucasia,* I cannot tell you what I suffer'd when I was alone; Rage and Madness seiz'd me, Revenge and Malice was all I thought upon; inspir'd by an evil Genius, I resolv'd his Death, and pleas'd myself in the Fancy of a barbarous Revenge, and delighted myself to think I saw his Blood pour out of his false Heart. In order to accomplish this detestable Freak, I snatch'd up a Steel Rapier,[1] which stood in the Hall, and walk'd away towards the Place of his Abode, saying to myself, The false *Bosvil* shall disquiet me no more, nor any other of my Sex; in him I will end his Race; no more of them shall come to disturb or affront Womankind. This only Son shall die by the Hands of me an only Daughter; and however the World may call it Cruelty, or Barbarity, I am sure our Sex will have Reason to thank me, and keep an annual Festival, in which a Criminal so foul is taken out of their Way. The Example, perhaps, may deter others, and secure many from the Wrongs of such false Traytors, and I be magnify'd in future Times. For it was for ridding the World of Monsters that *Hercules*[2] was made so great a Hero, and *George*[3] a Saint; then sure I shall be rank'd in the Catalogue of Heroines, for such a Service done to my Sex; for certainly, the Deserts of *Arabia* never produc'd so formidable a Monster as this unaccountable *Bosvil.* Behold what Sophisms[4] one can find to justify any Attempt, tho' never so mad or desperate; and even affront, if not quite reverse the Laws of Nature. That if the Feebleness of our Hands did not moderate the Fury of our Heads, Women sometimes would exceed the fiercest

---

1. **Rapier:** dueling sword.

2. **Hercules:** in classical mythology, hero of enormous physical strength who killed the Hydra, a sea monster, and subdued the wild bull of Crete.

3. **George:** Christian martyr and patron saint of England (third century), legendary slayer of a savage dragon.

4. **Sophisms:** plausible but fallacious arguments.

Savages, especially when affronted in their Amours; which brings into my Mind a Verse or two on such an Occasion.

> *A slighted Woman, oft a Fury grows,*
> *And, for Revenge, quits her baptismal Vows,*
> *Becomes a Witch, and does a Fiend espouse.*

In these wild Thoughts I wander'd, 'till Weariness made me know my own Weakness and Incapacity of performing what Fury had inspir'd, and forc'd me to seek Repose under the first convenient Shade; where my flowing Tears mitigated the Heat of my Rage, washing away those extravagant Thoughts, and made me turn my Anger against myself, my wretched self, that woful and unworthy Thing, the Scorn of my Kinsman, Lover, Friend; which Thoughts I branch'd into many Reflections against myself, and him, and hard Fortune, which at last turn'd to these kind of Words:

> *Why was I born, or why a Female born,*
> *Or why not Piece-meal*[1] *from my Mother torn;*
> *Or did I not with Teeth, or Rickets*[2] *die,*
> *Or other Accidents of Infancy;*
> *Or why not lame, hum-back'd, pock-broken Face,*
> *Or else in Morals infamous and base,*
> *Or ne'er had Being among human Race.*
> *Had I been lewd, unfaithful, or unjust,*
> *To Friend, or Lover, or betray'd my Trust,*
> *I then might well expect the Lot I have,*
> *But not for being vertuous, chaste, and grave.*[3]

With many Things more I utter'd of this Kind, almost complaining of Providence; and wish'd some kind Serpent would creep out of its Hole, and sting me to Death; or Thunder descend, and strike me into

---

1. **Piece-meal:** When a fetus was expected to be still-born, it might be dismembered in the womb.

2. **Rickets:** softening of the bones.

3. **Why…grave:** "Fidelia in St. Germains garden lamenting her misfortunes," Magdalen 343, Part 2, page 29, lines 18–28.

the Ground, and at once perform my Death and Funeral. O! no, (said I) that will render *Bosvil* too happy: I will go Home, and write the whole Scene of this Treachery, and make myself the last Actor in the Tragedy. With these foolish Thoughts I return'd home very weary: I threw myself on my Bed, where, in a little Time, all my Resentments became a Prey to gentle Slumbers, which much refresh'd my weary Body and more weary Mind, rendering me a little capable of acting according to the Dictates of Reason, but not without a large Mixture of Passion. When I awak'd, I writ to him after this Manner:

Cousin,

I thought you had been so well acquainted with my Humour touching a marry'd Life, as to know it is my Aversion; therefore wonder you should make such a Proposal to my Father on your Friend's Behalf. Perhaps you will say it was but in Jest, and I believe it to be no more; but I beg you to make something else the Subject of your Raillery,[1] and leave me out, 'till Misbehaviour renders me the proper Object of Ridicule, which it has not hitherto; for I have done nothing dishonourable to myself, nor disobliging to you; therefore ought rather to be the Subject of Civility than Banter, which, perhaps, Distance and Absence may accomplish; therefore, I beg you to see me no more, 'till Fortune commission you, by the Change of your Condition. In the mean Time, I remain, your Kinswoman and humble Servant,

Galecia.

In the Simplicity of these Words lay much Cunning, and under the Shadow of Frowardness[2] much Kindness; which I knew he must discern, if he had any real Affection for me in his Heart: For Love is like Ghosts or Spirits, that will appear to those to whom they have a Mind to speak, and to others are quite invisible. I pleas'd myself that I had taken this Occasion, at once to command his Absence, and, in a covert Manner, testify my Affection; for I knew that was the natural Interpre-

---

1. **Raillery:** banter.
2. **Frowardness:** stubbornness.

tation of these Words, *See me no more;* for nothing but a real Mistress could pretend to use them, and nothing but a fond Mistress could pretend to be displeas'd at the Presence of a Kinsman or a Friend, for having offer'd an advantageous Marriage in the Person of his Friend. Here was now no Medium, no Space left between open Lover and open Enemy; here was no more Love-Frolicks to be acted under the Disguise of a Friend or Kinsman; if he came to me after such a Prohibition, he must come upon the Pikes of my Anger, which he cou'd not pretend to appease by any other Atonement but that of his everlasting Love in holy Marriage-Vows. If he stay'd away, I had my Ends I had long sought, the being rid of one that gave me so much Disquiet. Thus I satisfy'd myself in Expectation of his Answer, which came next Day in these Words:

Madam,

I am extreamly astonish'd to find you so displeas'd at what pass'd the other Day, which was no Way meant to your Prejudice, but, on the contrary, much to your Advantage. However, Madam, I shall not justify what you are pleas'd to condemn; but add also to the Testimony of my Obedience, in submitting to your Prohibition, and not presume to see you more, tho' in it I sequester[1] myself from those Charms I have so long ador'd, and only at a Distance admire what your Rigour forbids me to approach, and so rest,

Madam,

Your Kinsman, and humble Servant,

Bosvil.

This complying with *See me no more,* gave me the same Satisfaction that a Patient has when his Limbs are cutting off, the Remedy and the Disease being both grievous: However, I knew now what I had to trust to, and therefore study'd to make a Vertue of this Necessity, and consolate myself with patient suffering what I cou'd no ways avoid: I experienc'd amply the Words of the Sage, that all was Vanity and Vexation of Spirit, and every Act of our Loves Folly, except design'd and offer'd to the Glory of God.[2] I reflected on my late extravagant Rage, when I

---

1. **sequester:** isolate, separate.

2. **Words . . . God:** "Vanity of vanities, saith the preacher; all is vanity." Eccles.12.8.

design'd his Death, and knew I ought to cry most earnestly to be deliver'd from Blood-guiltiness. I retir'd into myself, and return'd to my Studies; the Woods, Fields, and Pastures, had the most of my Time, by which Means I became as perfect in rural Affairs as any *Arcadian*[1] Shepherdess; insomuch, that my Father gave into my Power and Command all his Servants and Labourers; it was I that appointed them their Work, and paid them their Wages; I put in and put out who I pleas'd, and was as absolute over my Rusticks,[2] as the Great *Turk*[3] over his Subjects; and tho' this was a great Fatigue, yet it gratify'd my Vanity, that I was suppos'd able to perform Things above my Age and Sex, and tho' it was an Impediment to my Studies, yet it made Amends, it being itself a Study, and that a most useful one: The Rules to sow and reap in their Season; to know what Pasture is fit for Beeves,[4] what for Sheep, what for Kine,[5] with all their Branches, being a more useful Study than all the Grammar Rules, or Longitude or Latitude, Squaring the Circle,[6] &c. The Former, according to the Utility of his Occupation, deserves to hold the first Rank amonst Mankind: That one may justly reflect with Veneration on those Times, when Kings and Princes thought it no Derogation to their Dignities. The Nobles, in ancient Times, did not leave their Country-Seats to become the Habitation of Jack-daws,[7] and the Manufactory of Spiders, who, in Reproach to the Mistress, prepare Hangings, to supply those the Moth has devour'd, thro' her Negligence, or Absence. But to return from when I digress'd. This rural Business was so full of Imployment, that its continual Fatigue contributed very much to the Ease of my Thoughts touching *Bosvil,* beyond all that Reason, Devotion, or Philosophy could procure. For the constant Incumbrance which

---

1. **Arcadian:** pertaining to Arcadia, actual location in Greece, symbolic of rural peace and simplicity in Virgil's *Eclogues* and numerous English authors, including Philip Sidney.

2. **Rusticks:** agricultural workers.

3. **Great Turk:** the Sultan.

4. **Beeves:** cattle intended for slaughter.

5. **Kine:** cows.

6. **Squaring the Circle:** in mathematics and geometry, converting a circle into a square of equivalent size.

7. **Jack-daws:** crows.

attended this Station, left no Space for Love to agitate my Interiour: The Labour of the Day was recompens'd with sound Sleep at Night; those silent Hours being pass'd in Sleep's Restorative, the Day provided new Business for my waking Thoughts, whilst Health and wholsom Food repaid this my Industry. Thus, in a Country-Life, we roll on in a Circle, like the heavenly Bodies, our Happiness being seldom eclips'd, unless by the Interposition of our own Passions or Follies: Now, finding myself daily to get Ground of my sickly Thoughts, I doubted not of a perfect Recovery, if I continu'd the constant Application of this wholsom Receipt of laborious Industry, which made me reflect on those Words of the Poet,[1] as the Author of this incomparable Remedy,

> *Fac monitis fugias otia, &c.*[2]
> *Ovid* Remed Amoris.

> *Fly Sloth if thou wilt* Cupid *overthrow,*
> *Sloth points his Darts, but Business breaks his Bow,*
> *Imployment to his Flame is Ice and Snow.*

> Cupid *and* Venus *are to Sloth inclin'd,*
> *From both, in Bus'ness, thou mayst Safety find;*
> *For Love gives Place, where Business fills the Mind.*[3]

Moreover, that which contributed much to this Victory over myself, was the Return of my Brother from *France;* his dear Company, which I had long wanted, exterminated that Melancholy which had too long perplex'd me; the little Rarities he brought, adorn'd my Person, and garnish'd my Closet; he frequently entertain'd me with Descriptions of Places, and Customs of *France,* in particular, Convents, and their Way of Living, which I so admir'd, that I wish'd for such Places in *England;* which, if there had been, 'tis certain I had then become a Nun, and under a holy Veil bury'd all Thoughts of *Bosvil:* In this, my dear

---

1. **Poet:** Ovid (43 B.C.–A.D. 17), Roman poet, author of *Metamorphoses*.

2. **Fac monitis fugias otia, &c.:** Ovid, *Remedia Amoris* (*The Remedies for Love*), line 136: Obey my counsel and fly from sloth, etc. A humorous sequel to *Ars Amatoria, Remedies* demonstrates that love's victims can escape their predicament through activity, such as farming.

3. **Fly…Mind:** *The Remedies for Love*, lines 138–44.

Brother's Company, I daily improv'd my Studies; so that I began a little to understand an Author, of which none pleas'd me more than those of Physick,[1] in particular, *Harvey,*[2] his *Circulatio Sanguinis;* all which serv'd to fill my Head with Notions, and, perhaps, my Heart with Pride, at best, but a mispending of Time, Learning being neither of Use nor Ornament to our Sex; but on the contrary, many count a studious Woman as ridiculous as an effeminate Man, and learned Books as unfit for our Apartment, as Paint, Washes,[3] and Patches for his: In fine, the Men will not allow it to be our Sphere, so consequently we can never be suppos'd to move in it gracefully; but like the Toad in the Fable,[4] that affected to swell itself as big as the Ox, and to burst in the Enterprize: But let the World confine or enlarge Learning as they please, I care not; I do not regret the Time I bestow'd in its Company, it having been my good Friend to bail me from *Bosvil's* Fetters, tho' I am not so generous, by Way of Return, to pass my Word for its good Behaviour in our Sex, always, and in all Persons; for sometimes it becomes a Rival to their Duty, deluding them from the Care of their Children and Families, the Business allotted them by the Hand of Heaven.

Now *Bosvil* having been sometime absent, our Family, Friends, and Neighbours, began to take Notice of it, and more especially at my Brother's Return, when every Body came to bid him Welcome, not only the Gentlemen, but even the Ladies, at least to congratulate my Mother on his safe Arrival.

Now it was that his pretended Mistress, the fair Mrs. *Lowland* was marry'd, which you will believe was a certain Satisfaction to me, as Mischief is to Witches, though they get nothing by it; much I long'd to banter and insult him on this Occasion, but his constant Absence depriv'd me of that Pleasure; however, I could not pass over such a Field of full ripe Content, without cropping some few Ears: Wherefore I writ him a Letter in a counterfeit Character, and withal sent him a

---

1. **Physick:** medicine.

2. **Harvey:** William Harvey (1578–1657) articulated his theory of the circulation of blood in *Exercitatio Anatomica de Motu Cordis et Sanguinis* (1628).

3. **Washes:** treatments for the complexion.

4. **Toad in the Fable:** "Frog and Ox," *Fables of Aesop.*

Willow Garland[1] to crown the forsaken Lover, which, indeed, was so well made of Gum-work,[2] that one might take it for a real Branch of that forsaken Tree. This, with diverse other Emblems and Mottos, I sent him to *London* by the Carrier.

How he receiv'd this I know not, neither did I care; but I was told afterwards, That he laugh'd, and told his Companions what a pretty Present he had receiv'd from an unknown Hand, and withal, that he would secure himself from such Attacks by his speedy Marriage; and accordingly proceeded with a young Gentlewoman at *London:* And at his Return, acquainted his Friends, and in particular, a young Gentlewoman, one of our Relations, who, with many others, mistrusted him of an Amour with me; but I not having told her of it, who was in all Things else my Confidant, she laid aside that Thought, especially now since he declar'd to her his approaching Nuptials: However, she and every Body were amaz'd at his long Absence from our House, and ask'd him the Cause; to which he answer'd indirectly, and with divers Shuffles, but the vertuous *Towrissa* (our said Cousin) press'd him from Time to Time, till he, no longer able to resist her Importunities,[3] told her that his Cousin *Galesia* had forbid him; at which she was much surpriz'd, but said it should not rest so, for (said she) I will have you go to her this very Day along with me, that I may obtain the Blessing of a Peacemaker. He comply'd with her, and came to make me a Visit. Our Interview, after a whole Year's Absence, was surprizing to us both; for we trembled, blush'd, and faulter'd in our Words, that it was with the utmost Difficulty we perform'd the Civilities of the Occasion. After being seated, I remember he gaz'd with all the Eagerness, or rather Distraction, of youthful Eyes instigated by a tender Passion, which so dazled and confounded me, that I was every Moment afraid I should sink down in the midst of Company, who sate talking of Things indifferent: Having, for some Time, thus planted the Batteries[4] of our Eyes

---

1. **Willow Garland:** a crown of willows, symbolizing unrequited love.
2. **Gum-work:** artwork formed of materials stiffened with dried tree or plant gum.
3. **Importunities:** persistent and inappropriate questions.
4. **Batteries:** weapons for use in military attacks.

against each others Hearts, he gave the first Shot by a deep Sigh, saying, O cursed Love, that will never leave a Man! and rose from his Seat, as it were, to disperse those Vapours which seem'd to oppress him; to which I reply'd, (foolishly enough, with a feign'd Laugh, to stifle a real Sigh) that I hoped he had no Reason to complain of Love's Tyranny, Yes, yes, said our Cousin *Towrissa,* know you not that our Cousin *Bosvil* is shortly to be marry'd, so thinks every Moment a Martyrdom till the Day arrives? Therefore, dear Cousin (continu'd she) get your Dancing-shoes, if you mean to be a Bride-maid, ready. To which my Mother gravely answer'd, That it must needs be a Satisfaction to his Parents, to see their only Child well settled in the World.

What a Shock this Discourse gave me, I cannot describe, but 'tis certain I never felt any Thing like it: Behold now, my *Lucasia,* what was to become of all my Resolutions and fancy'd Indifferency; see what all my Anger, Fury, Scorn, Revenge, prohibiting him to see me, the fancy'd Satisfaction I took in his Absence; behold, I say, what all this came to, even just as much as the Lord *Rochester*[1] says of Court-Promises, and Whores Vows, which all *end in Nothing;*[2] so these my Resolutions were all meer Fantomes, compos'd of Vapours, and carry'd about with Fancy, and next Day reduc'd to nothing; but thus it is in most Things of human Life, we know not ourselves and our own Incapacities; we think ourselves able to perform this or that, or to look even Death in the Face, and when we have most Need of our imaginary Fortitude, we find ourselves most destitute and feeble, as I experienc'd in this Rencounter; for I was ready to die in the Place, but durst not remove, fearing my Legs should fail me, which I perceiv'd all in Convulsions and trembling: I was like a Horse in a Stable on Fire, burnt if he stays, yet dares not go out: At last, holding by Tables and Chairs, with feign'd Smiles in my Face, and jocose Words in my Mouth, I made a Shift to pass the Gantlet, and got into my Chamber, where God only was Witness of my Complaints, and Succour in the Midst of my Sighs and Tears. I threw myself on the Bed, roll'd on the Floor, hoped that every Cramp I felt

---

1. **Lord Rochester:** John Wilmot, second earl of Rochester (1647–80), libertine and poet, a favorite in the court of Charles II.

2. **Nothing:** Rochester, "Upon Nothing" (1679).

would be my Death's Convulsion, utter'd a Thousand Imprecations against him and my hard Fortune, and contrary to that Philosopher,[1] who thank'd the Gods that made him a Man and Not a Beast; I say, quite contrary to him, over and over, I thus expostulated,

> *O wherefore was I born of human Race,*
> *If doom'd to labour under such Disgrace:*
> *For what is more disgraceful to a Maid,*
> *Than to be scorn'd like me, like me betray'd?*
> *'Tis Heaven alone my Innocence can know,*
> *The World can ne'er believe that I am so;*
> *But Heaven knows all, and knows my vertuous Soul*
> *Does every vicious Act of Love controul;*
> *Knows the just Schemes of my intended Life,*
> *To be the chast, the chearful, faithful Wife:*
> *A vertuous Matron to my Houshold good,*
> *A helpful Neighbour in my Nighbourhood.*
> *With hospitable Table, open Door,*
> *One for my Friends, the other for the Poor.*
> *To teach my Family to lead good Lives;*
> *And chiefly teach my Maids to make good Wives:*
> *In doing which, a gen'ral Good I do;*
> *When Wives are good, they make good Husbands too,*
> *That, by Degrees, Mankind wou'd be all so.*
> *But Hell, or Fate, sure, plot to undermine,*
> *To baffle me in every just Design,*
> *And mark me out the Jest of Human Kind.*
> *Methinks I hear the People, pointing, say,*
> *That that's the fond, but scorn'd, Galesia.*

---

1. **Philosopher:** Roman writer, Lucretius (ca. 99–55 B.C.) in praise of Epicurus (341–271 B.C.), *De Natura Rerum* (*On the Nature of Things*) 1:72–74. A commonplace in Lucretius, Cicero (106–43 B.C.), Juvenal (ca. 55–ca.140), and others was that humankind was superior to beasts. Rochester's "A Satyr Against Mankind," based on the eighth satire of Boileau, challenges Lucretius and others, opening with the premise that he'd rather be a beast.

> *That's she whose Beauty lately made such Noise,*
> *Amongst the Inns of Court and College Boys,*
> *And made the Gallants their dear Town despise,*
> *Behold her now, a poor Abject,*[1] *Forlorn,*
> *The Object of each Country Ploughman's Scorn.*
> *To hear this said, what Flesh and Blood can bear?*
> *O no, I will myself in Pieces tear,*
> *And now begin with my dishevel'd Hair.*

After this Hurricane, and divers Gusts of Sighs and Tears, I began to flatter my Fancy that all this might be a Composition like that of *Lowland*, who was now actually marry'd to another Man; and when by this Means the Torments of my distorted Mind were a little appeas'd, I endeavour'd to clear my Countenance, wash'd my Face, took the Air at the Window, and came down to the Company; some Time pass'd in Discourse of Things indifferent, and then *Bosvil* took Leave, and went that Evening to his Father's House.

Towrissa stay'd to bear me Company, and was my Bedfellow that Night, the greatest Part of which we pass'd in Discoursing of *Bosvil;* she relating to me how seriously he had told her and her Mother of his intended Marriage, together with all the Circumstances of Portion and Jointure, Description of the Lady's Person and Family, &c. That there was no Place left for Doubt, for any one but me, who had the Eyes of my Understanding shut and seal'd up by the former Farce he had acted about Mrs. *Lowland;* nevertheless, I suffer'd great Distractions in my Mind; and when Length of Prattle had lull'd *Towrissa* asleep, I refresh'd my weary Spirits with weeping.

After two or three Days, the News came that *Bosvil* was sick of a violent Fever, even so bad that all despair'd of his Life. This was a new Stroke of Fortune, and she was arm'd with a Weapon against which I had never contended; I griev'd, and at the same Time was angry with myself for grieving: Ah, foolish *Galesia*, (said I to myself) Ah, silly Girl, to grieve for him who deserves thy Scorn and Hatred, for him that has robb'd thee of thy Quiet three whole Years, for him that swore to love

---

1. **Abject:** downcast, in low spirits.

thee, that languish'd and dy'd at thy Feet, expressly to make thee miserable; for him that obstructed the Amours of the first and second *Brafort,* that thy Ruin might be the more compleat; for him that was treated by thy hospitable Parents more like their own Child than an adventitious Guest, by which means the Traitor had Opportunity to steal away the Heart of their only Daughter! And is it possible that thou should'st grieve for such a Wretch as him? One that Heaven has now mark'd with its just Vengeance, and has sent this Sickness as a Scourge to his Falshood. But notwithstanding all this I must grieve and pray for him: Which I am sure I did with more Earnestness than I ever did for my own Soul; in which I did but pay a Devotion which he had advanc'd; for he has often assur'd me, that he offer'd me daily in his Prayers; the Consideration of which holy Kindness made me redouble my Request to Heaven to spare his Life, tho', at the same Time, I had much rather he should have dy'd, than not live mine. However, I did not pretend to capitulate with the Almighty, but ask'd his Life in general Terms, without including or excluding his Person, which, by Intervals, I hop'd might yet one Day be mine; for I still sooth'd my Fancy that he lov'd me, and that the Sight of me, after so long an Absence, was the sole Cause of this his Illness; and then made wild Resolutions to visit him, fancy'd myself there, figur'd to myself the Transports of Joy he would be in to see me so kind, imagin'd his Father and Mother embracing me as their own Child; then immediately drawing the Curtain, beheld myself rejected by them, as the Plague of their Family, perhaps refus'd and slighted by him, rebuk'd and wonder'd at for my coming, scorn'd and laugh'd at by all the World, severely treated by my Parents, or perhaps put out of Hopes of ever seeing them again; for I very well believ'd there was no Medium after such an Exploit, between being receiv'd by his Parents, and abandon'd by my own: And for me to have propos'd this Visit to them, I knew was vain, having no Pretence to justify the Request; the whole Amour having been a continu'd Act of Folly on the one Side, and Treachery on the other; and the last Scene a Declaration of Scorn instead of Kindness, he having own'd in the Presence of my Mother and other Friends his Design of marrying another; and then repeat in my Thoughts all his Crimes, and with my best Malice enlarge upon his Treachery, Falshood, and Cruelty; look upon him dead by the

Hand of Heaven, just and good in taking him away from a Possibility of accomplishing his Perjury in this his pretended Marriage; then in an Instant turn over the Leaf, and read him dead; dead as my faithful Lover, recount all our tender Words and Actions that had pass'd in our three Years Conversation; blame all my feign'd Indifferency and forc'd Coldness towards him; fancy'd he thought on me in his Agony, and nam'd me with his dying Breath; believe I saw his much-griev'd Parents cursing me as the Author of their Affliction, and after a Thousand of these tragical Notions, which presented themselves to my distracted Imagination, my Fancy wou'd open another Scene, and make me think I saw him alive, and happy in the Arms of his *London* Mistress, living in all the Felicity that a happy Espousal could procure. Thus my Thoughts play'd at Racket,[1] and seldom minded the Line of Reason; my Mind labour'd under a perpetual shaking Palsy of Hope and Fear; my whole Interiour was nothing but Distraction and Uncertainty. At last I resolv'd to send a Messenger secretly, to know how he did; in which I did a great Penance for all the proud Actions of my Life, not only in shewing that kind Concern for him, but a greater Difficulty yet, which was, to be oblig'd to a Servant, in making him Confidant of this Secret. However, this Occasion made me do Violence to my Nature, and engag'd one of my Father's Men to go secretly on this Errand: But first I order'd him to go to *Bosvil's* own Dwelling, which was near us, and there enquire after his Health; and if there he heard of his being better, then to go no farther, otherwise, to make the best of his Way to his Father's. The Man perform'd my Orders exactly, and hearing at this Place that he was something better, went no farther; with which I remain'd satisfy'd, 'till Time brought him to our House perfectly recover'd. But, ah, this Recovery was a Death to all my Hopes; for the first Use he made of his new-restor'd Health, was to go marry his Mistress at *London;* making our House in his Way, and me the Auditor of that horrid News; which at first shock'd me, but I had been so often put upon by false Alarms, that I was now grown like the Country-men to the Shepherds in the

---

1. **play'd at Racket:** referring to tennis or badminton, disjointed thoughts and indecision.

Fable, who, when the Wolf really came, stirr'd not, having been often deluded by the Shepherds, and call'd without Occasion; for I thought it impossible that he could come to tell me such News to my Face. But what is most astonishing, I have been told since, that in his Sickness he gave all he had to me, and recommended me to his Parents as their own Child, and they promis'd to receive me as such. Now, after all this, to go, directly after his Sickness, and be marry'd to another, is a Transaction most unaccountable. But I knew nothing of this at that Time, for I was told it afterwards, and that he had been extreamly concern'd on my Account in this his Sickness. However, ignorant as I was of these Circumstances, I did not in the least believe that his going to *London,* when he pass'd by our House, was to be marry'd, but look'd upon it as a meer Jest or Banter, such as was that of Mrs. *Lowland,* and others; wherefore, I could not pass over this Subject of Frolick or Mirth, without adding to the Jest, and as I had sent him a Willow Garland, on the Marriage of Mrs. *Lowland,* so now I sent him a pretty Pair of Horns,[1] neatly made of Bugles,[2] by which I meant to joke and banter him on his pretended Marriage; but, alas, it prov'd more than a Pretence, and the Horns came to him just upon his Wedding-Day, in the Presence of his Bride and all the Company; as also several Emblems and Mottos on that Subject, the Horns being fasten'd on a Head-band, as a sovereign Remedy for the Head-ach, to which marry'd Men are often very subject, especially those who marry Town-Coquets; all which, I protest, was without any malicious Intent, not thinking in the least that he was really about Marriage, but only design'd to render Jest for Jest, believing his Discourse of Marriage had only been a Banter, such as that of Mrs. *Lowland,* and the rest before-mention'd.

Now tho' all this came from an unknown Hand, no Question but he believ'd it came from me; and by his Behaviour I concluded as much, for he always avoided my Presence, and shunn'd my Company as much as possible, almost to the Breach of common Civility, by which I fancy'd

---

1. **Horns:** symbols of the cuckold, a man whose wife has committed adultery.
2. **Bugles:** horns of a wild ox, or beads in the shape of these horns.

I was the Object of his Aversion; tho' a Confidant of his, assur'd me of the contrary, and that *Bosvil* had told him, That Love had taken such deep Root in his Soul, that in spight of all his Efforts, even Marriage it self, he could not eradicate it, and therefore avoided my Presence, because he cou'd not see me with Indifferency; moreover, he told him what Conflicts he underwent during his Sickness; but on his Recovery, finding that I had taken no Notice of him, he resolv'd to shake off those Fetters, and abandon one that had never shew'd any Kindness to him, but treated him always with such an Air of Indifference, as seem'd rather the Effect of Prudence than Affection; and that he had invented that Story of Mrs. *Lowland* to try if Jealousy would work upon me, but all my Conduct had been with Caution and Circumspection, quite different from Passion or Tenderness; that he thought, (with others) that all Amourous Inclinations were bury'd with *Brafort,* and that he cou'd never hope farther than for a second Place in my Affections. How far this was sincere or pretended, I know not, but I rather think he set it up as a Screen to his own Falshood; for the meerest Dunce in the School of Love could not but spell Affection in all these three Years Transactions, especially in this Age, where Men are apt to interpret Things in favour of themselves, and believe Women forwarder than they really are, taking Civilities for Affection, and Affection for Passion; but he thought fit to give an Overturn, perhaps to hide his Falshood from the Sight of my Friends, and the rest of the World, by laying the Blame on me; which Way he meant it I know not, but I may justly say with Mr. *Cowley,* to myself,

> *Three of thy loveliest Years*
> *Were toss'd in Storms of Hopes and Fears.*[1]

But to return, he was marry'd at *London,* and brought Home his Bride. Now it was that I was forc'd to act the Part of patient *Grizel,*[2] and go, with other Relations, to bid her Welcome, throw the

---

1. **Three...Fears:** paraphrase of Cowley, *The Mistress,* "Love given over," Stanza 2, lines 1–2. "Three of thy lustiest and thy freshest years,/Tost in storms of *Hopes* and *Fears.*"

2. **Grizel:** Griselda; virtuous, long-suffering wife who submits to repeated tests of her obedience by her husband. See Chaucer, "The Clerk's Tale," *Canterbury Tales,* and Boccaccio, "Day 10," *The Decameron.*

Stocking,[1] eat Sack-Posset,[2] and perform all the Farce of a well pleas'd Kinswoman, invite her to our House, prepare Dinners and Treats for her, and in all Things seem easy and satisfy'd: All which I was constrain'd to do, or lay my Disgrace open to all the World.

Thus, my *Lucasia,* I have brought you to the Confines[3] of this Part of my Story; how far I may stand justify'd or condemn'd in your Thoughts I know not, but I do remember nothing in which I can accuse myself, even now that I am free from Passion, and capable to make a serious Reflection.

The only Thing (reply'd *Lucasia*) that I blame you for, is, that you did not consult your Mother, whose Wisdom might have found out a Way to have accommodated Things to all your Satisfactions. Alas, answer'd *Galesia,* I often reflected on that, but thought it his Business, or his Parents, to discover it to mine, and always expected such an Address; for if I had told my Father or Mother, I shou'd but have embarrass'd them in a difficult Business, for it ill befitted them to profer their Daughter in Marriage, and disagreeable, to leave me to struggle with my own Passion, and his Pretences, without taking any Notice; these Considerations made me let it remain a Secret, in Expectation of their making the Discovery. Nevertheless, I now believe it to be the safest and most commendable Way in any the like Case; and if I was to act the Part over again, I shou'd certainly proceed on that Footing; for in so doing my Duty I hope for a good Event from the Hand of Providence, for I believe wiser Heads than mine wou'd have been puzled in so difficult a Case, and found enough to do to pass through such a Labyrinth as *Bosvil's* subtile Turnings had compos'd: But where we take Vertue for our Guide, God and our good Angels helps us thro'; and tho' we meet with many

---

1. **Throw the Stocking:** early form of tossing the garter or bouquet to celebrate a marriage and denote the next to marry.

2. **Sack-Posset:** sherry or canary wine.

3. **Confines:** limits, end.

Rubs to make us stumble or reel, yet the good Hand of Providence is ready to lend Support, that we shall not fall into Ruin or Confusion.

FINIS.

A

Patch-Work SCREEN

FOR THE

LADIES;

OR,

LOVE and *VIRTUE*

Recommended:

In a COLLECTION of

Instructive NOVELS.

RELATED

After a Manner intirely New, and
interspersed with *Rural* POEMS, describing the *Innocence* of a *Country-Life.*

By Mrs. JANE BARKER, of *Wilsthorp,*
near *Stamford,* in *Lincolnshire.*

'Tis *Love* does all that's Noble here below;
Love is the *Steel,* that strikes upon the *Flint;*
Gives Coldness *Heat,* exerts the hidden *Flame,*
And spreads the *Sparkles* round to warm the *World.*

DRYDEN.

LONDON:

Printed for E. CURLL, over against *Catherine-
street* in the *Strand;* And T. PAYNE, near
Stationers-Hall. 1723. [Pr. *2s. 6d.*]

This page is an approximation of the title page of the 1723 edition of *A Patch-Work Screen for
the Ladies.* Epigraph. The last three lines are from John Dryden (1631–1700), *Love Triumphant;
or, Nature Will Prevail* (1694) 3.1.139–41. Accused of incestuous desires between brother and
sister, the speaker Victoria claims that Alphonso's love is noble and has inspired him to achieve
great deeds for his country. The two are in love but not, it is discovered, brother and sister.

TO THE READER.

My Two former Volumes[1] of Novels *having met with a favourable Reception, (much beyond their Desert) encourages me to perform my Promise in pursuing* The Sequel of Galesia's Story.[2]

But I doubt my Reader will say, Why so long about it? And why a History[3] *reduc'd into* Patches? *especially since* Histories *at* Large *are so Fashionable in this Age; viz.* Robinson Crusoe, *and* Moll Flanders; Colonel Jack,[4] *and* Sally Salisbury;[5] *with many other* Heroes *and* Heroines? *Why, truly, as to the* First, *I had lost my* Galesia, *she being gone from St. Germains,[6] and I retir'd into an obscure Corner of the World.[7] As to the* Second, *you'll find in the following Pages, by what Steps and Means it was framed into this Method. And now, having given you this Account, I think I ought to say something in Favour of* Patch-Work,[8] *the better to recommend it to my Female Readers, as well in their Discourse, as their Needle-Work: Which I might do with Justice, if my Genius were capable: But indeed, I am*

---

1. **My Two former Volumes:** *Love Intrigues; or, The History of the Amours of Bosvil and Galesia* (1713) and *Exilius; or, The Banish'd Roman* (1715). The novels appeared together in *The Entertaining Novels of Mrs. Jane Barker* (1719).

2. The last Novel in Mrs. *Barker's* 2d. Volume. [Publisher's note.] This reference is to *Love Intrigues.* **The Sequel of Galesia's Story:** *A Patch-Work Screen for the Ladies* is the sequel of *Love Intrigues.* **Galesia:** Barker's semi-autobiographical literary persona, first in print in *Poetical Recreations* (1688). Also the Numidian princess, huntress, and student of philosophy and law in *Exilius.* The name recalls the feminine form of Galaesus, prophet and son of Apollo, Greek god of poetry.

3. **History:** term applied to many fictional narratives in the period that claimed to be the story of actual people and times.

4. **Robinson Crusoe, and Moll Flanders; Colonel Jack:** novels (1719, 1722, 1723) by Daniel Defoe (1660?–1731).

5. **Sally Salisbury:** famous prostitute and criminal, likely model for Defoe's *Moll Flanders* (1722) and *Roxana* (1724), figured in the semi-fictional *Authentick Memoirs of…Sally Salisbury* (1723) by Capt. Charles Walker (pseudonym?).

6. **St. Germains:** town near Paris where James II (1633-1701), deposed in December 1688, installed his court-in-exile.

7. **obscure Corner of the World:** Lincolnshire, where Barker leased agricultural property.

8. **Patch-Work:** needlework consisting of pieces of fabric, varying in size, shape, color and type of cloth, applied to a single-fabric background; in Barker's time, the pieces were appliquéd directly to the background rather than pieced together first and then sewn to the background.

not much of an Historian; *but in the little I have read, I do not remember
any thing recorded relating to* Patch-Work, *since the Patriarch* Joseph,[1]
(*whose Garment was of sundry Colours*) *by which means it has not been*
common *in all Ages; and 'tis certain, the* Uncommonness *of any* Fashion,
renders it acceptable to the Ladies.

And I do not know but this may have been the chief Reason why our
Ladies, *in this latter Age, have pleas'd themselves with this sort of Entertainment; for, whenever one sees a Set of Ladies together, their* Sentiments *are
as differently mix'd as the* Patches *in their Work: To wit,* Whigs[2] *and*
Tories,[3] High-Church[4] *and* Low-Church,[5] Jacobites[6] *and* Williamites,[7]
and many more Distinctions, which they divide *and* sub-divide, *'till at last
they make this* Dis-union *meet in an harmonious* Tea-Table *Entertainment. This puts me in mind of what I have heard some* Philosophers *assert,
about the* Clashing *of* Atoms,[8] *which at last* united *to compose this glorious
Fabrick of the* UNIVERSE.

---

1. **Joseph:** favorite son of Jacob, whose gift of a fine, ornamental coat aroused the jealousy of
Joseph's brothers; see Gen. 37:3. The King James version of the Bible (1611) translated the
Hebrew "ornamental" and "long-sleeved" as "of *many* colours."

2. **Whigs:** traditional champions of Parliament and dissenting Protestants outside the Church
of England, often allied with the rising powers of mercantile interests.

3. **Tories:** often from the rural gentry, traditional champions of the Crown and the Church of
England.

4. **High-Church:** pertaining to the Church of England, emphasizing the role of tradition, the
sacraments, and authority; set in bitter opposition to Low Church and most sympathetic with
Tory politics.

5. **Low-Church:** pertaining to the Church of England, believed that the Church should be
surbordinate to the State and that voluntary societies for "reformation of manners" were more
effective than Church courts; increasingly sympathetic with Whig politics.

6. **Jacobites:** from the Latin *Jacobus* for James; supporters of the House of Stuart after the
Revolution of 1688.

7. **Williamites:** supporters of William of Orange (1650–1702), Protestant nephew of James II,
who became William III and co-ruled with his wife Mary II (1662–94), Protestant daughter of
James II.

8. **Clashing of Atoms:** referring to ancient and late seventeenth-century atomic theories.
Greek philosophers Democritus (460–ca. 357 B.C.) and Epicurus (341–271 B.C.), and Roman
poet Lucretius (ca. 99–ca. 55 B.C.), argued that phenomena in the universe are explained by the
random rearrangement of the smallest observable units, or atoms. English natural philosopher,
Robert Boyle (1627–91) articulated an atomic theory of matter, and his student Robert Hooke
(1635–1703) posited the kinetic hypothesis of gases.

Forgive me, kind Reader, for carrying the Metaphor too high; by which means I am out of my Sphere, and so can say nothing of the Male Patch-Workers; *for my high Flight in Favour of the Ladies, made a mere* Icarus[1] *of me, melted my Wings, and tumbled me Headlong down, I know not where. Nevertheless my* Fall *was amongst a joyful Throng of People of all Ages, Sexes, and Conditions! who were rejoycing at a wonderful* Piece *of* Patch-Work *they had in Hand; the Nature of which was such, as was to compose (as it were) a* New Creation, *where all Sorts of People were to be* Happy, *as if they had never been the* Off-spring *of fallen* Adam. [2]

I was greatly rejoyc'd at this my Fall, *when I found my-self amongst these happy Undertakers,[3] and hop'd to unite my-self in their Confraternity;[4] but they finding some Manuscript* Ballads[5] *in my Pocket, rejected me as one of that Race of Mortals who live on a certain barren Mountain 'till they are turn'd into* Camelions;[6] *so I was forc'd to get away, every one hunching and pushing me, with Scorn and Derision. However, as the Sequel prov'd, I had no small Reason to rejoice at being thus used; for soon after, their* Patch-Work Scheme,[7] *by carrying the Point too high, was blown up about their Ears, and vanish'd into Smoke and Confusion; to the utter Ruin of many Thousands of the Unhappy Creatures therein concern'd.*

When I was got out of this Throng into the open Field, I met with the poor Galesia, *walking to stretch her Legs, having been long sitting at her Work. With her I renew'd my Old Acquaintance; and so came to know all*

---

1. **Icarus:** in Greek mythology, prideful mortal who flew too close to the sun, thereby melting the wax attaching his artificial wings and plunging him to his death in the sea west of Samos (now the Icarian Sea).

2. **fallen Adam:** Adam was expelled from Paradise for having disobeyed God; see Gen. 2–3.

3. **Undertakers:** those who undertake projects.

4. **Confraternity:** association, company.

5. **Manuscript Ballads:** unpublished verse, in Barker's hand.

6. **Camelions:** small, lizard-like animals that change color to blend into the background; supposedly nimble-tongued and living on air; a common metaphor to describe self-interested changing or concealing of political or religious allegiances. See Dryden's allusion in defense of his conversion to Catholicism in *The Hind and the Panther* (1687) 3:788. A less common allusion to poetic imagination; see Sir John Davies, "Orchestra" (1596).

7. **Scheme:** possibly referring to the South Sea Bubble, when thousands of investors lost heavily in speculative stock of the South Sea Trading Company (1720).

this Story of her Patch-Work: *Which if you like, I will get the remaining Part of the* SCREEN;[1] *for they are still at Work:*[2] *And, upon my Word, I am glad to find the Ladies of* This Age, *wiser than* Those *of the* Former; *when the working of* Point[3] *and curious* Embroidery, *was so troublesome, that they cou'd not take* Snuff *in Repose, for fear of soiling their Work: But in* Patch-Work *there is no Harm done; a smear'd Finger does but add a* Spot *to a* Patch, *or a* Shade *to a* Light-Colour: *Besides, those curious Works were pernicious to the Eyes;* they *cou'd not see the* Danger themselves *and* their Posterity might be in, a Thousand Years hence, about I know not what—*But I will inquire against the next Edition; therefore, be sure to buy these* Patches *up quickly, if you intend to know the* Secret; *thereby you'll greatly oblige the* Bookseller, *and, in some degree, the* Author. *Who is,*

RICHMOND,[4]   Your humble Servant,
Candlemas-Day,   JANE BARKER.
1722–23.[5]

---

1. **Screen:** a large ornamental piece that displayed the maker's feminine talents in sewing and signified her family's social position. Screens from the period often had several panels that could measure 9 feet by 2 feet and took several years to finish.

2. **Work:** general term for needlework. To be "at her work" means that a woman or girl is at her needlework.

3. **Point:** from the French for stitch, thread lace made wholly with the needle.

4. **Richmond:** fashionable town near London.

5. **Candlemas-Day:** 2 February, a feast of the Virgin, marked by an abundant display of candles. **1722–23:** i.e., 1723 new style.

INTRODUCTION.

When we parted from *Galesia* last, it was in St. *Germain's Garden;* [1] and now we meet with her in *England,* travelling in a Stage-Coach from *London* Northward; where she had the Luck to meet with good Company, who entertained each other agreeably with Things indifferent, suitable to the Times; thereby beguiling the Tediousness of the Way, and the tiresome Rocking of the Vehicle they were in, 'till they came where the Road extended it-self between Two Woods, a Place well known for the many Robberies which had been there commited.

Here our Passengers began to fear it was now their Turn to be rifled of what they had, especially when they saw divers[2] Horsemen, well mounted, crossing the Way backward and forward, in and out of the Woods, whooping and hollowing to one another; 'till the Sight of a Huntsman with his Horn, and a Pack of Hounds rushing out of the Wood, in Pursuit of a Hare which was gone a little while before, eas'd them of their Apprehensions, and convinc'd them, That the Horsemen they had seen, were only some of the Gentry of that Neighbourhood, diverting themselves with their Dogs. However, this Accident put them in Mind of many criminal Adventures and Robberies, which they related, one Story bringing on another, as is usual amongst Company; some of which, perhaps, will not be disagreeable to the Reader; and therefore I shall insert them here; beginning with the following, as related by one of the Gentlemen.

A certain Robber that lived in *Wales,* knowing the Day of *Shrewsbury-Fair*,[3] came down from the Mountains in the Night, that he might be at the Town early enough to slip no Opportunity that might be to his Advantage; the *Graziers-Fair*[4] beginning early in most Places, and it

---

1. See The Amours of *Bosvil* and *Galesia,* one of Mrs. *Barker's* Novels. Printed 1719. [Publisher's note.]

2. **divers:** diverse; numerous.

3. **Shrewsbury:** town in central England. **Fair:** periodic event of festivities and agricultural commerce, authorized by the charter of a town or borough.

4. **Graziers:** those who graze animals to be sold.

being the Business of Cheats and Robbers to watch who buys, and who sells, who receives Money, and where they carry or deposite it.

When he was got within Eight or Ten Miles of *Shrewsbury*, he saw grazing in a Farmer's Ground a Yoke or two of large Fat Oxen; these he thought would be ready Money at the Fair, and accordingly drove them away, 'till he came to a Publick House[1] in the Road, near the Town, where he called to drink, and asked the Landlord, If he had any Pasturage, where he might graze his Oxen a while, to plump them so as to make them appear better at the Fair? Hereupon the Landlord put them in a very good Pasture just by his House; and then our *Mountainier* went into the Fair, amongst the Farmers and Graziers, and met with a Chapman,[2] who was buying from one Farmer to another, in order to make up his Droves;[3] so our Thief told him, That he had some very good Oxen feeding just without the Town-Gate, where he had left them to rest a while, they being heavy and weary. The Grazier went readily along with him, and, in few Words, bargained for the Beasts, paid down the Money, and, finding the Pasture good, desired the Landlord to let them rest there, and he would send more to them, 'till he had compleated his Drove: So both went their Way, one about his Honest Calling, the other to pursue his Wicked Projects.

What other Advantage this Thief made at the Fair, is not come to our Knowledge: But having taken Notice of a very pretty Mare that ran in the same Ground with the Oxen, he thought he would not miss that Booty, and went in the Evening to the same House, ordering a good Supper, and treated himself and his Landlord very well. In the Night he got up, and having remarked where a Bridle and Saddle hung, he went into the Ground, took the Mare, and away he rode, 'till he arrived pretty near the Place where he had taken the Oxen. He there met the Owner of them, who inquir'd of him concerning his Beasts, (as he had done all about those Parts, of every one he met) describing to him their Age, Shape, and Marks. To which our Thief reply'd, That in such a

---

1. **Publick House:** tavern.

2. **Chapman:** merchant.

3. **Droves**: herds.

Ground, belonging to such a Man, near *Shrewsbury*, there were just such Oxen as he described. The Farmer, overjoy'd to hear of his Cattle, began to lament that his Horse was so ridden down, that he fear'd, he would not be able to carry him to *Shrewsbury*. Ah me! said he, if I had my good Horse I was bid Money for t'other Day, he would have done my Business. The Mountainier presently formed another Cheat in his Head, and seem'd to pity the good Man, telling him, He would lend him that Mare on which he rode, provided he would give him some Mark or Token, by which he might have the Horse he mentioned. The Farmer, much rejoyced hereat, told him, That he should go to his Wife, and give her that tired Horse, and bid her deliver the bald Horse which was in the Stable; by the same Token, *That he was bid Ten Guineas for him such a Day, she being by, making up her Butter.* By these punctual Tokens, the Thief got the good Horse, and away he rode to the Mountains with his Booty.

And now let us follow the Farmer; who soon arrived at the Place where his Oxen were grazing; and challenging them, the Landlord refus'd to deliver them, as not being put there by him; and, on the other Hand, seiz'd his Mare, and the Farmer for the Thief that stole her. This created a great deal of Trouble between the Landlord, the honest Farmer, and the Grazier who had bought the Beasts; and, one may suppose, took up much Time and Money before the Right could be understood. But, in Conclusion,

The Man had his Mare again.

From whence, I suppose, said the Gentleman, arose that Proverb.

The Gentleman having thus finish'd his *Proverbial-Story*, another of the Company was incited thereby to call to Mind a *Proverbial-Story* of later Date; but first asked the Company, If they knew how ill-dress'd Perukes[1] came to be called *Kaxtons?*[2] To whom all answering No; he began his Story as follows.

There is, said he, a good Farm-House just by the Road near *Kaxton;* the honest Master of which, having, at some Market or Fair, received

---

1. **Perukes:** wigs.
2. **Kaxton:** Caxton, Cambridgeshire.

Money for Goods he had sold, was telling it over on *Saturday* Night, and put up in a Bag as much as would pay his Half-Year's Rent, telling his Man, That on *Monday* he should carry it to his Landlord; and, at the same Time, ordered his Labourer, (who was then receiving his Wages) to be sure to come early on *Monday* Morning to take Care of the Yard, while his Man was out.

Next Day, being *Sunday*, the Young Man went, in the Afternoon, to visit and divert himself amongst his Friends and Companions; and coming home a little late, he found the Gates shut fast, that he could not get in; and knowing that his Mistress Lay-in, he would not make a Noise by knocking, lest it should disturb or fright her, but went quietly away, and lay with some of his Companions.

Next Morning he came again, thinking to go about his Business, but found all fast shut still; and though he knock'd often and loud, could make No body hear: He saunter'd about 'till towards Noon, and still it was the same; no Noise was to be heard but the Herds lowing in the Yard for Fodder. Hereupon he went to the Town, and informed several People of the Matter, who all agreed to take a Constable and some of the best of the Parish, and if they could make No-body hear by knocking, e'en to break open the Gates and Doors, and see what should be the Matter; some conjecturing one thing, some another; but most concluding with the Servant, That the good Man was gone to carry his Rent, and the good Woman fallen into some grievous Fit, if not dead.

In short, They broke open the Gates, and while some went to force the House-Doors, others proceeded to the Barn for Straw to throw into the Cribs, and there they beheld the most amazing Sight imaginable; the Good Man and his Wife both murder'd on the Floor, and two Forks[1] broken! Hereupon, they went towards the House, and passing cross the Yard, they saw the Child's Swath[2] dropt, and when they came into the House, found the Babe in the Cradle, with its Neck wrung behind it. They proceeded then to search the House; The Goods all

---

1. **Forks:** pitchforks.
2. **Child's Swath:** swaddling clothes.

remain'd; but the Money, and divers Silver Things, as Spoons, Porrin-gers, Cups, and the like, were gone.

Upon due Consideration, they suspected the Labourer, he being no where to be found; Hereupon Hue-and-Cries[1] were sent forth, every way describing his Person, Age, and Cloaths: But all in vain; no News could be heard. The Manner of the Murder, they conjectur'd, was on this wise: That the Labourer was in the Barn, and when the good Man went to give his Beasts Fodder, the Villain fell upon him, and he resist-ing, caus'd the two Forks to be broke. The poor Woman sitting in the House with her Child on her Lap, hearing the Noise in the Barn, rose hastily, and clapping the Child in the Cradle, with its Clouts[2] hanging loose about it, ran to the Barn, and dropt the Swath; which was found as aforesaid: And so met her poor Husband's Fate.

Thus Things pass'd without Discovery for Seven Years, all which Time the Villain liv'd beyond Sea. At the Seven Years End, thinking the Matter might be forgot, he came into *England,* and being a North-country Man, directed his Journey towards *Kaxton;* And calling at an Alehouse in a Village near that Town to drink and rest himself, it so happen'd, that the Master of the House was Constable at the Time he fled, when the Hue-and-Cries were after him; and now, in Seven Years Time, the Office having been round the Village, was come to him again. By what Spirit or Genius this Constable was inspired, cannot be guess'd; but so it was, he thought this Man answer'd the Character of the Hue-and-Cry which came to his Hands Seven Years before, of which, perhaps, he had the Copy by him; Wherefore, by Virtue of his Office, he seiz'd him, and carry'd him before a Justice, who examin'd and committed him: But the Crime of which he was suspected being committed Southward, near *Kaxton,* he was conveyed thither to be Try'd; At what Time, there were many Witnesses appear'd to testify that he was the Labourer in that Farmyard, when this Murder was commit-ted; all which he most stedfastly deny'd, protesting, that he never was there in his Life, nor knew the Place. At last, the Servant of that Farm,

---

1. **Hue-and-Cries:** warrants for the pursuit and arrest of a criminal.

2. **Clouts:** swaddling clothes.

who knew him very well by his Face and Speech, added one Circumstantial more, saying, That the Man who then thrash'd in the Barn, had a Running-Sore on his Side; which, said he, I have divers times help'd him to dress; so that if the Sore should be heal'd, there must needs be a Scar. Hereupon the Part being search'd, and the Scar plainly appearing, he could no longer oppose or deny so manifest a Truth. He was hang'd in Chains by the Road-side near *Kaxton;* an Example of the most vile Cruelty that could be committed.

There happen'd to pass some *Cambridge* Scholars[1] that Way to visit some Friends thereabouts; and the Weather being a little turbulent, the Wind and Wet so discompos'd their Wiggs, that when they came in, they fancy'd them to look like that on the Head of the Hang'd Man. This Fancy they carry'd back with them to *Cambridge,* and there broach'd it amongst the Youth of their Time; which, by Degrees, spread over the Nation. Afterwards, by reason of many of our young Gentlemen going into the Wars in divers and distant Countries, this Fancy was carried with them, so that in most Parts of *Europe,* to this Day, an ill-dress'd Wigg is call'd

A Caxton, or Kak.

According to the usual Proverb as aforesaid, *One Story begets another,* so it happen'd amongst this Company: The next Gentleman said, That forasmuch as the two former had embellish'd their Stories by Proverbs, he would not offer to the Company a Relation but what he knew to be Truth.

There was, said he, a certain Gentleman of Distinction, who at his Death, left three Daughters Coheiresses, under the Guardianship of their Uncle his Brother. The Gentleman being dead, the young Ladies, by Advice of their Uncle, broke up House, and sold their Goods, in order to put themselves into Places of polite Education,[2] thereby to improve themselves before they entred into a Married State.

In order to which, their Family was retrench'd, Servants paid off, and

---

1. **Cambridge Scholars:** students at Cambridge University.

2. **Places of polite Education:** private English schools or French convents where girls and young women would learn genteel accomplishments such as fine embroidery, music, and French. Barker had attended such a school in Putney, near London.

Goods sold; And every Thing being thus dispos'd, and they ready to leave the House, there came one Evening, a Gentleman that had lost his Way, and, driven by ill Weather, begg'd Refuge at this House. The young Ladies were fearful to receive him, their Family being small, and the Situation distant from Neighbours: But Commiseration of the Gentleman's distrest Condition moving them, at last they entertain'd him very kindly, made a handsome Supper, and lodg'd him in a good Room; but withal, took Care to fasten his Door, and all Passages that led to it, in order to secure themselves from any wicked Intention he might possibly have to let in any Gang of Villains to destroy or disturb them: And, for their better Security, they resolv'd not to go to Bed that Night; but sate up, often descanting on their Folly, in having admitted this Stranger, which was the Cause of their Discomposure. Then would they reflect on his Horse, Pistols, and Accoutrements, all which, they fancy'd, had more the Air of an Highway-man, than a solitary unfortunate Traveller. Then again, they would reflect on the Genteelness of his Person and Behaviour; the Honesty and Integrity of his Countenance; the Agreeableness of his Discourse, all tending to Vertue and Honesty, and adorn'd with Wit and good Humour.

Thus, *Pro* and *Con,* they entertain'd and rejected their Fears, 'till after Midnight; and then their wavering Apprehensions were turn'd into a substantial thorow Fright; for they heard at the Drawing-room Door, which open'd into the Garden, a Noise of breaking open; which made them presently conclude it to be some of the Traveller's Companions, who, because he could not let 'em in, being fast lock'd up, had betaken themselves to this forcible Entry.

Thus being frighted, distressed, and distracted; they went to see what was become of the Traveller; but they peeping and listening at the Door, could perceive nothing, but that he was fast asleep; Whereupon they took Courage, enter'd his Chamber, awak'd him, and told him their Distress. He immediately got up, took his Sword and Pistols, went with them to the Drawing-Room, and found the Door almost ready to give the Villains Entrance: The Door and the Jaumb[1] being shatter'd, the

---

1. **Jaumb:** jamb; sidepost of a doorway.

Gentleman had the better Opportunity to let fly at them; which he did, and with such Success, that one of them fell down dead, or sore wounded; and the others had enough to do to get him away, and themselves off clear.

We may imagine how they spent the rest of the Night; the least Part of which, we may suppose, pass'd in Sleep. Next Morning, they earnestly invited the Traveller to stay with them the coming Day, to prevent any farther Frights, though, we may reasonably suppose, they provided themselves of Assistance for the ensuing Night. The Gentleman was too Generous to refuse their Request, at least for a Day, hoping their Spirits, which were greatly disorder'd by the Night's Distractions, might be restored in that Time.

They had scarce din'd, when a Messenger came from their Uncle, who liv'd about Four Miles off, to invite them to his Son's Funeral the next Day. They were greatly surprized at this sudden and unexpected News; and divers Questions they ask'd the Messenger; testified much Grief for the Death of their dear Cousin; promis'd to go and pay that last Respect to his Memory; and with many dutiful and compassionate Services to their Uncle, dismiss'd the Messenger.

Then they desir'd the Traveller to go along with them on the Morrow, that they might present him to their Uncle, as the Author of their Safety. He was not hard to be persuaded to defer his Journey, or suspend his Business; Beauty and Fortunes being always most powerful Rhetoricians.

In short, he went along with them; where, we will suppose, they found all the Desolation suitable to such an Occasion. The Ladies desired to see their Cousin, e'er he was interr'd; but he was fasten'd up before they came: This increas'd the Gentleman's Suspicion, who having laid many Ends together, began greatly to believe there was some foul Play. Wherefore, without saying a Word, he went to some Officers of Justice, which he brought along with him, and commanded the Coffin to be open'd, and the Corps search'd: In so doing, they found a Wound in the Body, which had been his Death; upon which surprizing Spectacle, the whole Family was seized; And now, being in the Hands of Justice, the old Man's Grief and Remorse would not permit him to conceal any-thing; but he freely and openly own'd, That he and his Son design'd to murder the young Ladies, and so become Lords of their Inheritance.

This free Confession soon put a Period to his Afflictions, by the Help of a Shameful Death; and the young Gentleman, who was a younger Brother,[1] made his Fortune and himself Happy in the Marriage of one of the Ladies. And thus, according to the Proverb,

One good Turn deserves Another.

The Company having return'd the Gentleman Thanks, told *Galesia,* That they hop'd she had some Story or Adventure wherewith to oblige them. To which she reply'd, That, truly, she had pass'd so many Years out of *England,* that she should be obliged to conduct their Attention as far as *Paris.* And so proceeded.

I suppose, said she, you all know there is a great Fair, in the *Faux-bourgh Saint Germains*[2] at *Paris,* kept at a certain Time of the Year; wherein there are, besides all sorts of Merchandize, Shews, Games, and Raffling, *&c.*

Hither it was that a Gentlewoman and I were going, a little to divert ourselves amongst other Holy-day[3] Fools, and passing through *Luxem-bourg-Garden,*[4] we sate down on a Bench, a-while to rest ourselves: Where, regarding the well-built House of *Luxembourg,*[5] wherein lived the Princess *Madamoiselle de Monpensier,*[6] we began to reflect on the Folly of that Lady, for adhering to the Rebels in the King's Minority,[7] and how unfortunate she had made herself in having lost his Majesty's

---

1. **younger Brother:** because of the law of primogeniture, which entitles the eldest son to inherit his parents' entire estate, a younger brother would have to make his fortune on his own.

2. **Fauxbourgh Saint Germains:** fashionable Parisian neighborhood.

3. **Holy-day:** holiday.

4. **Luxembourg-Garden:** public park, once the grounds of a palace built for Marie de Médicis (1573–1642), queen of Henri IV (1553–1610).

5. **House of Luxembourg:** Luxembourg Palace.

6. **Madamoiselle de Monpensier:** Anne-Marie Louise d'Orléans (1627–93), Duchesse de Montpensier, known as La Grande Mademoiselle, supported rebel princes in the Fronde, a series of civil wars, 1648–53, that attempted to check the power of royal government. She once ordered a cannon to be turned against royal troops to save the Condé, a rebellious prince and her relation. She was exiled from court.

7. **King's Minority:** Louis XIV (1638–1715) inherited the throne at age five. His mother Anne d'Autriche (1601–66) ruled as regent until his majority in 1651.

Favour for so doing. Whilst we were in this Discourse, a Gentleman of our own Country came to us, and asked, If we were design'd for the Fair? We told him Yes. There has been, said he, a great Bustle in the Fair to Day. Whereupon we desired him to sit down, and tell us what was the Occasion.

Last Night, said he, there were Gentlemen raffled[1] in a Booth 'till it was pretty late. At last, the Losers having pretty well emptied their Pockets, departed. He that was the chief Winner, was also about to go; but the Master of the Booth dissuaded him, telling him, That there were many Spies about the Fair, taking Notice of those that were Winners; and when they went away, took Opportunity to rob, and sometimes murder them: And you, Sir, continued he, having won considerable, will be in Danger; wherefore, I beg you to remain here 'till Day-light. The Gentleman found the Advice very reasonable, and sate himself down in an Easy-Chair, and bid them make him a Pot of Chocolate, and he would there get a little Sleep.

So said, so done; but in the Chocolate, they put a good Dose of *Opium;* and when he was fallen into a sound Sleep, they murder'd him, cut him in Pieces, and carry'd him out to a Common Shore,[2] into which they threw him.

In the Morning, a Foot of him was seen by Passengers, who calling Officers of Justice, got out the Body Piece-meal as it was, as also the Head; and amongst all this, a Plate, which was writ on, belonging to such a Cook.

The Cook and his Family were hereupon seiz'd and examined, who knew nothing of the Matter, but call'd to Mind to whom they had sent out Meat that Day, and who had, or had not return'd the Plates. At last the People of the foresaid Booth were seiz'd and examin'd: Conscience, which flew in their Faces, would not permit them to deny it much: The Maid own'd, that she carried the Head out upon a Plate, which Plate slipp'd out of her Hands when she threw the Head into the Common Shore.

---

1. **raffled:** gambled.
2. **Common Shore:** sewer.

Thus Murder will out.

Thus Four of our Passengers told their melancholy Stories, which the Danger of the Road had first brought into their Memories. There was a Fifth, a young Lady Daughter to one of the Gentlemen; so they ask'd, If she had not a Story wherewith to oblige the Company? To which she reply'd, That she had no Story of that kind; being but, lately come out of a Nunnery, (where her Father had plac'd her for a safe Education, Death having depriv'd her of her Mother); but she would relate a Transaction which happen'd in the said Convent.

There was a beautiful young Lady said she, and a Gentleman, suitable in Years, Quality, and all other Accomplishments of Mind and Person, who contracted a mutual Affection for each other; but the Gifts of Fortune were not such as could probably make them happy; for which Reason, the Parents on both Sides oppos'd their Espousals.

The young Lady, finding that she could not give her Person to him to whom she had surrender'd her Affections, implored the Favour of her Parents, to let her enter into a Convent, where, amongst those holy Votaries,[1] she might endeavour to overcome her Passion. Her Friends consented to the Proposal, concluding that Time and perpetual Absence might give her that Tranquility which could not be had otherwise.

Our young Lady being in the Convent, began to be charm'd with that devout and heavenly Way of Living: Such Regularity and Exactitude in their Religious Performances: Such Patience; such Obedience: Such Purity of Manners; by which those holy Souls climb to Heaven; that, considering the Difficulty, or rather, Impossibility of ever possessing her Cavalier, she resolved to bury all Thoughts of him, together with her own Beauty, under a holy Veil: To which her Friends giving Consent, though very unwillingly, she betook herself to a Religious Habit,[2] in order to perform her Time of Probation.[3] In the mean time, our Cavalier was ingaged in the Army far distant, both performing their Duties according to their Stations.

---

1. **Votaries:** those who make a sacred vow.

2. **Religious Habit:** nun's clothing.

3. **Time of Probation:** until she could take final vows.

And now, behold the Vicissitude of Human Affairs: Our Cavalier, by his valiant and noble Achievements, was advanc'd to great Honours in the Army, and at the same Time he had an Uncle dy'd, who left him an Estate that seem'd to put him above the Reach of adverse Fortune; and not knowing the Fate of his Beloved Mistress, he returned Home, not fearing any Obstacle in his Addresses, (after such Acquisitions of Glory and Fortune) either from the young Lady or her Parents.

But, alas! when he came and found his dear Mistress ingaged in a Religious Order, how great his Affliction was, is hard to describe. Ah! said he, had she been taken Prisoner by the *Turk*, one might hope, by Valour or Money, for her Inlargement: or had she been married to some old unworthy Rival, Time or Death might provide her a Release; or was she confin'd or forbidden by the Caprice of humoursome Parents, Respect, Duty, and Indearments to them, might gain not only their Consent, but their Affections. But, as it is, (O wretched as I am! unfortunate and miserable!) I am not only deprived of all Hopes of injoying her, but of ever seeing her; Nor can so much as the least Line from me reach her Hands; Nay, so unhappy I am, that it is said to be a Crime in me even to complain to my-self. Unhappy that I am! to have mov'd and acted in Showers of Bullets untouch'd, and now to sink under the most incurable of all Wounds! I coveted the Glory of Conquest, and the Riches of Reward, for no other End, but to render me more acceptable to her, and her Parents. I have no Taste of the Glory of Victory, or the Pleasure of Plenty, since she is not to be Copartner in my Glory or Abundance.

These and a thousand such Lamentations he utter'd when alone, or only in the hearing of a little pretty Hugonot-Page,[1] which he had taken whilst in the Army, who hearing his Complaints, took the Liberty to speak to his Master, telling him, That he doubted not but by his Means he might find a way to correspond with this his Religious Mistress, and know, at least, whether she had thus sequester'd her self from him out of real Devotion, or the Persuasions of her Parents, or Despair of the Continuation of his Kindness; for the last of which he thought she had no

---

1. **Hugonot-Page:** Huguenot; a French Protestant serving as a personal attendant.

Reason; for though he was long absent, and far distant, yet he had not fail'd to give her perpetual Assurances in Writing, not reflecting how difficult, if not impossible, it is in those Places for Letters to come to the Hands of the Beloved. But to return to our Page:

The Master and he agreed, that he should be dress'd like a Girl, and put into that Convent, to be educated in good Manners, and instructed in Religion. This they contriv'd with the utmost Dexterity, and executed with Success. And now behold our Page-Damsel is got into the Convent with full Instructions from his Master, to the young Nun, or rather Novice; for, as Luck was, she was not yet profess'd, though she had been there above a Year; the Order of that House requiring Two Years Probation.

And here the young Gentlewoman who related the Story, read to us the following Letter, which the Cavalier intrusted to the young Hugonot, which, she said, she had procured a Copy of.

The *Letter.*

Madam,

I cannot tell whether Grief or Surprize have the greatest Share in my Breast, to find you ingaged in a State so absolutely destructive to my Happiness; but both exceed all Degrees of Comparison. Ah! my fair and dear Creature, how could you be so cruel to your self and me! For I flatter my self, it was and is a Cruelty to You as well as to Me your fond Lover: I say, How could you abandon me to Despair? In which I would say (if I durst) that you are not only Unkind, but Criminal: For you ought not thus to have given yourself away without my Consent or Knowledge. Recollect, how often you have assured me of your Affections, and everlasting Love; and that the only Objection you or your Parents had against our Espousals, was Narrowness of Fortune. But that Objection being remov'd, you ought to be wholly Mine; You ought not to give away that which is not your own. Stollen Goods are an unworthy, nay, an impious Offering to Heaven. King Saul[1] sav'd that which was none of his, to sacrifice to the Lord, and how unacceptable it was, I desire you to consider, and make the Application.

---

1. **King Saul:** first king of the ancient Hebrews, usurped priestly functions to make untimely sacrifices, unpleasing to God; see 1 Sam. 10:8, 13:8–14.

Think on these Things, my Bright, my Fair, my Dear Charmer: And think what Injustice you do me, every Moment you deprive me of your Person. And, believe it, you are but a Murderer, as long as you seclude yourself from me, who cannot live without you: Therefore, bethink yourself of the Injury you do me; and repair all, by the Surrender of your Person to me, who have the True and Real, though not the common Legal Right to alledge.

The young Lady that gives you this, will take Measures with you; Take Courage then, my dearest Life! to put in Practice what is so well-contrived; and so make Happy the most Faithful of Lovers, even

Your Constant and Passionate,
CHEVALIER.

This Letter our young Hugonot found an Opportunity, to deliver, though with great Difficulty; for in those Houses they correspond very little, but live in Solitude and Silence, nor ever go into each other's Cells,[1] those Places being the Recesses for solitary Meditation: But more especially the Religious Dames converse not with the young Ladies who are there for Education, except those that are placed over them, as Teachers and Governesses. Nevertheless, our fair Messenger, found some lucky Moment to deliver the Letter, and recount to her the Griefs her Cavalier suffer'd for her sake, the many Sighs he breath'd, the many Tears he shed, and Groans he utter'd, with continual Languishing in Discontent and Despair; All which so touch'd our Novice, that she began to regret what she had done, and to wish she could find a Way, handsomely and without Contempt, to undo what she had done.

Millions of Things she revolved in her Mind, discuss'd the Matter between the poor State of a Religious Life, destitute of all Comforts, and those Pleasures which are to be found in a Plentiful Fortune, with a noble young Husband, honour'd with Wreaths of martial Glory; In all which she made her own Inclinations Arbitrator between Heaven and Earth, God and the World, *&c.*—After many Debates with herself, she wrote to her *Cavalier* as follows.

---

1. **Cells:** small bedrooms where nuns slept and reflected.

Sir,

Your Letter has so ruffled my whole Interior, that I know not how to write common Sense: Therefore, if my Answer be unintelligible, blame me not, for I am utterly lost in an Abyss of Confusion: The Thoughts of breaking my holy Resolutions on one Hand, and the Sufferings which the keeping them, makes us both undergo, on the other, distracts me. My dear Chevalier! *change your Reproaches into Pity: I will endeavour to repair my Faults: Faults! did I say? Ah me! it is a Crime, to call this my Religious Enterprize a Fault! My Thoughts, Words, Writings, on this Occasion, are Faults! The very Corresponding with the young Lady you placed here, is a Fault! Yet, a Fault so sweet, so delicious, that I cannot refrain, because she recounts a thousand tender Things of you; repeats your Sighs and Grief in such soft and melting Words and Accents, as would soften the most obdurate Heart.*

Then, what Effect, think you, must it have on Mine, which is prepared to be set on Fire by the least Spark struck from your dear Assurances, which she most industriously blows into a Flame, not to be suppress'd by any devout Sighs, Tears, or other Religious Mortifications; by which I suffer a perpetual Martyrdom, and see no Way of Delivery, but by adhering to your Advice sent by her, and come to your Arms: Those dear glorious Arms! those Arms, that have honoured your Family, Friends, and Native Country! Those Arms, that have crown'd the Hero with Lawrels,[1] and the Lover with Myrtles.[2] Those Arms, that have greatly help'd to subdue the Enemies of France, *and built Trophies in the Hearts of the Fair.*

O! can I refuse my Hero? Can I refuse my Lover? Can I refuse my dear Chevalier? *Indeed, I cannot! No, no, I cannot! I will not! The Temptation is too great to be resisted by frail Mortality.*

Wherefore, my beloved Chevalier, *I will comply with those Measures you and your young* Hugonot *have taken.*

This Letter being writ, our Two young Ladies were greatly embarrass'd how to get it to the Cavalier's Hands: At last, they thought on the

---

1. **Lawrells:** laurels; emblems of victory.

2. **Myrtles:** plants sacred to Venus, goddess of love.

following Means. The Hugonot work'd a curious fine Purse, and begg'd Leave of the Abbess to present it to her Patron the Cavalier. So between the Lining and the Out-side they plac'd this Letter, writ on fine Paper and in a small Character, and so convey'd it to the Cavalier.

Now the Way, contriv'd to extricate the Fair Novice from the Convent, was thus; That the Cavalier should be present at the Altar, when she should come to take her Religious Vows; At what Time, she declar'd before the whole Congregation, That all the Vow she meant to take, should be in Holy Marriage to that Gentleman, taking him by the Hand. This surpriz'd the whole Congregation; in particular, her Parents, and the Quire[1] of Nuns. Some blam'd the Boldness of that Proceeding, saying she might have gone out quietly and privately: Others prais'd the generous open Way she had taken. The Clergy, which were there assembled, all told her Parents, That they could not refuse their Consent, since she had demanded him at the Altar of God. All the Quality[2] there (which were many, who came to assist and grace the Ceremony) said the same. The Parents were very well content, only wish'd she had proceeded otherwise, and not made herself the Publick Subject of a Nine Days Wonder.[3]

In short, all were pleas'd, and the Marriage was accomplished to every Body's Satisfaction, except to that of the young Hugonot; Who came forth, and, on her Knees, begg'd Pardon for having deluded her Master; For, indeed, said she, I am not a Boy, as I pretended to be, but a foolish Girl, that took that Disguise upon me to be near your Person; that illustrious Person, which not only dazled the Eyes of me, an unthinking Maid, but which, joyn'd with your Noble Actions, made all Hearts rejoice. But when I came to be Witness of your Grief for this Lady, Pity and Generosity supplanted Affection, and made me undertake this Enterprize; for which, I humbly beg Pardon of all these holy Votaries; and that they will receive me a Member of their Pious Society; in which

---

1. **Quire:** choir.

2. **Quality:** people of high social standing.

3. **Nine Days Wonder:** a novelty, indicating the time in which it was said to attract attention; subject of gossip.

Station, I shall offer my daily Prayers for the Happiness and Prosperity of this Noble Couple.

This Discovery was a Surprize greater than the other; But there being many of the dignified Clergy as well as Quality, all interceded so, that, in short, the Nuns received the Hugonot; the Couple was married; and Things were brought to a happy Conclusion.

The Company return'd Thanks to the young Lady, for her diverting Story: And by this Time, the Coach was got to the Town, where the Company were all to alight, except *Galesia,* who was to go alone in the Coach to the End of the Stage. It happen'd, that there was another Stage-Coach stopp'd at the same Place, and set out at the same Time with hers; and whether the Bounty of the Passengers had over-filled the Heads of the Coach men, or what other Freak, is unknown; but they drove the Two Coaches full Gallop, 'till they came to a Bridge, and there one Coach jostled the other so, that that in which was our *Galesia,* fell, together with its Horses, off the Bridge into the River.

By good Luck, this Bridge was at the Entry of a little Village, so that People hastened to their Assistance; some helping the Horses, some the Coach, and some with Difficulty getting out *Galesia;* Who however, when she was got out, found no Hurt, only was very wet: She was much pity'd by the good People; amongst whom there was a poor Woman took her under the Arm, and told her, she would conduct her to a House, where she might be accommodated with all Manner of Conveniencies.

All wet and dropping, she got to this House, which was a poor Village-Alehouse; and a poor one indeed it was; It being Evening, the Woman of the House was gone out a Milking, so that the good Man could come at no Sheets, that she might have got rid of her wet Cloaths, by going to Bed; However, he laid on a large Country Faggot;[1] so she sat and smoaked in her wet Cloaths, 'till the good Woman came; who hasten'd and got the Bed Sheeted, into which she gladly laid herself; but the poorest that her Bones ever felt, there being a few Flocks[2] that stank;

---

1. **laid on a large Country Faggot:** placed a large bundle of twigs on the fire.
2. **Flocks:** coarse bedclothes.

and so thin of the same, that she felt the Cords[1] cut through. The Blankets were of Thread-bare Home-spun Stuff, which felt and smelt like a Pancake fry'd in Grease; There were Four Curtains at the Four Corners, from whence they could no more stir, than Curtains in a Picture; for there were neither Rods nor Ropes for them to run upon; no Testern,[2] but the Thatch of the House; A Chair with a Piece of a Bottom, and a brown Chamberpot, furr'd[3] as thick as a Crown Piece.

However, all this was a better Lodging than the Bottom of the River; and great and many Thanks were due to God for it. The good Woman was kind, and brought *Galesia* a good wooden Dish-full of boil'd Milk, well crumb'd with brown Barley-Bread; which she persuaded her to eat, to drive out the Cold. She took Care to get her Cloaths dry, and brought them to her, e'er she went a Milking. And notwithstanding all these Hardships, she got no Cold, Cough or Lameness; but arose well-refresh'd; took Leave of her Landlord and departed, directing her Steps and Intentions towards the Town were the Stage-Coach'd Inn'd.

But it so happen'd, in this her Journey, that she lost her Way, and got, she knew not how, into a fine Park,[4] amongst Trees, Firs, Thickets, Rabbet-burrows, and such like; nor knew she where she was, nor which Way to go; but standing still a little while to consider, she heard a *Tomtit* sing in a Tree, as her musing Fancy made her imagine,

> *Sit thee down, sit thee down, sit thee down, sit.*

At the same time looking on one Side, she saw a handsome Seat at a very little Distance, to which she went, and obey'd the threefold Advice. As she sat there to rest herself, revolving divers Thoughts, a little Hedge-Sparrow in a Bush, sung, *Chear-up, Chear-up;* Ah! poor Bird! said she, thou givest me good Counsel; but that is all thou hast to give; and bare Words help little to a hungry Stomach, and I know not where to fill mine, unless I could eat Grass like the Four-footed Beasts.

---

1. **Cords:** rope supports of a bed.

2. **Testern:** canopy; covering.

3. **furr'd:** covered with fungus.

4. **Park:** extensive grounds surrounding a country estate.

As she was in these Thoughts, a Crow sitting in a Tree, with a hoarse Voice, seem'd to say *Good-Luck, Good-Luck!* If thou art a true Prophet, said *Galesia*, the Birds of thy Colour, shall no more be counted Birds of Ill Omen, but the Painters shall put a long Tail to you, and the Poets shall call you *Birds of Paradise*.

As she was thus musing on the Language of the Birds, she heard a Noise of Hunting in the Park, Horns winding, Men hollowing, and calling *Ringwood, Rockwood, ho! Boman! Blossom, ho.* She then began to reflect how necessary this Diversion was: Alas! said she, if it was not for this, we might all lodge as bad as I did last Night. We are beholden to *Ringwood* and *Jowler*,[1] for many a Dainty Morsel which *Reynard*[2] would deprive us of, if it were not for this Pack of Allies, who oppose his Tyranny; Who otherwise would not only over-run the Woods, and Farmers Yards, 'till there is neither Cocks nor Hens, but would also ravage the Fens and Islands, the Habitations of Ducks and Geese; Then long live *Ringwood, Rockwood, Boman* and *Jowler,* by whose Industry we eat good Bits, and lie on good Beds.

Whilst *Galesia* was in these Cogitations,[3] the Dogs and Hunters came very near where she was sitting; amongst whom, was a Lady, mounted on a beautiful Steed, who beginning to grow weary of the Chace,[4] order'd her Servants to stop, and help her off her Horse, resolving to walk home over the Park, it being a fine smooth Walk betwixt two Rows of Lime trees, planted and grown in exact Form, agreeable to the Eye, pleasing to the Smell, and making a most delightful Shade. The Lady directing her Eyes and Steps towards this Walk, she saw *Galesia* sitting in the disconsolate Posture aforesaid, and being not a little surpriz'd to see a Gentlewoman all alone in that desolate Place, could not avoid interrogating her thereupon.

---

1. **Ringwood, Rockwood . . . Boman . . . Blossom . . . Jowler:** names of hunting dogs.

2. **Reynard:** fox, from the name of that animal in the French medieval poem, *Roman de la Rose* (ca. 1230–40) by Guillaume de Lorris.

3. **Cogitations:** reflections; thoughts.

4. **Chace:** chase; hunt.

Galesia, in few and respectful Words, inform'd the Lady of her Disaster of being overthrown into the River the Day before, and her bad Lodging at Night, and her losing her Way that Morning, all which made her betake herself to that Seat. The Lady most courteously and charitably took her along with her to her House, which was a Noble Structure, situate in the midst of that Park. Here she entertain'd her very kindly; assuring her of all Assistance to convey her to the Place to which she was design'd, when she had rested and recover'd her Fatigue. In the mean Time, she diverted her, by shewing *Galesia* her Gardens, House, and glorious Appartments,[1] adorn'd with rich Furniture[2] of all Sorts; some were the Work of hers and her Husband's Ancestors, who delighted to imploy poor Gentlewomen, thereby to keep them from Distress, and evil Company, 'till Time and Friends could dispose Things for their better Settlement.

At last, the Lady shew'd her an Appartment embellish'd with Furniture of her own making, which was PATCH-WORK, most curiously compos'd of rich Silks, and Silver and Gold Brocades: The whole Furniture was compleated excepting a SCREEN, which the Lady and her Maids were going about. Her Ladyship told *Galesia,* She would take it kindly if her Affairs would permit her to stay with her some time, and assist her in her SCREEN. Which Invitation *Galesia* most gladly accepted, begging the Lady to send to the next Stage of the Coach and Carrier, for her Trunks and Boxes, which contained her Wearing Cloaths. The Lady forthwith sent for the Things, hoping that therein they might find some Bits of one thing or other, that might be useful to place in the SCREEN. But when the Trunks and Boxes came, and were opened, alas! they found nothing but Pieces of *Romances, Poems, Love-Letters,* and the like: At which the good Lady smil'd, saying, She would not have her Fancy balk'd, and therefore resolved to have these ranged and mixed in due Order, and thereof compose a SCREEN.

And thus it came to pass, that the following SCREEN was compos'd.

---

1. **Appartments:** a suite of private rooms.

2. **Furniture:** decorations, especially needleworked pieces.

A *Patch-Work Screen* for the *Ladies*.

Leaf I.

The *Continuation* of the *History* of *Galesia*.

The good Lady and *Galesia* being thus sate down to their Work, and the Trunks open'd, the first Thing they laid their Hands on, was a Piece of a *Farce*,[1] which the Lady would have put by, for another Opportunity; and desired *Galesia* to begin where *Lucasia*[2] and she broke off in *St. Germains-Garden*: To which *Galesia* readily comply'd without Hesitation.

Having disingag'd my Thoughts from *Bosvil*,[3] said she, I had nothing to disturb my Tranquility, or hinder me from being Happy, but the Absence of my dear Brother,[4] who was gone a second Time beyond Sea, to study at the University of *Leyden*,[5] that being the Third Place where he endeavour'd to inrich his Mind; having before gathered a Treasure of Learning from those Two inexhaustible Fountains, *Oxford* and *Paris*: thereby to inable him to perform, what he shortly intended to practise, the Cure of Human Maladies; in which he began already to be known and esteemed.

It would be too tedious to give your Ladyship a Character of this excellent Man, whose Learning grac'd his natural Parts, and his vertuous Life was an Honour to his Learning. His Philosophy and Medicinal Science did not supplant Civility, but cultivated and inrich'd his natural pleasant Humour. He was in every thing a Gentleman and a Christian, so that Envy herself could not find a feeble Side whereon to plant her Batteries, to attack or deface that Esteem his Merits had rais'd in the Hearts of all that knew him; which serv'd to make me more sensible of his Absence.

However, I comforted my self with the Hopes of his Return; and in

---

1. **Farce:** broadly comic play.

2. **Lucasia:** probably the literary name for an actual friend of Barker, from the pseudonym of Anne Owen, friend addressed in the poetry of Katherine Philips.

3. **Bosvil:** Galesia's suitor in *Love Intrigues*.

4. **Brother:** Edward Barker (1650–75?).

5. **Leyden:** city in Holland, noted for advanced medical studies.

the mean time, corresponded as often as I cou'd in Writing, passing the rest of my Time in my shady Walks, Fields, and Rural Affairs. The Pleasure of which was greatly improv'd by reading Mrs. *Phillips*.[1] I began to emulate her Wit, and aspir'd to imitate her Writings; in doing of which, I think, I deserv'd *Arachne's* Fate,[2] or at least to be transform'd into one of the lowest of *Mack-Fleckno's* Followers:[3] Her noble Genius being inimitable; especially in Praise of a Country-Life, and Contempt of human Greatness; all which I swallow'd as Draughts of rich Cordial, to enliven the Understanding. Her Poetry I found so interwoven with Vertue and Honour, that each Line was like a Ladder to climb, not only to *Parnassus*,[4] but to Heaven: which I (poor Puzzle as I was!) had the Boldness to try to imitate, 'till I was dropp'd into a Labyrinth of Poetry, which has ever since interlac'd all the Actions of my Life. Amongst other Fancies, I took into my Head, to draw a Landskip[5] in Verse, beginning with a GROVE. [6]

The *Grove*. [7]

> Well might the *Ancients* deem a *Grove* to be
> The sacred Mansion of some DEITY;
> Its pleasing Shades, and gloomy Terrors, move

---

1. **Mrs. Phillips:** Katherine Philips (1632–64), "the Matchless Orinda," poet, translator, and writer of letters. She was admired for her poetry and its moral excellence.

2. **Arachne's Fate:** in Greek myth, Arachne was a mortal weaver and embroiderer who challenged the goddess Athena to a contest to see whose art was best. Infuriated by the excellence of her challenger's tapestry, Athena turned her into a spider, condemned to spin eternally; see Ovid, *Metamorphoses* 1:1–142.

3. **Mack-Fleckno's Followers:** in Dryden's *Mac Flecknoe; or, A Satyr upon the True-Blew Protestant Poet, T.S.* (1682), playright and poet Thomas Shadwell (1640–92) manifests the worst of dull and stupid verse inherited from Richard Flecknoe (ca. 1620–78).

4. **Parnassus:** a mountain in Greece, sacred to the Muses. One of its peaks was sacred to Apollo.

5. **Landskip:** landscape.

6. **Grove:** in Roman mythology, a *lucus,* or shady sacred area that served as a retreat from culture; was sometimes associated with Diana, the goddess of the hunt.

7. This poem is a revised version of "The Prospect of a Landskip, Beginning with a Grove," *Poetical Recreations,* Part 1 (hereafter cited as *PR*1). Barker revised numerous poems from *PR*1 for part three of the Magdalen MS and included them in *Patch-Work Screen.*

Our *Souls* at once to *pious Fears* and *Love:*
Betwixt these Passions, rightly understood,
Lies the streight[1] Road to *everlasting Good.*
Fear frights from *Hell,* and *Love* exalts to *Heav'n;*
Happy the Soul to whom *these Two* are giv'n!
Beside the Pleasure of the Present Time,
To walk and muse, describe its Sweets in Rhime;
Where nought but Peace and Innocence obtrude,
The worst that can be said of it, 'tis *rude.*
Yet *Nature's Culture* is so well express'd,
That *Art* herself would wish to be so dress'd.

Lo! here the *Sun* conspires with ev'ry Tree,
To deck the *Earth* in Landskip-Tapistry:
Then thro' some Space his brightest Beams appear,
Erecting a bright golden Pillar there.
Here a close Canopy of Boughs is made;
There a soft grassy Cloth of State is spread;
With Gems[2] and gayest Flow'rs imbroider'd o'er,
Fresh as those Beauties honest Swains adore.
Here Nature's Hand, for Health and Pleasure, sets
Cephalick *Cowslips,* Cordial *Violets.*[3]
The cooling Diuretick *Woodbine* grows,[4]
Supported by th'Scorbutick[5] *Canker-Rose.*
Splenetick[6] *Columbines* their Heads hang down,
As if displeas'd their Vertue should be known.
Pinks, Lillies, Daisies, Bettony, Eye bright,[7]

---

1. **Streight:** strait; narrow.

2. **Gems:** flower buds.

3. **Cephalick:** pertaining to the head; **Cowslips:** wild, fragrant yellow flowers; **Cordial:** stimulus to the heart and blood circulation.

4. **Diuretick:** stimulating discharge of the urine; **Woodbine:** climbing ivy.

5. **Scorbutick:** pertaining to scurvy; **Canker-Rose:** wild rose.

6. **Splenetick:** pertaining to the disorder of the spleen, and tending toward melancholia.

7. **Bettony:** plant with blue spiked flowers; **Eye bright:** plant reputed as remedy for weak eyes.

To purge the Head, strengthen or clear the Sight.
Some mollify, some draw, some Ulcers[1] clear,
Some purify, and some perfume the Air.
Of which some gentle Nymph the fairest takes,
And for her *Coridon*[2] a Garland makes:
Whilst on her Lap the happy Youth's Head lies,
Gazing upon the Aspects of her Eyes;
The most unerring, best *Astronomy,*
Whereby to calculate his Destiny.
Whilst o'er their Heads a Pair of *Turtles*[3] coo,
Which with less Constancy and Passion wooe.
The Birds around, thro' their extended Throats,
In careless Consort, chant their pleasing Notes;
Than which no sweeter Musick charms the Ear,
Except when Lovers Sighs each other hear;
Which are more soft than austral Breeses[4] bring,
Altho' 'tis said, they're Harbingers o'th' Spring.

Methinks, I pity much the busy Town,
To whom these Rural Pleasures are not known.
But more I pity those whom Fate inthralls,
Who can't retire when Inclination calls,
By Business, Families, and Fortune ty'd;
Beset, besieg'd, attack'd on ev'ry Side,
By Friends & Foes; Wit, Beauty, Mirth & Wine,
Piques, Parties, Policies, and Flatterers join
To storm one's Quiet, Vertue undermine.

'Tis hard we must, the World's so vicious grown,
Be complaisant in Crimes, or live alone!
For those who now with Vertue are indu'd,

---

1. **Ulcers:** internal or external erosion on the body that forms an open sore.

2. **Coridon:** Corydon; conventional name for a rustic in pastoral literature; see Virgil, *Eclogues* 6, and Theocritus.

3. **Turtles:** turtledoves.

4. **austral Breeses:** mild, southerly winds.

Do live alone, tho' in a Multitude.
Then fly, all ye whom Fortune don't oblige
To suffer the Distresses of a Siege;
Fly to some calm Retreat, and there retrieve
Your squander'd Time; 'Tis ne'er too late to live.
Free from all Envy, and the tiresome Noise
Of prating Fools, and Wits that ne'er were wise:
Free from Ambition, and from base Design,
Which equally our Vertue undermine,
In Plenty here, without Excess, we dine.
If we in wholsome Exercise delight,
Our Sleep becomes more sound & sweet at Night;
Or if one's Mind to Contemplation leads,
Who has the Book of God and Nature, needs
No other Object to imploy his Thought,
Since in each Leaf such Mysteries are wrought,
That whoso studies most, shall never know
Why the strait *Elm's* so tall, the *Moss* so low.
     I farther cou'd inlarge upon this Theme,
But that I'm, unawares, come to the Stream,
Which at the Bottom of this *Grove* doth glide:
And now I'll rest me by its flow'ry Side.

Thus, Madam, I have given you the first Taste of my Country-Poetry, which to your Ladyship (who is furnish'd with all the fine Pieces that come out) must needs be as insipid as a Breakfast of Water-gruel to those that are us'd to Chocolate and rich Jellies.[1]

It will do very well, reply'd the Lady, a Landskip in a SCREEN, is very agreeable; therefore let me have the rest.

The next Madam (reply'd *Galesia*) is the *Rivulet*[2] at the Bottom of the GROVE, which I try'd to mould into *Pindarick:*[3] I suppose, out of

---

1. **Jellies:** nutritive gelatins, often made of animal parts or sweet fruits.

2. **Rivulet:** small river.

3. **Pindarick:** an ode or other poem in imitation of the metre or verse of the Greek lyric poet Pindar (ca. 522–ca. 442 B.C.).

Curiosity; for I neither love to read nor hear that kind of Verse. Methinks, it is to the Ear like Virginal Jacks[1] to the Eye; being all of irregular Jumps, and Starts, sudden Disappointments, and long-expected Periods, which deprives the Mind of that Musick; wherewith the good Sense would gratify it, if in other Measures. But since your Ladyship commands, be pleas'd to take it as it is; next to Blank Verse[2] disagreeable: (at least, to my Ear) one sort spoils good Verse, the other good Prose; whereas the regular Chime[3] of other Verse, helps to make amends for indifferent Sense: Wherefore, fit to be courted by me; whose Fingers ought to have been imploy'd rather at the Needle and the Distaff,[4] than to the Pen and Standish,[5] and leave these Enterprizes to the Learned, who know how to compose all Measures, thereby to please all Palates. However, at present, I shall sacrifice this Aversion to the Obedience due to your Ladyship's Commands.

The *Rivulet.* [6]

I.

Ah! lovely Stream, how fitly may'st thou be,
  By thy Immutability, [7]
Thy gentle Motion and Perennity,
  To us the Emblem of Eternity?
   And, to us, thou dost no less
A kind of Omnipresence, too, express,
   For always at the Ocean, thou
Art ever here, and at thy Fountain too;

---

1. **Virginal:** musical instrument related to the spinet and harpsichord. **Jacks:** pieces of wood fitted with a quill that plucked the string when the key was pushed down.

2. **Blank verse:** poetry in unrhymed iambic pentameter.

3. **Chime:** rhythm or music of verse.

4. **Distaff:** long wooden implement held under the worker's arm while she spun wool or flax; figurative for women's work and for the female sex.

5. **Standish:** inkstand or container for writing implements.

6. The poem is a revised version of "Sitting by a Rivulet," *PR* 1.

7. **Immutability:** not subject to change.

Always thou go'st thy proper Course,
Most willingly, and yet by Force,
Each Wave forcing its precursor on;
Yet each one freely runs, with equal haste,
As if each fear'd to be the last;
With mutual Strife, void of Con-ten-ti-on,
In Troops they march, 'till thousand, thousand's past,
 Yet, gentle Stream, art still the same,
 Always going, never gone:
 Yet do'st all Constancy disclaim,
Wildly dancing to thine own murmuring tuneful Song,
 Old as Time, as Love and Beauty young.

II.

But chiefly thou to Unity lay'st claim,
 For though in Thee
Innumerable Drops there be,
 Yet still thou art but One,
Th' Original of which, from Heav'n came;
 Whose purest Transcript we
I'th' Church may wish, but never hope to see,
 Whilst each Pretender[1] thinks himself alone
  To be the True Church Militant:[2]
  Nay, well it is, if such will grant,
That there is one elsewhere Triumphant.[3]

III.

Ah, gentle Stream! ah, happy we!
 Cou'd we but learn of thee,
As thou dost Nature, we our God obey;
 Gently rolling on our Way:

---

1. **Pretender:** claimant.
2. **Church Militant:** the earthly embodiment of the church.
3. **Triumphant:** the Church Triumphant, or the church in heaven.

And as we pass, like thee do good,
Benign to all our Neighbourhood;
To God and Man, our Love and Duty pay:
Then at our Ocean we Repose shall find,
The Ocean Grave, which swallows all Mankind!

Thus, Madam, I trifled my Time, 'till the Return of my Brother from *Leyden,* which was to me like the Return of Spring to Northern Climes. His Presence rais'd my drooping Spirits, and dispers'd those Clouds of Sorrow gather'd in my Heart by *Bosvil's* Falshood. I began to delight myself in Dressing, Visiting, and other Entertainments, befitting a young Gentlewoman; nevertheless, did not omit my Study, in which my Brother continued to oblige my Fancy,[1] and assisted me in *Anatomy* and *Simpling,*[2] in which we took many a pleasing Walk, and gather'd many Patterns of different Plants, in order to make a large natural Herbal. I made such Progress in *Anatomy,* as to understand *Harvey's* Circulation of the Blood,[3] and *Lower's* Motion of the Heart.[4] By these and the like Imployments, I began to forget and scorn *Bosvil.* If I thought on him at all, it was with Contempt; and I wonder'd how it came to pass that I ever lov'd him, and thought myself secure the rest of my Days from that Weakness.

As I thus betook myself to an Amusement different from my Sex and Years, my other young Companions, began to look grave upon me; or I, perhaps, look'd so upon them. Our little Follies of telling our Dreams; laying Things under each other's Heads to dream of our Amours; counting Specks on our Nails, who should have the most Presents from Friends or Lovers; tying Knots in the Grass; pinning Flowers on our Breasts, to know the Constancy of our Pretenders;[5] drawing Husbands

---

1. **Fancy:** desires, inclinations.

2. **Simpling:** the study of simples or medicinal plants; herbal medicine.

3. **Harvey's Circulation of the Blood:** William Harvey (1578–1657) articulated his theory of the circulation of blood in *De Motu Cordis* (1628).

4. **Lower's Motion of the Heart:** Richard Lower (1631–91), noted London physician, author of *Tractatus du Corde* (1669), and pioneer in blood transfusions.

5. **Pretenders:** suitors.

in the Ashes; St. *Agnes's* Fast;[1] and all such childish Auguries,[2] were now no more any Diversion to me; so that I became an useless Member in our Rural Assemblies. My Time and Thoughts were taken up in *Harvey, Willis*,[3] and such-like Authors, which my Brother help'd me to understand and relish, which otherwise might have seemed harsh or insipid: And these serv'd to make me unfit Company for every body; for the Unlearned fear'd, and the Learned scorn'd my Conversation; at least, I fancy'd so: A Learned Woman, being at best but like a Forc'd-Plant,[4] that never has its due or proper Relish, but is wither'd by the first Blast that Envy or Tribulation blows over her Endeavours. Whereas every Thing, in its proper Place and Season, is graceful, beneficial, and pleasant. However, my dear Brother humouring my Fancy, I pass'd my Time in great Satisfaction. His Company was my Recreation, and his wise Documents my Instruction; even his Reproofs were but as a poignant Sauce, to render his good Morals the more savoury, and easier digested. Thus we walk'd and talk'd; we laugh'd and delighted our-selves; we dress'd and visited; we received our Friends kindly, and by them were generously treated in their turn: all which was to the Satisfaction of our endearing tender Parents. But, alas! short was the Continuance of this Happiness; for my dear Brother died. And now, Madam, forgive these flowing Tears, which interrupt my Discourse.

Galesia having discharg'd a Torrent of Tears, the usual Effect of any Discourse for so great a Loss, she endeavoured to compose her-self, dry'd her Eyes, and return'd to her Story.

This, Madam, was such a Grief as I had never felt; for though I had suffer'd much in the Transactions of *Bosvil;* yet those Sorrows were allay'd, in some degree, by the Mixture of other Passions, as Hope, Fear, Anger, Scorn, Revenge, *&c.* But this was Grief in Abstract, Sorrow in

---

1. **St. Agnes's Fast:** according to legend, a young woman going to bed without eating on the night of 21 January would dream of her future husband.

2. **Auguries:** practice of divining the future from omens.

3. **Willis:** Thomas Willis (1621–75), physician and one of the founders of the Royal Society. With the assistance of Richard Lower, he wrote *Cerebri anatome hervorumque descripho et usus* (1664), which described the arterial system at the base of the brain.

4. **Forc'd-Plant:** a plant artificially grown to produce flowers or fruit out of season.

pure Element. I griev'd without ceasing; my Sighs alternatively blew up my Tears, and my Tears allay'd my Sighs, 'till fresh Reflections rais'd new Gusts of Sorrow. My Solitude was fill'd with perpetual Thoughts of Him;[1] and Company was entertain'd with nothing but Discourses of this my irreparable Loss. My sleeping, as well as waking Hours, were fill'd with Ideas of him! Sometimes I dream'd I saw his Ghost, come to visit me from the other World; sometimes I thought I assisted him in his Sickness; sometimes attending at his Funeral; then awake in a Flood of Tears; when, waking, I cou'd form no Thought or Idea, but what Grief suggested. In my Walks and Studies, it was still the same, the Remembrance of some wise Documents, or witty Entertainment, roused up my Grief, by reflecting on my great Loss. No Book or Paper cou'd I turn over, but I found *Memorandums* of his Wisdom and Learning, which served to continue and augment my Grief; and so far transported me sometimes, that I even wish'd for that which is *the Horror of Nature,* that I might see his *Ghost.* I experienced what the Philosophers assert, *That much reflecting on* Death, *is the way to make it less terrible;*[2] and 'tis certain, I reflected so much on his, that I wish'd for nothing more; wish'd to be with him; wish'd to be in that happy State, in which I assur'd my self his Vertues had plac'd him. But in vain I wish'd for Death; I was ordain'd to struggle with the Difficulties of Life; which were to be many, as I have since experienced; Heaven having taken away from me, Him, who seem'd by Nature ordain'd to conduct me through the Labyrinth of this World, when the Course of Nature should take my dear indulgent Parents from me, to their Repose in *Elysium.*[3] And now, instead of being a Comfort to them in this their great Affliction, my Griefs added Weight to theirs, such as they could hardly sustain.

I read those Books he had most studied, where I often found his Hand-writing, by way of Remarks, which always caus'd a new Flux of Tears. I often call'd upon Death; but Death was deaf, or his Malice oth-

---

1. **Him:** her brother.

2. **That much . . . less terrible:** commonplace in both Stoic and Epicurean philosophies; see for example Lucretius, *On the Nature of Things* 3.

3. **Elysium:** in Greek myth, paradise; home of the blessed after death.

erwise imploy'd on more worthy Prey; leaving me a useless Wretch; useless to the World; useless to my Friends, and a Burden to myself: Whilst he that was necessary to his Friends, an Honour to his Profession, and beneficial to Mankind, (but chiefly to me) the Tyrant Death had seiz'd and convey'd away for *ever!* —O that Word *Ever!* that Thought *Ever!* The Reflection of *Ever* and *Never,* devour'd all that cou'd be agreeable or pleasing to me: *Ever* to want his wise Instructions! *Never* to injoy his flowing Wit! *Ever* to regret this my irreparable Loss! *Never* to have his dear Company in my shady Walks! This *Ever* and *Never,* star'd in my Thoughts like Things with Saucer-Eyes in the Dark, serving to fright me from all Hopes of Happiness in this World.

In these and the like anxious and melancholy Amusements, I pass'd my woeful Days, 'till Length of Time, which changes and devours all Things, began a little to abate my Grief, and the Muses began to steal again into my Breast; and having, as I said before, affected to study those Books, on which I had seen my Brother most intent, I at last resolv'd to begin with a Body of *Anatomy,* and between whiles, to reduce it into Verse: Perhaps, reflecting on what is said of *Ovid,*[1] that he writ *Law* in Verse: And *Physick*[2] being as little reducible to that Softness as *Law,* I know not what Emulation or Fancy excited me; but thus I began:

An *Invocation* of her *Muse.* [3]

Come, gentle Muse! assist me now,
A double Wreath plait for my Brow,
Of *Poetry* and *Physick* too.

Teach me in Numbers to rehearse
Hard Terms of Art, in smooth, soft Verse,
And how we grow, and how decrease.

---

1. **Ovid:** Publius Ovidius Naso (43 B.C.–A.D. 17), Roman poet, had studied law.

2. **Physick:** medicine.

3. This poem is a revised version of "A Farewell to Poetry, with a long Digression on Anatomy," *PR* I. The "Invocation" replaces lines 1–14 of the original poem, and the section on "Anatomy" begins at line 15 of the original.

Teach me to sing APOLLO*'s Sons,* [1]
The *Ancient* and the *Modern*-ones,
And sing their Praise in gentle Tones.

But chiefly sing those *Sons* of *Art,*
Which teach *the Motion of the Heart,*
Nerves, Spirits, Brains, and every Part.

Anatomy.

Now BARTHOLINE,[2] the first of all this Row,
Does to me *Nature's Architecture* show;
How the *Foundation,* first, of *Earth* is laid;
Then, how the *Pillars* of *Strong-Bones* are made.
The *Walls* consist of *Carneous-Parts*[3] within,
The Out-side *pinguid,*[4] overlay'd with *Skin;*
The *Fret-work,*[5] *Muscles, Arteries* and *Veins,*
With their Implexures;[6] and how from the *Brains*
The *Nerves* descend; and how 'tis they dispense
To every *Member* Motive-Power, and Sense.
He shews the Windows in this Structure fix'd,
How *trebly glaz'd,*[7] and Curtains drawn betwixt
Them & Earth's Objects: All which prove in vain
To keep out *Lust,* or *Innocence* retain.

---

1. **Apollo's Sons:** physicians and medical scientists. Apollo was the Greek god of medicine and poetry.

2. **Bartholine:** Caspar Bartholin (1585–1629), Danish physician and anatomist, author of *Anatomicae Institutiones Corporis Humani* (1611). His son, Thomas (1616–80), also an anatomist, supported Harvey's theory of blood circulation.

3. **Carneous-Parts:** fleshy parts.

4. **pinguid:** fat.

5. **Fret-work:** in architecture, carved work with intricately intersecting lines.

6. **Implexures:** things entwined.

7. The *Three Humours* of the *Eye,* with the *Tunicle.* [Author's note.] **Humors:** fluids. **Tunicle:** skin that covers the eye.

For 'twas the *Eye*, that first discern'd the *Food* ,[1]
As *pleasing to itself,* for eating *good,*
Then was persuaded, that it wou'd refine
The *half-wise Soul,* and make it all Divine.
But O how dearly *Wisdom's* bought with Sin,
Which shuts out *Grace;*[2] lets *Death* & *Darkness* in.
And 'cause *our Sex*[3] precipitated first,
To Pains, and Ignorance *we* since are curs'd.
Desire of *Knowledge,* cost *us* very dear;
For *Ignorance,* e'er since, became our Share.
　　But as I was inlarging on this Theme,
WILLIS and HARVEY bid me follow them.
　　They brought me to the *first* & *largest Court*[4]
Of all this *Building,*[5] where, as to a Port,
All *Necessaries* are brought from afar,
For *Susentation,*[6] both in *Peace* and *War.*
For *War*[7] this Common-wealth, doth oft infest,
Which pillages one Part, and storms the rest.
　　We view'd the *Kitchen* call'd *Ventriculus;*[8]
Then pass'd we through the Space call'd *Pylorus;*[9]

---

1. **For . . . Share:** These ten lines allude to the Fall and Expulsion of Adam and Eve from Eden; see Gen. 2-3 and Milton, *Paradise Lost* (1667).　**Food:** fruit of the Tree of Knowledge.

2. **Grace:** God's benevolence, especially through the sacrifice of Christ, unmerited by humankind.

3. **our Sex:** women, since Eve first ate of the forbidden fruit and bade Adam eat.

4. *Ad infimum ventrem* [Author's note.] The innermost part of the abdomen (Latin). In the next fifty lines, Barker conducts a house tour of the body—beginning with the abdomen, continuing to the heart and brain, and returning to the abdomen—based on theories of the organs and circulation of blood.　**first & largest Court:** cardiac or uppermost section of the stomach.

5. **Building:** the body.

6. **Susentation:** maintenance of human life.

7. *Morbi infimo ventri Diarrhoea,* &c. [Author's note.] Diseases of the lowest or smaller intestine, including diarrhea, etc. (Latin).

8. **Ventriculus:** pyloric section of the stomach.

9. **Pylorus:** valve which leads to the intestines.

And to the *Dining-Room*[1] we came at last,
Where the *Lacteans*[2] take their sweet Repast.
From thence we thro'a *Drawing-room*[3] did pass,
And came where *Jecur*[4] very busie was:
Sanguificating[5] the whole Mass of *Chyle*,[6]
And severing the *Crural Parts*[7] from *Bile:*
And when she's made it tolerably good,
She pours it forth to mix with other *Blood.*
This & much more we saw; from thence we went
Into the *next Court*[8] by a small Ascent.
Bless me! said I; what Rarities are here!
A *Fountain* like a *Furnace*[9] did appear,
Still boiling o'er, and running out so fast,
That one wou'd think its Eflux,[10] cou'd not last:
Yet it sustain'd no Loss, as I cou'd see,
Which made me think it a strange Prodigy.
Come on, says HARVEY, don't stand gazing here;
But follow me, and I thy Doubts will clear.
　　Then we began our Journey with the *Blood,*
Trac'd the Meanders of its Purple Flood. [11]

---

1. **Dining-Room:** duodenum or upper small intestine.

2. **Lacteans:** lymphatic vessels.

3. **Drawing-room:** hepatic portal to the liver.

4. **Jecur:** the liver.

5. **Sanguificating:** mixing of blood. **Chyle:** a milky white fluid formed in the process of digestion.

6. *Secundum Opinionem* Galen. contra Recep. commun. [Author's note.] According to Galen's view, against common belief (Latin). Galen believed that the blood formed in the liver. Harvey disputes this theory in *De Motu Cordis.*

7. **Crural Parts:** relating to the blood. **Bile:** fluid secreted by the liver to aid in digestion.

8. *Per* Diaphragmata. [Author's note.] Through the diaphragm (Latin). **Next court:** the thoracic cavity.

9. The *Heart.* [Author's note.] **Fountain like a Furnace:** the heart, pumping blood.

10. **Eflux:** a flowing out, in this instance, into the aorta.

11. **Meanders of its Purple Flood:** from the wandering and winding river in ancient Phrygia, the sinuous path of the blood.

Thus we thro' many Labyrinths[1] did pass,
In such, I am sure, old *Dædalus*[2] ne'er was.
Sometimes i'th' Out-works,[3] sometimes the *First-Court*,
Sometimes i'th' *Third* these winding Streams would
    sport.
Such Rarities we found in this *Third Place*, [4]
As put ev'n *Comprehension* to disgrace.
Here's Cavities,[5] said one; And here, says He,
Is th' Seat of *Fancy, Judgment, Memory.*
Here, says another, is the *fertile Womb*,
From whence the *Spirits-Animal*[6] do come:
Which are mysteriously ingender'd here,
Of Spirits, from *arterial Blood* and Air. [7]
Here, says a third, Life made her first approach,
Moving the Wheels of her *triumphant Coach.* [8]
But HARVEY that *Hypothesis* deny'd,
Say'ng 'twas the *Deaf-Ear* on the *Dexter-side.*[9]
Then there arose a trivial small Dispute, [10]
Which he by Fact and Reason did confute.
This being ended, we began again

---

1. **Labyrinth:** in Greek myth, complex palace of mazes, designed for King Minos of Crete.

2. **Daedalus:** designer of the Labyrinth.

3. **Out-works:** the arms, legs and other areas distant from the heart.

4. **Third Place:** the brain. The following fifteen lines examine theories of the starting point of life, including those posited by the Greek philosopher, Plato (ca. 427–347 B.C.) and the Greek physician and surgeon Galen (A.D. 129–ca. 199), which were modified or challenged by Willis. Galen's theories, based on dissection and scientific observation, were still important in medical education of Barker's day.

5. **Cavities:** the interconnected ventricles of the brain.

6. **Spirits-Animal:** it was believed that three spirits of the body—animal, vital and natural—regulated different physical functions.

7. **arterial Blood and Air:** Galen proved that the arteries carried blood, not air, as previously thought.

8. **triumphant Coach:** the prime mover of life.

9. **Deaf Ear on the Dexter-Side:** the right auricle, atrium of the heart.

10. **trivial small Dispute:** contemporary controversy over Harvey's theories.

Our former Progress, and forsook the *Brain;*
And after some small Traverses about,
Came to the Place where we before set out:
Then I perceiv'd, how HARVEY all made good,
By th' Circles of the Circulating Blood,
As Fountains have their Water from the Sea,
To which again they do themselves convey.
And here we found great LOWER,[1] with much Art,
Surveying the whole *Structure of the Heart.*
Welcome said he, dear *Cousin!*[2] Are you here?
Sister to *Him*,[3] whose Worth we all revere:
But ah, alas! So short was his Life's Date,
As makes us since, almost, our Practice hate;
Since we cou'd find out *nought* in all *our Art,*
That cou'd *prolong* the *Motion* of his *Heart.*

This latter Line, Madam, *was,* and *is,* and *ever will be,* my *great Afflic-tion.* So dear a Friend, shining with such Brightness of Parts, cut off in his Bloom! Ah Me! I cannot *think* or *speak* of *him* without *weeping;* which if I did not in abundance, I shou'd not be just to his Memory; I shou'd be unworthy of that Fraternal Love he express'd to me on all Occasions; so that it is fit I should weep on all *Occasions;* especially when I reflect how much I want[4] him in every Circumstance of Life. The only Comfort I have, is, when I think on the Happiness he enjoys by Divine Vision; All Learning and Science, All Arts, and Depths of Philosophy, without Search or Study; whilst we in this World, with much Labour, are groping, as it were, in the Dark, and make Discoveries of our own Ignorance. Which Thoughts wou'd sometimes fold themselves in these or the like Words.

---

1. **great Lower:** Richard Lower.
2. **dear Cousin:** Barker and Lower were related through their mothers, both from Cornwall.
3. **Him:** Edward Barker.
4. **want:** miss.

I.

Thou know'st, *my Dear,* now, more than *Art* can!
THOU know'st the *Essence* of the *Soul* of *Man!*
And of its *Maker* too, whose powerful Breath
Gave Immortality to sordid Earth!
    What Joys, *my Dear,* do THEE surround,
    As no where else are to be found?
    Love, Musick, Physick, Poetry,
    Mechanicks,[1] grave Philosophy;
And in each Art, each Artist does abound;
Whilst All's converted to Divinity.
    No drooping Autumn there,
    Nor chilling Winter, does appear;
    Nor scorching Heat, nor budding Spring,
    Nor Sun does Seasons there divide;
Yet all Things do transcend their native Pride;
    Which fills, but does not nauseate;
    No Change nor Want of any Thing,
Which Time to Periods, or Perfections, bring.
    But yet Diversity of State,
And Soul's Felicity There has no Date.

II.

Shou'dst THOU, *my Dear,* look down on *us* below,
    To see how busie *we*
    Are in *Anatomy,*
Thou woud'st despise our Ignorance,
Who most Things miss, and others hit by chance,
For *we,* at best, do but in Twilight go:
Whilst *Thou* see'st all by most transcendant Light;
Compar'd to which, the *Sun's* bright Rays are Night.
    Yet so Celestial are thine Eyes,

---

1. **Mechanicks:** the engineering of machines.

That Light can neither dazle nor surprize;
  For all Things There
  Most perfect are,
And freely their bless'd Quality dispense,
Without the Mixture of Terrestrial Dross, [1]
  Or without Hazard, Harm or Loss.
  O Joys eternal, satiating Sense!
And yet the Sense, the smallest Part ingross!

Thus, Madam, my worthless Muse help'd me to discharge my Griefs. The writing them in this my lonely State, was like discoursing, or dis-burthening one's Heart to a Friend. Whether your Ladyship will like to have them plac'd in your SCREEN, you yourself must determine.

By all means, reply'd the Lady, these melancholy *dark Patches*, set off the light Colours; making the Mixture the more agreeable. I like them all so well, I will not have *One* lay'd aside. Therefore, pray, go on with your Story.

Madam, said *Galesia*, It was at this Time, that I had a Kinsman[2] a Student at the University; who at certain Times, frequented our House; and now and then brought some of his young Companions with him; whose youthful and witty Conversation, greatly help'd to divert my Chagrin. Amongst these vertuous young Gentlemen, there was one,[3] whose Merit ingaged my particular Esteem, and the Compassion he had for my Griefs, planted a Friendship, which I have ever since culti-vated with my best Endeavours. When he was thus become my Friend, I unbosom'd my self to him, acquainted him with the Story of *Bosvil*, not concealing the least Weakness in all that Transaction, which was an Indiscretion I can hardly forgive my self; and I doubt not, but I shall stand condemn'd in your Ladyship's Judgment: For a young Gentleman is certainly a very unfit Confidant of a young Gentlewoman's Amours: The best she can expect from such a Discovery, is his Pity, which is one

---

1. **Dross:** impurities, waste products.

2. **Kinsman:** This relation, yet unidentified, introduced Barker to Cambridge University students. *PR* (1688) grew out of this literary friendship.

3. **one:** identified by his literary name Exilius in *PR.*

Step towards Contempt; and that is but a poor sort of Consolation, or Return of that Confidence she reposes. However, his generous Soul, gave it another Turn; and instead of despising my Foible, valued my Frankness, and abhorr'd *Bosvil's* Unworthiness, continuing to divert me with his Wit, whilst my Kinsman and he joyn'd to consolate me with repeated Proofs of their Friendship; all which my dear Parents approv'd; and promoted their Visits to our House by a generous and kind Reception at our Country Retreat; where they came now and then, a little to relax their College Discipline, and unbend the Streightness of their Study; bringing with them little Books, new Pamphlets, and Songs; and in their Absence, convers'd with me by Writing; sometimes Verse, sometimes Prose, which ingaged my Replies in the same manner. And here, amongst these Papers, appear several of them; out of which, perhaps, your Ladyship may chuse some *Patches* for your SCREEN.

An *Invitation* to my Learned Friends at *Cambridge.* [1]

> If, Friends, you wou'd but now this Place accost,
> E'er the *Young* Spring that Epithet[2] has lost,
> And of my Rural Joys participate,
> You'd change your learn'd Harangues for Country Chat,
> And thus with me salute this lonely State:
> Hail SOLITUDE! where *Peace* and *Vertue* shroud
> Their unvail'd Beauties, from the censuring Croud;
> Let us but have their Company, and we
> Shall never envy this World's Gallantry.
> Tho' to few Objects here we are confin'd,
> Yet we have full Inlargement of the Mind.
> From varying Modes, which oft our Minds inslave,
> Lo! here, a full Immunity we have:
> For here's no *Pride*, but in the *Sun's bright Beams*,
> Nor *murmuring*, but in the *Crystal-Streams*.
> No *Avarice*, but in the hoarding *Bees*,

---

1. This poem is a revised version of "An Invitation to my Friends at Cambridge," *PR* 1.

2. **Epithet:** brief term used to characterize a person.

Nor is *Ambition* found, but in the *Trees*.
No *Emulations* ever interpose,
Except betwixt the *Tulip* and the *Rose*.
No *Wantonness*, but in the *frisking Lambs;*
Nor *Luxury*, but when they suck their *Dams*. [1]
No *politick Contrivances* of *State*,
Only each *Bird* contrives to *please* its *Mate*.
No *Shepherd* here of scornful *Nymph* complains,
Nor are the *Nymphs* undone by *faithless Swains*.
NARCISSUS[2] only, is that sullen He,
That can despise his amorous, *talking She*.
But all Things here, conspire to make us bless'd;
Whilst *true Content* is *Musick* to the *Feast*.

    Then hail sweet *Solitude!* all hail again,
All hail to every Field, and Wood, and Plain;
To every beauteous Nymph, and faithful Swain. [3]
Then join with me; come, join with me, and give
This Salutation; or at least believe,
'Tis such a kind of *Solitude* as yet
Romance ne'er found where happy Lovers met.
Yea, such a kind of solitude it is,
Not much unlike to that of *Paradise;* [4]
Where Nature does her choicest Goods dispense,
And I, too, here, am plac'd in *Innocence*.
I should conclude that such it really were,
But that the *Tree of Knowledge*[5] won't grow here.
Though in its Culture I have spent some Time,

---

1. **Dams:** ewes.

2. **Narcissus:** in Greek myth, he was condemned by Aphrodite to fall in love with his own image as punishment for spurning the love of Echo, one of her nymphs.

3. **Swain:** sweetheart, lover.

4. **Paradise:** the Garden of Eden; see Gen. 2:8–10, 16.

5. **Tree of Knowledge:** tree of universal knowledge, of all good and bad.

Yet it disdains to grow in *our*[1] *cold Clime,*
Where it can neither Fruit nor Leaves produce,
Good for its Owner, or the publick Use.
Whilst *God* and *Nature* for You[2] constitute,
Luxurious Banquets of this *dainty Fruit.*
Whose *Tree* most fresh and flourishing is found,
E'er since 'twas planted in your fertile Ground.
Whilst you in *Wit,*[3] grow, as its *Branches,* high,
Deep as its *Root,* too, in *Philosophy.*
Large as its *spreading Arms,* your *Reasons* show;
Close as its *Shade,* your well-knit *Judgments* grow;
Fresh as its *Leaves,* your *sprouting Fancies* are;
Your *Vertues* like its *Fruit,* are *bright* and *fair.*

This my Invitation they all accepted, plain and innocent as it was, like those Cates,[4] wherewith they were treated; for we search'd not Air, Earth, and Water to gratify our Palates with Dainties, nor ravag'd *Spain, France,* and the *Indies,* for Diversity of Liquors: Our own Product, in a cleanly wholsome manner, contented our Appetites; such as serv'd the Conveniency of Life, not superfluous Luxury. Our Correspondence was of the same Piece, vertuous and innocent: No Flear[5] or Grimace tending to Lewdness, or cunning Artifice, out of the Way of Rural Simplicity: But pure and candid, such as might be amongst the Celestial Inhabitants. In this manner it was, that these vertuous Youths relieved my *Solitude,* and, in some Degree, dissipated that Melancholy wherewith I was oppress'd: And in their Absence (as I said before) visited me with Letters, and little Presents of the newest Pieces of Diversion that came to their Hands. And some of them having complimented me with an Epistle, I wrote the following Answer.

---

1. A Female Capacity. [Author's note.]

2. The Men.[Author's note.]

3. **Wit:** knowledge, understanding.

4. **Cates:** delicate or dainty food.

5. **Flear:** mocking look.

To my Young *Lover.*[1]

Incautious Youth! why dost thou so misplace
Thy fine Encomiums,[2] on an o'er-blown Face?
Which after all the Varnish of thy Quill,
Defects and Wrinkles shew conspicuous still;
Nor is it in the Power of Youth, to move
An age-chill'd Heart, to any Strokes of Love.
Then chuse some budding Beauty, which in Time,
May crown thy Wishes, in thy blooming Prime.
For nought can make a more prepost'rous Show,
Than *April Flow'rs*, stuck on St. *Michael's Bough.*[3]
To consecrate thy first-born Sighs to me,
A super-annuated[4] *Deity,*
Makes that *Idolatry* and *deadly Sin,*
Which otherwise had only *venial* been.

This, and some other such, obtain'd of them a friendly Rebuke, for making my self Old, when I was but little more than Twenty. The Truth is, I believe Grief made me think the Time tedious, every Day of Sorrow seeming a Year; insomuch that, according to that Account, I was as old as the *Patriarchs*[5] before the *Flood.*[6] I believe it is in this as in other things; we judge according to our Passions, and imagine others should do the same. The *fearful Man* thinks he sees Spirits, Thieves, and Murderers: The *angry Man*, if he sees a Straw lie in his Way, believes his Enemy laid it to affront him: The *jealous Man* mistrusts, and misconstrues even his Wife's Kindness and Caresses: And so it is on all Occa-

---

1. This poem is a slightly revised version of "To My Young Lover," *PR*1.

2. **Encomiums:** high praises.

3. **St. Michael's Bough:** the fruit of a variety of pear tree that ripens around Michaelmas, 29 September.

4. **super-annuated:** old, obsolete.

5. **Patriarchs:** Long-lived figures, including Enoch, Seth, and Methuselah in Genesis.

6. **Flood:** catastrophic deluge resulting from God's decision to destroy all living creatures, save Noah and those he collected on the ark, because of the great wickedness of humankind; see Gen. 5:28–9:29.

sions of Passion and Fancy. So that when I was out of my Teens, I thought all the Days of Youth were past, and those that could write Twenty, ought to lay all Things youthful and gay aside. But it seems these my young Friends were not of the same Sentiment; but treated me in their eloquent Letters and poetical Epistles, like a very young and beautiful Lady, equal in Years to themselves. Which caus'd me to make this following Reply to one of their Epistles.

> To praise, sweet Youth, do thou forbear, [1]
>   Where there is no Desert;
> For, alas! Encomiums here,
>   Are Jewels thrown i'th' Dirt.
>
> For I no more deserve Applause,
>   Now Youth and Beauty's fled,
> Than does a *Tulip* or a *Rose*,
>   When its fair Leaves are shed.
>
> Howe'er, I wish thy Praises may,
>   Like Prayers to Heaven borne,
> When holy Souls, for Sinners pray,
>   Upon Thy-self return.

These, Madam, were the little Adventures of my Country Life; not fit Entertainments for your Ladyship, but that your Commands stamp the Character, and make current the meanest Metal, and render that acceptable, which otherwise would hardly be excusable. The Compassion your Ladyship seem'd to have for my Griefs, encourag'd me to let you know by what Steps I climbed out of the deepest Gulph of Sorrow; and how this my *mournful Tragedy* was chang'd into a kind of *innocent Pastoral;* [2] as appears by the Ballad I sent to these my young Friends to *Sturbridge-Fair.*

---

1. This poem is a slightly revised version of "To My Young Lover. A Song," *PR* 1.

2. **Pastoral:** drawn from ancient Greek literature, celebration of idealized simplicity of rural life, often peopled with shepherds and shepherdesses.

A *Ballad.*

By Way of *Dialogue* between Two *Shepherd-Boys.*[1]

First Boy.

I wonder what *Alexis* ails,
    To sigh and talk of Darts; [2]
Of Charms which o'er his Soul prevails,
    Of Flames and bleeding Hearts.
I saw him Yesterday alone,
    Walk crossing of his Arms;
And Cuckow-like,[3] was in a Tone,
    Ah, *Celia!* ah, thy Charms!

Second Boy.

Why, sure thou'rt not so ignorant,
    As thou wou'd'st seem to be:
Alas! the Cause of his Complaint,
    Is all our Destiny.
'Tis mighty LOVE's all pow'rful Bow, [4]
    Which has *Alexis* hit;
A powerful Shaft will hit us too,
    E'er we're aware of it.

First Boy.

Why, LOVE! —Alas! I little thought
    There had been such a Thing;
But that for Rhime it had been brought,
    When Shepherds us'd to sing.
And, sure, whate'er they talk of *Love*,
    'Tis but *Conceit* [5] at most;

---

1. This poem is virtually unchanged from "A Pastoral Dialogue Betwixt Two Shepherd Boys," *PR*1.

2. **Darts:** the arrows shot by Cupid's bow, inflicting love upon those they strike.

3. **Cuckow-like:** like a cuckoo bird, known for its distinctive mating call.

4. **Love's all powerful Bow:** Cupid's bow.

5. **Conceit:** idea, notion.

As *Fear* i'th' *Dark* our *Fancies* move
    To *think* we see a *Ghost.*

Second Boy.

I know not; but the other Day,
    A *wanton Girl* there were,
Which took my *Stock-Dove's* Eggs[1] away,
    And *Black-bird's* Nest did tear.
Had it been Thee, my dearest Boy,
    Revenge I should have took;
But She my *Anger* did destroy,
    By the Sweetness of her Look.

First Boy.

So t'other Day, a *wanton Slut,*
    As I slept on the Ground,
A *Frog* into my Bosom put,
    My Hands and Feet she bound:
She hung my Hook upon a *Tree;*
    Then, laughing bid me wake;
And though she thus abused me,
    Revenge I cannot take.

Chorus.

Let's wish these *Overtures* of *Fate,*
    Don't *luckless Omens* prove;
For *those* who *lose* the *Power* to *Hate,*
    Are soon made *Slaves to Love.*

    The young Gentlemen receiv'd it kindly, and return'd me Thanks in these Words.

---

1. **Stock-Dove's Eggs:** eggs of a wild pigeon.

Dear *Galesia*,

We all return you Thanks for your Ballad; to which our Friend Sam. Set-well, *put a Tune, and we sung it in a Booth*[1] *merrily, 'till the* Proctor[2] *had like to have spoil'd the Harmony. But he finding no Female amongst us, drank the innocent Author's Health, and departed. The whole* Chorus *salute you, with the Assurance of being*

Your Humble Servants.

This Conversation, and Correspondence, Madam, infused into me some Thoughts, befitting my Sex and Years, rendering me fit for Company, and to live like the rest of my Fellow-Creatures; so that being one Day where there was a young Gentleman, who did not think me so much a *Stoick*[3] as I thought myself, he so far lik'd my Person and Humour, that altho' he had been a very loose Liver, he began to think he could endure to put on Shackles, and be confin'd to *one:* But being perfectly a Stranger, and knowing not well how to introduce himself into my farther Acquaintance, he took this odd Method.

There was a certain Gossip in those Parts, that used to go between the Ladies and Gentlewomen, with Services, and How-d'ye's; always carrying with her the little prattling News of Transactions where she frequented. This Woman coming to our House, was receiv'd with a good Mien,[4] and the best Chear our Larder[5] would afford, which was my Office to perform. She took the Opportunity to tell me, that her coming at that Time was particularly to Me, from Mr. *Bellair*,[6] who had seen me the other Day at such a Place, since which time he had had no Repose, nor none could have, 'till I gave him Leave to make me a Visit, which he begg'd most earnestly. To which I reply'd, That though Mr. *Bellair* had seen me, he was perfectly a Stranger to me, otherwise he had not sent

---

1. **Booth:** tent or other temporary covered dwelling.

2. **Proctor:** university officer charged with student discipline and maintenance of peace.

3. **Stoick:** Stoic; referring to a school of philosophy in Greco-Roman antiquity that stressed austere living and patient endurance of hardships.

4. **Mien:** air; manner.

5. **Larder:** room or closet in which provisions are stored.

6. **Bellair:** name suggests handsome appearance or manner.

such a Message; he knowing that I lived in my Father's House, not in my own; therefore had no right to invite or receive any-body unknown to my Parents, much less young Gentlemen; that being an Irregularity mis-becoming my Sex and Station, and the Character of a dutiful Daughter: This I desir'd her to tell him, with my Service; which Answer I utter'd with a little Sharpness, that the Woman could not but see her Errand was disobliging, as it was, and ought to be; such a Message looking more like a dishonourable Intrigue, than an Address to a vertuous Maiden-Gentlewoman. The Truth is, I always had an Aversion to those secret Addresses, as all vertuous Maids ought, and was resolved as carefully to avoid them as Mariners do Rocks; for 'tis certain, that Parents are natu-rally willing to promote their Childrens Happiness; and therefore, that Lover who desires to keep the Parents in the Dark, is conscious to him-self of something that has need to shun the Light; for his Concealing his Pretensions from the Mother, looks as if he meant an unworthy Con-quest on the Daughter; and especially those of Mr. *Bellair's* Character.

However, I mistook my young Gentleman, his Intentions being more sincere than I expected: For upon that Answer to my Gossip, he took the first Occasion to discover his Sentiments to his Father; who did not only approve, but rejoyced thereat, hoping that he was in a Dis-position to reclaim himself from his loose Way of Living; and that the Company of a Wife, and Care of a Family, wou'd totally wean him from those wild Companions, in whom he too much delighted: Not but that his Father had divers times offered, and earnestly persuaded him, to dis-pose himself for a Married Life, having no Son but him, to inherit his Riches, and continue his Family. To which the young Man was ever averse; counting Marriage as Fetters and Shackles, a Confinement not to be borne by the Young and the Witty; a Wife being suppos'd to be the Destruction of all Pleasure and good Humour, and a Death to all the Felicities of Life; only good in the Declension of Years, when Coughs and Aches oblige a Man to his own Fire-side: then a Nurse is a most necessary Utensil in a House. These and the like, us'd to be the wild Notions, wherewith he oppos'd his Father's indulgent Care, when-ever he went about to provide for his happy Establishment: So the good old Gentleman was overjoy'd at his Son's own Proposal, and took the first Opportunity with my Father, over a Bottle, to deliver his Son's

Errand. To which my Father answer'd, like a plain Country Gentleman, as he was (who never gilded his Actions with fraudulent Words, nor painted his Words with deceitful or double Meanings;) and told him, "That he was very sensible of the Honour he did him in this Proposal; but that he cou'd not make his Daughter a Fortune suitable to his Estate: For, continued he, that becoming Way in which we live, is more the Effect of prudent Management, than any real Existence of Riches." To which the old Gentleman reply'd, "That Riches were not what he sought in a Wife for his Son; Fortune having been so propitious to him, that he needed not to make that his greatest Care: A prudent, vertuous Woman, was what he most aim'd at, in his Son's Espousals, hoping that such an one, would reclaim and wean him from all those wild Excursions to which Youth and Ill-Company had drawn him, to his great Affliction. But, methinks, continu'd he, I spy a Dawn of Reformation in the Choice he has made of your Daughter; who, amongst all the young Gentlewomen of these Parts, I value, she having a distinguishing Character for Prudence and Vertue, capable to command Respect and Esteem from all the World; as well as does her amiable Person ingage my Son's Affections. Wherefore, said he, I hope you will not refuse your Concurrence, thereby to make my Son happy." My Father making him a grateful Acknowledgment, told him, "He wou'd propose it to my Mother and me; and added, That his Daughter having been always dutiful and tenderly observant, he resolv'd to be indulgent, and impose nothing contrary to her Inclinations. Her Mother also, continu'd he, has been a Person of that Prudence and Vertue, that I should not render the Justice due to her Merit, if I did any thing of this kind, without her Approbation."

This my Father related to me, with an Air full of Kindness, telling me, That he wou'd leave the Affair wholly to my Determination; adding, That there was an Estate, full Coffers, and a brisk young Gentleman; So that I think (said he) I need say no more to a Person of common Sense, to comply with what is so advantageous.

To which I reply'd, "That these or any of these, were above my Desert; and your Recommendations, Sir, redouble the Value; upon whose Wisdom and paternal Care I ought wholly to depend: But his particular loose Way of Living, I hope will justify me, when I lay that before you, as a Cause of Hesitation." To which my Mother reply'd, "That it must be my Part, with Mildness and Sweetness, to reclaim him: That he having now *sow'd his wild Oats,* (according to the Proverb) wou'd see his Folly; and finding there is nothing to be reap'd but Noise, Vanity, and Disgrace, in all Probability, wou'd apply himself to an other Way of Living; especially having made the Proposal to his Father of settling with a Person of his own choosing, where no Interest nor Family-Necessity had any Hand in the Election."

These and the like Discourses and Considerations, pass'd among us; we having his Father's serious Proposal for our Foundation; which, join'd with the Message he himself had sent me by the Gossip, we had Reason to believe the Superstructure would not be defective.

Nevertheless, though I was but an innocent Country Girl, yet I was not so ignorant of the World, but to know or believe, that often those Beau Rakes,[1] have the Cunning and Assurance to make Parents on both sides, Steps to their Childrens Disgrace, if not Ruin: For very often, good Country Ladies, who reflect not on the Vileness of the World, permit their Daughters to give private Audiences, to their Lovers, in some obscure Arbour[2] or distant Drawing room; where the Spark[3] has Opportunity to misbehave himself to the Lady; which, if she resent, there is a ready Conveniency for him to bespatter her with Scandal. And I did not know but *Bellair* might have some such thing in his Thoughts, out of Malice for my having rejected his Intrigue by the Gossip. For I could not fancy my-self endow'd with Charms sufficient to hold fast such a Volage;[4] however, I knew my self safe under my Mother's Prudence, and my own Resolution.

And thus I expected my *pretended Lover*[5] some Days; But instead of his personal Appearance, News came, That he was taken in a Robbery on the

---

1. **Beau Rakes:** dissipated men of fashion.

2. **Arbour:** a shady retreat surrounded by closely intertwined trees or shrubs.

3. **Spark:** suitor or dandy.

4. **Volage:** that which is flighty, unpredictable.

5. **pretended Lover:** professed suitor.

High-way, and committed to the County-Gaol:[1] And all this out of a Frolick; for tho' he had all Things necessary, both for Conveniency and Diversion, nevertheless, this detestable Frolick must needs be put in Practice, with some of his lewd Companions; for which at the next Assizes,[2] he receiv'd the Reward of his Crimes at the Place of publick Execution.

I have told you this Transaction, that your Ladyship may not be ignorant of any thing that appertains to me, though this was an Affair utterly unknown to all the World; I mean his Proposal of Marriage; nor does any of my Poems take the least Notice, or give any Hint of it; for there was no Progress made by any personal Correspondence, nor can I persuade my-self he meant any thing but Mischief.

I cou'd recount to your Ladyship another Story or two of odd Disappointments; but, they will take up too great a Place in your Screen, and render the View disagreeable.

---

1. **Gaol:** jail.

2. **Assizes:** county-based court hearing or judicial inquest.

A *Patch-Work Screen* for the *Ladies*.
Leaf II.

It was not long after these Turns of Fortune, that I had the real Affliction of losing my dear and indulgent Father; and so was left the only
Consolation of my widow'd Mother. I shall not mention the Grief,
Care, and Trouble which attended this great Change; these Things
being natural and known to every-body: Therefore, I shall pass them
over in Silence, as I was forced to undergo it with Submission.

When our Griefs were a little compos'd, and our Affairs adjusted, so
that the World knew what Fortune I had to depend upon, and that in
my own Power, there wanted not[1] Pretenders to my Person; so that now
was the Time to act the *Coquet*,[2] if I had lik'd the Scene; but that never
was my Inclination; for as I never affected the formal *Prude*, so I ever
scorn'd the impertinent *Coquet*. Amongst this Train of Pretenders,
(some of which address'd to my Mother, and some privately to me) I
think there is nothing worth Remark, but what your Ladyship may
guess, by a Copy or two of Verses writ on these Occasions.

To my *Indifferent Lover,* who complain'd
of my *Indifferency.*[3]

> You'd little Reason to complain of me,
> Or my Unkindness, or Indifferency,
> Since I, by many a Circumstance, can prove,
> That *Int'rest*[4] was the *Motive* of your *Love.*
> But Heav'n it-self despises that Request,
> Whose sordid Motive's only Interest.
> No more can *honest Maids* endure to be
> The *Objects* of your *wise Indifferency.*
> Such wary Courtship only shou'd be shown

---

1. **wanted not:** lacked not.

2. **Coquet:** flirt.

3. This poem is a slightly revised version of "To Dr. R.S. my indifferent Lover, Who
complain'd of my Indifferency," *PR 1.*

4. **Int'rest:** self-interest.

To *cunning, jilting Baggages*[1] o'th' Town.
'Tis *faithful Love's* the *Rhetorick* that persuades,
And charms the Hearts of silly *Country Maids.*
But when we find, your *Courtship's* but *Pretence,*
Love were not *Love* in *us,* but *Impudence.*
At best, I'm sure, to *us* it needs must prove,
What e'er you think on't, most *injurious Love.*
For had I of that gentle Nature been,
As to have lov'd your Person, Wit, or Mien,
How many Sighs & Tears it wou'd have cost,
And fruitless Expectations by the Post?
Saying, *He is unkind.*—O no! *his Letter's lost;*
Hoping him sick, or lame, or gone to Sea;
Hop'd any thing but his *Inconstancy.*
Thus, what in *other Friends,* cause *greatest Fear,*
To *desperate Maids,* their only *Comforts* are.
This I through all your Blandishments[2] did see,
Thanks to Ill-Nature, that instructed me.
Thoughts of your Sighs, sometimes wou'd plead for you;
But Second Thoughts again wou'd let me know,
In gayest *Serpents* strongest *Poysons* are,
As sweetest *Rose-trees,* sharpest *Prickles* bear.
And so it proves, since now it does appear,
That all your *Flames* and *Sighs* only for *Money* were.
As Beggars for their Gain, turn blind and lame,
On the same score, a *Lover* you became.
Yet there's a Kindness in this feign'd Amour,
It teaches me, ne'er to believe Man more:
Thus *blazing Comets* are of *good Portent,* [3]
When they excite the *People* to *repent.*

---

1. **Baggages:** disreputable women, strumpets.
2. **Blandishments:** gently flattering speeches.
3. **blazing Comets:** omens of disaster and death. **Portent:** omen, clue to the future.

These Amours affected me but little, or rather not at all; For the Troubles of the World lighting upon me, a thousand Disappointments attended me, when deprived of my Father. Alas! we know not the real Worth of indulgent, tender Parents, 'till the Want of them teach us by a sad Experience: And none experienc'd this more than myself: deceitful Debtors, impatient Creditors, distress'd Friends, peevish Enemies, Lawsuits, rotten Houses,[1] Eye-servants,[2] spightful Neighbours, impertinent and interested Lovers, with a thousand such Things to terrify and vex me, nothing to consolate or assist me, but Patience and God's Providence.

When my Mother and I had accommodated our Affairs, we endeavour'd to make ourselves easy, by putting off our Country Incumbrance, and so went to live at *London.*

Here I was, as if I was born again: This was a new Life to me, and very little fitted the Shape of my Rural Fancy; for I was wholly form'd to the Country in Mind and Manners; as unfit for the Town, as a Tarpaulin for a States-man; the Town to me was a Wilderness, where, methought, I lost my self and my Time; and what the World there calls Diversion, to me was Confusion. The Park,[3] Plays, and Operas, were to me but as so much Time thrown away. I was a Stranger to every-body, and their Way of Living; and, I believe, my stiff Air and awkard Mien, made every-body wish to remain a Stranger to me. The *Assemblèes,*[4] *Ombre,* and *Basset-Tables,*[5] were all *Greek* to me; and I believe my Country Dialect, to them, was as unintelligible; so that we were neither serviceable nor pleasant to each other. Perhaps some or other of the Company, either out of Malice to expose me, or Complaisance to entertain me in my own Way, would enter into the Praise of a Country Life, and its plentiful Way of Living, amongst our Corn, Dairies, and Poultry, 'till by Degrees, these bright *Angels* would make the *Ass* open its

1. **rotten Houses:** houses in decay.

2. **Eye-Servants:** domestics who spied on their employers.

3. **Park:** St. James's Park, scene of fashionable promenades, sport, and procurements.

4. **Assemblèes:** fashionable social gatherings (French).

5. **Ombre, and Basset:** fashionable card games at which one could lose a good deal of money.

Mouth, and upon their Demand, tell how many Pounds of Butter a good *Cow* would make in a Week; or how many Bushels of *Wheat* a good *Acre* of *Land* would produce; Things quite out of their Sphere or Element: And amongst the rest, the Decay of the *Wooll-Trade* is not to be omitted; and, like a true Country Block-head, grumble against the *Parliament*, for taking no better Care of the *Country-Trade*, by prohibiting *Cane-Chairs* and *Wainscot;*[1] by which means, the *Turkey-work,*[2] *Tapistry*,[3] and *Kidderminster Trades*[4] were quite lost; and in them the great Manufacture of the Nation; and not only so, but perpetual Fires[5] intail'd on the City of *London.* Thus I, one of the *free-born* People of *England,* thought I had full Privilege to rail at my *Betters.* Sometimes, and in some Places, perhaps, Part of the Company, who knew a little of my Bookish Inclinations, would endeavour to relieve that Silence which the Ignorance of the Town laid upon me; and enter into a Discourse of Receipts,[6] Books, and Reading. One ask'd me, If I lik'd Mrs. *Phillips,* or Mrs. *Behn*[7] best? To whom I reply'd, with a blunt Indignation, That *they ought not to be nam'd together:* And so, in an unthinking, unmannerly Way, reproach'd the Lady that endeavour'd to divert and entertain me; she having that Moment been pleased to couple them. By this Blunder, Madam, said *Galesia,* you see how far one is short, in Conversation acquired only by Reading; for the many Plays and pretty Books I had read, stood me in little stead at that Time, to my great Confusion; for

---

1. **Wainscot:** panel work made from superior quality imported oak.

2. **Turkey-work:** imitation of tapestry, originating in Turkey, often used for chair and sofa coverings.

3. **Tapistry:** woven textiles.

4. **Kidderminster Trades:** a special kind of carpet, named after a village in Worchestershire where it was manufactured.

5. **Fires:** the most devastating of numerous fires was the Great Fire of 1666 that killed nine people and destroyed almost 400 acres of buildings within the city walls.

6. **Receipts:** recipes.

7. **Mrs. Behn:** Aphra Behn (1640–89), also known as "Astrea," popular playright, poet, novelist and translator. She was considered the first woman author in English to earn her living by her pen. Behn's plays openly portrayed sexuality, and her life provided a contrast to the image of the chaste life of Katherine Philips.

though Reading inriches the Mind, yet it is Conversation that inables us to use and apply those Riches or Notions gracefully.

At the *Toilet*,[1] I was as ignorant a Spectator as a Lady is an Auditor at an *Act-Sermon* in the University,[2] which is always in *Latin;* for I was not capable to distinguish which Dress became which Face; or whether the *Italian, Spanish,* or *Portugal* Red, best suited such or such Features; nor had I a Catalogue of the Personal or Moral Defects of such or such Ladies, or Knowledge of their Gallantries, whereby to make my *Court* to the *Present,* at the *Cost* of the *Absent;* and so to go the World round, 'till I got thereby the Reputation of *ingaging* and *agreeable* Company. However, it was not often that the whole Mystery of the *Toilet,* was reveal'd to my Country Capacity; but now and then some Aunt, or Governess, would call me to a Dish of Chocolate, or so; whilst the Lady and her officious Madamoiselle, were putting on those secret Imbellishments which illustrated her Beauties in the Eyes of most of the fine-bred Beholders. But some petulant, antiquated Tempers, despised such Ornaments, as not having been used in good Queen BESS's Days;[3] nor yet in the more Modern Court of *Oliver Cromwel.*[4] As to myself, I was like a *Wild Ass* in a Forest, and liv'd alone in the midst of this great Multitude, even the great and populous City of *London.*

When Duty and good Days call'd me to Church, I thought I might find there some Compeeresses, or Persons of my own Stamp, and amongst the Congregation behave my self like others of my Sex and Years; But, alas! there were Locks and Keys, Affronts from Pew-keepers, crowding and pushing by the Mob, and the gathering Congregation gazing upon me as a Monster; at least I fancied so. When patient waiting, and Pocket opening to the Pewkeeper, had got me a Place, I thought to exercise the Duty that call'd me thither: But, alas! the Curte-

---

1. **Toilet:** fashion, including clothing and grooming.

2. **Act-Sermon in the University:** the public presentation of one's learned thesis; on Act Sunday, new Doctors of Divinity would publicly preach their theses.

3. **Queen Bess:** Queen Elizabeth I (1533–1603).

4. **Oliver Cromwel:** Oliver Cromwell (1599–1658), Puritan, Parliamentary general in the Civil Wars (1642–49) and one of those responsible for the execution of Charles I (1649); he became dictatorial Lord Protector of the Commonwealth (1653–58).

sies, the Whispers, the Grimaces, the Pocket Glasses, Ogling, Sighing, Flearing, Glancing, with a long &c. so discompos'd my Thoughts, that I found I was as unfit for those Assemblies, as those others before nam'd, where a verbal Conversation provided against those mute Entertainments; which my Clownish Breeding made me think great Indecencies in that Sacred Place; where nothing ought to be thought on, much less acted, but what tended to Devotion, and God's Glory; so that I was here likewise alone in the midst of a great Congregation. Thus you see, Madam, how an Education, purely Country, renders one unfit to live in the great World, amongst People of refin'd and nice Breeding; and though I had bestow'd Time and Pains in Book-Acquests,[1] a little more than usual; yet it was but *lost Labour* to say the *best of it:* However, I did not repent; for though it had suppress'd and taken Place of that nice Conversation belonging to the Ladies, yet it furnish'd me with Notions above the Trifles of my Sex, wherewith to entertain my self in *Solitude;* and likewise, when Age and Infirmities confin'd my dear Mother within-doors, and very much to her Chamber, I paid my Duty to her with Pleasure, which otherwise might have seem'd a Constraint, if not in some Degree omitted, had my Thoughts been levell'd at those gaudy Pleasures of the Town, which intangle and intoxicate the greater Part of Woman-kind. Now, I believe, it was this retired Temper which pleas'd a certain Person a little in Years, so as to make his Addresses to me, in order to an Espousal. This was approv'd of by my Friends and Relations; amongst the rest, my young Kinsman, whom I mention'd to your Ladyship, a Student at the University, writ me a very fine persuasive Copy of Verses on the Subject of *Marriage,* which I have lost; but the Answer to those Verses appear here amongst the other Paper-Rubbish.

---

1. **Book-Acquests:** acquisition of book knowledge.

To my Friend *Exilius,* On his persuading me to marry Old *Damon*[1]

When *Friends Advice* with *Lovers Forces* joyn,
They *conquer Hearts* more *fortified* than *mine.*
Mine open lies, without the least Defence;
No *Guard* of *Art;* but *its own Innocence;*
Under which *Fort* it could fierce *Storms* endure:
But from thy *Wit* I find no *Fort* secure.
Ah! why would'st thou assist mine Enemy,
Whose Merits were almost too strong for me?
For now thy *Wit* makes me almost adore,
And ready to pronounce him Conqueror:
But that his Kindness then would grow, I fear,
Too weighty for my weak Desert to bear:
I fear 'twou'd even to Extreams improve;
For *Jealousy,* they say's th'Extream of *Love.*
Even *Thou,* my dear *Exilius,* he'd suspect;
If *I* but look on *thee,* I *him* neglect.
Not only *Men,* as innocent as thou,
But *Females* he'd mistrust, and *Heaven* too.
Thus best things may be turn'd to greatest Harm,
As the *Lord s Prayer* said backward, proves a Charm.[2]
Or if not thus, I'm sure he wou'd despise,
And under-rate the easy-gotten Prize,
Forgetting the Portent o'th' *willing Sacrifice.*[3]
    These and a thousand Fears my Soul possess;
But most of all my own Unworthiness:
Like *dying Saints,* that wish for *coming Joys,*

---

1. This poem is an extensively revised version of a poem by the same name in *PR 1*.   **Exilius:** identified in *PR* as "*a Gentleman* of St. John's *College,* Cambridge."   **Damon:** common figure in pastoral; rural singer of love in Virgil, *Eclogues* 8 (37 B.C.).

2. **Charm:** magical spell.

3. When Sacrifices went willingly to the Altar, it portended Good. [Author's note.]

> But *humble Fears* their *forward Wish* destroys.
> What shall I do, then? Hazard the Event?
> You say, old *Damon's* All that's excellent.
> If I miss him, the next some '*Squire* may prove,
> Whose *Dogs* and *Horses*, shall have all his *Love*.
> Or some *debauch'd Pretender* to lewd Wit,
> Or covetous, conceited, unbred Cit.[1]
> As the brave Horse, who late in Coach did neigh,
> Is forc'd at last to tug a nasty *Dray*.[2]

I suppose, I need not desire your Ladyship to believe, that what seems here to be said in Favour of *Damon,* is rather Respect to my Kinsman's Persuasions, than any real Affection for him; who being a little in Years, was not much capable of raising a Passion in a Heart not hospitable enough to receive a Guest of this kind; especially having found so much Trouble with those that had lodg'd there heretofore. Wherefore this Affair pass'd by, with Indifference on both Sides: And my Mother and I remain'd at Quiet, we not thinking of any-body; nor any-body thinking of us: And thus we liv'd alone (at least in our Actions) in the midst of Multitudes.

Our Lodging was near *Westminster-Abbey,*[3] for the Benefit of those frequent and regular Services there performed. For my own Part, I chose the early Prayers, as being free from that Coquettry, too much appearing at the usual Hour: Besides, there one has the Opportunity, to offer all the Actions of the Day to Heaven, as the First-fruits, which heretofore was a most acceptable Sacrifice. By this, methought, all the Actions of the following Day were sanctified; or, at least, they seem'd to be agitated by a Direction from Heaven. The Comers thither appear'd to me to resort really there about what they pretended; and *the Service of God* seem'd to be the *true Motive* of their Actions. But, good Heaven! how was I surpriz'd at a Transaction I will relate, though not appertaining to my-self or my Story.

---

1. **Cit.:** citizen (pejorative).

2. **Dray:** sled or cart without wheels.

3. **Westminster-Abbey:** medieval church adjacent to Parliament House and Westminster Palace.

There was an elderly Man, in a graceful comely Dress suitable to his Years, who seem'd to perform his Devotions with Fervor and Integrity of Heart; nevertheless, this wicked Wight,[1] pick'd up a young Girl in order to debauch her; which was in this manner. Immediately when they came out of the Chapel, he began to commend the young People he saw there, for leaving their Morning-Slumbers, to come and serve God in his Sanctuary: "In particular, You, Sweet-heart, (addressing to one lately come out of the Country) have hardly yet any Acquaintance, to ingage you to meet upon an Intrigue or Cabal;[2] (at least I guess so by your Mien and Garb) but come hither purely for God's Worship, which is extremely commendable, and ought to be encourag'd. Come, pretty Maid, come along with me, and I will give you a Breakfast, together with good Instructions how to avoid the Vices of the Town, of which I am convinced you are thoroughly ignorant." Thus this old Whorson[3] play'd the *Devil for God's sake,* according to the Proverb, and took this young Innocent into a House of very ill Repute. [4]

It was not long e'er this poor Wretch began to find herself ill and out of Order: She came to me, hearing that I had some Skill in Physick; but I perceiving her Distemper[5] to be such as I did not well understand, nor cared to meddle withal, recommended her to a Physician of my Acquaintance, who was more used to the immodest Harangues necessary on such Occasions. I calling to mind, that this was she, who had been seduced at the early Prayers, was a little curious to know the Manner of her Undoing.

She told me, That the Person who misled her, was a Goldsmith, living in good Repute in that Quarter of the Town. He gave her a great deal of good Counsel to avoid the Beaus and Gallants of the Town; which if she did, and behav'd herself modestly and discreetly, he said, she should want for nothing; for he would be a Father to her: bad[6] her

---

1. **Wight:** demonic person.
2. **Cabal:** secret intrigue of sinister nature by a small group of persons.
3. **Whorson:** literally, son of a whore; despicable character.
4. **House of very ill Repute:** brothel.
5. **Distemper:** disease.
6. **bad:** bade.

meet him again on the Morrow, and he would bring a Ring, and therewith espouse her. Which accordingly he did, and put the Ring on the Wedding Finger, and took her for his Left-hand Wife.[1] By this Fallacy, was this silly Girl ruin'd. They continued this their Commerce for some time; he giving her many Treats and Presents; 'till, by degrees, he grew weary, diminished his Favours, met her but seldom, and at last took no Notice of her. Whether she was lewd with any other Person, and got the Venereal Distemper, and so disoblig'd him, or what other Reason, I know not; but she being abandon'd by her Gallant, and disabled by her Illness, was reduc'd to great Distress, and from Time to Time was forced to sell what she had to relieve her Necessities. The Ring she kept 'till the last, that being the Pledge of his Love, and pretended Constancy; but then was forc'd to seek to make Money of that vile Treasure, the *Snare* that had intangled both *Body* and *Soul*. Now this silly Creature never knew directly where this her Gallant liv'd. I suppose his Cunning conceal'd that from her; whether by Sham[2] or directly refusing to tell her, I know not: But she ignorantly stumbled on his Shop to sell this Ring; where finding an elderly Matron, she address'd herself to her to buy it. The good Gentlewoman seeing her Husband's Mark on the Ring, and calling to mind, that she had miss'd such a one some time ago, seiz'd the Girl, in order to carry her before a Justice to make her prove where, and how, she came by that Ring. The poor Wretch, all trembling, told her, That a Gentleman had given it her; but indeed, she did not know where he lived. Whereupon the Gentlewoman reply'd, That if she could not produce the Person that gave it her, she must be prosecuted as a Felon, and as such, undergo what the Course of Law should allot her; and accordingly order'd her immediately into the Hands of a Constable, to have her before a Justice. At this Moment, it so happen'd, that the Master of the Shop came in; at which the poor trembling, frighted Creature, cry'd out, O Madam! this is the Gentleman that gave me the Ring. *You impudent Slut,* reply'd he, *I know you not; get you gone out of my Shop!*

---

1. **Left-hand Wife:** mistress or woman who lives with man as his wife without benefit of marriage.

2. **Sham:** lie, falsehood.

and so push'd her out. She being glad to get thus quit, hasted away, leaving the Man and his Wife to finish the Dispute between themselves.

Behold, Madam, what an odd Piece of Iniquity[1] was here. That a Man in Years shou'd break his Morning's Rest, leave his Wife, House, and Shop at Random, and expose himself to the chill Morning Air, to act the Hypocrite and Adulterer; ruin an innocent young Creature, under the Pretence of a ridiculous Sham-Marriage, and at the same Time exhaust that Means which should support his Family and his Credit, is to me wonderful to conceive. At last the poor Creature was abandon'd to all Misery, even Hunger and a nauseous Disease; between which she must have inevitably perish'd, a loathsome Example of Folly and Lewdness; but that the Doctor to whom I had recommended her, got her into an Hospital, from whence, after her Cure, she went away to the Plantations,[2] those great Receptacles of such scandalous and miserable Miscreants.[3]

Pardon, Madam, this long Digression, which is not out of an Inclination to rake in such Mud, which produces nothing but Offence to the Senses of all vertuous Persons; but it came into my Way to shew how much I was mistaken, in the Vertue and Piety of some of those early Devotees. Not that I mean by this or the like Example, to condemn all who there daily make their Addresses to Heaven: But to shew you, that in all Places, and at all Times, my Country Innocence render'd me a kind of a *Solitary* in the midst of Throngs and great Congregations. But though I found my self thus alone in Morals, yet I no where found a *personal Solitude;* but all Places full; all Persons in a Hurry; suitable to what that great Wit, Sir *John Denham,*[4] says;

——With equal Haste they run,
Some to undo, and some to be undone.[5]

---

1. **Iniquity:** evildoing.

2. **Plantations:** colonies, especially in North America and Ireland.

3. **Miscreants:** villains, criminals.

4. **Sir John Denham:** poet and translator (1615–69), best known for his long topographical poem, *Cooper's Hill* (1642), and his paraphrase of the *Aeneid.*

5. **With...undone:** These lines are a paraphrase of *Cooper's Hill,* lines 31–32.

At home, at our own Lodging, there was as little Quiet, between the Noise of the Street, our own House, with Lodgers, Visiters, Messages, Howd'ye's,[1] Billets,[2] and a Thousand other Impertinencies; which, perhaps, the Beau World wou'd think Diversion, but to my dull Capacity were mere Confusion. Besides which, several People came to me for Advice in divers sorts of Maladies, and having tolerable good Luck, I began to be pretty much known. The Pleasure I took in thus doing good, much over-balanced the Pains I had in the Performance; for which benign kind Disposition, I most humbly bless my great Creator (the free Disposer of all Blessings) for having compos'd me of such a Temper, as to prefer a vertuous or a charitable Action, before the Pomps or Diversions of the World, though they shou'd be accompanied with Riches and Honours; which, indeed, I did not injoy, nor expect; therefore happy, that my Inclinations corresponded with my Circumstances. The Truth is, I know not but that Pride and Vanity might, in some Degree, be united to this Beneficence; for I was got to such a Pitch of helping the Sick, that I wrote my *Bills*[3] in *Latin*, with the same manner of *Cyphers* and *Directions* as Doctors do; which Bills and Recipes[4] the Apothecaries fil'd amongst those of the Doctors: And this being in particular one of my Sex, my Muse wou'd needs have a *Finger in the Pye;*[5] and so a Copy of Verses was writ on the Subject; which, perhaps, your Ladyship may like so as to put them in your SCREEN. They are as follow:

On the *Apothecaries* Filing my *Recipes*
amongst the *Doctors.*[6]

I hope I sha'n't be blam'd, if I am proud
To be admitted in this learned Croud.

---

1. **Howd'ye's:** notes inquiring into correspondent's health.

2. **Billets:** brief letters.

3. **Bills:** list of drugs to be mixed to compose a medicine.

4. **Recipes:** medical prescriptions.

5. **Finger in the Pye:** finger in the pie; meddling.

6. This poem is a revised version of the poem by the same name in *PR 1*.

For to be proud of Fortune so sublime,
Methinks, is rather Duty than a Crime.
Were not my Thoughts exalted in this State,
I should not make thereof due Estimate:
And, sure, one Cause of *Adam's Fall,* was this,
He knew not the just Worth of *Paradise.*
But with this Honour I'm so satisfy'd,
The Ancients were not more, when *Deify'd.*
'Tis this makes me a fam'd Physician grow,
As *Saul* 'mongst Prophets turn'd a Prophet too.

    The *Sturdy Gout,*[1] which all Male-Power withstands,
Is overcome by my soft Female Hands.[2]
Not *Deb'rah, Judith,* or *Semiramis,*[3]
Cou'd boast of Conquest half so great as this;
More than they slew, I save, in this Disease.

    Now Blessings on you All, you Sons of Art,
Who what your selves ne'er knew, to me impart.
Thus Gold, which by th'Sun's Influence does grow,
Does that i'th'Market, *Phoebus*[4] cannot do.
Bless'd be the Time, and bless'd my Pains & Fate,
Which introduc'd me to a Place so great!
False *Strephon*[5] too, I almost now cou'd bless,
Whose Crimes conduc'd to this my Happiness.
Had he been true, I'd liv'd in *sottish Ease,*
Ne'er study'd ought, but how to *love* and *please*;
No other *Flame,* my *Virgin Breast* had *fir'd,*

---

1. **Gout:** disease characterized by painful inflammation and swelling of the joints.

2. Having a particular *Arcanura* for the Gout. [Author's note.] **Arcanura:** secret remedy. Barker developed a plaster to treat gout.

3. **Deb'rah, Judith, or Semiramis:** Each acted decisively and forcefully. Deborah was a prophetess and military advisor; see Judges. Judith cut off the head of the general Holofernes to deliver the Hebrew people from Nebuchadnezzar; see Judith, the *Apocrypha.* Semiramis was a mythical Assyrian queen and military leader.

4. **Phoebus:** Apollo, Greek god of the light, poetry, and medicine.

5. *Bosvil* call'd *Strephon* in her Verses. [Author's or Publisher's note.] **Bosvil:** her suitor in *Love Intrigues.*

But *Love* and *Life* together had *expir'd.*
But when, false *Wretch!* he his forcd Kindness *pay'd,*
With less *Devotion* than e'er Sexton[1] *pray'd,*
Fool that I was! to sigh, weep, almost dye,
Little fore-thinking of this present Joy;
Thus happy Brides shed Tears, they know not why.
Vainly we praise this *Cause,* or laugh at that,
Whilst the *Effect,* with its *How, Where,* & *What,*
Lies *Embrio* in the Womb of Time or Fate.
Of future Things we very little know,
And 'tis Heav'ns Kindness, that it should be so;
Were not our *Souls,* with *Ignorance* so *buoy'd,*
They'd *sink* with *Fear,* or *overset* with *Pride.*
So much for *Ignorance* there may be said,
That large Encomiums might thereof be made.
But I've digress'd too far; so must return,
To make the *Medick-Art* my whole Concern,
Since by its Aid, I've gain'd this honour'd Place,
Amongst th'immortal *Æsculapian*-Race:[2]
That if my Muse, will needs officious be,
She must to this become a *Votary.*
In all our Songs, its Attributes rehearse,
Write *Recipes,* as OVID *Law,* in Verse.
To *Measure* we'll reduce *Febrific Heat,*[3]
And make the *Pulses* in true *Numbers* beat.
Asthma and *Phthisick*[4] chant in Lays most sweet;
The *Gout* and *Rickets*[5] too, shall run on Feet.

---

1. **Sexton:** church officer responsible for maintenance of the premises, ringing of the bells, and burying of the dead.

2. **Æsculapian-Race:** physicians. In classical myth, Aesculapius was a god of healing and medicine.

3. **Febrific Heat:** feverish heat.

4. **Phthisick:** wasting disease of the lungs, tuberculosis.

5. **Rickets:** softening of the bones.

In fine, my Muse, such Wonders we will do,
That to our *Art*, Mankind their Ease shall owe;
Then praise and please our-selves in doing so.
For since the Learn'd exalt and own our Fame,
It is no Arrogance to do the same,
But due Respects, and Complaisance to them.

Thus, Madam, as People before a Looking-glass, please themselves with their own Shapes and Features, though, perhaps, such as please no-body else; just so *I celebrated my own Praise,* according to the Proverb, *for want of good Neighbours to do it for me;* or rather, for want of Desert to ingage those good Neighbours. However, I will trouble your Ladyship with relating one Adventure more, which happen'd in this my Practice.

There came to me a Person in Quality of a Nurse who, though in a mean servile Station, had something in her Behaviour and Discourse, that seem'd above her Profession: For her Words, Air, and Mien, appeared more like one entertaining Ladies in a Drawing-Room, than a Person whose Thoughts were charg'd with the Care of her sick Patients, and Hands with the Pains of administring to her own Necessities. As we were in Discourse of the Business she came about, we were interrupted by a certain Noise in the Street, a little more than usual; which call'd our Curiosity to the Window; where pass'd by a noble fine Coach, with many Foot-men running bare-headed on each side, with all other Equipage and Garniture[1] suitable; which made a splendid Figure, deserving the Regards of People the least curious. The Coach being pass'd, I turn'd me about, and found the good Nurse sunk in a fainting Fit, which was a little surprizing; but calling my Maid, with a little Endeavour, we brought her to herself; we ask'd her the Cause of this sudden Disorder? Whether she was accustom'd to those Fits? or, Whether any sudden Surprize or Reflection had seiz'd her? She reply'd, That indeed it was a sudden Surprize: The Sight of that great Coach, had affected her Spirit, so as to cause in her that Disorder. Whereupon I told her, I should be oblig'd to her, if she thought fit to inform me what Person or Occasion

---

1. **Equipage and Garniture:** equipment, elaborate furnishings.

had caus'd in her so violent an Effect. To which she reply'd, That a Person of his Grandeur who was in the Coach, ought not to be nam'd with one of her mean[1] Condition: Nevertheless, said she, you appearing to be a Gentlewoman of Prudence and Vertue, I will tell you my Story, without the least Disguise.

My Father, said she, was the younger Son of a Country Gentleman, and was a Tradesman of Repute in the City: He gave me a Gentlewoman-like Education, as became his Family, and the Fortune he was able to bestow upon me; for he had no Child but my self, which, perhaps, was the Cause that I was more taken Notice of than I should have been otherwise. Amongst many that cast their Eyes upon me, a certain young Clerk of the Inns of Court,[2] of a piercing Wit, graceful Mien, and flowing Eloquence, found Opportunity to make an Acquaintance with me, and as soon to make his Addresses to me. Alas! my unguarded Heart soon submitted to the Attacks of his Wit and ingaging Behaviour; and all this without the Knowledge of my Father; which was the easier accomplish'd, I having no Mother. I will not repeat to you, continu'd she, the many Messages, Letters, and little Presents, which attended this secret Amour, there being therein no more than ordinary on such an Occasion.

Now though we had been careful and cunning enough to keep this from the Knowledge of my Father, yet Jealousy soon open'd the Eyes of a Lover; for the Foreman of my Father's Shop, designing me for himself, found out our Correspondence, and discovered the same to my Father: At which he was very much displeas'd, knowing that the young Gentleman had little or no Foundation, but his own Natural Parts, and his Education, to recommend him for a Husband to a City Heiress. Hereupon my Father forbad me his Company, charging me to have no manner of Correspondence with him, upon pain of his utmost Displeasure. But, alas! my Affections were too far ingag'd, to let Duty have the Regency; and not only my Affections, but my faithful Word given in

---

1. **mean:** humble.

2. **Clerk of the Inns of Court:** law student at one of the four law societies: Lincoln's Inn, the Middle Temple, the Inner Temple, and Gray's Inn.

Promise of Marriage to this young Gentleman; which I kept from my Father, assuring him of a ready Obedience to his Commands.

Thus things pass'd some time in Silence and Secrecy, 'till my Father had an Opportunity to marry me to a wealthy Citizen; wherewith he press'd me very earnestly to comply. But his Trade was none of the Genteelest, neither his Education nor Person at all polite, nor was he very suitable in Years: These Things were disagreeable in themselves; but worst of all, my Word given to my young Lawyer, render'd the Difficulty almost unsurmountable. I had not Courage to let my Father know the Truth; which if I had, perhaps, I had been never the better; for the more I seem'd to dislike this other Proposal, the more my Father's Aversion grew towards my young Lawyer, as supposing him to be the Obstacle that barr'd me from my Duty, as he really was, in a great degree. But Things did not hold long in this Posture; for my Father press'd on the Marriage with the utmost Earnestness, using Promises and Threatnings, 'till at last my *Weakness* (for I cannot call it *Obedience*) made me comply. After I was married, I lived in plenty enough for some Years. In the mean Time, my Father married a young Wife, by whom he had many Children, which depriv'd me of all future Hopes of receiving any Benefit by his Bounty. But to shorten my Story, by such time as I had liv'd a Wife about Seven Years, my Father dy'd, and my Husband broke, by which I was reduc'd to a low Ebb of Fortune; and he being a Man of no Family, had no Friends to assist or raise him; and with this Fall of Fortune, his Spirit sunk withal, so that he had not Courage to strive or grapple, or turn any thing about, 'till he had spent the utmost Penny. Whether this Ruin proceeded from Losses by Sea and Land, to which great Dealers are obnoxious, or from the immediate Hand of Heaven, for my Breach of Vow to my young Lawyer, I know not; but our Distress grew greater and greater, 'till I was forc'd to betake my self to the Imployment of a *Nurse;* and my Husband to be *Labourer* at St. *Paul's,*[1] which is his present Occupation. In the mean time, my young Lawyer grew into Fame, by his acute Parts, which he imploy'd in serving the

---

1. **Labourer at St. Paul's:** manual laborer helping rebuild St. Paul's Cathedral, destroyed by the Great Fire.

Royal-Cause,[1] 'till he is become that great man you saw pass by: which sudden Sight gave me such Confusion, that I cou'd no longer support my self, but sunk into the Chair next the Place where I stood.

Thus ended she her Story; which is indeed not a little extraordinary, though scarcely sufficient to merit your Ladyship's Attention. Nevertheless, the good Woman's Humility, Patience, and Industry, are greatly to be commended, and ought to be an Example to many, even her Superiors as well as her Inferiors; she being so true a Pattern of Patience, humble Condescension, and Diligence, that I think I may apply to her a Couplet I wrote on a particular Occasion, amongst some of my Poems:

> Where *Fortune* wou'd not with her *Wish* comply,
> She made her *Wish* bear *Fortune* Company.[2]

Thus, Madam, I rubb'd on, in the midst of Noise and Bustle, which is every where to be found in *London;* but Quiet and Retreat scarce any where. At last I found out a Closet[3] in my Landlady's Back Garret[4] which I crept into, as if it had been a Cave on the Top of *Parnassus;* the Habitation of some unfortunate Muse, that had inspir'd *Cowley, Butler, Otway,* or *Orinda,*[5] with Notions different from the rest of Mankind; and for that Fault, were there made Prisoners. Here I thought I found my own poor despicable Muse given to *Orinda* as her Waiting-maid; and it was, perhaps, some of the worst Part of that great Lady's Punishment, to be constrain'd to a daily Correspondence with so dull a Creature. However, this Hole was to me a kind of Paradise; where I thought I met with my old Acquaintance as we hope to do in the other World.

---

1. **Royal-Cause:** the King's business.

2. **Where . . . Company:** See *Love Intrigues,* page 8, and "A dialogue between Fidelia and her little nephew Martius," lines 40–41, page 315. The pronouns vary, depending upon the context: she, he, they.

3. **Closet:** small room.

4. **Garret:** area on the top floor of a house, typically under a pitched roof; attic.

5. **Cowley, Butler, Otway, Orinda:** Abraham Cowley (1618–67), popular playwright and lyric poet. **Samuel Butler** (1612–80), author of *Hudibras,* the celebrated satire in three parts (1663, 1664, 1678) that criticizes Presbyterians and Independents. **Thomas Otway** (1652–85), popular playwright, especially remembered for the tragedy *Venice Preserv'd* (1682). **Katherine Philips** (1632–64), "the Matchless Orinda." All were Royalists.

Here I tumbled over *Harvey* and *Willis* at Pleasure: My impertinent Muse here found me; and here we renew'd our old Acquaintance. Sometimes I wou'd repel her Insinuations; and sometimes again accept her Caresses; as appears by the following Invocation.

To my *Muse*.[1]

Cease, prithee, Muse, thus to infest
The barren Region of my Breast,
Which never can an Harvest yield,
Since Weeds of Noise o'er-run the Field.
If *Interest* wont oblige thee to it,
At least let *Vengeance* make thee do it;
'Cause I thy Sweets and Charms oppose,
In bidding Youth become thy Foes.
But nought, I see, will drive thee hence,
Threats, Business, or Impertinence.
But still *thou* dost thy Joys obtrude
Upon a Mind so wholly rude,
As can't afford to entertain
Thee, with the Welcome of one Strain.

   Few Friends, like *thee,* wou'd be so kind,
To come where Interest does not bind;
And fewer yet return again,
After such Coldness and Disdain.
But *thou,* kind Friend, art none of those;
Thy Charms thou always do'st oppose
Against Inquietude of Mind;
If I'm displeas'd, still thou art kind;
And with thy Spells driv'st Griefs away,
Which else wou'd make my Heart their Prey.
And fill'st their empty Places too,
With Thoughts of what we ought to do.
Thou'rt to my Mind so very good,

---

1. This poem is a revised version of "To the Importunate Address of Poetry," *PR 1*.

Its Consolation, Physick, Food.
Thou fortify'st it in Distress;
In Joy augment'st its Happiness:
Inspiring me with harmless Rhimes,
To praise *good Deeds,* detest *all Crimes.*
Then, gentle *Muse,* be still my Guest;
Take *full Possession* of my *Breast.*

Thus, Madam, in my Garret-Closet, my *Muse* again took Possession of me: Poetry being one of those subtle Devils, that if driven out by never so many firm Purposes, good Resolutions, Aversion to that Poverty it intails upon its Adherents; yet it will always return and find a Passage to the Heart, Brain, and whole Interior; as I experienced in this my exalted Study: Or, to (use the Phrase of the Poets) my *Closet* in the *Star-Chamber;*[1] or the *Den* of *Parnassus.*

Out of this Garret, there was a Door went out to the Leads;[2] on which I us'd frequently to walk to take the Air, or rather the Smoke; for Air, abstracted from Smoke, is not to be had within Five Miles of *London.* Here it was that I wish'd sometimes to be of *Don Quixote's* Sentiments,[3] that I might take the *Tops* of *Chimneys,* for *Bodies* of *Trees;* and the *rising Smoke* for *Branches;* the *Gutters of Houses,* for *Tarras-Walks;* and the *Roofs* for stupendous *Rocks* and *Mountains.* However, though I could not beguile my Fancy thus, yet here I was alone, or, as the Philosopher says, never *less alone.*[4] Here I entertain'd my Thoughts, and indulg'd my solitary Fancy. Here I could behold the *Parliament-House,*[5]

---

1. **Star Chamber:** King's council in its judicial function, abolished in 1641, sitting in closed session to pass judgment on those accused of crimes against the state.

2. **Leads:** both the passageways on a roof and the lead sheets that compose the covering of a roof.

3. **Don Quixote's Sentiments:** Don Quixote, impractical hero of Cervantes' Spanish picaresque novel (1605–15), imagined that windmills were giants and a serving wench was a gracious lady.

4. **never less alone:** "Never less idle than when wholly idle, nor less alone than when wholly alone," *De Officiis* 3.1.1, by Cicero (106–43 B.C.), Roman writer on philosophy, rhetoric, and law.

5. **Parliament House:** Royal Chapel of St. Stephen, part of the Palace of Westminster, meeting place of the House of Commons until destroyed by a fire in 1834.

Westminster-Hall,[1] and the *Abbey,*[2] and admir'd the Magnificence of their Structure, and still more, the Greatness of Mind in those who had been their Founders; one Place for the establishing good Laws; another for putting them in Practice; the Third for the immediate Glory of God; a Place for the continual singing his Praise, for all the Blessings bestow'd on Mankind. But with what Amazement did I reflect, how Mankind had perverted the Use of those Places design'd for a general Benefit: and having been reading the Reign of King *Charles* the First, I was amaz'd, to think how those *Law Makers* cou'd become such *Law-Confounders,*[3] as the History relates. Was it Ambition, Pride or Avarice? For what other wicked Spirit entred amongst them, we know not; but something infernal sure it was, that push'd or persuaded them to bring so barbarous an Enterprize to so sad a Conclusion. Ambition sure it cou'd not be, for *every one* cou'd not be *King,* nor indeed cou'd *any one* reasonably hope it. Neither cou'd it be Pride, because in this Action they work'd their own Disgrace. It must certainly therefore be Covetousness; for they hop'd to inrich themselves by the Ruins of the *Church* and *State,* as I have heard; though the Riches were of small Durance. These kind of Thoughts entertained me; some of which, I believe, are in Writing, amongst my other Geer.[4]

Upon *Covetousness.*

Covetousness we may truly call, The *Dropsie*[5] of the *Mind,* it being an insatiable Thirst of Gain: The more we get, the more we desire, and the more we have, the less willing are we to part with any. It was a wise Remark of him that said, *A Poor Man wants Many things, but the Covetous Man wants All things;* for a *covetous Man* will want *Necessaries,* rather than part with his *Gold;* and unless we do part with it, it is of no use to

---

1. **Westminster-Hall:** part of the Palace of Westminster, site of the Law Courts and booksellers' stalls in Barker's time.

2. **The Abbey:** Westminster Abbey.

3. **Law-Confounders:** in their open debate, legislative decisions, and political intrigues, many members of the Protestant Parliament sought to undermine the power of Catholic James II.

4. **Geer:** gear.

5. **Dropsie:** dropsy; disease characterized by extreme lethargy.

us; since we can't eat, drink, or warm ourselves by it: And, as of itself it can neither feed, warm, nor cloath us, so neither can it make us Ploughshares, Pruning-hooks, Weapons of Defence, or other Utensils worthy the Value we set upon it. Yet this *shining Earth*[1] commands this *Lower Orb,*[2] and for it we often sell our Friends, King, Country, Laws, and even our eternal Happiness. Thus *Avarice* brings *many* to that *Region* where the Coveting of *Thirty Pieces of Silver*[3] brought the *most abominable* of all *Traitors.*

Then I turn'd my Eyes on *Westminster-Hall,* that noble Structure, which contains the several Courts of Justice, where those good Laws, made in the other High Court,[4] are put in practise. But how far this Intention is perverted, God knows, and the World daily informs us. For Truth is too often disguised, and Justice over-ballanced, by means of false Witnesses, slow Evidences to Truth, avaritious Lawyers, poor Clients, Perjury, Bribery, Forgery, Clamour, Party, Mistakes, Misapprehensions, ill-stating the Case, Demurrs, Reverses, and a thousand other Shifts, Querks and Tricks, unknown to all but Lawyers.

From hence I turn'd my Eyes on the *Abbey,* and wondred to behold it standing; when so many stately Edifices and stupendous Piles were demolished. Whether its Revenues were *too small* to be *coveted,* or *too large* to be *hop'd for,* I could not tell; but I believe the Stones were neither more nor less Criminal than those of their Fellow-Dilapidations. So I concluded these Considerations, with a Couplet of Sir *John Denham's.*

> Is there no *temp'rate Region* to be *known,*
> Betwixt their *torrid* and our *frigid Zone?* [5]

I return'd into my Closet, or rather my Den of Dulness, for the Retreat of such a Student deserves not the Name of a *Study.* Here I cast

---

1. **shining Earth:** gold, which is mined from the earth.

2. **Lower Orb:** earth.

3. **Thirty Pieces of Silver:** the amount of money Judas Iscariot received for betraying Christ; see Matt. 26:14, Mark 14:10, and Luke 22:3–6.

4. **High Court:** referring to Parliament and suggesting God's court.

5. **Is there ... Zone?:** Denham, *Cooper's Hill,* lines 139–40.

mine Eyes on a very fine Epistle in Verse from my Friends at *Cambridge;* whereupon I sat me down to answer it, which was to dissuade them from Poetry, notwithstanding their great Genius towards it, express'd even in that Epistle. Which Answer be pleas'd to take as follows.

To my *Friends*, against *Poetry*. [1]

Dear Friends, if you'll be rul'd by me,
Beware the Charms of *Poetry;*
And meddle with no fawning Muse,
They'll but your harmless Love abuse.
Tho' *Cowley's* MISTRESS had a Flame,
As pure and lasting as his Fame;
And to *Orinda*[2] they were ty'd,
That nought their Friendship cou'd divide;
Yet now they're all grown Prostitutes,
And wantonly admit the Suits
Of any Fop,[3] that will pretend
To be their Lover, or their Friend.
Tho' they to *Wit,* no Homage pay,
Nor can the *Laws of Verse* obey,
But ride poor *Six-foot* out of Breath,[4]
And rack a *Metaphor* to Death;
Yet still, as little as they know,
Are Fav'rites of the Muses now.
Then who wou'd honour such a *She,*
Where *Fools* their happier Rivals be?
We surely may conclude there's none,
Unless they're drunk with HELICON;[5]
Which is a Liquor that can make

---

1. This poem is a revised version of poem by the same name, *PR 1.*

2. Mrs. *Katherine Philips.* [Author's note.]

3. **Fop:** foolish and conceited man, pretender to wit and excessively attentive to fashion.

4. **Six-foot:** six metrical units in a line of poetry.

5. **Helicon:** mountain of Bœotia, sacred to the Muses.

A Dunce set up for Rhyming Quack;
A Liquor of so strange a Temper,
As all our Faculties does hamper;
That whoso drinks thereof is curs'd
To a continu'd Rhyming Thirst.
Unknown to us, like Spell of Witch,
It strikes the Mind into an *Itch;*
Which being *scrubb'd* by *Praise,* thereby
Becomes a spreading *Leprosy;*
As hard to cure, as Dice or Whore,
And makes the Patient, too, as poor:
For *Poverty* as sure attends
On *Poets,* as on *Rich-Mens* Friends:
Wherefore I'd banish it my Breast.
Rather than be to Fools a Jest,
I'd to old *Mammon*[1] be a Bride,
Be ugly as his Ore untry'd;
Do every Thing for sordid Ends,
Caress my *Foes,* betray my *Friends;*
Speak fair to *all;* do good to *none;*
Not care who's happy, who's undone; }
But run where *Int'rest* pushes one;
Do any thing to quench poetick Flame,
And beg my Learned Friends to do the same.

Looking over what I had wrote, I remember I did not like it; for instead of praising what they had sent me, as it deserv'd, giving them Thanks, begging them to continue the same Favour to me and the World, I, in an uncouth, disobliging Manner, oppos'd their Ingenuity; by which I very little deserved any more such agreeable Entertainments. Moreover, casting an Eye on the other Poem, which I had wrote but a Day or two before, in which I had kindly treated and cajol'd my Muse; and then again on my Friends witty Epistle; so that between these

---

1. **Mammon:** Aramaic for riches, personification of materialism and covetness; see Matt. 6:24, Luke 6:9–13, and Milton, *Paradise Lost* 2 (1667).

Three, my Thoughts *danc'd the Hay*,[1] like the *Sun* and *Moon* in the *Rehearsal,* and thereby made an *Eclipse* in my *Resolution.* But as I have heard, that in some Countries they go with Pans and Kettles, and therewith make a Noise; whether to wake the Sun out of his imagin'd Sleep, or raise him from the Dead, I know not: But, in like manner, a hasty Knocking at the Door of the Leads; disappointed this my Ecliptick Dance. I speedily open'd the Door, and there found a Gentlewoman of a graceful Mien and genteel Dress: She hastily rush'd in, and begg'd me to fasten the Door, and then to introduce her to the Gentlewoman of the House: To which I consented, and so descended with her to my Landlady's Apartment, where we found her, together with my Mother. After I had inform'd them of the Adventure of her coming over the Leads, in at the Garret-Door, they courteously receiv'd her, and desir'd to know wherein they cou'd be further serviceable.

She told them, That although her Crimes render'd her too confus'd to relate her Story; yet, her distressed Condition obliged her to an undisguised Recital.

The *Story* of *Belinda*.[2]

I am, said she, Daughter to a worthy Country Gentleman, of an ancient Family and large Possessions; who lived suitable to the Rank and Station in which Heaven had plac'd him. He and my Mother were esteemed by Persons of all Ranks, as indeed they deserv'd; for they were beneficent to every body; Neighbours, Relations, Servants, Poor and Rich, all had a Share in their Generosity, Kindness, or Charity. Their Tenants gather'd Estates[3] under them; Their Servants gain'd wherewith to become Masters in their Old Age; Their Table and Cellar were always free and open to the Freeholders,[4] and Tradesmen, who came to pay their Respects to them; Their Park and Gardens were at the Service of any of the neighbouring Gentry, that were not Masters of such Conve-

---

1. **danc'd the Hay:** performed winding or sinuous movements around objects, as in a dance.
2. **Belinda:** conventional name of romance heroine.
3. **gather'd Estates:** accumulated wealth and property, prospered.
4. **Freeholders:** tenants who hold a life interest in property.

niences: Their Persons were amiable, and their Discourse agreeable and entertaining. Thus they pass'd their Days in Plenty and Honour, 'till their unhappy Off-spring gave a new *Byass* to their *Bowl* of Life,[1] which had hitherto *rolled on* with such Evenness, as testified the steady Hand of those that gave the *Cast*.[2] My Brother being grown to Years of Maturity, listed[3] himself in all the Lewdness of the Age; by which he contracted so many and such gross Infirmities, that a thorough Recovery of his Health is despaired of.

Now my Parents, who had been always affectionate towards me, became extreamly fond, humouring me even to a Fault, especially since I made such ill Use of their Tenderness: For by means of this extraordinary Indulgence, I grew troublesome to Servants, impertinent to my Betters, rude and disobliging to my Equals, harsh and insulting to my Inferiors; in short, I behav'd my self, as if all the World were created for me only, and my Service. In the mean Time, Fondness so blinded my Parents, that they saw no Fault in me, nor I in my self, which was my great Misfortune.

Now, whether this humoursome, impertinent way made me disagreeable to Young Gentlemen, I know not; but though my Fortune was considerable, and my Person such as you see, not contemptible, yet nobody made any Overtures of Marriage to me, or to my Parents on my behalf; at least, that I know of.

Amongst, many whom my Father's Quality and Munificence brought to our House, there was a certain fine Gentleman cast his Eyes on me, with a Tenderness unbefitting my Youth, and his Circumstances, he being a married Man; but notwithstanding that, I suffered his Insinuations to penetrate my Soul. His Looks and Gestures demonstrated a violent Passion; but his Words were always dress'd up in Vertue and Honour; and the frequent Theme of his Discourse was on *Platonick Love*,[4] and the happy State any *Two* might injoy, that lived together in

---

1. **new Byass to their Bowl:** term from lawn bowling, referring to altered path of the ball.

2. **Cast:** pitch or toss of the ball.

3. **listed:** enlisted.

4. **Platonick Love:** after the Greek philosopher, Plato, a love without sensuality that would lead one to contemplation of higher Love and Goodness.

such a chaste Affection. In these kind of Discourses we pass'd many Hours; sometimes in Walks, sometimes in Arbours, and oftentimes in my Chamber, 'till very late Hours. At last, the Mask of *Platonick Love* was pull'd off, and a personal Injoyment concluded the Farce, compos'd of many deceitful Scenes, and wicked Contrivances. In a little Time I began to perceive my self pregnant, to that degree, that I daily fear'd others should take notice of it. There was no way left to escape the Fury of *my* Parents and *his* Wife, but by Flight, which we put in Execution, pretending to go beyond-Sea, the better to avoid Search. But instead thereof, he brought me to a House in your Neighbourhood; and there left me. What is become of him, I know not, nor dare inquire. The Officers of the Parish being inform'd of my being here, in this Condition, came to inquire into the Matter; but my Landlady being aware thereof, convey'd me through her Garret over the Leads of *Westminster-Hall,* and so into your Garret.

And now, Gentlewomen, behold what a miserable Creature is before you. I cannot bear being carried before a Justice on this Account; I shall sooner lay violent Hands on my self; which I pray God forbid. Therefore, dear Ladies, advise me what to do, or how to proceed.

After a little Consideration, my Landlady, with much Goodness, sent for the Officers of the Parish, to ingage on her behalf; that they might leave her in Repose, 'till Time should find out the Gentleman; or get some Accomodation with her Parents; after which she sent her Maid with her to her Lodging; recommending her to the Care of her Landlady, with Assurance of Payment.

She being gone, we began to descant on the poor miserable Creature's Distress; withal much applauding the Charity of our good Landlady, to a Person so wholly a Stranger. No, indeed, reply'd the good Gentlewoman, she is not quite a Stranger to me, for I was heretofore very well acquainted with her Parents, who were really worthy good People; but since the Birth of this Girl, her Father has chang'd his generous beneficent Temper; and as she grew up in Beauty, he grew the more Niggardly;[1] of which I could give you a particular Instance, but

---

1. **Niggardly:** miserly.

shall reserve it to another Opportunity; and always wish, that Parents would never set their Hearts so much on great Provisions for their Children, as to refuse Charity to any miserable Object that addresses them, as did this Gentleman; but rely on God's Providence for their Posterity, as well as their own Riches, Frugality or Industry.

This Adventure, Madam, as it prov'd a Consolation to this distressed Creature; so it prov'd a Misfortune to me; for hereupon my Mother prohibited me my Garret-Closet, and my Walk on the Leads; lest I should encounter more Adventures, not only like this, but perhaps more pernicious: So that being depriv'd of my solitary Retreat, your Ladyship cannot expect much of Verse or Poetick Fancies whereof to make *Patches* at present.

Methinks, reply'd the Lady, I should expect some doleful Ditty, upon being depriv'd of this your beloved *Solitude*. On this Occasion I fancy you like *Ovid*,[1] when banish'd from all his Pleasures and Injoyments in the glorious City of *Rome*; you being depriv'd of what you preferr'd before all them; which shews, there is no Possibility of making People happy against their Will. Some are happy in a Cottage; others can scarce endure Life but in a Palace. Some take great Delight in Fields, Woods, and Rural Walks: others again, in lofty Buildings, glorious Apartments, sumptuous Entertainments, Balls, Dancings, Shows, and Masquerades.

'Tis true, Madam, reply'd *Galesia*; and this makes me reflect, how useless, or rather pernicious, Books and Learning are to our Sex. They are like Oatmeal or Charcoal to the deprav'd Appetites of Girls; for by their Means we relish not the Diversions or Imbellishments of our Sex and Station; which render us agreeable to the World, and the World to us; but live in a Stoical Dulness or humersome[2] Stupidity. However, I comply'd with my Mother, and made Inclination submit to Duty; and so endeavour'd to make a Vertue of this Necessity, and live like others of my Rank, according to Time, Place and Conveniency.

---

1. **Ovid:** Roman poet, banished by Emperor Augustus (8 A.D.).

2. **humersome:** humorsome, peevish.

My dear Mother now growing aged, began to be very desirous to see me established in a married State; daily inculcating to me, That we, in a manner, frustrate the End of our Creation, to live in that uncouth kind of *Solitude*, in which she thought I too much delighted, and which she believed would grow upon me, when God should take her away: At what Time, I should then have no body to consolate, protect or assist me; urging, That I ought not to pass my Time in idle Dreams on *Parnassus*, and foolish Romantick Flights, with *Icarus*; whose waxen Wings fail'd him so as to let him fall into the Sea; which indeed purchas'd him a Name, but became the perpetual Record of his Folly: And such a Name, such a Record, I should be glad, said she, you would avoid, by becoming a good Mistress of a Family; and imploy your Parts in being an obedient Wife, a discreet Governess of your Children and Servants; a friendly Assistant to your Neighbours, Friends, and Acquaintance: This being the Business for which you came into the World, and for the Neglect of this, you must give an Account when you go out of it. These were Truths which Reason would not permit me to oppose; but my Reflections on *Bosvil's* Baseness, gave me a secret Disgust against Matrimony. However, her often repeated Lectures, call'd for Compliance, especially Fortune seeming at that Time to concur with my Mother's Counsel, in the following manner.

A *Patch-Work Screen* for the *Ladies.*
Leaf III.

The *History* of *Lysander.*[1]

There was a certain Widow-Gentlewoman, who had but one only Son, who should have been the Staff of her Age. This Son she had educated to the Law, and placed him in handsome Chambers in the *Temple.*[2] But the young Gentleman, instead of studying the Laws of his Country, practis'd the Mode of the Times, and kept the Wife of an unhappy Citizen, made so partly by her Vanity and Coquettry, 'till he was forced to seek his Fortune in the Plantations, whilst she found hers in the wicked Embraces of this young Gentleman; who hired a very handsome House for her, furnished it genteely, and when he pleas'd, there pass'd his Time, making her his Study, Practice and Diversion. In this guilty Correspondence,[3] they had Children; in particular one, who grew a great Girl, and was put to a Boarding-School, amongst young Gentlewomen of Vertuous Descent.

Now this kind of Life was very grievous to his good Mother, and as it caus'd her to shed many Tears, so it obliged her, from Time to Time, to use many Reprehensions suitable to her maternal Affection; sometimes sharp, sometimes soft, sometimes persuasive, sometimes menacing: But all in vain; for he still went on in the same Road, supporting this Adultress in all her Extravagancies, humouring her in all her Whimsies and Caprices, 'till the Diminution of his Circumstance, began to call on him for a Retrenchment of his Expences. His Lands were mortgaged, his Houses decay'd, his Debts increased, his Credit diminished, Duns[4] attack'd him in every Quarter, Writs[5] and Bayliffs[6] follow'd him, Vexa-

---

1. **Lysander:** name common in heroic romance, including Barker's *Exilius*.

2. **Temple:** referring to one or both of two legal societies of the Inns of Court, the Inner and the Middle Temple, so-called because built on the site once occupied by the Knights Templar.

3. **Correspondence:** illicit sexual intercourse.

4. **Duns:** bill collectors.

5. **Writs:** legal documents instructing the person to whom they are addressed to do or refrain from performing specified acts.

6. **Bayliffs:** bailiff, a warrant officer or sheriff's deputy.

tions of all Sorts met and overtook him: Nevertheless, her Riot, Vanity, and chargeable Diversions must not be abated; so great an Ascendant she had got over him, that (according to the Proverb) *He scarce durst say his Soul was his own.*

One time, being under an Arrest for some Debt contracted by means of her Extravagancy; he sent to her to come and lay down the Money, which he knew she could do with Ease, she having Cash by her, or at least he knew she could raise it speedily, out of those rich Presents he had made her from Time to Time; but she boggled,[1] and made many frivolous Excuses, which would not hold Water: At last she plainly refused, unless he would grant her a Judgment of all that he had, *Real* and *Personal,* Body and Goods, alledging (no doubt) That it was the safest Way to secure to himself a Livelihood, and balk his Creditors. He depending on the Belief of her Affection, and the manifold Obligations she lay under, comply'd with this Proposal, thinking it a proper Blind or Sham, to secure himself, and defraud others.

This being done, the gay Serpent began to shew her Sting, and treated him with less Respect and Complaisance. Those Caresses and Endearments, which hitherto had shone in her Looks and Actions, began to be overcast with cold Clouds and a careless Behaviour; and, by Degrees, to a disdainful Neglect; scarce containing herself sometimes within the Bounds of common Civility. This Treatment awaken'd him out of his Lethargick Slumber, opened his Eyes, and made him see all at once the many false Steps he had taken in his Life's Travels: In particular, The Griefs he had given his Mother; the Disgrace to his Education and Profession; and, in short, the total Ruin of his Family, which was like to be extinct in him; and himself become a miserable Dependant on the Charity of an insolent Strumpet.[2] Alas! what Charity, what Kindness can be expected from such a Creature? For when a Man's Fortune fails, that he can no longer bribe her Pride or Luxury, there is no more Kindness to be hop'd for, than a poor Client, when Fees fail, can hope from an avaritious Lawyer. And now he begins to consider how he

---

1. **boggled:** hesitated.

2. **Strumpet:** prostitute, whore.

shall repair or stave off his utter Ruin; which he concluded was no way to be done, but by closing with his dear Mother's Advice, in betaking himself to some vertuous Woman in Marriage. Being thus resolved, he took the first Opportunity to communicate his Thoughts to his Mother, making a Merit of this Necessity, by a pretended Obedience to her often-repeated Counsel; assuring her, that he would submit his Inclinations to her wise Election.

The good Gentlewoman was transported at this hopeful Change in her Son, and casting about in her Thoughts, at last pitch'd upon this your Servant *Galesia;* a Person not worthy such Esteem, only favour'd by the Opinion she had of my Vertue and Innocence. When she propos'd it to her Son, he seem'd as much pleas'd with his Mother's Choice, as she was at his seeming Reformation; and ingaged her to agree upon a Day to come along with her to make me a Visit.

The Day appointed, he dined with his Mother, in order to wait on her to our Lodging in the Afternoon: But e'er they had well din'd, a Messenger came to him from a Tavern over-the-way, bringing word, that there were Gentlemen had Business of Consequence, and desired to speak with him: Which Gentlemen were only this Adultress, who having got Intelligence of this design'd Visit, came to disappoint it with her alluring Cajoleries;[1] making him send Word to his Mother, that he would wait on her another Day; pretending, that the Gentlemens Business ingag'd his Attendance at that Time. Behold in this Transaction, what Power these Creatures have over Men! Notwithstanding those Reasons he had to abhor and detest this his false *Dalilah,*[2] was he again deluded by her; so that one may truly say with the wise Man, *Whosoever is fetter'd by a lewd Woman, is led like a Beast to the Slaughter, never to return.*[3]

Thus Things pass'd quietly for a while: At last he found an Opportunity to come along with his Mother to make me a Visit or two; of which

---

1. **Cajoleries:** false, flattering words used to get one's way.

2. **Dalilah:** Delilah; woman to whom Samson revealed the source of his strength and who betrayed him to the Philistines for money; see Judg. 16:4–22.

3. **wise Man . . . return:** Solomon; see Prov. 7:21–22.

by the Treachery of his Man,[1] and her Vigilance, she (I mean the Harlot) got Notice, and quarrell'd with him about it very sharply, and then again wheedled, courted and caress'd him, and sometimes with Smiles, sometimes with Tears, besought his Constancy, sometimes with Fits, and melancholy Vapours, ingag'd his Pity: Then again, with opprobrious[2] and violent Words reproach'd his Falshood, reviling him for all his broken Vows; alledging, That her Ruine, Life and Health would all lie at his Door; That for his sake she had cast herself out of the Protection of her Friends, and forfeited their Favour and Kindness: That for his sake she had disgrac'd herself in the Face of the World, offended God, and greatly wrong'd her Husband; in all which, she had affronted Heaven and Earth, and flown in the Face of her Family, abus'd her Birth and vertuous Education, and wasted her Youth in the Embraces of a perjur'd Wretch, who now abandon'd her to Grief, Shame and Poverty; with many such grating Reflections, and violent Speeches, wherewith from time to time she persecuted him. Which sometimes he endeavoured to moderate by Arguments, sometimes alledging Religion, sometimes Reason, sometimes Necessity, and the Impossibility of doing otherwise: Now cajoling her with the Pretence of Sorrow and Regret, and buoying her up with Hopes that he found himself not able to leave her; and then again plunging her into Despair, by alledging his Duty to his Mother, and the Anxiety of a tormented Conscience. Thus they argued this Way and that, from side to side, like a Ship that goes to fetch a Wind, which never sails directly to the Point.

At last the Gentleman resolv'd to be thoroughly plain with her, and accordingly told her, without any Varnish of Words or Shadow of Disguise, that he was fully resolv'd to marry; but that he would not abandon her to Misery or Distress; but would settle such a Pension on her, as might support her in a decent, honest Way of Living; and that he would likewise take Care to provide for her Daughter, in giving her such a Portion[3] as might marry her to some honest Tradesman in a good Station of

---

1. **Man:** manservant.

2. **opprobrious:** abusive.

3. **Portion:** dowry; the amount pledged by her family that a bride will take to her husband.

Life; and with this he charged her to be content, without meddling with him in his married State, but live retir'd, vertuously and modestly, and it should be the better for her and her Daughter.

The Creature being thus provoked, fell into violent Words and Actions; told him, That he shew'd his Falshood and Baseness too late, he having put his Person and Fortune out of his own Power, and into hers; wherefore she would take care of herself, by securing both to her own Advantage. Being thus stung to the Quick, he left her House in great Vexation of Spirit: And in the midst of his Fury, went forthwith and shot himself.

This was the fatal End which his Lewdness and Folly brought upon him! This was the Conclusion of his guilty Embraces! Thus a filthy Strumpet shewed herself in her Colours! And thus was he bullied out of his Estate, Life, and Honour; his Life lost, his Debts unpaid, his Estate devour'd by a lewd Harlot! A very fatal Warning to all unwary Gentlemen.

I suppose, Madam, you cannot imagine, that his Death affected me much as a Lover, there being but little of that in the Story; but one must have been without Humanity, to be unconcern'd at such an Accident, and not have borne some part in his Mother's Affliction; especially since the good Gentlewoman had pitch'd upon me amongst all her Acquaintance, for so near an Alliance. I could not omit reflecting on *Job* and *Tobit*,[1] as if the Almighty had permitted some *Satan*, or *Asmodas*[2] to persecute me in the Persons of all that pretended to love or like me. Which way soever it was, I endeavour'd to be resign'd; this being the Duty of a Christian in all Conditions. However, it contributed to make me the more despise the World, with all its gaudy Trappings; or, perhaps, with the *Fox*, thought the *Grapes sowre*,[3] because *I could not reach*

---

1. **Job. . . Tobit:** two righteous men who were tested severely, remained devout and were vindicated. The Book of Job is canonical. Barker, as a Catholic, should have accepted the Greek Book of Tobit, considered apocryphal by the Church of England.

2. **Asmodas:** Asmodeus; the evil demon that killed the first seven husbands of Sarah on their wedding nights; see Tob. 3:8.

3. **Fox . . . them:** referring to "The Fox and the Grapes," one of the *Fables*, Greek moral tales ascribed to legendary compiler Aesop (sixth century B.C.); the fox, unsuccessfully reaching for hanging grapes, insisted he didn't want them after all because they were sour.

them. The Truth is, I had found so many Disappointments, that I began to be displeas'd at my-self, for hoping or expecting any thing that tended to Happiness: I thought with Mrs. *Phillips,*

> If with some *Pleasure* we our *Griefs* betray,
> It *costs* us *dearer* than we can *repay:*
> For *Time* or *Fortune*, all Things so devours,
>> Our *Hopes* are *cross'd,*
>> Or else the *Object* lost,
>> E'er we can *call it ours.*[1]

Which indeed was always so with me, not only in this, but in all other Enterprizes and Transactions of Life: I could *hope* nothing, *propose* nothing, but I was cross'd or disappointed therein, e'er I could arrive at Accomplishment. Therefore, Madam, you need not think it strange that I began to believe Providence had ordain'd for me a *Single Life. Began*, did I say? No, rather *continued* in that Sentiment ever since the Disappointment of *Bosvil.* And I think here are a few Lines something tending to that Subject:

A *Virgin Life.*[2]

> Since, O good Heavens! you have bestow'd on me
> So great a Kindness for *Virginity,*
> Suffer me not to fall into the Powers
> Of Man's almost Omnipotent Amours.
> But let me in this happy State remain,
> And in chaste Verse my chaster Thoughts explain;
> Fearless of *Twenty-five*,[3] and all its Rage,
> When Time with Beauty lasting Wars ingage.
> When once *that Clock has struck*, all Hearts retire,
> Like *Elves* from *Day-break*, or like *Beasts* from Fire,
> 'Tis Beauty's *Passing-Bell;* no more are slain;

---

1. **If . . . ours:** "Song to the Tune of Adieu Phillis," *Poems By the most deservedly Admired Mrs. Katherine Philips*, lines 7–12.

2. This poem is a revised version of the poem by the same name in *PR 1.*

3. **Twenty-five:** age 25.

But dying Lovers all revive again.
Then every Day some new Contempt we find,
As if the Scorn and Lumber[1] of Mankind.
These frightful Prospects, oft our Sex betray;
Which to avoid, some fling themselves away;
Like harmless *Kids,*[2] who when pursu'd by *Men,*
For Safety, run into a *Lyon's Den.*

   Ah! *happy State!* how strange it is to see,
What mad Conceptions some have had of *Thee!*
As if thy Being was all Wretchedness,
Or foul Deformity, in vilest Dress:
Whereas thy Beauty's pure Celestial,
Thy Thoughts Divine, thy Words Angelical:
And such ought all thy Votaries to be,
Or else they're so but for Necessity.
A *Virgin* bears the Impress of all Good,
Under that Name, all Vertue's understood.
So equal all her Looks, her Mien, her Dress,
That nought but Modesty is in Excess;
The Business of her Life to this extends,
To serve her God, her Neighbour and her Friends.

Indeed, said the Lady, the Transactions of thy Life hitherto seem a perfect Chain of Disappointments. However, the Almighty has been gracious in giving thee a Mind submissive and resign'd; for which thou art bound to glorify his Goodness, and hope for more prosperous Days for the Time to come. As they were about to proceed in their Discourse, and look for more *Patches* to carry on their Work, the Lady's Butler came from his Master, saying, He was about to make a Bowl of Punch, and sent to the Stranger-Gentlewoman for her Receipt,[3] which she was talking of the Night before; which *Galesia* readily rehears'd:

---

1. **Lumber:** useless odds and ends.

2. **Kids:** baby goats.

3. **Receipt:** recipe.

The *Czar's Receipt* to make *Punch*.

Take Three Bottles from *Spain*, and one from *France*,
Two from the *Rhine*, and one from *Nance:*[1]
No Water at all, but a little from *Roses;*
A red-nos'd Sea-Captain, to mingle the Doses;
Limons,[2] *Nutmeg*, and *Sugar*, with a *Toast* to float on it;
And a Knot of good Fellows, that will not shrink from it.

With these Instructions, the Butler made his *Exit*, making a low Bow according to the old Fashion.

The Butler being gone, the Lady desired *Galesia* to return to her Discourse: To which she readily accorded, saying, After this unexpected Accident of the said unhappy Gentleman, my Mother began to think that Heaven had design'd me for a *Single Life*, and was a little more reconcil'd to my studious Way; saying, with the Proverb, *It is in vain to strive against the Stream; or oppose Providence.* Sometimes she regretted that ever she had promoted, or consented to that Proposal, the Business having prov'd so fatal both to the Gentleman and his good Mother, whose Griefs, said she, methinks I feel; which Reflection would sometimes draw Tears from her Eyes. And one Day, my Compassion uniting with hers, caus'd me to take out my Handkerchief, and with it fell the following Verses.

The *Necessity* of *Fate*.[3]

I.

In vain, in vain it is, I find,
To strive against our Fate;
    We may as well command the Wind,
The Sea's rude Waves, to gentle Manners bind,
Or to Eternity prescribe a Date;

---

1. **Nance:** Nancy, a town in eastern France.

2. **Limons:** lemons.

3. This poem is a slightly revised version of a poem of the same name in *PR 1*.

As frustrate ought that Fortune has design'd:
For when we think we're Politicians grown,
    And live by Methods of our own,
    We then obsequiously obey
Fate's Dictates, and a blindfold Homage pay.

II.

Were it not so, I surely could not be
Still Slave to Rhime, and lazy Poetry:
    I, who so oft have strove
    My Freedom to regain;
And sometimes too, for my Assistance took
    Obedience, and sometimes a Book;
    Company, and sometimes Love:
    All which, still proves in vain;
For I can only shake, but not cast off my Chain.

III.

All this, my *Fate,* all this thou didst foreshow,
    Ev'n when I was a Child,
    When in my *Picture's* Hand,
    My Mother did command,
There should be drawn a *Lawrel Bough.*[1]
Lo! then my *Muse* sat by, and smil'd,
To hear how some the Sentence did oppose,
    Saying an *Apple, Bird,* or *Rose,*
Were Objects which did more befit
My childish Years, and no less childish Wit.

IV.

For then my *Muse* well knew, that *constant Fate*
    Her Promise would compleat:
    For *Fate* at my Initiation

---

1. **Lawrel Bough:** laurel bough; symbol of poetry.

> Into the Muses Congregation,
> As my Responsor promis'd then for me,
>   I should forsake those *Three*,[1]
> Soaring Honours, vain Persuits of Pleasure,
>   And vainer Fruits of worldly Treasure,
> All for the Muses *melancholy Tree,*
> E'er I knew ought of its *great Mystery.*
> Since, O my Fate! thou needs wilt have it so,
> Let thy kind Hand exalt it to my Brow.

To which my Mother reply'd, I think, *Fate* would be more kind to set a Basket, or a Milk-pail, on thy Head; thereby to suppress those foolish Vapours that thus intoxicate thy Brain: But if there be a *fatal Necessity* that it must be so, e'en go on, and make thyself easy with thy fantastick Companions the Muses: I remember, continued she, I have been told, that one of the ancient Poets says:

> Thrust *Nature* off, with Fork, by Force,
> She'll still return to her old Course:[2]

And so I find it in the whole Course of thy Life. And, as thou sayest in this Poem, thou hast tryed divers means to chase away this unlucky Genius that attends thee; and, I am sensible, out of a true design'd Obedience to me: But since it will not do, I shall no more oppose thy Fancy, but comply and indulge so innocent a Diversion. As I was about to return her my Thanks, a Gentleman that had married our Kinswoman, came in.

As *Galesia* was about to proceed, the Lady rang for a Servant; and bad him go to her House-keeper, and tell her to get a Dish of the *Welsh* Flummery[3] ready, which *Galesia* had taught her last Night, and set it in an Arbour; and when 'tis cool, said she, call us. And now, continued the Lady, give me the Receipt, for it shall make a *Patch* in the SCREEN, as well as does that of the *Punch.* To which *Galesia* readily agreed.

---

1. Referring to the *Apple, Bird,* or *Rose.* [Author's note.]

2. **ancient . . . Course:** Roman author, Horace (65–8 B.C.), *Epistles* I.10.24.

3. **Welsh Flummery:** sweet dish taken at the end of a meal.

The *Receipt* for *Welsh* Flummery, Made at the Castle of *Montgomery*.[1]

Take Jelly of *Harts-horn*,[2] with *Eggs clarify'd,*
Two good Pints at least; of *Cream,* one beside.
Fine *Sugar* and *Limons,* as much as is fit
To suit with your Palate, that you may like it.
Three Ounces of *Almonds,* with *Orange Flow'r*-Water,
Well beaten: Then mix 'em all up in a Platter
Of *China* or *Silver;* for that makes no matter.

The Lady was pleas'd with the Receipt, and bad[3] *Galesia* return to her Story, of the Gentleman that had married her Friend.

The Unaccountable *Wife.*

This Gentleman, said *Galesia,* had married a young Gentlewoman of Distinction, against the Consent of her Friends; which she accomplish'd by the Help of her Mother's Maid-Servant. To say the Truth, though her Birth was very considerable, yet her Person was not at all agreeable; and her Fortune but indifferent: her Parents, I suppose, thinking, that more than just enough to support her, would but betray her to an unhappy Marriage. In short, married she was to the foresaid young Man, whose Person was truly handsome; and with Part of her Fortune he plac'd himself in the Army, bestow'd another Part in furnishing her a House, and so liv'd very decently; and notwithstanding her indifferent Person, he had Children by her, though they did not live long. Thus they made a pretty handsome Shift in the World, 'till a vile Wretch, her Servant, overturn'd all; as follows. This Servant, whether she was a Creature of her Master's before she came to her Mistress, is not known; but she became very fruitful, and had every Year a Child; pretending that she

---

1. **Montgomery:** castle in Wales, dismantled in 1649 by Parliamentary forces in the English Civil Wars.

2. **Jelly of Harts-horn:** a nutritive gelatin made of the shavings of the horn of a red deer.

3. **bad:** bade.

was privately married to an Apprentice. Whether the Wife knew the whole of the Matter, or was impos'd upon, is uncertain; but which way soever it was, she was extremely kind to this Woman, to a Degree unheard-of; became a perfect Slave to her, and, as if she was the Servant, instead of the Mistress, did all the Household-Work, made the Bed, clean'd the House, wash'd the Dishes; nay, farther than so, got up in the Morning, scour'd the Irons, made the Fire, &c. leaving this vile Strumpet in Bed with her Husband; for they lay all Three together every Night. All this her Friends knew, or at least suspected; but thought it Complaisance, not Choice in her; and that she consider'd her own Imperfections, and Deformity; and therefore, was willing to take no Notice of her Husband's Fancy in the Embraces of this Woman her Servant. But the Sequel opens quite another Scene: And now I come to that Part of the Story, where he came to my Mother. His Business was, to desire her to come to his Wife, and endeavour to persuade her to part with this Woman; For, said he, she has already Three Children living, and God knows how many more she may have: Which indeed, Madam, said he, is a Charge my little Substance is not able to sustain; and I have been using all Endeavours to persuade my Wife to part with her, but cannot prevail: Wherefore I beg you, as a Friend, Relation, and her Senior in Years, to come, and lay before her the Reasonableness of what I desire, and the Ridiculousness of her proceeding. Good Heaven! said my Mother, can you think thus to bore my Nose with a Cushion? Can you imagine me so stupid, as to believe your Wife can persist in such a Contradiction of Nature? It is impossible a Wife should oppose her Husband's Desire in parting with such a Woman. Madam, reply'd he, I beg you once more to be so good as to come to my Wife, and then condemn me if I have advanc'd a Falshood. Well, reply'd my Mother, I will come; though I doubt not but upon due Inspection, the whole, will prove a Farce compos'd amongst you, in which your Wife is to act her Part just as you between you think fit to teach her; which she, out of Fear, or some other Delusion, is to perform. But he averr'd again and again, that, without Fraud or Trick, the Thing was as he said. In short, my Mother went; and there she found the Servant sitting in a handsome Velvet Chair, dress'd up in very good lac'd Linnen, having clean

Gloves on her Hands, and the Wife washing the Dishes. This Sight put
my Mother into such a violent Passion, that she had much ado to
refrain from laying Hands on her. However, she most vehemently chid
the Mistress; telling her, That she offended God, disgrac'd her Family,
scandaliz'd her Neighbours, and was a Shame to Woman-kind. All
which she return'd with virulent Words; amongst other Things, she
stood Buff[1] in Favour of that Woman; saying, That she had been not
only a faithful Servant, but the best of Friends, and those that desir'd to
remove such a Friend from her, deserved not the Name of Friends, neither did she desire they should come into her House: All which she
utter'd with such an Air of Vehemency, that there was no Room left to
doubt of the Sincerity of her Words; but that all proceeded from an
Interiour thoroughly degenerated. All which my Mother related to me
with great Amazement: But withal, told me, that she would have me go
to her on the Morrow; and with calm and friendly Words, endeavour to
persuade her to Reason; for, said she, I was in a Passion at the disagreeable View; but you, who have naturally more Patience than my-self,
pray put on the best Resolutions you can to keep your Temper, whatsoever Provocations shall occur. Thus instructed, thus resolved, I went
next Day, hoping that a Night's Repose would calm the Storm my
Mother's Anger might have rais'd. But when I came, I found it all the
same: Though I took her apart, and with the utmost Mildness, persuaded her, and us'd the best Reasons I could think on to inforce those
Persuasions, yet all was in vain; and she said, We all join'd with her Husband to make her miserable, by removing from her, the only Friend she
had in the World; and passionately swore by Him that made her, that if
we combin'd to send the Woman away, she would go with her. I would
try that, reply'd I, were I in your Husband's Place: At which her Passion
redoubled; and she, with violent Oaths, repeated her Resolution; desiring, that her Friends would meddle with their own Business, and let her
alone, to remain in Quiet in her House, and not come to give her Disturbance. After these uncouth Compliments, I left her, carrying with
me the greatest Amazement possible. After this, the Husband came to

---

1. **Buff:** defiant, like a buffalo.

us, and ask'd, If we did not find true what he had told us? Indeed, replied I, true, and doubly true; such a Truth as I believe never was in the World before, nor never will be again. In this Case, said he, What would you counsel me to do? Truly, said my Mother, it is hard to advise; for to let the Woman live there still, is not proper; nor can your Circumstances undergo the Charge: And if your Wife should do as she says, and go with her; I should in some Degree be accessary to the parting Man and Wife. I would venture, said I, for when it comes to the Push, I warrant her she will not go. Hereupon the Man said he would try; and accordingly, hired a Place in a Waggon to carry the Creature into her own Country; hoping, as I suppose, that his Wife would have rested herself contented with him, when the Woman had been gone; but instead thereof, she acted as she said, and went along with her.

This Transaction was so extraordinary, that every-body was amazed at it; and when they had been gone some time, there arose a Murmuring, amongst Friends, Neighbours and Acquaintance, as if he had made his Wife away; and when he told them the Manner of her Departure, they would not believe him, the thing in itself being so incredible.

But we will leave him to make his Party good, as well as he can, amidst the Censure of his Neighbours, the Threats of her Friends, and the Ridicule of his Acquaintance; and follow the Travellers, into the Country whither they were gone.

They arrived safe at the Woman's Father's, where they found as kind a Reception as a poor Cottage could afford; and a very poor one it was, there being no Light but what came in at the Door, no Food but from the Hands of Charity, nor Fewel[1] but what they pilfer'd from their Neighbours Hedges.

Now what this unaccountable Creature thought of this kind of Being, is unknown, or what Measures she and her Companion thought to take, or what Schemes they form'd to themselves, is not conceivable: But whatever they were, the discreet Neighbourhood put a Period to their Projects; for they got a Warrant to have them before a Justice, in order to prevent a Parish Charge;[2] there being two Children there

---

1. **Fewel:** fuel.

2. **Parish Charge:** poor person aided by local authorities, often ecclesiastical.

already, which they had sent some time before; and now two helpless Women being come, they knew not where the Charge might light, and therefore proceeded as aforesaid. It happen'd as the Constable was conducting them to the Justice, with a Mob at their Heels, that they pass'd by the House of a Lady of Quality, who looking out of her Window, saw in the midst of this Throng, this unfortunate Wife, whom she immediately knew to be the Daughter of her Friend; knew to be the Child of an honourable Family. It is impossible to describe what Amazement seiz'd her: She call'd out to the Constable and other Neighbours there, bidding them bring that Gentlewoman to her, which they immediately did. This good Lady, out of Respect to her old Friends, a worthy Family, bid them discharge her, telling them, That her-self would be bound that she should be no Parish Charge; so took her into her House, treated her kindly, and offer'd her all she could do on such an Occasion: For all which she return'd the Lady but cold Thanks, and begg'd her Ladyship's Assistance to convey her to *London* along with the other Woman, who, she said, was the truest Friend in the World. The Lady knowing nothing of her Story, with much Goodness provided for her Departure, together with her Companion. In this manner, loaden with Disgrace, they came back to *London,* to her Husband, from whom, no doubt, she found Reproaches suitable to her Folly.

Long it was not, e'er Death made a true and substantial Separation, by carrying the Husband into the other World. Now was the Time to make manifest, whether Promises, Flatteries or Threatnings had made her act the foresaid Scene: But it appear'd all voluntary; for when he was dead, her Friends and Relations invited and persuaded her to leave that Creature and her Children, and come to live with them, suitable to her Birth and Education. But all in vain; she absolutely adher'd to this Woman and her Children, to the last Degree of Folly; insomuch, that being reduc'd to Poverty, she begg'd in the Streets to support them. At last, some Friend of her Family told the Queen of the distressed way she was in; and in some Degree, how it came to pass, that neither her dead Husband nor her Relations might be blameable. The *Queen,* with much Goodness, told her Friend, That if she would leave that Woman, and go live with some Relation, she would take Care she should not want; and withal sent her Five Guineas, as an Earnest of a Monthly Pension; but notwithstanding, this infatuated Creature refus'd the *Queen's* Favour, rather than part with this Family: And so, for their Support, begg'd in the Streets, the Remainder of her Days.

Sure, said the Lady, This poor Creature was under some Spell or Inchantment, or she could never have persisted, in so strange a manner, to oppose her Husband, and all her nearest Friends, and even her *Sovereign*. As they were descanting on this Subject, a Servant came and told them, that all was ready in the Arbour; and that the Gentlemen having finish'd their Bowl of *Punch*, were attending their coming, to share with them in a Dish of *Tea*, and *Welsh Flummery*.

Accordingly, the Ladies went thither, where they were saluted with a most pleasant Consort of chirping Musicians, whose wild Notes, in different Strains, set forth the Glory of their great Creator, exciting the whole Company to certain Acts of Joy and Thanksgiving: Amongst which Quire, none seem'd so harmonious as the soft Strains of the delightful *Philomel*,[1] whose various Notes ingag'd every one's Attention; insomuch that the Lady call'd to her Page, to sing that old Song, the Words of which held due Measure with the Tunes and different Changes of the *Nightingale*.

The *Song*.

> It was on a Day,
> When the Nymphs had leave to play,
> As I walk'd unseen,
> In a Meadow green,
> I heard a Maid in an angry Spleen,
> Complaining to her Swain,
> To leave his toiling Vein,
> And come and sport with her upon the Plain.
> But the silly Clown
> Lay delving[2] of the Ground,

---

1. **Philomel:** Philomela; in Greek myth, she was changed by the gods into a nightingale, known for its sweet song.

2. **delving:** digging.

Regardless of her Moan,
   When she cry'd,
Come away, bonny Boy, come away.
   "I cannot come, I will not come;
   I cannot leave my Work undone."
And that was all, this silly Clown could say.

II.

   Thus vexed in her Mind,
   To see him so unkind,
   To *Venus*[1] she went,
   In a Discontent,
To get her *Boy*,[2] with his Bow ready bent,
   To take a nimble Dart,
   And to strike him to the Heart,
For disobeying her Commandement.
   Cupid then
   Gave the Boy such a Bang,
   As made him to gang[3]
   With the bonny Lass along.
   When she cry'd,
Come away, bonny Boy; come hither.
   "I come, I come, I come."
And so they gang'd along together.

The Company were all pleas'd with the Lad's Performance, in which he imitated the *Nightingale* to Admiration. Thus they diverted themselves, 'till Chariots came to carry them out to take the Evening Air.

---

1. **Venus:** goddess of love and mother of Cupid.

2. **Boy:** Cupid, god of love.

3. **to gang:** to walk.

A *Patch-Work Screen* for the *Ladies*.
Leaf IV.

The Ladies having pass'd their Evening's Diversion, and their Night's Repose, dispos'd themselves in the Morning to go on with their *Patch-work;* the Lady ordering *Galesia* to resume her Story. Which she was about to do, when the Cook came to inquire, what shou'd be for Dinner; telling her Ladyship, That Two of the *South-Sea* Directors[1] had sent his Master Word they wou'd dine with him to Day. They think themselves Great-Men, said the Lady, that they did not suppose we had a Dinner worth their eating, without sending us Word. But since they have taken Care to give us this Notice, we will do the best we can; therefore, if you can tell my Cook how to make a very good *French* Soup, prithee do.

A *Receipt* for *French Soup.*

Take a large Barn-door Cock, and all his Bones break;
Of *Mutton* and *Veal,* each one a good *Neck:*
Of these, then, Two Quarts of *strong Broth* you may make;
Next, another full Quart of good *Beef Gravey* take;
Of right *Vermicelli,* a Quartern[2] at least:
Then season all these as best likes your Taste:
A *Fowl* in the Middle, to swim like a Toast,
It matters not whether it boil'd be or roast.
With *Bacon* and *Balls,* then garnish it well.
Add *Toasts* fry'd in *Marrow,* and *Sweet-breads*[3] of *Veal,*
And what else you please: for I cannot tell.

This is a chargeable Soup, said the Lady, but one wou'd not stick at Expence to obtain the Favour of one of these *Directors.* My Husband is about to lay a Debt upon his Estate, to put into this profitable Fund:

---

1. **South-Sea Directors:** managers and part-owners of a trading company that collapsed in 1720 after a speculative frenzy over its stock. Investors lost millions of pounds in this "South Sea Bubble."

2. **Vermicelli:** long, thin pasta. **Quartern:** the quarter part.

3. **Sweet-breads:** the thymus gland, an edible organ meat.

He has, with much ado, got the Promise of a Subscription[1] for 10,000 *l.*[2] for this Purpose. Madam, reply'd *Galesia,* I beg you to use your utmost Endeavours to prevent this Proceeding: I beg you for God's Sake, your own Sake, your Childrens Sake, and for the Sake of all the Poor, that depend upon your Charity, to endeavour to disappoint this Design. I know not what to say (reply'd the Lady) to these your earnest Entreaties; but for the Sake of this your Solicitation, I shall consider very well upon it, together with my Husband. And now we are alone and quiet, turn over your Papers, and look out some *Patches.* Accordingly *Galesia* went about it, and, lo! the first thing she laid her Fingers upon, was a Prophesy, which she read, after the Lady had discharg'd her Cook with due Orders about the Dinner.

The *Prophesy.*

When a Noise in the *South*
Shall fill ev'ry one's *Mouth,*
Then *England* beware of *Undoing,*
Your Sins shall be *scourged,*
Your Pockets well purged,
And, *ev'ry one seek his own Ruin.*

I suppose, said the Lady, this Prophesy gives you so great an Aversion to the *South-Sea.* I cannot deny, said *Galesia,* but it strikes my Thoughts so far, that if I had never so much to spare, I wou'd not put a *Shilling* into *that* or *any other* Bubble.[3] I will not inquire into your Reasons, said the Lady; it will but hinder our Diversion: So pray go on with your Story.

Alas! said *Galesia,* the next is so melancholy, that I care not how long I keep from it; for now it was that the Death of King CHARLES II.[4] put a Stop to the Wheel of all Joy and Happiness in *England:* And it more

---

1. **Subscription:** commitment to purchase stock.

2. **l.:** pounds sterling.

3. **Bubble:** questionable scheme.

4. **King Charles II:** the Stuart king (1630–85), son of beheaded Charles I, whose brother James II succeeded him in 1685.

particularly affected me, because the Death of this our Gracious Sov-
EREIGN, seiz'd my dear aged Mother with such a Storm of Grief, that
she fell into a languishing State, in which she continu'd for many
Weeks, e'er Death releas'd her. During her Illness, whilst I watch'd her
Slumbers, divers Reflexions accosted me, some of one kind, some of
another; in particular, What a new Face the World had at present: It was
but t'other Day, said I to myself, that all the World was in Gaiety, and
the *English-Court* in Splendor. The KING reverenc'd; the Courtiers
belov'd; the Nation seeking after them for Places and Preferments: Glittering Coaches crowding before *White-hall-Gate*,[1] discharging out of
their sides *Beaus* and *Belles,* in the most sumptuous Apparel, as if they
meant to vie with *Phoebus* in his Meridian.[2] And now, behold how wonderful[3] is the Change! as if *Dooms-day* had discharg'd it self of a Shower
of black walking Animals; whose Cheeks are bedew'd with Tears, and
whose Breasts are swollen with Sighs! Amongst these, none griev'd more
sincerely than my Mother, for the Death of this her *Royal Lord*,[4] for
whose dear Sake, and that of his Father, so many Heroes of her Family
had shed their dearest Blood.[5] Then wou'd she remark upon, and recite
the Villainies of those Times, 'till Faintness call'd her Spirits to some
reviving Slumbers. In the mean time my Pen wou'd discharge itself of
one sort of Scribble or other; and I think here is one appears:

On the *Follies* of *Human-Life.*

To trace but out the Follies of Mankind,
Whether in the Common-Mass, or else disjoyn'd,
Is an *Abyss,* wherein to drown the Mind:
A *Lab'rinth* wild, obscure, to lose one's Sense,
A *Wilderness* of thick Impertinence.

---

1. **White-hall-Gate:** turreted gateway that gave access to Whitehall Palace, the royal
residence.

2. **Phoebus in his Meridian:** the god Apollo in his chariot.

3. **wonderful:** astonishing.

4. **Royal Lord:** Charles II.

5. **so many . . . Blood:** the Connocks of Cornwall were fervent Royalists who had served in
the military for Charles I and II.

Tho' we pretend we'ave *Reason* for our *Guide,*
When *Passions* get the *Reins,* they drive *aside,*
O'er *dang'rous Ways,* and *Precipices* run,
'Till *Reason* is by *Passion* overthrown.

No Animals such *Bubbles*[1] are, as *Man;*
They strive to save *themselves,* in all *they* can;
But *we* in *our own* Snares, *our selves* trapan.[2]
We're Heav'n's *Clock-work,* too, too finely wrought,
Seldom *strike true,* in *Deed,* in *Word* or *Thought.*
But *clash* and *clatter, contradict* and *prove,*
Then *say* and *unsay,* as *our Fancies move.*
Sometimes we glory of *Immortal Souls,*
Whilst *every* Action, *every* Word controuls.
Above all *Sense,* we of our *Reason* boast,
Whilst by our *Deeds,* we shou'd think *both* were lost,
Some, with *Respect to God,* their *Words* will place,
Whilst some again, his *Entity* disgrace,
And All, in *Deeds,* affront him to his Face.
Then to excuse ourselves of all these Crimes,
We *lay* the Fault on *Devils* or the *Times.*
When *false Ideas,* our *frail Minds* persuade,
And *Lust* or *other Crimes* our *Wills* invade,
The *Devils* are aspers'd, and *Panders* made.

'Tis true, e'er since the *Fall,* we are his *Fools,*
He *plots our Ruin,* and make *us* his *Tools.*
For oft'ner *we* betray ourselves than *he*
(Deforming th' Image of the *Deity*);
And so make *Brutes,* much happier than *we.*
Than 'tis not strange, if we *this Being* hate,
Since *brutal Happiness* is more compleat.

---

1. **Bubbles:** fragile, foolish beings.

2. **trapan:** entrap.

After a little Reflection, recollecting my scatter'd Thoughts, I broke out into the following Contemplations:

Whither, O whither! do my Thoughts ramble!—Into what strange, unfrequented Desarts does my Imagination wander!— *Desarts*, never trodden but by one *Wild* Passenger.[1] He, indeed, has told the World of one *Jowler*, a *Happy Creature*.[2]

But I dare ingage, if it were in *Jowler's* Power, he would most readily change with the most contemptible of Human Creatures, (setting a happy Immortality aside). I have heard say, That a *Butcher's* Dog, and a *Brewer's Hog*, are the Happiest of *Brute Animals:* But which of us wou'd change with either of them, if *Transmigration* were in our Power? Not one I dare answer; no, not even of those who daily make themselves in *Fact,* what those Animals are in *Form;* and by their repeated Excesses, become of so deprav'd a Nature, that they are scarce distinguishable (at least in their Actions) from those poor Brutes. And tho' these are Vices which all the World explode in *Words,* yet very few do in *Acts.* And what is more detestable, (if true) I have heard that our Women begin to be Practitioners in this Vice; which is but lately, if at all; for 'till now, their Manners never suffer'd the least Blemish of that kind, but were as perfect, as to any such Taint, as an untouch'd Plumb, or Grape, in a fair Summer's Morning; *Pride* having been the only Vice imputed to the Fair Sex. And indeed at some Times, and on some Occasions, is so far from being a Vice, that it is a Vertue of great Magnitude, shining in the Horizon of their Affairs. However, I dare ingage, there is not one of either Sex wou'd injoy the utmost Pleasures, attending the Perpetration of these Crimes, at the Price of their *Humanity.*

---

1. The Earl of ROCHESTER [Author's note.] **John Wilmot** (1648–80), libertine and poet, was a favorite at the court of Charles II, and author of "A Satire Against Mankind" (1675).

2. Alluding to these Verses in his *Satire against Man:*
> Those Creatures are the Wisest, who attain,
> By surest Means, the Ends at which they aim.
> If, therefore, *Jowler* finds and kills his Hare,
> Better than *Meers* supplies Committee-Chair;
> Tho' one's a *States-Man,* t'other but a Hound,
> *Jowler,* in Justice, wiser will be found. [Author's note.] *Satire,* lines 117–22.

And as to *Pride,*

A crime most laid at the Ladies Door; 'Tis said, they love Dressing, gaudy Apparel, Preference of Place, Title, Equipage, *&c.* But which of them wou'd be a *Peacock* for the sake of his *Plumes?* a *Lark* for its *high flying?* or an *Owl* for the sake of the *great Equipage* of *Birds* that *fly after him?* Alas! not one. The meanest Servant in a Family, wou'd not change her Station, to be the Happiest of these Animals. Then let us value our *Humanity,* and endeavour to imbellish it with vertuous Actions; by which means we shall be far from seting our-selves on the Level with mere Animals, much less giving them the Preference. But e'er I leave this Reflection on *Pride,* we must remember, That there is a great Difference between the Use and Abuse of those Things, which seem the Concomitants of *Pride;* for Cloaths, Place, Equipage, &c. in some Cases, and to some Persons, are Necessaries almost to a Necessity; as the Gospel testifies, *Soft Rayment*[1] *is for King's Houses:* For *God* is pleas'd to place different Persons in different Stations; and every one is to accommodate themselves according to their Station; it wou'd as ill befit a *Hedger*[2] to wear a *Velvet Coat,* as a *Courtier* to wear a *Leathern one;* for if *over-doing* our Condition, may ascend to *Pride, under-doing* may descend to *Sloth* or *Slovenliness:* Therefore, with Care, we are to chuse the *Medium.* I doubt not but *Diogenes*[3] was as proud in his *Tub,* as *Alexander*[4] in his *Palace.* To find a right *Medium,* is sometimes hard; for very often *Vice* dresses her self in the Apparel of *Vertue;* and, in a special manner, *Pride* puts on the Mask of *Honour:* And though one be a direct *Vice,* and the other a *Vertue,* yet they are not distinguishable to every Capacity, but often *one* passes for the *other. Lucifer,*[5] the Author of this *Sin,*

---

1. **Rayment:** raiment, clothing.

2. **Hedger:** laborer who maintains hedges.

3. **Diogenes:** Greek philosopher (ca. 400–325 B.C.), who claimed that happiness lay in the most austere life; famous for owning little more than a tub.

4. **Alexander:** known as the Great (356–323 B.C.), conqueror of an empire that stretched from Greece to India; he supposedly met Diogenes and failed to impress him.

5. **Lucifer:** Satan, the archangel cast out from Heaven for leading a revolt among the angels against God; see Isa 14:12–15 and Milton, *Paradise Lost* I.

having taken Care to gild it over double and treble, with the refulgent Brightness of *Honour, Magnanimity,* and *Generosity:* Which so dazles our Interiour, that we are not always able to distinguish between the Crime of this *Apostate Angel,*[1] and the Vertue of *Seraphims;*[2] the *one* by his *Pride* having thrown himself into utter Darkness, and eternal Misery; the *other,* by their *Obedience,* maintaining their Seraphick Glory in the highest Heavens. By mistaking these, we often deprive ourselves of the Benefit of our well-form'd Intentions. Again, sometimes, the beauteous Face of Vertue presents her-self in an obscure Light, without the Sun-shine of happy Circumstances. We then let her pass unregarded, and so lose the Opportunity of making our-selves happy in her Embraces. Which puts me in mind of a Distich[3] or two.

> If Chance or Fore-cast, some small Good produce,
> We slip it by unknown, or spoil it in the Use.
> When many Years in Toils and Cares are pass'd,
> To get of Happiness some small Repast,
> Our Crimes or Follies always spoil the Taste.

Now these Oversights and Mistakes, are not only in the Case of *Pride* and its *opposite Vertues;* but in other Cases, a false Light or a false Appearance deceives us; we mistake *Cunning* for *Wisdom,* and a *mean Selfishness,* for a *discreet Precaution; Fury* and *Rashness* for *Valour; Vainglory* for *Charity;* and a thousand Things of the like Nature. But having mention'd *Charity,* here appears a little Slip of Verse; which, I think, refers rather to the *forgiving,* than the *giving Part* of *Charity.* However it will make a *Patch.*

Upon *Charity.*

> This *Vertue* does above all others climb;
> To *give* is Noble, to *forgive* Sublime.
> The *Giving,* one may call *Religion's Heart;*

---

1. **Apostate Angel:** Lucifer had renounced his religious faith.
2. **Seraphims:** highest order of angels.
3. **Distich:** in verse, a couplet, usually containing a complete idea.

The *Pardoning,* the *Animating Part.*
These *Two* conjoyn'd, make *Charity* complete,
By which our Souls of Heav'n participate.
A *Vertue* kind, soft, gentle, debonair,
As *Guardian Angels* to their *Pupils* are,
Or faithful Swains, to their lov'd, *faithful-Fair.*
To chast Affection, 'tis as *Oyl* to *Fire,*
But *Ice* and *Water* to all foul Desire.
Of Friendship and fraternal Love the Source,
And Marriage Vows, it waters with its Course;
Like *Aqua-fortis,*[1] graving on the Mind,
The Character of all good Deeds and kind.
But otherwise it does a *Lethe*[2] prove,
And makes us quite forget *forgiving Love.*
These Blessings are th' Effects of *Charity;*
But nought compar'd to Heav'n's unbounded Joy,
Surpassing Sense! which those participate,
Who shar'd this Virtue in their Earthly State.

Joys! not only *surpassing Sense!* but too high for Humane *Thought!* O
the transcendant Joys of a bless'd *Eternity!* How inconceivable to our
weak Capacities, are the ineffable Pleasures of the bright Regions of
Eternity! Eternity of *Time,* and *Infinity* of *Space,* who can comprehend?
Reason can climb high, and *Thought* can extend far; but neither *Reason*
nor *Thought* can reach the *Altitude* of *Heaven,* nor the *Extent* of the
Almighty's Dominions. To say nothing of His Justice, Mercy and Wisdom, and His Power to execute whatsoever His Wisdom determines
from and to all *Eternity:* Where the Righteous injoy all Happiness, and
the Wicked all Misery. All this we risque, for a little Shining Earth, or,
what is less worthy, a little empty Fame; the one being the Aim of the
Covetous, the other of the *Ambitious* Man; of which the latter is the
worst, because his Vice affects whole Countries and Kingdoms; whereof
we have but too pregnant an Example at this Time, in the Person of the

---

1. **Aqua-fortis:** strong water (Latin); nitric acid, a powerful solvent and corrosive used in
engraving.   **graving:** engraving.

2. **Lethe:** in Greek myth, the river in Hades that causes forgetfulness.

Duke of *Monmouth.*[1] Unhappy Young Prince! to be possess'd with this Devil of *Ambition,* which makes him become the *Phaeton*[2] of our Age; to set these Kingdoms in a Combustion. [For it was at this Time, Madam, added *Galesia,* that the Duke of *Monmouth's* Enterprize began to be talk'd of.] Whether *Ambition* be a Branch of *Pride,* or *Pride* a Branch of *Ambition,* I know not: They *both* partake of the *same Quality;* so which is *Root,* or which is *Branch,* it matters not; since it may be determin'd, that the *Tree* produces the worst of *Fruit.*

As I was going on in these wandring Thoughts, during the Intervals of my grieved Mother's Slumbers, I heard a little mumbling Noise in the next House, in a Room joyning to ours; which mumbling at last ended in a *Hymn:* Then I concluded it to be the *Prayer* of an Old Gentlewoman who lodg'd on the same Floor in the next House. But the *Hymn* being distinct, I cou'd hear the Words perfectly; which are these:

A *Hymn.* Sung in a *Psalm* Tune.

> Preserve thy Holy Servant *Monmouth,* Lord,
> Who carries for his Shield thy *Sacred Word.*[3]
> Preserve him from the *Lyon* and the *Bear.*
> From *Foxes* and from *Wolves,* who daily tear
> Thy *little Flock;* and for him whet[4] thy Sword,
> That *we* may be *Thy People,* Thou *our Lord.*
> Do thou the *Red-Coats*[5] to Confusion bring,
> The *Surplices, Lawn-Sleeves,* and eke their *King;*[6]
> Whilst in thy *Sion*[7] we thy Praises sing.

---

1. **Duke of Monmouth:** James Scott (1649–85), illegitimate son of Charles II who attempted to seize the throne from James II at his father's death; defeated at the Battle of Sedgemoor, he was then executed for treason.

2. **Phaeton:** in Greek myth, borrowed a chariot from his father Phoebus (god of the sun); unable to control the horses in a wild ride, he was thrown to his death.

3. It was said, that a Bible was carry'd before him. [Author's note.]

4. **whet:** sharpen.

5. **Red-coats:** soldiers.

6. **Surplices:** loose clerical vestments of white linen worn over a cassock. **Lawn-Sleeves:** sleeves of a Bishop's robe made of lawn, a fine fabric. **eke:** also. **King:** James II.

7. **Sion:** Zion, the tradiional name of one of the hills of Jerusalem on which the city of David was built.

Wicked Song! said I; and wicked Wretch that sings it; in which she curses the Lord's Anointed, and all his Adherents, the Church and all her Children. Graceless Woman! that dares lift up Hands, Eyes, and Voice to Heaven with such Maledictions! But sure, it is her Ignorance; Nobody can be so designedly wicked. Happy had such been to have died in their Infancy, before the Baptismal Water was dry'd off their Face! But, ah! if I think on that, who is there so Righteous, but that they may wish they had dyed in the State of Innocency?

In these Reflections, a certain drousy Summons to Sleep seiz'd me; and having watch'd long with my dear sick Mother, I comply'd with my Weakness, and fell fast asleep; and having been just before reflecting on Baptismal Innocence, I fell into the following Dream.

The *Childrens,* or *Catechumen's Elysium.*[1]

> Methought I pass'd thro' that *Elysian* Plain,
> Which to the *Catechumens* appertain;
> And is to those, likewise, the soft Abode,
> Who ignorantly serve the *Unknown God.*
>
> Lo! here the Souls live in eternal Peace,
> Almost tir'd out with everlasting Ease;
> Exempt from Griefs, but no true Joys possess;
> Which is, at best, but half true Happiness.
>
> When in my Dream, I thought I enter'd here,
> All that was charming struck my Eye and Ear;
> Large Walks, tall Trees, Groves, Grots,[2] and shady Bow'rs,
> Streams in Meanders, Grass, and lovely Flow'rs,
> Babes unbaptiz'd (like Birds from Tree to Tree)
> Chirp here, and sing in pleasing Harmony.
> Long Walks of *Roses, Lilies, Eglantines,*
> *Pinks, Pansies, Violets* and *Columbines,*

---

1. **Catechumen's Elysium:** a paradise for converts, especially children. This poem is a slightly revised version of "A dream, Of the Cattacumens Elesium," Magdalen MS 343, part 2, page 33.

2. **Grots:** grottos, small caves or caverns.

Which always keep their perfect Beauty here,
Not subject to the Changes of the Year.
In fine; Here's all Things that can Fancy please,
Rooms of Repose, and Canopies of Ease;
Towers, Terrasses, arch'd Roofs, and Theatres,
Well-built Piazzas, lofty Pillasters;
Statues, and Stories of terrestrial Pride,
Of such who follow'd *Virtue* for their Guide;
At last, against their Wills, were *Deify'd.*
Sumptuous Apparel, Musick, Mirth and Balls,
Exceeding *Londoners* in Festivals,
The *Temple-Revels;* foreign *Carnivals.*
The Swains, too, had their *Country-Wakes*[1] and Chear,
Th'Apprentices *Shrove-Tuesday*[2] all the Year,
And every one was happy in his Sphere:
That is to say, if Happiness can be,
Without th'Enjoyment of a *Deity.*

Small Joy can *Immaterial Beings* find,
Till with their *Immaterial Center* joyn'd.
The *Soul* of Man is a *Celestial Flame,*
Without *true Joy,* 'till it goes *whence it came.*
As *Fire* ascends, and *Earth* and *Water* fall,
So must *we* join with our *Original.*[3]
This Truth poor *mortal Lovers* represent,
Whom nought but the *lov'd Object* can content.

In these Reflections, many a Path I trod,
And griev'd to think *they ne'er must see their God.*

---

1. **Country-Wakes:** festivities following a funeral.

2. **Shrove-Tuesday:** in Christian tradition, day of exuberance and excess in food and drink before the Lenten fast that precedes Easter.

3. **Original:** God.

This melancholy Reflection awaked me; when I was in Amaze to find my self in my Mother's Chamber; having had such an absolute and perfect Idea of that *happy Place*, where, amongst the *rest*, I thought *I had seen my Mother;* that I wonder'd to find her *asleep in her Bed,* and I *in a Chair by her;* and some little Time it was, e'er I cou'd believe that I had *Dream'd* and was now *Awake.* But at last, convincing my-self, I compos'd these Verses upon the Occasion.

On *Dreams.*

> A *Dream* to me seems a *Mysterious Thing,*
> Whate'er the *Naturalists*[1] for *Causes* bring.
> Whilst *Sleep's* dull Fetters, our frail Bodies tye,
> The *Soul,* inlarg'd, finds pleasant Company.
> With *Comrade-Spirits,* midnight Revels make,
> And see Things pass'd, and Things to come forespeak.
> Sometimes in merry *Jigs* and *Gambols,*[2] they
> Present th'Events of the approaching Day:
> Sometimes they mount e'en to the Place of Bliss;
> Then sink again into the deep Abyss;
> With such Agility and Ease they go,
> The piercing Lightning seems to move more slow,
> Yet as they *pass,* all Things they *See* and *Know.*
>
>   But as a Country Lady, after all
> The Pleasures of th' *Exchange, Plays, Park,* and *Mall,*[3]
> Returns again to her old *Rural Seat,*
> T''instruct her *Hinds,*[4] and make 'em earn their Meat,
> So comes the *Soul* home to her *coarse Retreat.*

---

1. **Naturalists:** those who believed in rational explanations for all phenomena.

2. **Gambols:** leaps in dances.

3. **Exchange:** the New Exchange, site of innumerable shops. **Mall:** fashionable London promenade adjacent to St. James's Park, created in 1660.

4. **Hinds:** farm laborers.

A coarse Retreat indeed! Where Sin, Sorrow, and Sufferings, of all Kinds, and from all Quarters, accost and attack *her,* and from which *she* is perpetually wishing to be delivered; and yet is loth to quit this *her* Earthly Mansion: Which Fondness for this transitory Life, and Fear to imbark for a Better in the Ocean of Eternity, must surely proceed from a Deficiency of *Faith,* and the Want of a firm Belief of *Future Happiness.*

As I was going on with these Reflections, my Mother, with a most piercing Groan, awaked, and faintly calling me to her Bed-side, I had the inexpressible Affliction to see her last Moments drawing on:—Pardon, *said* Galesia, *wiping her Eyes,* these briny Ebullitions:[1] The next most shocking Grief was now approaching to torture my labouring Spirits.—To be short—for who can dwell on such a Subject!—My dear Mother, in the midst of her Blessings poured on me, and Prayers for me, recommending her Soul to Divine Mercy, was interrupted by Death, and looking wistfully upon me, and grasping my Hand, expired!—

Hereupon *Galesia* fell into a Flood of Tears, which suspended her Discourse. And the good Lady, being unwilling to press her any farther on that melancholy Theme, took her by the Hand, saying, Come, my *Galesia,* we will go and inquire how forward Dinner is; and whether the Gentlemen who have invited themselves, are yet come, or not.

Accordingly, they went out together; but *Galesia* rising from her Seat, dropp'd the following Verses; which the Lady took up, saying, Well! Here I see, is Matter for another *Patch,* which we will peruse on our Return.

On the *Difficulties* of *Religion.* [2]

O Wretched World! but Wretched above All,
Is Man; the most unhappy Animal!
Not knowing to what State he shall belong,

---

1. **briny Ebullitions:** sudden flood of tears.

2. This poem is a shorter version of 79-line "Fidelia arguing with her self on the difficulty of finding the true religion," Magdalen MS 343, part 1, page 8. Fidelia, whose name is from the Latin for *faithful,* is Barker's persona as reflective Catholic. The 1680s–1720s were a period of conflicting views about the role of religion, the authority of the Church of England, and personal moral reform and salvation.

He tugs the heavy Chain of Life along.
So many Ages pass, yet no Experience shows
From whence Man comes, nor, after, where he goes.
We are instructed of a Future State,
Of Just Rewards, and Punishments in That;
But ign'rant How, or Where, or When, or What.
I'm shew'd a Book,[1] in which these Things are writ;
And, by all Hands, assur'd, all's True in it;
But in this Book, such Mysteries I find,
Instead of Healing, oft corrode the Mind.
Sometimes our *Faith*[2] must be our *only* Guide,
Our *Senses* and our *Reason*[3] laid aside:
Again to *Reason* we our *Faith* submit,
This spurs, that checks, we curvet,[4] champ the Bit,
And make our future Hopes uneasy sit!
Now *Faith*, now *Reason*, now *Good-works*,[5] does All;
Betwixt these Opposites our Virtues fall,
Each calling each, *False* and *Heretical.*[6]

And, after all; What Rule have we to show,
Whether these Writings Sacred be, or no?
If we alledge, The Truths that we find there,
Are to themselves a Testimony clear,
By the same Rule, such all good Morals are.
Thus we by Doubts, & Hopes, & Fears, are tost,
And in the Lab'rinth of Disputes are lost.

---

1. The BIBLE. [Author's note.]

2. **Faith:** in the belief of some Protestant sects, faith alone could enable a believer to enter Heaven.

3. **Reason:** referring to Deism, a religious position that celebrates rationality, rejects mystery and revelation, and posits that God turned away from human affairs after the Creation.

4. **curvet:** referring to a horse's complicated leap, an advanced movement in training.

5. **Good-works:** in some Christian beliefs, including Catholicism, good works during one's lifetime could help a believer to enter Heaven.

6. **Heretical:** departing from church dogma.

> Unhappy! who with any Doubts are curst!
> But of all Doubts, *Religious* Doubts are worst!
> Wou'd I were dead! or wou'd I had no Soul!
> Had ne'er been born! or else been born a Fool!
> Then future Fears, wou'd not my Thoughts annoy,
> I'd use what's truly mine, the present Joy.
> Ah! happy *Brutes!* I envy much your State,
> Whom Nature, one Day, shall Annihilate;
> Compar'd to which, wretched is Human Fate!

Dinner not being quite ready, the good Lady conducted *Galesia* again into her Appartment, and they being seated, she read the foregoing Verses, which, she said, should serve for another Patch in her Screen: And as she was laying it by for that Purpose, she cast her Eye on the Backside of the same Paper, and there found the following Lines, which seemed, by the Tenor of them, as well as by the Writing, to be the Product of the same melancholy Frame of Mind with the former, as well as to be written at the same Time. After a sort of *Chasm,* they began thus.

> But what does most of all my Spirit grieve,
> Is, That I must my Dear *Fidelius*[1] leave!
> My Dear *Fidelius!* Witty, Young, and Gay,
> To whose Embraces Virtue chalks the Way.
> In loving Him, I answer Heaven's Call;
> For Love's allow'd, for Virtuous Ends, to All:
> And Heav'n, perhaps, has rais'd him up Express,
> By Force of Love, to prop my Feebleness,
> And stop my Fall into this Precipice.
> But how know I, he's not set on by Hell,
> To stop the Progress of my doing well?
>
> Thus I'm, alas! by diff'rent Passions mov'd,
> And hope, and fear, and love, and am belov'd.

---

1. **Fidelius:** from the Latin, a masculine name suggesting one who is faithful.

Yet if I own I love, I ruin Him,
And to deny the Truth, is, sure, a Crime.
My Sufferings are great: Heav'n pity me!
But whatsoe'er I bear, let him go free!

Hereupon the Lady looking over the Work, and finding there was enough to make Four Folds of a *Screen,* she said, she would have it made up, and fram'd, to see how it would look before they proceeded any farther. And now, said she, the Players are come into the Country, and the Assembleés and Horse-Races will begin; so we will defer our Work 'till those Diversions are over. But, however, continued she, since I have received so many Favours from you, my dear *Galesia,* in this Way, and that I may contribute a little to divert you in your melancholy Hours, when the Remembrance of so sad an Occasion as your Mother's Death, crouds too heavily upon your Thoughts, I will shew you a Poem that was presented me on New-Year's Day last, by an Excellent Hand, in Commemoration of the Nativity of our Blessed SAVIOUR; Which, added the good Lady, I question not, but will give you as much Pleasure and Consolation, as it has frequently done me.

An *Ode*

In *Commemoration* of the *Nativity* of *Christ*.[1]

Magnus ab Integro Sæc'lorum nascitur ordo.

VIRG.[2]

I.

Well dost thou do, my Muse;
Ne'er envy Tuneful Bards, whoe'er they be.
That Vain and Earthly Subjects chuse,
    Yet vainly hope for Immortality.
Some sooth with Magick Sounds, the Virgin's Breast,
Which self-bewitching Thoughts before possest;
    Adore the transient Pageant of a Day,
    And Idolize a Piece of Painted Clay.
Another lifts some Hero to the Skies,
And a Man-slaughterer Deifies,
    Sent in God's Vengeance, when, by his Command,
    Tempests of War invade a Guilty Land.
      Another tunes his Mercenary Strings,
To act that Worst of Witchcraft, flatter Kings.
But Thou yield'st all thy Praise, and offer'st all thy Love,
    Where it is only due, ABOVE!
Yet, O thou Virgin! O thou Vestal-Muse!
    That won't profane thy Voice, with Things below,
One Theme, as Low as Earth can yield, I chuse,
    And yet as High as Heav'n can e'er bestow.
Therefore, begin from Earth: But know, Thy Flight
Shall tow'r beyond Day's blazing Orb of Light.
The Lark so flickering o'er its Grounded Nest,
First ope's its little Lungs, exerts its Breast,
    Then rising on its Saily Wings,

---

1. **Nativity of Christ:** See Matt. 2, Luke 2.

2. **Magnus ab Integro Sæc'lorum nascitur ordo:** "The last great age, foretold by sacred rhymes," Virgil (70–19 B.C.), "The Fourth Pastoral," *The Works of Virgil* (trans. Dryden), 4.5.

It meditates the Sky;
As still it rises, still it sings,
   'Till its small Body leaves the Eye;
And when it does near Heav'n appear,
Its finest Notes desert the Human Ear.
Say, Wouldst thou know this Happy Theme,
That thus shall wing thee above mortal Fame?
   Sing thou the Child, that seem'd like Mankind's Scorn,
   At Depth of Winter in a Stable born;
   Born among Beasts, and in a Manger laid:
   Yet if that Child will thee, inspiring, aid,
   The lovely Theme, exalting, shalt thou raise,
   Above the Kings and Heroes others praise.

II.

Let each King's Bard reap, as he gives, Renown,
   While Flatt'rers, like himself, with shortliv'd Fame,
His Lawrel hail, as he the Regal Crown,
   Giving each Toy what neither Toy can claim;
Myriads of Spirits, that e'er Men were made,
E'er the Foundations of the Earth were laid,
   Far brighter had, for Ages, shone
Than a vain Monarch on a Birth-day shines,
   Whose Forms outdo the Day-bestowing Sun,
And shall, when Nature, sunk in Years, declines;
Shall, when that Sun is blotted from the Sky,
   When the Blue *Æther*, reddning, melts in Flame;
When all Created Worlds are bid to die,
   Shine on for all Eternity the same:
All these bright Spirits, whose each Single Voice,
Can make Spheres dance, make Heav'n and Earth rejoyce;
These shall thy Song upon this Babe refine,
Shall All in One great Chorus join;
   Humbly they too shall own

Him the Immortal Heir of *David's* Throne,[1]
And that to Him their Song is Low as thine.
For, know, That Infant, poorly as it lies,
In Spirit treads the Stars, and walks the whirling Skies!
That Babe, on Earth expos'd in this Abode,
Is now in Heaven—He is the Almighty God.

III.

Yes, Mortals, Yes, who deigns thus Mean to be,
Mysterious Change, O Man! But 'tis, 'tis He,
To whom the Thought-transcending Being said,
The Being that his Angels Spirits made,
That made his Ministers a Flame of Fire,
"Thou art than all these Angels Higher,
Thou my Son, and I thy Sire:
To me a Son for Ever shalt thou be,
And I for Ever Sire to Thee."
Still farther, Heaven's High King proceeded on,
And thus to his Coequal Son
     The Son's Coequal Father spake,
"O God! for Ever is thy Throne,
     Thy Foes thy Footstool will I make:
Be seated here at my Right Hand;
Where'er there's Light, Air, Sea, or Land,
Thou Always shalt and All Command."
This said, Choirs that fill'd the bright Abode,
Worshipp'd, at his Command, this Babe, and
     worshipp'd him a God.

IV.

And is it thus, thou Mighty Helpless Thing!
Thou less than Beggar, and thou more than King!
Canst Thou yon Starry Region term thy Throne?

---

1. **Immortal Heir of David's Throne:** the Messiah; see Matt. 1.

Claim, as thy Footstool, this vast Globe of Earth?
Call all the spacious Globe contains, Thy own?
Thou! Cradled in a Manger at thy Birth,
As feeble Man, can't tow'r a God. How can
The God of Nature sink to feeble Man?
Oh Wondrous! Oh Mysterious Change!
Yet as Eternal Truth no Wrong can know,
Strange as it seems, it is as true as strange;
It is——It must be so.
Long e'er this World the World's Redeemer blest,
Old Prophets, Sign delivering after Sign,
His Coming, and his Acts, when come, exprest,
That all might know the Man who was Divine.
When this was made, beyond disputing, plain,
Then Endless Woes were doom'd, by God's Award,
To be the stubborn Unbeliever's Pain,
And Endless Joys Believers great Reward:
These, by his Prophets Mouths, the Father swore,
That, trusting in his Son, obey'd his Lore,
These He, His Sacred Oath confirming, said,
Should Uncorrupted at the fatal Day,
Which shall the World itself in Ashes lay,
From the Corrupted Regions of the Dead,
Rise and Immortalize their Mortal Clay.
But *those,* in Bitterness of Wrath, He vow'd,
Whom no Rewards could win, or Threats could awe,
To take the Paths, propounded for their Good,
But, heedless, stubbornly would spurn his Law,
Should be condemn'd to wander round the Earth,
And when they dy'd, be doom'd to go,
To Endless Gulphs of Fire below.

V.

O LORD! who meditates what Thou hast wrought,
That Man is God, and God is Man;

Who knows, if he believes not what You taught,
    Tho' more than bounded Reason e'er can scan,
He shall the Object of thy Wrath remain,
Immortal made to feel Eternal Pain.
    But if, confiding in the Word
    Of Truth, Itself's ne'er-failing Lord,
He own'd this Wonder, he should be
Heir to a bless'd Eternity.
O Lord! who meditates what thou hast wrought,
Is lost at first in pleasing, dreadful Thought;
But feels a Particle within, that tells,
His Soul is lasting as his God reveals:
From thence he does the boundless Pow'r confess,
May do what he can't think, as what he can't express;
And owns the Greater Wonder from the Less:
    Thus when he finds, that the Immortal Son
Grew Mortal, to make Men Immortal grow;[1]
Straight does his grateful Breast with Ardor glow,
    His Fears are vanish'd, and his Terrors gone.
        The Man who thus conceives
Christ's Goodness, and this Mystery believes,
Nor menac'd Pains, nor promis'd Joys controul;
Fix'd by Affections rooted in his Soul,
He his Redeemer views, with Joy, Above,
And, swallow'd in the Ocean of his Love,
Needs nothing else his working Faith to move.

VI.

    'Tis in this Light, O Saviour! that we view,
We, who are honour'd with the Christians Name,
    The wondrous Acts that You vouchsafe to do,

---

1. **Immortal Son...grow:** The gospel or good news of the New Testament was that the death and resurrection of Christ, son both of God and mortal flesh, would bring salvation to believers.

To pay our Forfeit, and redeem our Claim.
Then we recount the Wonders of that Age,
When Heav'ns High Lord trod on this Earth's Low
    Stage.
We read, How Men, quite Lame, did Christ pursue,
Ran, by one Miracle, to see a New.[1]
When straight Blind Mortals feel the visual Ray,
And the First Man they see, is Author of the Day.
The Dumb, lamenting Silence, this behold,
When straight their Loosening Tongues new Miracles
    unfold.
Dœmoniacks foam'd and curst to see the Deed,
But blest the Author when from Doemons freed.
Up from the Dead a Carcass newly rais'd,
Join'd with the Living, and Death's Victor prais'd.
Man's Union hence with God ev'n Reason can,
Tho' but by Consequence and faintly, scan:
    Enough, howe'er, to lead to Faith's true Road,
Since this we find was done by Man,
    And could not but by God:
By these Reflections, which thy Preachers raise,
Those that were Dumb, sing out aloud thy Praise;
Those seek Thee that were in Devotion Lame,
Like bounding Roes,[2] that, thirsty, seek the Stream.
Those that were Blind, here get the Eye of Faith,
And, pressing forward to Salvation's Path,
The stubborn *Jews* they, left behind, invite
To follow them from Error's foggy Night:
Bid them from obstinate Delusions fly,
Who most are Proofs of what they most deny:
    Curs'd by the Lord, they live on Earth by Stealth,
Thro' the Wide World, like Vagabonds, they roam,

---

1. **a New:** anew, again.
2. **Roes:** small deer.

Princes and Lords in Wealth,
    But Lords without a Home:
Tho' suff'ring still, they still thy Laws despise,
Since Seventeen Cent'ries cannot make them wise:
Since from their rooted Sin they cannot part;
Melt (for Thou canst!) the hardest Heart,
    And open Blindest Eyes:
Make All on Earth, as All in Heav'n, join,
Since All in Heav'n and Earth alike are Thine.

FINIS.

THE
LINING
OF THE
Patch Work Screen;

Design'd for the Farther

ENTERTAINMENT

OF THE

LADIES.

By Mrs. JANE BARKER

LONDON,

Printed for A. BETTISWORTH, at the
Red Lion in *Pater-Noster Row.* MDCCXXVI.

This page is an approximation of the title page of the 1726 edition of *The Lining of the Patch Work Screen.* The ornament in the original is slightly different.

TO THE L A D I E S.

You may please to remember, that when we left our *Galecia*,[1] it was with the good Lady, to partake of the Autumn Diversions in the Country; as Horse-Races, Dancings, *Assemblées*,[2] Plays, Rafflings, and other Entertainments.

These being over, some Business of consequence call'd her to *London*, whether Masquerading,[3] or Tossing of Coffee-Grounds, I know not; but probably the latter; it being an Augury[4] very much in vogue, and as true, as any by which *Sidrophel*[5] prognosticated, even when he took the Boy's Kite for a blazing Comet[6]; and as useful too as Scates[7] in *Spain*, or Fans in *Moscovy*;[8] whatever was the Motive, our *Galecia* must needs ramble, like others, to take *London*-Air, when it is most substantially to be distinguished, in the midst of Winter.

Here it was I found her, and often had her Company, receiving from time to time an account of her Adventures; which I have kept together, in order to make a *Lining* for your *Patch-work Screen*.[9] But these Pieces being much larger than the others, I think we must call it *Pane-work*;[10] which, I hope, will be acceptable to your Ladyships, you having pleas'd

---

1. **Galecia:** Galesia, Barker's semi-autobiographical literary persona, first in print in *Poetical Recreations* (1688); also the name of the Numidian princess, huntress and student of philosophy and law, in *Exilius* (1715). The name recalls the feminine form of Galaesus, prophet and son Apollo, Greek god of poetry.

2. **Assemblées:** fashionable social gatherings (French).

3. **Masquerading:** attending a ball, play, or other event disguised in mask, the anonymity at times an excuse for lewd behavior.

4. **Tossing . . . Augury:** like the reading of tea leaves, interpreting coffee grounds to tell the future.

5. See *Hudibras*, Part 2. Canto 3. [Author's note.] **Hudibras:** three-part satire (1663, 1664, 1678) by Samuel Butler (1613–80), featuring **Sidrophel**, a crazed astrologer.

6. **blazing Comet:** omen of disaster and death.

7. **Scates:** ice skates.

8. **Moscovy:** Moscow.

9. **Patch-work Screen:** the large ornamental structure composed of appliquéd pieces of fabric and some of Galesia's literary works, first described in *A Patch-Work Screen for the Ladies* (1723). Screens were composed of several panels that could measure nine feet by two feet and take years to finish.

10. **Pane-work:** large squares of fabric, sewn together to form the lining.

your selves with this kind of Composure in your Petticoats; which, methinks, bears some resemblance to Old *London,* when the Buildings were of Wood and Plaister. I wish, Ladies, you don't condemn this my *LINING* to the same Fate.[1]

Well, be it so; if it have but the honour to light your Lamps for your Tea-kettles, its Fate will be propitious enough; and if it be thus far useful, I hope, you will not think there is too much of it. For my own part, I fear'd there would hardly be enough to hold out measure with the *SCREEN.*

This made me once think to have enlarg'd it, by putting in some Pannels of Verse; but, that I heard say, Poetry is not much worn at Court; only some old Ends of *Greek* and *Latin,* wherewith they garnish their Dedications, as Cooks do their Dishes with Laurel or other Greens, which are commonly thrown by, as troublesome to the Carver, whatsoever Poetry may be by the Reader.

Wherefore, I hope, your Ladyships will easily excuse the want of this kind of Embellishment in my Dedication; remembring, that

One tongue is enough for a Woman.

But perhaps, it may be said, that this is an old fashion'd, out-of-the-way Proverb, used only when Ladies liv'd at their Country-Seats, and had no occasion for the Jargon of *Babel*;[2] their Cooks, Gardiners, Butlers, Waiting-women, and other Servants all understood, and spoke the same Language, even old *English:* But now 'tis otherwise; and that which God sent for a Curse on those presumptuous Builders, is now become the distinguishing Mark of good Breeding.

How this Alteration came to pass, or when it began, I do not well know. But some say, it was in the Year when the first Colony of *BUGGS* planted themselves in *England.*[3]

---

1. **same fate:** allusion to London's numerous fires, including the Great Fire of 1666.

2. **Jargon of Babel:** confused, inarticulate speech, God's punishment of the Babylonians for presuming to build a tower reaching Heaven; see Gen. 11:1–11.

3. **BUGGS . . . England:** commonplace to describe troubles; also, likely reference to the invasion of William of Orange (1650–1702) in 1688 to depose James II; infectuous spread of Quakerism, debunked by former Quaker, Francis Bugg (1640–1742?); and actual infestations that brought typhus to England in the 1680s.

Others affirm, it was at the same time that *JINN*[1] broke down the Banks of our Female Sobriety, and overflow'd the Heads of the whole Populace, so that they have been brain-sick ever since: But I am not Antiquarian enough to enter into this Dispute, much less to determine it; only thus far, if I may speak my simple Thoughts, I believe it was in *Oliver's*[2] time, when the Saints and the Ungodly spoke a Dialect so different, that one might almost take it for two Languages.

But after all, Ladies, I should be very proud to find something amongst Authors, that might embelish my Dedication so as to make it suitable to your Merits, and my Book worthy your Acceptance.

I would most willingly, rifle *Boileau*, *Racine*, and hunt *Scaron*[3] through all his Mazes, to find out something to deck this my Epistle,[4] till I made it as fine as a *May day* Milk Pail,[5] to divert you with a Dance at your Closet-doors,[6] whilst my *Crowdero*-Pen,[7] scrapes an old Tune, in fashion about threescore and six years ago; and thereby testifie that I am passionately desirous to oblige you.

Since you have been so kind to my Booksellers in favour of the *SCREEN*, I hope, this *LINING* will not meet with a less Favourable Reception from Your Fair Hands: Which will infinitely oblige

Your Devoted Servant,
Jane Barker.

---

1. **JINN:** gin, a cheap and widely consumed alcoholic beverage brought from Holland by WIlliam III. A dramatic increase in robberies and personal degradation, including female drunkenness, was attributed to gin.

2. **Oliver:** Oliver Cromwell (1599–1658), Puritan, Parliamentary general, dictatorial Lord Protector of the Commonwealth (1653–58), and one of those responsible for the execution of King Charles I (1600–49).

3. **Boileau, Racine, . . . Scaron:** French neoclassical writers. Nicolas Boileau (1636–1711), author of *Art poétique* (1674). Jean Racine (1639–99), author of psychological tragedies, including *Phèdre* (1677). Paul Scarron (1610–60), author of comedies and a parody of Virgil.

4. **Epistle:** letter.

5. **May day Milk Pail:** referring to the 1 May celebration of the coming of spring, when the community decorated objects with flowers and greenery.

6. **Closet-doors:** doors to a private room.

7. **Crowdero-Pen:** Crowdero, one-legged fiddler and leader of bear-baiters in Butler's *Hudibras*.

The Lining to
the *Patch-Work Screen.*

Galecia one Evening setting alone in her Chamber by a clear Fire, and a clean Hearth, (two prime Ingredients towards composing the Happiness of a Winter-season) she reflected on the Providence of our All-wise and Gracious Creator, who has mercifully furnish'd every Season with its respective Comforts to sustain and delight us his poor Creatures: The Spring, for example, with its Sweets of Buds and Blossoms; the Musick of the singing Birds, which hold Concert with the whistling Plough-man, committing his Seed to the Earth, in hopes of a plentiful Harvest: Next, the Summer season, with its Fields cover'd over with shining Corn,[1] and the Meadows with Haycocks; all inviting the industrious Farmer to come and receive the Fruits of his Annual Toil and Sollicitude. This happy Season being past, comes the Autumn, with its laden Branches, to fill the Vats with Wine and Cyder; as also the Hogsheads[2] with well brew'd *October*,[3] to gladden the Feasts when seated with Friends by good Fires, those benign Champions that defend us from the Inclemencies of Winter's Fury. Thus the Year is brought about; and tho' I have not the Society of Friends by my Fire-side (said she to her self) yet God has given me the Knowledge of Things, so far as to be able to entertain my Thoughts in this Solitude, without regret; when the Coldness of Friends, or rather the want of Riches, deprives me of their Company these long Winter-Evenings.

In these Cogitations,[4] she cast her Eyes towards the Window, where she beheld the Full Moon, whose Brightness seemed a little to extend the extream Shortness of the Days, when Dusk calls for Candles to supply the Sun's Absence. This brought to her mind the Thoughts she had in her Childhood on this Subject: For then she had a Notion (whether

---

1. **Corn:** collective term for cereal plants such as wheat or barley.
2. **Hogshead:** large barrel, cask.
3. **October:** ale brewed in October.
4. **Cogitations:** reflections, thoughts.

taught by her Nurse, or otherwise) that the Old Moons were given to good Children to make them Silver Frocks to wear on Holidays.

As she reflected on this infant Conceit,[1] she began to consider whether she had improv'd in her riper Years. Alas, said she to her self, what have I spoke or acted more consonant to good Morality, than this Conceit in the State of mine Innocence? For after we have pass'd this contemptible Stage of Weakness both of Mind and Body, we enter into a State of Danger and Temptation; and if by chance we escape the Snares laid to catch our heedless Youth, we then walk on in a rough Road of consuming Cares and Crosses, in which we often stumble or fall; and if we rise again, perhaps it is to meet with greater Dangers, in Sickness, Sorrows, or divers Temptations, to which we too often submit, thro' our Rashness or Inadvertency.

When the Blossom of Youth is shed, do we bring forth the Fruits of good Works? Do we relieve the Poor, any way within our Power? Do we instruct the Ignorant, comfort the Afflicted, strengthen the Doubtful, or assist the Feeble, with other Works of Mercy corporal and spiritual?

She was thus ruminating, when a Gentleman enter'd the Room, the Door being a jar. He was tall, and stood upright before her; but not speaking a word, though she look'd earnestly upon him, could not call to mind that she knew him, nor could well determine whether he was a Person or a Spectre. At last she ask'd him, who he was; but he gave her no answer. Pray, said she, tell me; if you are a Mortal, speak; still no Answer. At last, with an amazed Voice, she said, pray, tell me, who, or what you are. I am, said he, your old Friend Captain *Manly:* At which she was extreamly confused, to think that she had so weak an *Idea* of so good a Friend, as not to know him, he having been many Years absent; not knowing whether it proceeded from a Change of his Person in that time, or Dimness of Sight, between Moon-shine and Fire-light. But calling for a Candle, she beg'd a thousand Pardons, engaged him to sit down, and let her know, what had so long conceal'd him from her Correspondence.

---

1. **Conceit:** notion, idea.

The *Story* of *Captain Manly.*

Dear *Galecia*, said he, though you partly know the loose, or rather lewd Life that I led in my Youth; yet I can't forbear relating part of it to you by way of Abhorrence.

Then it was I married a rich Widow-Lady, thereby to gratifie my Pride, Luxury and Ambition; for Love had no part in the Espousals.[1] I knew, that her Fortune, Friends and Interest would soon place me in a Station to my Liking, where I might enjoy my Bottle and my Friend, and, when I pleas'd, a little Cocquet-Harlot.[2] These things were the chief of my Ambition: For I did not aim at benefiting my King or Country by my Services, into what state soever I might be advanc'd; but to gratifie my Pride and Vanity in embroider'd Cloaths, long Wigs, fine Equipage,[3] and the like: Which Vanity is excusable also, when the intention is to grace the Monarch we serve, or to honour the Family of which we are descended: But my Design was only to please the Eyes of the Fair, and make me the Subject of their Prattle, when *Ombre*-Tables[4] and *Assemblées* call them together; or to over-hear them in the *Mall*,[5] saying, *No body had a better Fancy in Dress than Captain* Manly.

When Days of Muster[6] call'd us out to Review in the *Park*,[7] then the shewing our fine Saddles, Holsters and Housing,[8] were more my Concern, than teaching my self or my Soldiers their Duty. And when I returned, I fansied I had undergone a great Fatigue, and could go no further than *Locket's* or *Paulet's*,[9] send my Horses home, charge my Man

---

1. **Espousals:** marriage vows.

2. **Cocquet:** coquet, flirt.   **Harlot:** whore, prostitute.

3. **Equipage:** variously, articles for personal adornment, carriages, or a suite of attendants.

4. **Ombre:** fashionable card game.

5. **Mall:** The Mall, grand walkway for fashionable promenades and procurement in St. James's Park, London.

6. **Muster:** assembly of the militia for inspection and exercise.

7. **Park:** St. James's Park.

8. **Housing:** covering of fabric or leather for a horse's back.

9. **Locket's or Paulet's:** popular London taverns. Locket's, Charing Cross, held a warrant from James II to provide food and drink to the Horse Guards.

to be sure to have my Chariot ready to carry me to the Play in the Evening. And alas! my Business there, was not to admire the Wit of the Poet, or the Excellency of the Actors in their respective Parts; but to ogle[1] the Ladies, and talk to the Masks;[2] and when I found one witty or well-shap'd, take her with me to the next Tavern to Supper. Thus, at coming out, with my Strumpet[3] in my hand, assaulted and surrounded with a number of miserable Objects,[4] I could step into my Chariot without relieving their Wants, or considering them as my Fellow-Creatures. Now, was not this valiantly done, to venture without any Weapon, but scornful Looks, to charge through a Set of miserable Creatures, for daring to ask Alms[5] of so great a Beau? not reflecting, what great Lord had sent them, even the Lord of Heaven and Earth, whose Raggs were their Credentials, and their Sores the Badges of being his Messengers.

Thus far, *Madam*, I acted the Part of a Beau-Rake,[6] till a Salivation and a Sweating-Tub[7] call'd upon me for a more regular way of Intriguing: And even in this I ran the risque of a Chance-medly Venture,[8] like those that hope to make their fortune by Lotteries.

One Evening at the Play I saw a pretty young Creature, very well dress'd, without Company or Attendants, and without a Mask (for she had not yet learn'd so much Impudence, as to put on that Mark of Demonstration.) This Fort I attack'd, and found it not impregnable. She consented to a Parley[9] at the Tavern; but told me withal, that I was greatly mistaken if I took her for a lewd Person; for she was not so, but

---

1. **ogle:** leer.

2. **Masks:** women, assumed to be lewd, who hide their identities behind masks.

3. **Strumpet:** whore; prostitute.

4. **miserable Objects:** beggars.

5. **Alms:** charity.

6. **Beau-Rake:** dissipated man of fashion.

7. **Salivation and a Sweating-Tub:** treatments for venereal disease; the administration of mercury resulted in a discharge of saliva.

8. **Chance-medley Venture:** random or haphazard action in which good and bad luck prevail by turns.

9. **Parley:** meeting.

a vertuous Maiden-Gentlewoman. The truth is, I knew not how to spell, or put together this seeming Contradiction: For to pretend to Vertue, and yet consent to go to a Tavern with a Man wholly a Stranger to her, I did not understand. In short, we supp'd at the Tavern; but whether she or the Drawer,[1] by her Instigation, put any thing in my Liquor, I know not; but so it was, I went drunk to bed, and in the Morning had forgotten what had pass'd, and was greatly amazed to find a Woman in bed with me. We fell into Discourse; and she frankly told me her Name and Family, which greatly amaz'd me; and that she was a Virgin, which more and more confounded me; and then she told me the Cause of this Adventure: For, said she, I liv'd beyond my Fortune; and when that fail'd, I knew not what to do, for I could not work, and am asham'd to beg; nor, indeed, could I reasonably hope to be reliev'd, being in Youth and Health; for Charity is seldom extended to such Persons, be their Birth and Education what it will; Humility and Industry are the Lectures preach'd, and the Alms given on such Occasions: I will not argue (continu'd she) how far that way is right or wrong; but finding my self reduced to Distress, resolved to take hold on the first Opportunity that presented it self, either to marry, or live with any Gentleman that would like my Person so well as to take me either of these ways, into his Protection.

I extreamly lik'd the Frankness of the Girl, together with her Person, which was truly handsom; and after a little farther Discourse, I honestly told her, that I could not marry any body, having a Wife already; but the other way I was willing to take her, and therefore bid her look out for a House, and meet me again the next Night at the Play, and I would then take further measures: I offered her a Guinea; but she generously refus'd it, saying, *It was not come to that yet, to accept a Guinea for a Night's Lodging,* and so departed, promising to meet me at the Play.

This generous Behaviour surpriz'd me; and if at first I lik'd her, I now esteemed her, and thought there was something extraordinary in the Creature, thus to refuse the Figure of the most amorous Monarch[2] in

---

1. **Drawer:** one who draws liquor for customers at a tavern.
2. **most amorous Monarch:** the king's likeness on a coin.

the Universe, on a Piece of Gold, the Thing she so much wanted, as to
sacrifice her Vertue and Honour for its sake. I began to make her an
Heroine, or petty Goddess in my Thoughts; her Beauty stamping on her
the Character of one, and her Generosity of the other. I pleased my self
with the Thoughts of becoming a Beau of the First Rate, in having a
handsome House and a genteel *Mistress*, with whom to pass away my
idle Hours; or, properly speaking, to consume my time in wickedness. I
often recounted to my self the Charms of her Conversation, as well as
those of her personal Beauty; with a thousand other idle Ravings, which
being pass'd, I would return to my self, saying, *Fool that I am, thus to
delude my Fancy with the hopes of Happiness in a Strumpet, a cunning Jilt,
pretending to Vertue, the better to disguise her Vices; a Creature pickt up at
a Play, as one does any common Stroler.*[1] However, I resolved to keep my
Appointment, if it were but to divert my self in bantering her pretended
Vertue. When I came to the Play, I found my Mistress engaged with
another Spark:[2] Then I reflected what a Coxcomb[3] I had been, but was
glad things had gone no further. I should have hired a House, said I (in
reproaching my self) to have been the Receptacle of her numerous Cul-
lies,[4] and furnish'd it for the service of her Lewdness. O, what ridiculous
Creatures do we Cullies make of our selves, when we depend upon a
Creature that has abandon'd Vertue and Honour, in once becoming a
Prostitute! Ah, happy is the Man that has a vertuous and beautiful Wife:
Justly might the wise Man say, *Her Price is above Rubies.*[5] In which only
Sentence he has proved himself a *mighty Sage.*[6]

Thus a thousand Thoughts rambled in my Head, all the while keeping a spiteful Eye on my beautiful Deceiver. I watch'd her going out
with him, and saw them take Coach together in a dirty Hack;[7] which

---

1. **Stroler:** prostitute.

2. **Spark:** foolish suitor.

3. **Coxcomb:** fool.

4. **Cullies:** dupes.

5. **Her Price is above Rubies:** referring to the ideal wife, who is virtuous, loving, thrifty, and industrious; see Prov. 31:10–28.

6. **Sage:** wise man.

7. **Hack:** hackney; coach for hire.

grated my Pride, to see the Jilt prefer that to my fine Equipage, and a plain Country-Gentleman (as he seemed to be) before a Spark of the Town. I was much out of humour all the Evening, nor was it in the power of Bottle or Friend to divert me: If *Ben Johnson*[1] or *Hudibras*[2] had been there, I must have remained dull and ill-humour'd. I am ashamed to tell you, the great Anxieties of Thought in which I past that Night; but Sleep, I am sure, had a very small share of that time allotted by Nature for our Refreshment. The Morning was not much better: I could scarce be commonly civil to those Friends that did me the honour to come to my *Levée*.[3] When drest, I went to the Chocolate House,[4] in order to divert my self there amongst the Fops[5] that frequent that Place; which, indeed, in some degree quell'd my disturbed Thoughts, to observe the different Follies of the Town-Fools; some taking out their Pocket-Glasses to see how to place a Patch[6] right upon a Pimple, tho' there was none to be found on the Face; others talking of the Favours of their *Phyllis's* and *Bellinda's*;[7] some cursing the Treachery of the Sex; others taking out their Billets to read over, for want of Conversation to entertain the Company; and if there was one more ugly than the rest, be-sure he pretended to more Letters and Billets[8] than any body else, though, perhaps, written by himself, or some Friend for him; which way soever it was, it served to gratifie his Vanity. Here, perhaps, I met with some as idly dispos'd as my own *good-for-nothing self*, that when Dinner-time approached, were ready to go with me to *Locket's*; where,

---

1. **Ben Johnson:** Ben Jonson (1572–1637), dramatist, poet, scholar, and writer of court masques.

2. **Hudibras:** Samuel Butler, author of this satire.

3. **Levée:** reception of visitors after rising in the morning.

4. **Chocolate House:** along with coffee houses, popular meeting places for men. Chocolate was a seventeenth-century novelty.

5. **Fops:** foolish and conceited men, pretenders to wit, excessively attentive to fashion.

6. **Patch:** artificial beauty spot.

7. **Phillis's and Bellinda's:** conventional female names in pastoral and romance.

8. **Billets:** brief letters.

at a costly rate, we found Rarities enough to gratifie any luxurious Appetite.

Thus, I began by little and little to banish my false *CHLORIS*,[1] who by this time had but little Interest left in my Thoughts; so that I knew, a Game at *Hazard*[2] would utterly supplant her: For whether I should win or lose, I knew, the Pleasure or the Chagrin would equally out-rival her Charms. It was my luck to win; but I was too vain to carry off the Money; but immediately sent for my Barber to bring me one of his best Wiggs, and to my Semstress for a Suit of her finest Linen, whether Point[3] or Lace.

Thus equipt, I order'd my Equipage[4] to attend me to *Hide-Park*,[5] where in Fops-Ring[6] I might ogle[7] at my pleasure, and at the same time expected my Wigg and Linen should draw the Eyes of others, especially those of the Fair. No Author at *Will's*[8] listned more attentively to what was said of his New Book or Play, than I look'd to see who ogled these my New Trappings, or could have more Chagrin if neglected: But, I think, I was not mistaken; *Beaus* and *Belles*, *Prudes* and *Coquets*, all gave a Glance, at least I thought so; and that pleased my Vanity as well, as if really so: And now I began to wonder at my self for having had the least Disquiet for my Play-house Jilt. I began to be as impatient at my self, as ever I was at her, to think that such a worthless Thing should discompose the Thoughts of such a Hero, as I there counted my self: But behold what hapned in the midst of the high Conceits I had built on

---

1. **Chloris:** conventional female name in pastoral or romance.

2. **Hazard:** complicated game of dice.

3. **Point:** from French for stitch, thread lace made with a needle.

4. **Equipage:** carriage and attendants.

5. **Hide-Park:** Hyde Park, the largest of the Royal parks in London; fashionable gathering place and site of coach races and duels.

6. **Fops-Ring:** familiar term for the Ring, a circular carriage drive around which the fashionable used to parade.

7. **ogle:** stare admiringly.

8. **Will's:** known as the "Wits' Coffee House," famous London coffee house frequented by literary figures including John Dryden (1631–1700), William Wycherley (1640–1716), and Alexander Pope (1688–1744).

such a sandy Foundation. Here comes by my Miss, in a Coach, and the Spark I saw with her at the Play. Their Coach seem'd to be a Country-Gentleman's Vehicle; good Horses, but look'd as if us'd to a Plough and Cart more than a Coach. He, indeed, was handsome in Person, only wanted a little of the Air of our Town Gallants. And now, after all the Tranquillity in which I thought my self, the sight of this Slut discomposed me. I was enraged to think, that she should prefer his dirty Acres before all my shining Equipage, and costly Ornaments. I went out of the *Park* as sullen as a sick Monkey; I knew not whether to strole: The Play was my Aversion, fansying I should see my false *CHLORIS* there. Too soon to go to *Will's* or the *Rose*,[1] I resolved to take a Turn in the *Mall*, tho' too soon for the *Beau Monde*,[2] but good time for the City and Country-Ladies to gather the Dust, and spoil their fine Petticoats. Here I diverted my self as well as I could, to see the Intrigues, some beginning, some going on, though but an old sort of worn-out Diversion to me; yet it serv'd to sooth my surly Humour at that time.

I betook my self to a Seat, and there began to look back upon the Follies of my Life, and of all such as liv'd in that way, whose whole Business is Pride, Sloth and Luxury. We move in a constant course of Irregularity; I may say, as constant as the Sun, but with this distinction, his Motion is to do good, ours Mischief, to our selves, Neighbours and Families. Methought I wish'd my self in Shades[3] amongst the Poets and Philosophers, where wholsome Air and Innocence procured us Health, that first step to Happiness: Nay, I thought, if I had a Wife that was good-humour'd, how many other Disagreements soever she had belonged to her, I could make my self easie, and live honest, without considering that my Misbehaviour was the Cause of her ill Humour. I was in these Cogitations, when one of my wild Companions came and set himself by me, and ask'd, what made me so out of humour. Didst thou drink ill Wine last Night, says he, and so art Maw-sick?[4] Or has

---

1. **Rose:** tavern next to the Drury Lane Theatre, which developed a reputation as a dangerous place, site of assaults and duels.

2. **Beau Monde:** fashionable society.

3. **Shades:** from Roman myth, *lucus,* a shady sacred area that served as a retreat from culture.

4. **Maw-sick:** sick at one's stomach.

Miss jilted thee? Come, Man, let us go take a Bottle, wash down Sorrow, and talk of our Adventures over a brisk Glass of *Champagne:* For, to tell truth, Friend, I am almost resolved to marry, and so abandon this loose way of living. There's no way like it, replied I; and it is certainly in the Power of a sweet temper'd Woman to reclaim the worst of us; therefore be sure to secure that Point, whatever the rest may prove. That is a Quality I mightily esteem, replied my Friend, and I hope I have met with one to my purpose. Prithee where, or when, said I, tell me your Adventure; it is pleasant sitting here, and too soon for a Bottle, so tell me your Intrigue.

The other Night, said he, as I was walking here a little late, till the *Mall* began to empty: I took notice of two pretty young Creatures, very well dress'd in new Mourning, with Gold Watches and Tweezers.[1] They seemed in a great Consternation, that their Man did not bring 'em word he had got 'em a Coach ready at the other side of the Horse-Guard,[2] as they had appointed, and seemed very uneasie to go that way without Company or Attendance. I perceiving their Anxiety, offer'd to wait on them till they could get a Coach, which was readily enough to be had as soon as through the Guard. I put them in a Coach, and begg'd leave to see them safe to their Lodgings, which was but in the *Hay-Market*;[3] we arriv'd at a handsome House, and as handsomly furnish'd, a spruce Footman waiting, whom they rebuked for neglecting his Attendance in the *Park*, so that they were forced to be obliged to this Gentleman (meaning me,) for which they made me many grateful Acknowledgments in their North Country Dialect.[4] They asked me to drink a Dish of Tea, it being just ready, saying, they could not pretend to offer any thing else, they being Strangers in Town, Lodgers, and not House keepers: They offered and excused every thing in such a pretty Country Plainness as charmed me: So being desirous to creep further into their

---

1. **Tweezers:** cases for small implements, including tweezers.

2. **Horse Guard:** building that housed the Royal Household troops.

3. **Hay-Market:** Haymarket, center for commerce in hay and livestock, site of numerous taverns.

4. **North Country Dialect:** dialect of Ireland, Scotland, and the northernmost counties of England; thought to be rough and rude by fashionable Londoners.

Acquaintance, I refused Tea at that time, begging leave to wait on them in the Morning, when a Dish of Tea would be very acceptable: I took my leave, but with a certain tender Reluctance, such as I had been never sensible of before.

In the Morning I went, and found a civil Reception, mix'd with much Modesty; and in some turns of Discourse, I found that their coming to Town was to adjust some Law intanglements, and that their Stay would not be long: They desired of me to let them know the nearest Church, where they might go and offer themselves and their Affairs to the Protection of Heaven; so I gave them as good Directions as I could, withal promising to wait on them with my Chariot to *Westminster*[1] and *St. Paul's*,[2] and that it was at their service on all occasions, whenever they would honour me with their Acceptance. In short, they are so devout, sweet and innocent, that I have indulged my Fancy to that degree, so as to resolve to marry the Elder, who seems not averse to the Proposal; but will determine nothing till her Guardian comes to Town: But I hope to unrivet that Fancy; for you know that my loose way of living has made a great Hole in my little Estate, which her Guardian would soon find out, and perhaps I should be disappointed in the first Resolution I ever made of marrying.

He had scarce finish'd his Discourse, when two of the Marshal's Men brought these two Ladies by us to carry them to *Bridewell*,[3] which we found, upon Enquiry, was for having pickt a Gentleman's-Pocket of twenty Guineas, and withal giving him the Foul Disease.[4]

This was a surprizing Revolution, and it was with difficulty that I hinder'd this my Friend from going to their Rescue. I alledged to him all the manner of their first acquaintance, together with its Progress, as not being consonant to true Vertue and Modesty; and wonder'd, that he who knew the Town so well, should be so easily bubled;[5] but he had

---

1. **Westminster:** site of Westminster-Hall and Westminster Abbey.
2. **St. Paul's:** St. Paul's Cathedral.
3. **Bridewell:** notorious London prison.
4. **Foul Disease:** venereal disease.
5. **bubled:** duped.

attributed all their Freedom and Easiness of Acquaintance to proceed from a Country Simplicity, and Ignorance of the World. After having a a little descanted on this Adventure, we resolved to go to the *Rose*, to wash down our Disappointments, and try to meet some of our Acquaintance as they came out of the Play, and hear what Transactions, what Intrigues, and other little trifling News the House afforded that Evening. In order to which, we posted our selves in a Room just at the Stairs-head, where we sat talking over our respective Affairs, as I have just now related.

And, behold, the first that mounted was my *Mistress*, conducted by her Country-Squire: He bad[1] the Waiter tell his Master to make haste with Supper, for he did not intend to stay long. As soon as they were got into their Room, I asked the Waiter if he knew that Gentleman? Yes, Sir, said he, I was born in the same Town with him, my Father holds a good Farm under him. And do you know the Lady that is with him? Yes, said he, she is his Sister. Are you sure of it, said I? Yes, replied the Waiter, she and I are both of an Age; and I believe, said he, they both go out of Town to morrow early. This was such a double Surprize, as shock'd me beyond Expression: For 'tis certain, that, unknown to my self, I lov'd her as well as any Hero in a Romance; and had suffer'd as great Anxieties for the Falshood of which she seemed to have been guilty: And now, a little Spark of satisfaction, kindled by this Boy's Intelligence, was at the same moment extinguished, by the thoughts of her going out of Town, consequently out of my reach. Thus, we suffer our selves to be hurried by irregular Passions, throwing Reason out of her Regency, and permit our selves to be governed by a thousand Crimes, Follies and Impertinencies. In short, we sat down over our Bottle, to divert our Chagrin, and heighten our Satisfaction: For we had a mixture of both, his Mistress proving a vile Jilt; nevertheless, it being discovered in time, e're too late, was a Consolation; mine proving an honest Whore (if one may so word it:) But the Proof came too late to retrieve the Loss of her out of the Dominion of her Brother. In short, we pass'd our time as agreeably as our Circumstances would permit, till Sleep called us to our respective

---

1. **bad:** bade.

Lodgings, and mine that Night was at my own House: And, I believe, if my Wife could have received me with good Humour, I should then have become a tolerable good Husband: For I was so chagrin'd with this Adventure, that Lewdness became nauceous to me; and I believe, there are few Husbands so abandoned, but a sweet-tempered Woman might find an Interval to reclaim: But I was not so happy in this Juncture.

In the Morning, according to custom, to the Chocolate House I went; here a Letter was brought me by an elderly Woman, who told me, she was ordered to deliver it into my own Hands; which was to this purpose, as near as I can remember:

SIR,

You may very well reproach me, that you have not heard from me in so many Days, and for not having obey'd your Orders in seeking for a House: But when you know the Cause, I'm sure, you will readily forgive the Neglect. 'Tis this: My Brother having heard of my frequenting the Playhouse, and admitting the Courtship of several Lords and Gentlemen (tho' I can safely affirm, I never granted any Favours but to your self.) This brought him to Town, to persuade me to go with him into the Country, which is really my Aversion. Nevertheless, he treated me so kindly, entertaining me with all the Diversions of the Town, and us'd so many cogent Arguments, that I could scarce hold out against his kind Offers. How much I suffered in my Thoughts pro and con, is too tedious to repeat; laying before my self the poor Life I should lead under the Conduct of a Sister-in-law, wholly a Country-Gentlewoman, and a Prude into the bargain, and young Nieces growing up to despise, and perhaps grudge the Bread that I eat, and much more the Cloaths that I wear; and I knew I had not wherewith to bribe them to Respect by costly Presents. On the other hand, the Scandal of being a kept Miss, or Left-hand Wife,[1] the Decay of Beauty, which necessarily entails the Contempt of a Gallant, &c. In short, my Brother took me to the Play last Night, and was so very obliging, that I had resolved to go next Morning with him into the Country. But, Ah! coming up the Stairs at the Tavern, I saw you, my dear Captain. This dash'd in pieces all my Intentions toward the Country: I could not leave my Manly, my beloved Captain: No, I

---

1. **Left-Hand Wife:** mistress or woman who lives with a man as his wife, without marriage.

resolved to be Concubine, Strumpet, or whatever the malicious World would call me, Terms invented by great Fortunes and ugly Faces, who would monopolize all the fine Gentlemen to themselves. I say, for your sake, I will undergo the worst of our Sex's Character. And now, that my Brother is gone out of Town, I shall have Opportunity to take measures with you; and will meet you at the Play house this Evening, who am, Sir,

Your Humble Servant,
Chloris.

Thus was I again catch'd faster than ever: Her abandoning her self and her Family, drew fast that Snare, in which her Beauty had before intangled me. And sure, the most severe part of Mankind cannot wholly condemn me, though I greatly condemn my self, and humbly beg pardon of Heaven.

I met her according to Appointment; and not to clog your vertuous Ears with what amorous Nonsense pass'd, she told me, she had found a House for our purpose, in a Quarter of the Town where neither of us were known. I gave her a Purse of Gold wherewith to furnish an Appartment and other Necessaries; all which she perform'd with Expedition, and every thing was accomplish'd with Neatness and Conveniency; and thus, vile Adulterer as I was, I establish'd my self with my *Harlot.*

And now I liv'd in a regular way of Lewdness; I pass'd my Days in Jollity, and slept in the Bed of Adultery, till Heaven, all-just and good, awak'd me out of this my impious *Delirium*, by the Revolution[1] which soon follow'd. I will not tell you what different Thoughts attack'd me on this occasion, lest in some things I shou'd give offence; but I assure you, I was greatly embarrass'd between Love, Religion and Loyalty; that if I was to write down the many Disputes I had with my self, it wou'd make a Book as big as *Fox's Martyrology.*[2] Let it suffice to tell you, that my

---

1. **Revolution:** Revolution of 1688 which deposed James II and brought William of Orange, later William III, to the English throne.

2. **Fox's Martyrology:** In the *Book of Martyrs* (1563), clergyman John Foxe (1516–87) recounted the history of the Christian Church, with special reference to heroic sacrifices of Protestant martyrs.

Wife perceiving that I had some inclination to close with the new Government,[1] and my Miss, on the other hand, thinking I would go away, they both made their respective Interest according to their Fancies, my Wife to have me disobliged, that I might get me gone, and so rid her of the Company of an ill Husband; *Cloris*, that I might be prevented from going, that she might retain her beloved Gallant. But so it was, between these different Interests, I was clap'd into Prison even *Newgate*.[2] Thus, we see how different Extreams produce the same Effect, as Glass is made by the Extreams of Heat and Cold: When the Government had got their Affairs in a pretty good posture in *Ireland*,[3] that my Liberty could do the King no service, I was let out of Prison. However, the Confinement had so disobliged me, that it answered my Wife's Intentions; and I went away to St. *Germain's*,[4] leaving *Cloris* to shift for her self in finding a new Gallant.

When I came there, I found the Court in a melancholy way, things going but ill in *Ireland*, and long it was not e're the King came back to *France*. Here I found, I cou'd do his Majesty no Service, there being more Officers come out of *Ireland* than cou'd be imploy'd; so that many remain'd chargeable Pentioners;[5] amongst these, his Majesty offer'd me Subsistence, which was a Favour I did not accept, they having born the Heat and Burden of the Day, lost their Estates and many of them advanced in Years, &c. So that I being young enough, resolved, to try my fortune, as many others did, in a Privateer,[6] the *French* being then very successful against the *English* and the *Dutch*: But it so hapned that the *English* took a Privateer bearing King *James's* Commission, and hanged 'em all as Rebels to their Country. This disappointed us all, in

---

1. **Government:** that of William III.

2. **Newgate:** notorious prison in Newgate Street.

3. **Ireland:** where William's troops defeated James II, 1689–91, in his attempt to regain the throne.

4. **St. Germain's:** Saint-Germain-en-Laye; town near Paris where James II installed his court-in-exile.

5. **chargeable Pentioners:** unemployed soldiers, financially burdensome to the king.

6. **Privateer:** armed vessel, privately owned, authorized by the government to act against ships of hostile nations.

particular my self, who would not be a burden to the King in his narrow Circumstances:[1] Wherefore I resolv'd to try my fortune in a Voyage to the *Indies*; accordingly I went aboard a *French* Vessel, resolving to try what Success I should have in Merchandize: I lay'd out all the Money I had, and what I cou'd get out of *England:* And thus set sail from *Brest*[2] for *Martinico*,[3] a Settlement in the *North Indies* belonging to the *French*. The Weather was good enough, nor did we meet with any Accident so considerable, as to be worth repeating, till we got off the *Madera Islands*;[4] and then a vile Pyrate attack'd us: We made what resistance we could; but they soon became our Masters, carry'd us into *Algier*, and there sold us for Slaves. Judge, dear *Galecia*, what a poor Station this was to me, who had indulg'd my self in Delicacy and Luxury. However, of a bad station, it was not the worst; for the Person that bought me was a Widow, whose Husband dy'd a Christian, (as I learnt afterwards) which I suppose, made her more kind to Christian Slaves; for I was not employed in hard laborious work, but to feed the Hogs, fodder the Beasts, take care of the Poultry, &c.

We had another Christian Slave, who had been there some Years, and had by his just Dealings gain'd so far upon our *Mistress*, that she made him Ruler over the other Slaves; he govern'd and was obey'd as if he had been a circumcised Free-man or Native. By little and little this Man and I grew more acquainted; when I found he was a *Roman Catholick Priest;* and by degrees learn'd, that he had secretly converted and baptized our Mistress's Husband before he dy'd, who had recommended him to his Wife, to be good to him, and as soon as she had settled her Affairs, to give him his Liberty and wherewithal to convey him into his own Country, which was *Italy.*

This good Woman had a great Favour for the Christian Religion, but had not Courage to profess it. The truth is, the Severities against it are so great, that it is not to be done without Loss of all things and Hazard of

---

1. **narrow Circumstances:** having little money.
2. **Brest:** seaport on the northwestern tip of France.
3. **Martinico:** the island of Martinique.
4. **Madera Islands:** Madeira Islands off the northwest coast of Africa.

Life, to those that are Natives; But for others, as Traders, and Travellers, &c. they live there thoroughly at their ease, together with their Families; and walk their Processions even in the Streets of *Constantinople*.

The longer I lived here, the more I grew in favour with my *Mistress*; insomuch that I liv'd easie, and as happy as any of her Domesticks that were Free-men. She being thus good to us, we endeavour'd to compensate her Goodness, by giving her a thorough Understanding of our holy Religion. We got her the *New Testament* in the *Turkish* Language; the Story of which is so surprizing, and beyond all to which their *Alcoran*[1] can pretend, that she was almost perswaded to be a Christian. What stuck with her some time, was, she could not tell how to conclude this History Authentick, much less sacred; But we made it plain to her, how it had pass'd through so many Ages, though oppos'd by the greatest of Human Powers, subtilest Knowledge, and its Professors persecuted to Death; yet they never endeavoured by Rebellious Armies to establish their Doctrine; but by patient and meek Suffering, became victorious, and that thus the Kingdom of the Holy Crucified Jesus was establish'd almost throughout the Universe. This we demonstrated to her; as also, how, lastly, the *Ottoman* Empire[2] was set up, and how it began with Rebellion, was carry'd on with Injustice, War and Rapine,[3] and established in a compound Religion, of *Jew, Heretical Christian* and *Old Heathenism*.[4] These, and the like things the good *Italian* Priest made out to her so clear, that she no longer doubted the Truth of the Christian Religion; but durst not venture on it in that Country; but chose rather to make off, and convert her Estate into Money, and fly with us into *Europe*. But here started another Difficulty, that it wou'd look strange in the Eyes of the vertuous *European* Women, for her to come away and travel, by Sea and by Land with two Men, and neither of them her Hus-

---

1. **Alcoran:** the Koran, holy book of Islam.

2. **Ottoman Empire:** Turkish Empire, established 1299, that expanded by conquest in southwestern Asia, northeastern Africa and southeastern Europe.

3. **Rapine:** plunder.

4. **Heretical Christian and Old Heathenism:** a phrase reflecting the common assumption among European Christians that Mohammed had fabricated Islam for his own advantage from Judaism, Nestorian Christianity, and Arab polytheistic beliefs.

band, nor otherwise related to her. Hereupon she propos'd to make one of us Master of that considerable Fortune she possess'd, together with her Person, which, was truly agreeable; not, said she, that I have any affection for either of you, above that of Friendship: For, believe it, all amorous Inclinations, are gone into the Grave with my dear Husband; but for Security of my honour, I make one of you this Proposal. The good Priest answer'd her very respectfully, that He being an *Italian* Priest was vow'd to a single Life. Then she cast her Eyes on me, expecting my Answer; whereupon I threw my self at her Feet, saying, *Madam*, in this gracious Offer, you make me doubly your Slave; therefore I shou'd be the worst of Miscreants,[1] should I abuse your Bounty,[2] in concealing from you a material Truth, which prohibits me from accepting the Honour you offer. Be pleas'd to know, Madam, that I am a married Man, and have a Wife at *London*, so that according to our Christian Law I cannot be Husband to another, till well assured that she is no longer living: But as to that Scruple, you make of going along with us, I beg you to dismiss all apprehensions, and be assured, that you shall be very safe under our Conduct: (For I, *Madam*) will defend your Vertue and Honour to the last drop of my Blood. She paus'd a while, and said, she was extreamly satisfied with our open Sincerity, and was resolv'd to commit her self and her Fortune to our care, and with us take a Voyage into *Europe*, for the sake of that Holy Religion we had taught her; and accordingly, took convenient measures to dispose and make off this her Country-Estate, under pretence of retiring from the Fatigue of Rural Incumbrance.[3]

We concerted with her all due Measures for our Flight into *Europe*. Father *Barnard* (for that was the Name of the Priest) being better acquainted with the *Turkish* Ways and Language, undertook to get an *European* Vessel, which he soon did at the Port of *Algier*; thither we came to him, where we found he had got an *Italian* Ship ready to set sail: We had a fair Gale, a smooth Sea, and a pleasant Serene Air; all

---

1. **Miscreants:** villains, criminals.

2. **Bounty:** generosity.

3. **Incumbrance:** encumbrance; burdensome responsibilities.

which Heaven blessed us with for the sake, perhaps, of this good Woman, who for the cause of Truth, forsook Friends, Kindred, and native Country. When we were got off the *African* Coasts, she press'd to be baptized, which was perform'd by Father *Barnard*, in the Presence of most of the Ship's Crew, who devoutly joyn'd in Prayers and Praises to God. Thus we had a very pleasant Voyage, without Danger or Difficulty. However, there is a little remarkable Story the Captain of the Vessel told us which I cannot omit relating.

The Captain had a very pretty Boy with him, to whom he shewed great Kindness or rather Fondness; which made us at first take him for his Son; but when he undeceiv'd us, we asked him what degree of relation he bore to him? He told us, none at all; but, said he, I will give you a particular Account of this Child.

I had been a Voyage in the Northern Seas, and return'd safe with a good Cargo; when I came ashoar I met with some Merchants who bad me kindly welcome, and ask'd me if I had brought store of such and such Goods; I told them, yes. They desir'd me if it was possible, to help them to some Parcels of them, there being a great Fair or Mart to open at that Place the day following. Hereupon I call'd two or three Sailors, that were come ashoar with me, and told them these Merchants would reward them if they would go to the Ship, and fetch those Parcels of Goods ashoar, which they readily undertook. In the mean time, I went with the Merchants to take a Glass of Wine, bidding the Fellows come to us at such an Hour.

There we stay'd many Hours; we drank, we supp'd, and fretted at our staying so long; we play'd, we slept, still no Return of our Sailors. Thus we passed the Night in Expectation, to no purpose, and in the Morning we departed about our Business. I enquired from place to place wherever I thought of any probability to find them, but could get no intelligence;[1] I got a Boat to convey me to the Ship, not doubting but I

---

1. **intelligence:** information.

should find them there: but the Ship's Crew had neither seen nor heard of them, which greatly amazed me. I then lookt out[1] some Goods, and sent to the *Merchants*, regulated my Affairs in the Ship, and when it was Evening went to Bed, having wanted Rest the Night before: Where lying in my Cabbin between sleep and wake, I heard a Noise of Feet coming down the steps; but I kept my self quiet as if asleep, thereby to prevent any body speaking to me. But as I lay thus, one cry'd, *Master,* three or four times, before I would speak; then opening my Eyes, I saw the Three Sailors that had been sent the Day before to look the *Merchants* Goods; at which, my Anger excited me to use *Seamens* rough Language, in bidding them be gone, and leave me to my Repose. Patience, *good Master,* said they, and hear us; we are no longer *living Mortals:* For we, together with your Boat, were cast away Yesterday, and drowned. To which I replied with Scorn and Anger, that I doubted not but they had been drowned in good *Ale* or *Brandy,* by which their Senses were lost; therefore bid them be gone to sleep, and not stay there to disturb me who was sleepy, through their last Nights Negligence. Indeed, *Master,* said one of them, you judge amiss; for we are truly and really dead, and what you see, are only our Ghosts. Give me your hand, said I, that I may feel. Whereupon one of them held out his Hand, which I caught at, thinking to hold it fast, but I felt nothing; at which I was greatly amazed; nevertheless I did not lose the Power to speak to them; but ask'd them, why they came to trouble me, if they were dead. To which one of them replied, saying, *Master,* you know you owe me so many Months Pay; which Money I desire you to employ in paying my Debts. The next said, that the Money I ow'd him, he desired I would with it put his Boy to School, and when he was big enough, take him with me to Sea. I told him, I knew not how to promise him that, having Children of my own, in particular a Son, who would be of fit Age at the same time. To which he added to his Request, saying, Sir, if you should have a good Voyage next time you put to Sea, will you promise me then

---

1. **lookt out:** examined.

to take him? I told him I would: So this Boy to which you see me so kind, is he; for I had a very good Voyage, and failed not to perform my Promise. I ask'd the third Sailor what he wanted; but the other Two told me, that he was not permitted to speak. After this, they all three bow'd, and vanish'd, which greatly amazed me; for till then, I could not tell what to guess about their being cast away, they look'd so like true substantial Persons.

Thus I have told you all the Relation and Obligation I have to this Boy, excepting his own Obedience and Industry, which is very engaging.

This Relation was very amazing to us, especially being told by the Person who transacted it: For tho' we hear many Stories of Spirits and Apparitions, and greatly attested for Truth; yet we seldom meet with any body that can relate them of their own knowledge, as did this Captain.

Thus, in one Discourse or other, we entertained our selves, sailing with a prosperous Wind, till we arrived at *Venice.* Here our new made Christian was greatly delighted with the Beauty of this City, and in particular, with the Glory of the Churches, and the Solemnity of the Christian Service, which Father *Barnard* took great pains to explain to her; all which she comprehended extreamly well. And now, being in a strange Country, without any Friend or Acquaintance, but us two that had been her Slaves, she was unwilling to travel any farther, but determined to fix there in some Religious House,[1] and in a peculiar manner dedicate her self to the Service of the Almighty. Father *Barnard* soon found out a convenient Place for this her pious purpose. We went with her to the Abbess, who was reported to be (what she really is) a Person of great Prudence and Vertue. We told her Ladyship our Story in few words, and that of our New Convert; at which she seemed greatly pleased, giving Glory to God; adding, that it was her Luck to receive into her House Ladies of Foreign Countries: For, said she, I have a beautiful *English* Woman in my *Convent,* whom we beg'd leave to see, that we might introduce an early Acquaintance between these *two Strangers* of far dif-

---

1. **Religious House:** convent.

ferent Countries. Hereupon my Lady call'd for the *English* Gentlewoman, who approached with great Respect and Modesty. But, good Heavens! How was I surprized, when I found it was my *Chloris!* The first View was surprizing to us both; which my Lady Abbess perceiving, ask'd if we were Relations, or old Acquaintance? At which, *Chloris* cast her self at her Feet, and with a Flood of Tears, in few Words related to her the guilty Acquaintance between us; and how the Distractions in *England* at the *Revolution,* caus'd her to look into her self, and behold with detestation her former Life, which she resolved to change, from Vice to Vertue, from Vanity to Piety, and imitate the holy *Magdalen*[1] as near as she could. In order to which, said she, I resolved to seek a *Convent* wherein to pass my Days in Penance. But supposing you, (addressing her self to me) to be gone into *France,* after your Royal Master, I would not direct my Steps that way, but hither, where you now see me; where I have the Society of holy Virgins, and the Opportunity of pious Performances, which I would not change for all the Riches and Grandeur in the Universe.

I was greatly delighted with this her holy Enterprize and encouraged her in her pious Purposes, and assured her I would pray for her Perseverance; of which she had no need, for she was very firm.

I told her, I was going for *England,* with a resolution to live with my Wife justly, and faithfully, begged her Prayers for my Performance, and so took leave.

I saw her no more; but laid hold on the first Opportunity to come away for *England,* leaving Father *Barnard* to settle and establish his Convert, which I hear, he accomplish'd to all their Satisfactions.

Upon my Arrival in *England,* I found my Wife dead; and the good Woman, notwithstanding all the Wrongs I had done her, had not only forgiven me, but certified the same, by having made me a decent Settlement. And, what is particular, upon due Examination, I found, that this Settlement was made and signed, the very Day I had honestly own'd to the *Turkish* Lady, my having a Wife in *England;* that I cou'd not but

---

1. **Magdalen:** Mary Magdalen; one of the followers of Jesus, interpreted erroneously as a prostitute; see Luke 8:2.

count it proceeded from the Hand of Heaven, for my just Dealings toward that good Lady, at a time when Necessity urged me to transgress the Rules of Honesty and Honour.

This Settlement is now my support; without which I shou'd have been reduc'd to great Distress, for I had lost and spent all I had in the World; in which I verified the Old Proverb,

That a Rolling Stone never gathers Moss,

The Gentleman having finish'd his Story, *Galecia* waited on him to the Stairs head; and at her return, casting her Eyes on the Table, she saw lying there an old dirty rumpled Book,[1] and found in it the following *STORY:*

In the time of the Holy War[2] when Christians from all parts went into the *Holy Land* to oppose the *Turks;* Amongst these there was a certain *English* Knight, who had passed divers Campaigns, to the Advantage of the *Christians;* Detriment to the *Turks,* and Honour to himself; at last, being weary of the War, he return'd home, loaden with Services done his King, Country and Relations: He retired into his own Country, to his paternal Estate, and by way of Thanksgiving to Heaven, he erected a Religious House just by his own Habitation, that he might frequently join with them in their holy Offices: He married a fine young Lady, in order to establish his Family. Thus this pious good Knight liv'd in Tranquillity of Mind and Fortune till things took another turn.

There were two young Gentlemen, who out of a Design of Piety, and the Contempt of the World, placed themselves in this holy Retreat, in order to become Votaries[3] in this *Confraternity.*[4] But as Temptations pursue us in all Stations, so here it happened, that one of these Gentle-

---

1. **Book:** worn by frequent reading, book containing adaptations of popular tales, many of them translated from French or Spanish. Romances with knights from the Crusades, stories of the Moors in Spain, and tales of nuns beseiged by lovers' entreaties to leave their convents abounded in these popular books.

2. **Holy War:** Crusades; series of military expeditions undertaken by European Christians in the eleventh, twelfth, and thirteenth centuries to recover the Holy Land from Moslems.

3. **Votaries:** those who have taken sacred vows.

4. **Confraternity:** brotherhood, religious order.

men, during the time of his Probation,[1] cast an amorous Eye on this Lady, the good Knight's Spouse. How far he endeavour'd to overcome or indulge this guilty Flame, is unknown; but he grew daily more and more passionatly in love; which he durst not discover any way but by obsequious[2] Bows when he happened in her Presence, or to pass by her, or the like; which the Lady return'd with a gracious Mien[3] and Smiling Countenance, being in her nature courteous and affable. But as we are always ready to flatter our selves, so did our Lover, and took the Lady's Courtesie for Kindness, and her smiling Looks for interiour Affection. This he revolv'd in his Thoughts from time to time, and Fancy[4] upon Fancy augmented his Passion. At last, he took the boldness to write her a very amorous Letter; at which the Lady was greatly astonish'd and pro-vok'd, and in her Anger shew'd it to her Husband. The good Knight laughed at the Man's Folly, and advised his Lady to seem easie, and not discourage her Lover, till such time as he should contrive his Punish-ment.

The good Knight did not tell his Superiour his Fault, thinking that would be a continual Disgrace and Blot upon our young Probationer, and likewise a sort of Disgrace to himself and his Lady, that any one should dare to have a Thought so audacious, much more to have the Impudence to own it. Wherefore he resolved to mortifie our young Lover himself with a good dry Basting:[5] so he consulted with his Lady, and engaged her to write a kind Letter to him, and invite him to come to her such a Night, forasmuch as the Knight her Husband would then be from home. This Letter greatly transported our Lover: He wash'd, bath'd, perfum'd himself, and got him fine Linen; and thus equipp'd, he came late in the Night, when all were in bed, and quiet, only one Ser-vant to let him in; who conducted him into the Parlour to the Knight his Master, instead of the Lady's Bed-chamber. Here the Knight shew'd

---

1. **Probation:** trial period before final vows.

2. **obsequious:** submissive, dutiful.

3. **Mien:** air, manner.

4. **Fancy:** imagination, desire.

5. **Basting:** thrashing.

him his Crime, in that vile Letter he had written to his Wife, and forthwith began his Punishment with a good Cudgel, intending no farther Mischief: But how it hapned, is unknown; whether the Knight's Wrath rose to an Extremity, or an unlucky Chance-Blow; but so it was, the Lover was kill'd in the Rencounter.[1]

This put the Knight into a great Consternation, not knowing what to do. The Knight's Servant, persuaded him to lend him his Help, to get the dead Body over the Wall of the *Convent* into their Garden, which joined to the Knight's House, supposing that when the Religious should come in the Morning, and find him there, they would conclude, some sudden Sickness had seized him in that place.

Now, there was one in the *Confraternity*, who was always at variance with this *Robert*, which was kill'd, (the other's Name was *Richard*.) It hapned, that *Richard* had occasion to rise in the Night, and come to the little House, and there found *Robert* placed as aforesaid, *Richard* not thinking any thing, attended a while; then began to call, and bid him come away; but the dead Man not answering, the other thought he mock'd him: At last, being enrag'd at such behaviour, *Richard* took up a Stone, and threw at him, which hit him in such a manner, that he fell down off the Seat. *Richard* finding that he was really dead, believed that it was that Stone had done the Execution. This put him into a great Consternation, being assured that it would pass for Wilful Murther, by reason of that Variance in which they used to live. So casting in his mind what to do, he at length resolved to get the Body over the Wall into the Knight's Court, which accordingly he did, and went and placed it in the Porch of the Knight's House, where he left it.

Now, let us return to the Knight: He and his Man were extreamly uneasie at what had hapned, and by peep of Day open'd the Door, in order to go and listen at the Wall of the *Convent*, thinking to hear something of the dead Body; but, to their surprize, they found it sitting in their own Porch, at first not knowing what to think, whether it was the real Body, or a Spirit; but on Examination, they found it was the Body; and what to do with it they did not know: At last they thought on the following Expedient:

---

1. **Rencounter:** skirmish.

There was in the Stable, a Horse that had served his Master in the War: They saddled this Horse, with his war-like Accoutrements, and fastened the dead Body on him, with a Spear in his hand, and so turn'd the Horse out of the Stable, to run where he would.

Whilst this was in hand, *Richard*, who was in great perplexity what to do on this occasion, believing himself guilty of the Death of *Robert*, and so liable to the Punishment, if discover'd resolv'd to get away; Thereupon he went to the Miller,[1] that belong'd to the *Convent*, and told him in the Name of the Superiour, that he must let him have his Mare to go out this Morning on earnest Business for the *Confraternity*. Thus getting the Miller's Mare, away he rid; but was not got far e'er he came within view of the dead *Robert*, whose Horse ran neighing after the Mare. *Richard* thinking this to be the Ghost of *Robert*, which pursued him for his Murder, cry'd out, O *Robert*, forgive me! I did not Murder you designedly; O forgive me, good *Robert*; But if nothing will appease thy Ghost but my Blood, I am ready to resign my Life to the Stroke of Justice.

By this time the Morning was come fully on, and People being up about their business, seeing this Confusion, seiz'd *Richard*, who stedfastly own'd the Murder of *Robert*, for which he was carried away to Prison; and would, no doubt, have been executed as the Murderer of *Robert*; But the good Knight hasted away to the King, and laid the whole Transaction before his Majesty. The King graciously pardoned the Knight; *Richard* was kindly receiv'd into his *Convent*, and all things went on in good order: But from hence came the Proverb,

We must not strike Robert *for* Richard.

By this time *Galecia's* Maid brought up her Supper; after which she cast her Eyes again on the foresaid little Book, where she found the following Story, which she read through before she went to bed.

The Cause of the *MOORS*[2] Overrunning *Spain*.

KING ——— of *Spain* at his Death, committed the Government of his Kingdom to his Brother *Don* ——— till his little Son should come

---

1. **Miller:** one who mills grain.

2. **MOORS:** Muslim conquerors of Spain in the eighth century, last expelled from Grenada by King Ferdinand and Queen Isabella in 1492.

of Age, to take the Government upon himself. But *Don* ———prov'd a Traytor to his Trust; and by many false Stories invented against the Queen and the Prince, so brought things about, as to make himself be acknowledg'd and Crown'd King of *Spain.* Hereupon the distress'd Queen made her Escape to the *Moors,* imploring that King's Protection; which he not only generously gave her, but also aided her with a formidable Army wherewith to invade *Spain,* in right of the young Prince.

The Usurper of *Spain,* in the mean time, made great Preparations to oppose his Enemy and secure his Kingdom. He had a Noble General, a Person truly worthy in all things, excepting his adhering to the Usurper, and sustaining his unjust Pretentions: This General he sent with a well-appointed Army, to oppose the *Moors;* where we will leave him for the present, and return to what passed at Court.

This General had a very beautiful Daughter, whom the King took into his Protection in a pecular manner, both for her Father's Sake, and her own, promising her Father to marry her to one of the chief Grandees of *Spain,* if not to a Prince of the Blood Royal; in order to which, he plac'd her in a noble Appartment in the Royal Palace, gave her Equipage and Attendance suitable to a young Princess, that her Beauty might appear with greater Lustre to draw the Eyes and Hearts of those of the highest Rank and Quality. But the Success prov'd otherwise; this over-doing undid all: For every body began to look upon her as one prepared to be the King's Mistress, not the Wife of any Subject. Her Jewels, Riches, and Grandeur were look'd upon as the Garlands to dress her up a Sacrifice to the King's Pleasure. Now whither these Whispers first put it into his thoughts, or that it was his Design all along, is unknown; but the event makes it look more like the latter: For he began to make his amorous Inclinations known to her, with the utmost Gallantry and Assiduity,[1] which she rejected with true Vertue and Modesty, beseeching his Majesty to dismiss her the Court, and give her leave to retire into a *Convent,* or any distant Country-retreat, where her Vertue and Honour might be secure, and his Majesty released from the Sight of that Face which was a Snare to his Honour and Christian Profession, with divers

---

1. **Assiduity:** diligence.

Arguments from time to time to the same purpose. All which served to render her the more amiable, and the more inflam'd that wicked Passion, which already was become unextinguishable; insomuch that he resolv'd *bon-gre mal-gre*[1] to enjoy her; and accordingly executed his wicked Resolution. It is not recorded whether he subborn'd[2] her Slaves, or used open Force; but 'tis certain he had not her Consent; but on the contrary, she was so enraged in her mind, that she thought on nothing but revenge; in order to which she disguised herself in form of a Slave and so went directly to the Army, to her Father; where casting her self at his feet, she told him the whole Indignity: Whereupon the General summoned many of the principal Officers of the Army, to hear the Story of this young Lady his Daughter! who upon her Knees begg'd them, for the sake of their own Children, to repair the Dishonour done to her and her Family. This so touch'd the General, and those noble Officers about him, that with one accord they resolv'd on a Revolt, and to joyn with the *Moors,* to dethrone the Usurper, and establish their young lawful King. In this state we will leave the Army, and return to Court.

The King having news of this Revolt, was greatly embarrass'd, not knowing which way to turn himself: He endeavour'd to raise new Troops; but alas to little purpose; for the Hearts of the People were estranged, and the vile Act which caused the General, and other Persons of Honour to draw the Army into a Revolt, opened the Eyes of all, even his chief Adherents, both in Town, Country and Court, so that he was reduced to the utmost Distress, being contemned by his Servants, abhorr'd by his People, and the Army in open rebellion. In the midst of these *Dilemma's,* like King *Saul*[3] of old, he betook himself to consult the Devil.

There was a Hill on which stood a strong-built Tower; But by whom, or when erected, or how it came there, no Record, or Tradition, gave

---

1. **bon-gre mal-gre:** whether for good or ill (French).

2. **subborn'd:** suborned, bribed.

3. **Saul:** first king of the ancient Hebrews, he consulted the Witch of Endor to aid him in battle; see 1 Sam. 28:7.

account; only in general, 'twas called the *Devil's Tower.* The Entrance was so fast lock'd and barricaded, as render'd it very difficult to open, if attempted, which was never done, as being supposed a dangerous Enterprize. However, in this great Exigence to which this Usurper was reduced, he resolves to open this Place, be the event what it will; which was perform'd with great difficulty, and divers Persons entered, who were immediately suffocated, and fell down dead; which was surprizing at first; but on second thoughts, it was easily concluded to be the unwholsome Vapours, so long shut up from Air, which caus'd that sudden Stop of the vital Spirits.

Wherefore it was resolved to let it stand open a few Days, placing a Guard to prevent any body's Entrance. In the mean time, provision was made of many *Flambeaux*[1] and *Torches,* not only for the Service of their Light, but to help extenuate those poysonous Particles there gather'd by means of the want of Air. Thus they entered the Habitation of the Devil, or the *Devil's Tower,* vulgarly so called.

They went but a little space till it seem'd to wind on both hands, but they struck towards the left; where they beheld with great Horror a vast Cauldron full of Blood, which kept continually boiling, but no Fire was to be perceived: At the same time they heard a strange Noise of a distinct Thump, perform'd in exact time and measure. Then going a little farther, they met two Monsters dragging one another, who were lash'd on by other Monsters behind them, making them cry and howl in a dismal manner: For they were both to be put into that Cauldron of boiling Blood. The Passengers stood aside to give them way, and then pass'd on, meeting divers frightful Figures, whether real Monsters grown out of the foul Particles of that odious Enclosure, or Phantoms, or Spectres, they could not tell: But, amongst the many Yellings and Cries which they heard; the continual Thump ceased not. Sometimes they heard a Noise like the Falling of Water; and going on they perceiv'd a Machine like a vast Mill which was a most horrible Sight; for the Grist[2] that was here ground, seem'd to be Human Creatures. At another place was a

---

1. **Flambeaux:** torches.

2. **Grist:** normally, grain that has been ground or pulverized.

vast fiery Furnace, wherein were many Monsters marching about, whether *Salamanders,*[1] or what, they could not tell. There were many more strange and monstrous Appearances, not easily to be remember'd, much less to be describ'd; nor could any body conceive the true natural Cause of these Productions, whether a subterraneous Fire heated that Red Liquor, which appear'd like Blood, (which Liquor, perhaps, was only Water, so coloured by passing through Red Earth) no body could conclude; tho' every one made their several Conjectures thereon.

After many strange and astonishing Appearances, they came at last to a Gate, whereon were written in great Letters the following Lines:

> *Mortal, whoe'er thou art, beware,*
> *Thou go not in this Place too far:*
> *Yet bear this Warning in thy Mind,*
> *Be sure thou dost not look behind.*[2]

When they had read these Verses, they were not only much frighted, but found the Words reduced them to great Difficulties, seeming to forbid them to go back: For they could not do that, without looking behind; and then again, importing Danger if they went forward. They weighed these Considerations a while, till the King's Inclinations, together with their own Curiosity, turned the Balance to a Resolution of entring in, and proceeding farther. They soon conquered the Difficulties of getting the Gate open; so on they went, and found themselves within the Body of a large round Room, which was the *Tower* that appeared above-ground, the rest being a subterraneous Circle round this *Tower.*

In the midst of this Place stood a great Image of TIME, with a huge long Club in his Hand, which he raised and let fall in due measure; and this caused that astonishing Thump which they heard from the first Moment of their Entry. They kept in their mind, that they must not

---

1. **Salamanders:** fabled lizard-like creatures that live in fire but are never consumed.

2. **Mortal . . . behind:** recalls the legend of Orpheus, who lost his wife Eurydice forever by breaking his promise not to look back at her as he led her from the Underground; see Virgil (70–19 B.C.), *Georgics* 4.453 and Ovid (43 B.C.–A.D. 17), *Metamorphoses* 10.1.

look behind them, so resolved to walk round the Place; where on the Walls they found divers Inscriptions, all importing Warnings, Menaces and Miseries to those that came there. In reading which, they sometimes stopt to consider the Purport and dubious Meanings of these uncouth Writings. At last being got round a good part of the Circle, they cast their Eyes on the Shoulders of the Image, and there found the following Words, which the King read with an audible Voice:

> *All Tribulation shall they find,*
> *Who needs will look on me behind.*

At the reading hereof they all fell into a great Consternation, especially the King. They now very well understood what was meant by those Words written on the Gate, *Not look behind;* which they had mistaken, thinking they were prohibited looking behind themselves, or turning back the same way. Thus, the Devil's Oracles are always double and delusive, and such are all his Temptations, as this wretched King and all his Adherents soon afterwards found.

They hasted out of the *Tower* as fast as they could, fastned and barricaded it up close, as they found it, and so left it. The King returned home greatly troubled, and more embarrass'd now than ever. The next Day the *Tower* was totally sunk into the Ground, and no sign left to demonstrate there had ever been such an Edifice. Thus the little Story ended, without telling what Misery befel the King and Kingdom, by the *Moors,* who over ran the Country for many Years after. To which, we may well apply the Proverb,

> *Who drives the Devil's Stages,*
> *Deserves the Devil's Wages.*

The reading this Trifle of a Story detained *Galecia* from her Rest beyond her usual Hour; for she slept so sound the next Morning, that she did not rise, till a Lady's Footman came to tell her, that his Lady and another or two were coming to breakfast with her: Whereupon she hastned to get her self and her Tea-Table ready for her Reception.

It was not many Moments e'er they arriv'd, and the good friendly Lady presented one to *Galecia,* asking her if she remember'd this her old Friend, after so many Years Absence? Which at first a little surpriz'd her;

but she soon call'd her to mind. Ah, said *Philinda,* (for that was her Name) I do not wonder you could not know me, my Afflictions having made me almost a Stranger to my self: To which the good Lady replied, That whilst the Tea Kettle was on the Fire, she might tell *Galecia* her short Story e'er it boyl'd: But *Philinda* beg'd the Lady to pardon the Confusion which might occur in this Relation, and recount it to *Galecia* her self, her Ladyship knowing every the minutest Circumstance. To which the good Lady accorded. *Philinda,* in the mean time seeing the little Old Book lying on the Table, in which *Galecia* had been reading over-Night, took the same, and went into the next Room, and left them to their Story, being willing to be out of the hearing of those Calamities, in which she had been so great a Sufferer.

The *Story* of *Philinda,*
Related by the Lady *Allgood.*

This Gentlewoman (said my Lady) had out of her Frugality saved a little private purse to her self, unknown to her Husband; a way which many an excellent good Wife takes, whether to have something of their own fancied Property, and more directly at their Service, or only to have a little Cash to look on, matters not; but thus it happened: There was a Gentleman that wanted a little Sum of forty or fifty Pounds, wherewith to make up a Payment of Money unknown to his Wife. *Philinda* being this Gentleman's Friend, he applied himself to her to help him to this Sum; to which she accorded, and lent him the Money privately.

After a while she having occasion to dispose thereof advantageously, writ a Letter desiring him to meet her at the *Abby,*[1] where she would be at Morning-prayers. His Wife hapned to receive the Note, and had the Curiosity to open it, and was seiz'd with a Jealousie, which destroy'd her Quiet. However, she made it up again, gave it her Husband without taking any notice; he went to the Church as appointed, and there he met with this his Friend; she whispered to him, that she had now an Opportunity to dispose of her Money to advantage, and therefore desired him to help her to it if he could, without too great Inconve-

---

1. **Abby:** Westminster Abbey.

niency. He told her, that he had the Money ready at home, and would go and fetch it, and come back to her by such time as prayers were ended. So said, so done: He went home, and fetch'd it, and came back to her e'er the Congregation was dispers'd. They went into a publick House[1] to pay and receive this Money: But as ill luck would have it, chop'd[2] into a House of ill Repute,[3] and so unlucky it was, that in that critical Juncture there came Constables and Officers of Justice to search for Lewd People; and finding him and her together by themselves, carried her before a Justice of Peace: Where, she not reflecting on the Consequence, told a wrong Name, being loth to be known, in that odd Circumstance; and happen'd on a Name that had lately been before the same Justice. Wherefore, without delay he sent her to *Bridewell.* Thus was this good Woman brought into Distress, Disgrace, Horror and the utmost Confusion, before she was aware; For at their being first seiz'd, she desir'd the Gentleman to slip away, and take no notice of her; but to leave her without concern, as if she had been a common Woman; thinking to deal well enough with the Constables: For all that she aim'd at was but to keep it from her Husband's Knowledge: But matters going on as I told you before, she was reduced to this Distress and shameful Condition, not knowing which way to turn her self, to whom to address, or what method to take for her Enlargement: She thought, if she told her true Name, and sent for her Husband, she could hope for nothing but to be abandon'd, if not prosecuted by him as an Adulteress. To remain there, and undergo the Rigour of the Law, allotted for such Offenders, was hard, or rather insupportable for an innocent Person: Besides, it could not be; for her Absence from her House would soon stir up her Husband's Enquiry to find her out.

Thus she weigh'd every thing, but could pitch upon nothing that had any Face of probability, to do her any Service; At last, she resolv'd on the plain Truth, that being generally the best Advocate for Innocence; and so sent for her Husband, and told him the true State of the Case: But

---

1. **publick House:** tavern.

2. **chop'd:** entered hastily.

3. **House of ill Repute:** brothel.

alas, it was all Words to a Storm, or the North Wind. He resolv'd, and actually put in execution the utmost that Law could do in such a case; Not only being content to abandon her to the Disgrace which would naturally ensue; but persecuted her from Place to Place, from Prison to Prison; so that Poverty, Prosecution and Punishment of all sorts, was her lot; nay, even her own Friends and Relations were her Enemies, so grossly foul was the Appearrance of this Transaction.

Thus this good Gentlewoman suffer'd with great patience, her manifold Afflictions, attended with the utmost foul Disgrace; But good Heaven at last made way for her Justification. The Gentleman that had borrow'd the money of her, had been hurried by his superiour Officer to his Post in *Flanders*.[1] Which was the Cause he could not appear in her behalf, when things came to that great extremity. This Gentleman receiv'd a cruel Wound in some Skirmish, which happen'd there; so that the Surgeons despair'd of his Recovery. Hereupon he call'd some of his Friends, Gentlemen of undoubted Honour and Probity, and begg'd them to receive the Attestation of a dying Man; which was, that *Philinda* was a perfect vertuous Woman, to the utmost degree that he knew of her; and that for his own Part, he never had a thought towards her, other than towards a Mother or a Sister; And so he related to them the whole occasion and manner of that Transaction, which had made so much Noise in the World, calling the Gentleman to witness, to whom he had paid the Money he had thus borrow'd of *Philinda,* and had been present when she lent it to him; without which the said Gentleman could not have made his Campaign. This he charged them all on the Word of a dying Man, to report to *Philinda's* Husband and Friends; which they did with the utmost Sincerity.

Now this News, with the great danger the Gentleman was in, rous'd his Wife out of her Jealousie or *Delirium;* she went to *Philinda's* Husband, beg'd pardon for all the trouble she had caused him and his Wife, declar'd how she had intercepted the Letter, made them be dog'd to that place where the Constable found them, and that she sent him there to seize them, and at the same time caused her Husband to be commanded

---

1. **Post in Flanders:** military posting in the Low Countries.

into *Flanders;* For all which she profess'd her self truly sorry: and earnestly beg'd, that as she had contriv'd their Separation, she might cause their Re-union: which she was willing to cement with her Tears and constant Vows offer'd to Heaven for their Happiness.

Thus was the married Couple happily reconcil'd, and have liv'd together ever since in great Tranquillity. The Gentleman recovered of his Dangerous Wound, came home to pertake of, and increase their Happiness by reiterated Attestations of the Innocence of all the proceeding. On the other side, his Wife promis'd never to intercept his or any body's Letters, perceiving now it was not only a great Indignity and Breach of good manners, but a Crime that deserves a Punishment, equal to that of picking Pockets, breaking a Lock, or the like.

Philinda and her Husband resolv'd to have no more separate Purses each from other, whereby to cause Contention. Thus were these two Families reunited, and the Cause of their Disturbance wholly remov'd; in which the Proverb was fulfill'd,

After a Storm comes a Calm.

Breakfast being ready the Company call'd *Philinda* from her old Book, in which she was much engag'd, in particular in one Story, which (said she) being extraordinary, I will repeat to the Company as soon as we have done our Tea, which accordingly she did, as follows:

Philinda's Story out of the *Book.*[1]

At the time when the *Moors* invaded *Spain,* there were many Irregularities committed which are usual wherever the Seat of War is carried. By this means a beautiful young Nun, enter'd into an Intrigue with a Cavalier, of the Army, who found means, notwithstanding all the Care and Circumspection of those Places; I say, they found means to contract an Affection; nor did they stop there, but promis'd personal Enjoyment, and to live together as married People, if our Nun could find a way to get out of her Cloyster.

Now she that could suffer her self to consent to the Temptation of the Flesh, the Devil was at hand to help her through, and found a

---

1. **Story out of the Book:** the story closely resembles Aphra Behn's *The History of the Nun; or, The Fair Vow-Breaker* (1689).

means for her Escape, to the utter breach of her Solemn Religious Vow of Chastity. Thus they went away together, were married, and liv'd in the midst of Plenty and conjugal Happiness, till her Husband's Devoirs[1] called him to the Army.

At his going he left a Friend to consolate and assist her in his Absence; who truly perform'd the part of a good Man in all things within his power: The Army was encamp'd far off, and Correspondence difficult, which was a perpetual Affliction to her; many Battels and Skirmishes were fought, without any News from him: At last, some of his own Regiment, sent her word that he was kill'd. This was an inexpressible Grief to her: She liv'd many Days and Weeks in the utmost Disquietude, using all means possible to know the truth; but he was Universally believed to be dead, though his Body was never found amongst the Slain, nor yet heard of amongst the Prisoners. The Friend, that was left with her, was no less afflicted, and bore a true share of Grief with our disconsolate Relict: But Time, which devours all things, by degrees drank up the Tears of the Widow, and so far dissipated the Grief of the Friend, that he began to be sensible of her Charms, not only those of her Beauty, but was touch'd with that tender Affection which she daily express'd for the Loss of his good Friend her Husband: This Esteem by degrees ripened into Affection, and from Affection to Passion, till he could no longer resist making his Addresses to her. How she received these Addresses at first, or by what degrees or steps he climbed into her Affection, is yet unknown; but so it was, in some time they were married together, and lived happy enough, till the suppos'd dead Husband return'd, which was after they had been married but a few Weeks. We will not descant[2] either on the Cause of his Silence or Absence, whether dangerous Wounds, Imprisonment, or what else happ'ned; but he thought to bring her a pleasing Surprize in bringing himself into her Arms: But, alas! the Appearance of his Person was much more disagreeable, than if it had been his Ghost. However, she conceal'd her Sentiments, and receiv'd him kindly. After the first mutual Caresses were over, he said he was weary, having travelled far that Day; therefore

---

1. **Devoirs:** duties; military obligations or orders.
2. **descant:** comment upon at length.

would go lie down on a Couch, in the next Room, He being thus gone to Repose his poor weary Body, she in the midst of her Anxiety, took a wicked thought in her head, and resolved his death, before her other Husband should return; for he was gone abroad. This execrable[1] Thought she indulg'd, till he being fast asleep, she put in Execution, and murder'd this unfortunate Gentleman; even him, for whose sake she had broke through the Laws of God and her Country, dishonour'd her self and her Family; Him, for whom she had shed a Flood of Tears, utter'd millions of Sighs and Lamentations, and was for divers Months the most disconsolate Creature living; yet had the Cruelty now to shed his Blood, who had given her no provocation; but on the contrary, had fatigu'd himself to a great degree with travelling far that day, to arrive at her Embraces.

No doubt, but her thoughts were greatly perplex'd at what she had done, and what to do when the other Husband should come home; which we will leave to the Consideration of any that shall hear the Story.

When the Husband came, she receiv'd him with a frighted disconsolate Kindness; which he perceiving, press'd her to know the Cause. After some Sighs and Tears, she told him, that Excess of Love to him had made her act the most wicked and detestable of all Crimes, and thereupon opened the Door where the poor murder'd Body lay; which Sight fill'd him with the utmost Horror and Detestation. He look'd upon her as a bloody and a hateful Monster, never to be forgiven by God or Man; then again turning his Wrath upon himself, for having supplanted his Friend, before greater assurances of his death, he lamented him, reproach'd her, hated himself; she, on the other side, sigh'd, wept, tore her Hair, suffer'd convulsive Agonies, that between 'em, they acted a miserable Scene of Horror.

After the first Efforts of their Grief and Distraction were discharg'd, they began to consider what was to be done. The Gentleman thought it was cruel to expose her to the Hand of Justice, for a Crime she had

---

1. **execrable:** abominable.

committed for his sake, though in its self most enormous; beside, his Affection for her, joyn'd with Compassion, for the Foible of the Sex, he resolv'd on the following Measures: Which were, that in the dead of the Night, he himself would carry the murther'd Body to the River, which ran just by the Side of the Town, and cast it therein. This Resolution they put in practice; first drying up his bloody Wounds as well as they could, then wrapt him in a Sheet, and the Gentleman took him on his Back, and went softly down Stairs; but as she was following, she perceived a Foot hanging out, and immediately took a Needle and Thread, and sew'd it into the Sheet: But in her Fright, by mistake, took hold of the Gentleman's Coat, and so fastned that to the Sheet. He went on with his Load, got safe to the River, and with a hasty Cast, threw it off; but the Sheet being fastned to his Coat as before-said, the Weight of the Dead Body in that sudden Motion, drew in the living Man also; where he was soon drowned, not being in the least able to help himself, by means of his being fastned to the dead Body.

Next day these two Bodies being found thus fastned together, were soon known, Officers of Justice came to search the House, examine, and apprehend the Family; But the miserable Lady, soon confess'd, and told the Story, for which she received Punishment from the Hands of Justice, and in which she fulfilled the Proverb.

Marry in haste, and Repent at leisure.

The Ladies, having thus pass'd the greatest part of the Forenoon, resolv'd to go take a walk in the *Park*, to get them a good Stomach[1] to their Dinner. Here they found much Company, it being a very bright fine Winter's Day; and according to custom there were divers sorts of Dresses, Figures and Shapes of Persons, and as many different Discourses; Some admiring the Fineness of the Weather, others saying it was not natural at that time of Year; some praising this Lady for her excellent Fancy in her Dress, whilst others were blam'd for not suiting their Dress to their Complexion; one praised this Lady's Manteau-

---

1. **Stomach:** appetite.

maker,[1] another blam'd that Lady's Seamstress; some commended the
Chocolate they had for breakfast, others complaining of the Oysters
they had eat over Night; some talking of the *Opera*, some of the Play;
how generous my Lord such an one was to his New Mistress; how glorious she appeared in the Box; some talking of what such a Lady won at
Ombre, or lost at *Basset*;[2] Who was kept by the one, and who was jilted
by the other; Who had luck in the Lottery, and who lost in the *South-
Sea*;[3] Who had hang'd themselves for Love, and who drown'd themselves for Debt. Good Heavens! said our Ladies, who is there that talks
of any good or moral Vertues? Who serves God or their Neighbour,
who prays with Devotion, or relieves the Poor; who instructs the Ignorant, or comforts the Afflicted; who protects the Fatherless, or supports
the oppressed Widow; who visits the Sick, buries the Dead, or covers
the Naked with a Garment? Many more things of this kind they were
repeating, till they perceiv'd a pretty elderly Gentlewoman following
behind them, who for some time had over-heard their Discourse; for
which she humbly beg'd their pardon, telling them it was not the effect
of Curiosity, but that she had been a true Sharer in those Afflictions,
caus'd by being abandon'd by Friends and persecuted by Enemies; But
the Almighty had been her Assistance; that she might with great truth
repeat those Words, *When my Father and Mother forsook me, the Lord
cared for me.*[4] The Ladies being a little weary of walking, and very curious to hear the Gentlewoman's Adventures, betook themselves to a Seat,
desired her Company, and to relate her Story.

The *Story* of *Mrs. Goodwife*.

In the late Troubles of *Ireland,* said she, my Husband betaking himself to
King *James's* Party, we were stript of all we had, our Estate was forfeited,[5]

---

1. **Manteau-maker:** maker of cloaks and dresses.

2. **Basset:** fashionable card game.

3. **South-Sea:** trading company that collapsed in 1720 after a speculative frenzy over its stock.

4. **When . . . me:** see Psalms 29:10.

5. **King James's Party . . . forfeited:** Irish supporters of James II were stripped of their lands
and goods by Williamites.

our House plunder'd, even to our wearing Cloaths; so that we were reduced to the utmost Exigence.[1] Being thus distressed, we came away for *England;* and I being of an *English* Family, came amongst my Friends, to consult and take measures with them, what course to take to help us in this our Extremity. But, alas, being reduced to a deplorable Condition, with two small Children, we found but cold Reception, there having been several Changes in our Family; some Friends being dead, others grown up and married, which caused new Methods, new Establishments, *&c.* However, by their help we came to *London,* thinking to get away to *France;* but when we came hither, we heard that the King had a greater Burthen of poor Followers than he knew well how to sustain. We staid here some time, considering what to do, or which way to direct our Course, endeavouring to get some Place or Business for my Husband, or my self, till we had spent all we had in the World, and all that we could borrow of any Friend or Acquaintance; insomuch that we were forced to go often supperless to Bed. In the Morning, when our poor Babes wak'd, one cry'd, *Mamma, me want Breakfast, me is hungry;* the other cry'd, *Pappa, me want a Bit of Bread, me is hungry.*

These poor Infants thus pealing[2] in our Ears, my Husband one Morning leap'd out of Bed, saying, he had lived long enough, since he heard his Children cry for Bread, and he had none to give 'em. I seeing him in this desperate Condition, leap'd out also, put on my Cloaths, and pray'd him to look to the Children, whilst I went to seek out for something.

Thus, down stairs I went, not knowing whither, or what about. But as I pass'd in the Entry, my Landlady called to me, as she was in her Parlour, saying, Mistress, I believe you are going to the Baker's; pray do so much as bring me a Loaf with you. I went accordingly, and desir'd a Loaf for my Landlady, which the Baker's Wife delivered to me immediately. I stood a while looking on the Shop full of Bread; but had not Courage to beg, nor Money to buy. Whether the Mistress

---

1. **Exigence:** urgent need.

2. **pealing:** appealing noisily; crying.

saw, I look'd with a longing Eye, and a needy Stomach, I know not; but she said, Mistress, I believe you want a Loaf for your self; To which I answer'd with flowing Tears, yes; but I have no Money to pay for one; then the good Woman replied, In the Name of God, take one, and pay for it when you can; and gave me a good large Loaf, so I came away joyfully. Of this, with a little Salt, my Husband, my self and Children made a comfortable Repast, washing it down with clear Element.[1]

As soon as we had thus refresh'd our selves, the good Baker's Wife, who had taken notice of my dejected Behaviour, sent a Servant with some Flower[2] to make us a Pudding,[3] a Piece of Meat to make the Children some Broth, together with a Pound of Butter, in which was stuck an Half-Crown Piece, to buy us Drink. I was transported at the good Woman's Charity, got on the Pot with speed, and made us a sumptuous Meal, such a one as we had not tasted in many Days. When this our plentiful Dinner was over, I began to consider which way I might dispose of my Half Crown to make us live for the time to come: Which, you will say, was a very small Sum wherewith to begin any Business, for a Livelihood.

After revolving divers things in my Mind, I at last took it in my thoughts to go buy a little Wheat, and boyl[4] it, and try to sell Bowls of Wheat; which accordingly I did, and next Day when my Wheat was ready, I went with it, with a Basket on my Arm. I must confess, I had Confusion to knock at Doors, and ask if they wanted a Bowl of Wheat; and what was an additional Mortification, when I took off my Gloves to deliver my Merchandize, my Hands discover'd that I was not brought up to such Business; insomuch, that the Servants would sometimes take notice, and say, that these Hands look'd more like the Hands of one used to sit in a Drawing Room and play with a Fan, than of one who sells things about the Streets. How far these kind of Complements

---

1. **clear Element:** water.

2. **Flower:** flour.

3. **Pudding:** a bread-like concoction.

4. **boyl:** boil.

might have given me Vanity at another time, I know not; but now they were a true Mortification; for nothing made this humble Task sit more easie, than the Belief, that no body knew me. However, I got as much by this Day's Industry, as bought us Food the next. Thus I went on, daily leaving my Husband to take care of the Children, and get the Wheat prepar'd for the ensuing Day. And thus did my Husband content himself in this poor Employment, for the sake of his dear Babes, who himself had been bred a Gentleman.

In my going to good Houses to sell my Wheat, I got many a Piece of boyl'd, bak'd, and roast Meat, which I brought home to my hungry Children; nor did my Husband refuse his Share. By degrees frequenting those Houses, I got acquainted with the Maids, so that they trusted me to sell old things for them, paying me so much in the Shilling, as I could get for them. Thus I fell into a little way of Merchandize, selling at one House what I got at another. The Cook maid at one House wanted this thing, the House-maid that; the Chamber maid this thing to sell here, the Nurse had that thing to buy there; so that by degrees I fell into a pretty Trade of this kind of buying and selling old Cloaths, and grew so skill'd in it, that we took a Shop; and by such time as our Daughter was grown up, we had a Portion[1] to dispose of her handsomely in the City. Our Son is our Assistant in this our Trade, and is our Book-keeper. Thus Ladies (said she) we have made out the Proverb,

Something doing, something coming.

They were all thankful to the Gentlewoman for her Relation; and the Lady invited her, with the others, to dinner; but she excus'd her self to her Ladyship, it being inconsistent with some Affairs she had at that time. The Lady and her Friends, together with *Galecia,* went with my Lady to dinner where we will suppose, they regaled themselves very well; together with my Lady's Husband, and his Friends till the coming of the *Punch*-Bowl, drove the Ladies into the Drawing-room, where the Tea-table attended their approach. They were scarcely seated when a Lady came to make my Lady *Allgood* a Visit; (for that was our Lady's

---

1. **Portion:** used as dowry, daughter's share of parents' estate.

Name) who receiv'd her with Transports of Kindness, after a very long Absence, she being just come out of *France*, where she had been many Years following the Fortune of King *James*. They made her many Congratulations for her safe Arrival, and divers Inquiries after the Health and Circumstances of their Friends and Acquaintance in those Parts, and the Condition of the Court of St. *Germain's*, since the Death of the King.[1] To which she answer'd, that they all acted a melancholy Scene. However, they had this Advantage, the Change of Fortune brought every one to a right understanding of themselves, and a due Consideration of others. The Poor are become respectful, the Rich (if such there be) compassionate, Inferiours are humble, Superiours are affable, the Women vertuous, the Men valiant, the Matrons prudent, Daughters obedient, Fathers obliging, Sons observant, Patrons readily assisting, Supplicants gratefully accepting; whilst true Piety and Devotion are the Cement of all the other Vertues, to build up a holy Court, like those we read of in the time of *Constantine*[2] or *Theodosius*.[3] In short, there is a Pattern, by which every one may square their Lives, so as to make vertuous and honest Figures amongst Mankind, and in some degree honourable also, Vertue and Honour being inseparable Companions.

The Ladies proceeded to ask her, if she had had a happy Voyage by Sea and Land, without any dangerous Adventures? To which she replied, that all was very easie and happy; only in the Coach between *Paris* and *Callis*[4] there was a Lawyer, who told us a Story carrying something of Horror along with it; which being short, if your Ladyship please, I will relate it: It is something of the *Portugueze Nun*,[5] whose

---

1. **King:** James II died in 1701.

2. **Constantine:** Flavius Valerius Aurelius Constantinus, called "The Great" (ca. 280–337), Roman emperor who adopted Christianity.

3. **Theodosius:** Roman emperor, called "the Great" (ca. 346–395), he made peace with the Goths.

4. **Callis:** Calais, France.

5. **Portugueze Nun:** Several popular works were published on the Continent, which were later translated into English, including *Five Love-Letters from a Nun to a Cavalier* (1678) trans. Roger L'Estrange (1616–1704); *Seven Portugese Letters: being a second part to the Five Love-Letters from a Nun to a Cavalier* (1683), trans. Roger L'Estrange; and Delarivier Manley (ca. 1663–1724), *Letters, to which is added a letter from a supposed nun in Portugal to a gentleman in France, in imitation of the Nun's five letters in print, by Col. Pack* (1696).

amorous Letters have been the Entertainment of all the World. Her Story must needs be acceptable, replied the Ladies, wherefore, pray proceed to oblige us with the relation of it.

The *Story* of the *Portugueze Nun.*

This Young Lady was bred in a *Convent,* as are most in those Countries, the *Convents* being the general Places of Education for all Children of Distinction. When she came to Years of Maturity, her Parents took her home, in order to establish her in the World, by marrying her to some worthy Gentleman; of which there was one in the Neighbourhood, who greatly coveted this Espousal: But all the Persuasions of her Parents, joyn'd with the Gentleman's Courtship, availed nothing; she persisted in her Resolution of becoming a *Religious Dame.* Her Mother endeavour'd as much as possible, to extirpate these Thoughts, by carrying her into Company, buying her fine Cloaths, introduc'd her at Court, Comedies, *Opera's,* Balls, Masques,[1] and all sorts of Diversion, which diverts the greatest Part of Human kind: But nothing moved this young Lady from her Religious Purpose. For all these kinds of Glories seemed to her as Folly and Vanity, a Dream without any solid Satisfaction: That in the end, her Parents consented to her Return into the *Convent.*

Here she performed all the Duties of her Novitiate with perfect Obedience, to the satisfaction of the Abbess and all the Religious, that she was receiv'd, and in due time, profess'd a Member of their Holy Society, with Joy and Content: In which she behaved her self with great Prudence, Vertue and Piety, for divers Years, till the great War[2] between *France* and the *Allies* broke out. Then it was, that a certain military Officer came to visit a Relation of his in the *Convent,* and brought with him a *French Chevalier,* who was an *Hugonot,*[3] and came out of curiosity with his Friend, to see the manner of making a Visit at the Grate.[4] Now, as it is not permitted for any young Lady or Nun, to receive Visitors

---

1. **Masques:** dramatic entertainments, staged at court or in the homes of aristocrats, involving dances and disguises.

2. **great War:** probably the War of the League of Augsburg (1689-98).

3. **Hugonot:** Huguenot; French Protestant.

4. **Grate:** large iron lattice-worked door, permitting communication but preventing entry.

there, without some Companion, this our foresaid Nun was appointed to accompany the other. And, lo, this was the fatal Moment of our Nun's Ruin: For she no sooner saw the Beau *Hugonot*, but she felt an Emotion she had never been sensible of before.

When she came to know he was an *Hugonot*, she thought it was Compassion that had disturbed her Interiours, to think that so fine a Person should live in a wrong Religion. He, on the other side, was troubled, to see so beautiful a young Lady thus confined, out of a whimsical Conceit of devotion (as his Principles termed it.) Amongst these Thoughts, divers Glances shot each against other, and forbidden Sighs met in a sort of soft Union; whilst the other Couple of Friends talked of things indifferent, appertaining to the common Rode of Friendship. In this way they continued till the Bell called our Nuns to Choir and our Gentlemen to their respective Habitations.

We will not pretend to know or guess, by what steps of Fancy or Cogitation they climb'd up to an extream Passion, such as her printed Letters demonstrate, or how they first discover'd their amorous Sentiments each to other, things extreamly difficult in those Places: But so it was, that he desir'd to be inform'd of the Catholick Religion, pretending that no body gave him so rational an Account, and produced such cogent Arguments as this Lady. By this means he was permitted to have frequent access to the Grate, where she not only entertain'd him with many devout Discourses, and solid Arguments, but gave him Books to read, which he return'd in due time, giving an account of what he read, in those Books; what touch'd, and what displeas'd him. This manner of proceeding blinded the Understanding of those that accompanied her to the Grate, and it is to be suppos'd, that by means of these Books lent and return'd, Letters were convey'd backward and forward to each other; not only those in Print, but divers others, by which means (no doubt) her Escape was contriv'd; which was accomplish'd in this odd manner: an Opportunity offering when one of those Religious Dames died and was interr'd, that Night, before the Vault was made up, she took the pains to lift out the Body and lay it in her own Bed, and then plac'd a Train of Fire,[1] which she knew would catch and set fire of the Bed by

---

1. **Train of Fire:** a path of flammables which the fire would follow.

such time as she could be got over the Wall, by Ladders of Ropes there provided by her Lover, (if one may so call the Devil's Engineer.) Thus she left the House to be burnt with all the holy Inhabitants, therein contain'd: But Providence so order'd it, that it was discover'd before 'twas too late, and extinguish'd before much hurt, only that Cell with its Moveables was destroy'd, and the Body so disfigur'd, that it could not be known, but was much lamented by the good Dames, really supposing it to be this our Fugitive. They lamented their Loss in her as a Person of exemplary Prudence and Vertue, as one in whom shin'd Piety and Wisdom with their most refulgent Rays; a Person whose Aspect commanded the Youth, and her Actions taught obedience to all; In fine, much they lamented, much they regretted the Death of this Holy Associate. In the mean time, she got safe away with her Chevalier, he having provided for her all manner of rich Accoutrements,[1] and took the first opportunity to get married. Thus she broke her solemn Religious Vow of Chastity, and the Laws of her Country, betray'd the Honour of her Family; and disgrac'd her Sex and Quality.

They liv'd together in this State, and had divers Children, till an unfortunate Shot in the Army finish'd his Days; but not on such a sudden, but that he had time to send word to her, by a particular Friend that he dy'd with great Remorse for what had pass'd between him and her; and griev'd to leave her and her Children in so distress'd and abandon'd a Condition. She receiv'd this Information with utmost Grief; she fell into Convulsions, which attended her Fit after Fit, all the Hours she liv'd, which were not many. But in one of her Intervals, she call'd some Friends about her, related to them all the Story of her criminal Marriage, greatly lamenting over her Children; for by this her Confession they must become miserable Vagabonds on the Face of the Earth, having no right to the Estate of their Father's Family, which is considerable in *France*, as is that of my Family (said she) here in *Portugal:* But I know, the Law in both Countries looks on them as Bastards, I being incapable of contracting Marriage, after a solemn Religious Vow. O wretch that I was, who with so much Importunity obtain'd of my Parents Leave to

---

1. **Accoutrements:** apparel and equipment.

become a Religious; I, who lived Years in the same state, with satisfaction to my self, and the approbation of the whole Community. How was it possible, that for the Love of this one Man, a Stranger, of a different Country, a different Religion, different Language! How was it possible, I say, to break all Laws Divine and Human, and to become so great a Monster as to hazard the burning so stately an Edifice, and in so doing, murder so many excellent pious Persons! O miserable Wretch that I am, and so she fell into one of her Convulsions, of which she dyed. At the Conclusion of this Story, said the Gentlewoman, there was none in the Coach that did not shed Tears; some compassionating one part of the Story, some blaming another, every one pitying the Children, whose Cause was then depending in the Parliament of *Paris* (as the Lawyer in the Coach said) in which he was engaged; but feared he should be able to do no good on the Childrens behalf; for he was almost sure they would lose their Process;[1] and withal lose that Charity they might hope for amongst their Friends, by humble Supplication; to which he said, he would advise 'em, that they might not fall under that unlucky Proverb,

All covet, all lose.

This sorrowful Story affected the Company with Compassion almost to Tears; which, to divert, my Lady *Allgood* began to call for Cards; But Evening approaching, they were unwilling to stay, yet asked the Lady who had told the last melancholy Story, if she had not one that was less grievous, to entertain them a few Moments, till Night should call for their Departure. To which she replyed, that in the Coach between *Dover*[2] and Home, there was an ancient Gentlewoman told 'em a kind of an odd Transaction, which hapned in the Neighbourhood where she liv'd heretofore; which is as follows.

---

1. **Process:** legal case.
2. **Dover:** town on the English Channel.

The *History* of *The Lady Gypsie.*[1]

In my younger days, said she, I liv'd in the West of *England;* for there I was born; in which Parts there happen'd this odd Project of a young Lady, the only Child of her Parents, who were Owners of a considerable Estate. As she grew in Stature, she improv'd in Beauty, which caus'd her Father to keep a strict hand over her; nevertheless she was not so ignorant of the World, but that she desir'd to know more: She saw and convers'd with many young Ladies of her Neighbourhood, who talked of the bright Diversions of the Town; this Play, that Ball, this Treat, that Musick meeting, this Walk, that *Assemblée,* the Diversions of the *Park,* Plays, *Exchange,* Spring-garden, *&c.* These Discourses, set her on fire, to see such much talked of Places; and that she might thereby be able to entertain Company suitable to her Sex and Quality: Whereas she was now but a silent Auditor to others, whose Capacities, perhaps, were less susceptible than hers; only having been in those Places, and amongst such Company as had filled, nay, even overflowed them with Vanity, which discharged its Superplus[2] amongst the young Country-Ladies, whose lot had lain at home.

This Constraint and Home-breeding began to be very tiresome to the young Lady; but no Persuasions could prevail with her Parents to relieve this her Country-restraint, telling her, she must not think of going to *London* till she was married. How far she wish'd to be married for the sake of going to *London,* or for the sake of Marriage its self, is unknown; but perhaps neither: For she was no sooner arived to marriageable Years, but she was sought after by many; her young beautiful Person, with her Father's large Inheritance annexed to it, rendering her extreamly desirable. Amongst these, her Father pitched upon one whose Riches and Prudence recommended him to his approbation; but by no means to our young Lady's liking. He was perfectly Country bred like her self; He knew nothing of Publick Affairs, but what he learnt of the

---

1. **Lady Gypsie:** This story and the "History of Tangerine," which follows, contain elements of plot and character strongly resembling Aphra Behn's *The Wandering Beauty* (1698).

2. **Superplus:** surplus.

News papers: His chief Entertainment was of Dogs and Horses; whether *Roan*[1] or *Ball*[2] performed their Heats best in order to win the Plate at the next Horse race. Beside, he was a Widower, though not old; nor had his Lady left him any Child. Nevertheless, she thought her Youth and Beauty deserved an Husband wholly new, and not a Man at second hand. In short, one reason or another presented themselves to her Fancy, that she grew obstinate to her Parents Proposal; they on the other hand, pressed as positively. This her Refusal made them fancy she had some other Object of her Affection; which Fancy so prevail'd with them, that they threatned to confine her to her Chamber, thereby to discover or prevent any such Intrigue. This was a grievous Surprize, and Fright; but instead of bending her thereby, Despair, or at least, Fear, not only made her grow Stubborn, and absolutely refused marrying this her home bred Lover, but also dread the positive Temper of her Parents.

As she was one day walking in the outward Court, ruminating on divers impending Occurrences, she saw some *Gypsies* enter the Gates, who presently approaching, addressed her with their gibble-gabble Cant[3] after their accustomed manner; but she took one of them aside, as if to hear her Fortune; and ask'd her, if they would receive a distressed Person into their Clan; to which they readily accorded. She then asked them which way they were strolling? They said, towards *London*, to gather up some Rents[4] for some Nurse-Children[5] they had taken. This their going towards *London* pleased our young Lady extreamly, it being the Place she longed to see; so she promised to come to them that Night, where they lodged.

So said, so done; and (like an unthinking Wretch as she was) left her Father's House that Night, and so went to this Band of Strollers, carrying with her only what her Pockets would contain, as, Money, Rings, a Watch, &c. She travell'd with them several Days, her Person being disguised both in Habit and Complexion, (for that they took care to do

---

1. **Roan:** horse of sorrel, chestnut or bay color, sprinkled with gray or white.

2. **Ball:** horse with white streak on its forehead.

3. **gibble-gabble Cant:** secret language that seems senseless chatter to outsiders.

4. **Rents:** fees.

5. **Nurse-Children:** foster children.

the moment she came to them.) After a few Days Travel, she saw and felt her Folly, undergoing the Fatigue of Wind and Wet, Heat and Cold, bad Food, bad Lodging, and all things disagreeable to her Constitution and Education: She knew not what to do with her self; she durst not return to her Parents, nor inform any body of her Condition; her Money, and all that was valuable, they had gotten from her: So, what to do, she knew not. She had no prospect but of Misery and Disgrace: She pass'd her Nights in silent Tears, and her Days in Sighs and secret Lamentations: The wicked way in which these vile Wretches liv'd, cheating, stealing, lying, and all sorts of Roguery, was abominable to her vertuous Mind. Amongst these, there was one who seemed of a better mien than the rest, and was ready upon all occasions to befriend her in any thing within his power. He was something in Years, and not so well able to undergo the Fatigue as the others; nor could he ever compass the Art of cheating, canting and stealing, as the rest did: He was weary of these his wicked Companions; but knew not how to live without them: So one Day, he and she being tired with marching, and coming near a Village, set themselves down on a Bank by the Highway, whilst the Gang strolled about the Hedges and Out-places, to try what they could pilfer.

Sitting here, the old Man began to tell her how he came to be linked into this Band of Vagabonds; of which, he said he was very weary, but knew not how to extricate himself, they having gotten from him all the Money his evil Life had before procured; and he being now advanced in Years, was not able otherwise to get a Livelihood, but as they provided for him according to their Contract when they received his Money; to which Contract they were very just, added he, and in some degree kind, being considerate of my Years, and other Occurrences, as you will understand by my Story, which I will faithfully relate to you.

The *Story* of *Tangerine,*
The Gentleman Gypsie.

I took my Name, said he, from that renowned Garrison of *Tangier;*[1] where I was a Soldier. When the good and gracious King *Charles* was

---

1. **Garrison of Tangier:** English fortress in northern Africa, part of the dowry Portugal provided when Charles II (1630–85) married Catherine de Braganza (1638–1705) in 1662. It was evacuated in 1683 so Charles could raise money. Garrison veterans were known as Tangerines.

driven to a necessity of demolishing that Fort, and dismantling the Garrison, which was much against his Inclination, it being a greater Loss to *England* than that of *Dunkirk;*[1] though not so much taken notice of, as lying so much farther off. The parting with either was very grievous to the King: But the great Machine of State at that time between Court and Country partly moved in such manner, that his Majesty had not Money to support the said Garrisons, so that *bon-gre, mal-gre* he was forced to part with them. But to return to what appertains to my self, State-affairs being neither your, nor my province at this time.

I was born a Gentleman, and educated accordingly, but the Havock *Cromwell's* Party had made in my Father's Substance,[2] forced me (as well as many other younger Brothers) to seek my Fortune; and so I went with a Friend of my Father's, (an Officer of Note) to *Tangier,* where, I doubt not, but he would have endeavour'd for my Preferment, in time.

But now, give me leave to go back a little; Before my going to *Tangier,* the Beauty of a young Lady had fir'd my Heart to that degree, that I knew not how to go, or stay. I shall not repeat to you the manner of our Courtship, the many Hopes, Tears, Joys and Fears, which agitated our Interiours. In short, the Lady was willing to promise me Marriage, and to stay for me till my Return, or till I should be in a condition to send for her; but that was not sufficient; nothing would serve my turn, but to espouse her e'er my Departure; and this with the utmost Sincerity. I had great Difficulty to gain her Consent to this; and many Arguments passed backward and forward on both sides; but at last her Affections were so prevalent, as to make her submit to my Importunites, and so married we were, very privately, about a Week before my Departure. I will not repeat to you what tenderness pass'd between us that Week; it breaks my aged Heart to think of it; nor is my faltring Tongue able to express the Sorrows of this our Separation.

I got well to *Tangier,* lived happy with my Friend, and made my self

---

1. **Dunkirk:** Dunkerque, France; northwestern coastal town, given to England in 1658 as a settlement for aiding France against the Spanish; sold to France in 1662.

2. **Havock…Substance:** the loss of property as a consequence of supporting Charles I rather than Oliver Cromwell's Parliamentary party in the Civil Wars (1642–49).

many more in the Garrison, *&c.* but it was not long e'er we were all sent for home, the Garrison being to be destroy'd as I before said. When I got to *England,* the first News I heard, was, that my Father was dead, and my elder Brother married to this my Wife. I cannot express how greatly I was afflicted and amazed, even to Distraction; I knew not which way to go, nor to address my self; Father I had none, Heaven and the Course of Nature had depriv'd me of that Happiness; my Father's House a Den of Incest; my Brother my Rival; my Wife an incestuous Prostitute. To go near, or reproach them, was to make them miserable, and my self not happy.

In the mean time, I wanted[1] Bread: For the King, who was not able to maintain us in Garrison, when we did him and the Nation Service, was as little able, when we did him none. In such Afflictions, I joyned my self with some others of these my distressed[2] *Tangier-*Companions, and so went to seek Adventures on the High way.[3] Sometimes we went in little Parties, sometimes single. It was my luck one time to attack a Coach, whilst another or two remain'd perdue[4] at a distance: But how was I surpriz'd, when I found in this Coach my Brother and his Wife, or rather my Wife! Tho' I knew them, they knew not me: For the Weather had much alter'd me in travelling by Sea and Land, beside the little Disguise I wore. They readily gave me me what they had, which was considerable, and with which I departed, without demanding Watches, Rings, Necklace, or any thing else. But Hue and Cry[5] was soon out after me; which pursued me so close every way, that I had no hopes of escaping. At this juncture 'twas I met with this Band of Strollers,[6] and gave them all my Booty[7] to receive me into their Gang; which they soon did, and as soon disguised me from being known by my most intimate Acquaintance:

---

1. **wanted:** lacked, needed.
2. **distressed:** financially troubled.
3. **Adventures on the High way:** robbery.
4. **perdue:** as lookouts; sentinels.
5. **Hue and Cry:** warrant for the pursuit of a criminal.
6. **Strollers:** vagabonds.
7. **Booty:** plunder.

And thus I have lived amongst them ever since, till Old Age has put me on another Disguise more undiscoverable than the former.

He had scarce finish'd his Discourse, when a mourning Coach came driving on with a slow Pace, and in it an elderly Lady, with two young Ladies. The latter perceiving our two Gypsies, called out to stop the Coach, that they might divert themselves, by having their Fortune told. The old Gypsie approaching the Coach, saw his Wife in her Widow's Dress: He told them, that their Fortune was so extraordinary, that he desir'd a little longer time to consider of it, before he could inform them; so they let him know where they intended to lodge that Night, which was to be at the same great Town where our Gang of Strollers were going; then the Coach passed on, he promising to come to 'em.

Indeed, said the Old Gypsie, I shall tell them strange Fortune, when I let the Lady know, that I am her true and lawful Husband, and Father to that young Gentleman that rode by the Coach: For I have heard, that she was delivered of this her Son some Weeks too soon for her Credit; so that I doubt not but I left my Brother an Heir ready for his Estate, before I went to *Tangier.*

Thus, methinks, I see an End of this miserable Way of living, which always seemed odious to me; but the Shelter it gave me from the fore-mention'd Pursuit made me undergo it with Patience: For I am not vicious or unworthy in my Nature, having always had a constant Abhorrence of the other, as well as this vile Course; but a fatal Necessity compell'd me to it. I have often thought it a Defect in our Government, that there is not some method thought on or contriv'd for distressed young Gentlemen and Gentlewomen, to employ, and secure them from these or other wicked Actions, to which they are often exposed by hard fortune, or ill management, or the Cruelty or Caprice of Parents; the latter of which I take to be your case (continuing his speech to the young Lady Gypsie) But, be assur'd, when I get to my Estate, which I shall now soon do, my Brother being dead, (by making my Wife own this her Son to be my Son;) Be assured, I say, that I shall then take care of you, in my own House, and make your Beauty shine in the Eyes of this my Son (if he be not otherwise engaged) so as to make you become my Daughter: For which Kindness our Young Gypsie was very thank-ful: But Providence determined otherwise, as appears by the Sequel.

By this time our Strollers came to them, having pillaged the Hedges and Farmers Yards of what they could conveniently come at: So one Party of them was to go with their Booty to the next Town, whilst the other went into this Village, to cant, lye, tell fortunes, pick Pockets, *&c.* and so they were to meet all at their Rendezvous, at the Place appointed.

Here they came to a Lady's House, where they began (as usual) to tell fortunes among the Servants, who listned to them as so many divine Oracles. In the mean time, the Lady of the House came to chide them for hearkening to those deceitful Vagabonds. Now, so it hapned, that this Lady had sore Eyes; which our Gypsie remark'd; and having before learnt many fine Receits[1] of her Mother, took notice to the Lady of the Indisposition of her Eyes, telling her that she could cure them. Alas, said the Lady, I have try'd almost all things, without Effect, and therefore have little reason to put any confidence in what you offer. But our Young Gypsie press'd her with such agreeable Arguments, couch'd in modest respectful Terms, that the Lady was persuaded to make use of this poor Stroller's Receit. Now, the Preparation being to take some days time, the Lady received the Girl into her House, till the Medicine could be made. This was a great comfort to our Gypsie, hoping, perhaps, to have an Opportunity of ingratiating her self with the Lady.

Things succeeded well; the Lady's Eyes were cured, and then her Ladyship asked the Maid, why such a young Girl as she, did not rather betake her self to Service,[2] than lead such a vagrant scandalous Life, and offered her to remain amongst the Servants, till some Place might fall for her; in the mean time she was appointed to assist in the Kitchen.

Here she behaved her self with great Discretion, and was so ready at all Sauces and savory Meats, all manner of Pickling and Pastry, with whatsoever belong'd to a compleat[3] Cook, that she amaz'd all who beheld the manner of her proceeding.

---

1. **Receits:** formulas for medical compounds; prescriptions.

2. **Service:** domestic service.

3. **compleat:** accomplished, expert.

She had not been there many Weeks, e'er the Lady's House-keeper was married; after which the Lady prefer'd our Gypsie to her Place. Here she performed all to admiration, whether Sweetmeats,[1] Distillations,[2] Infusions,[3] or whatever else belong'd to a Person in that Station: she was a Stranger to nothing, but ill-manners; all Curiosities of the House-keeper's Closet was familiar to her, that her Lady and every body were amaz'd not knowing what to conjecture.

By this time the false Complexion the Gypsies had put on her was worn off; and in this genteel Post she began to get Cloaths suitable to her station; that now our Gypsie appear'd beautiful in her Person, as well as knowing in her Business, and prudent in her Actions. Now, as this Brightness of Person and Parts was visible to all, so in a peculiar manner it struck the eyes, of the young Gentleman her Lady's Son, who was lately come from Travel, he had seen the World, with its various sorts of Beauties; but none had touch'd him like our Gypsie's. However, he thought of no other Favours, but what might be, purchased at the price of a Guinea, or so.

But, alas, when he came to make attacks, he quickly found his mistake; For our Gypsie, was so affronted, that she told her Lady, that she must take her leave of her Ladyship, and desired to be dismissed. The Lady was surprized, and would not permit her to depart, till she asked her the reason of this her sudden Resolution; Much she press'd, and loath the Girl was to discover[4]: But in the end, she told the real Truth. The Lady rebuked her Son, for having such an unworthy thought towards the poor young Creature; and one that she loved and esteemed. The Gentleman promised that he would no more attack the Gypsie's Vertue; nevertheless, a while after, the Gypsie press'd for her Departure, which the young Gentleman oppos'd.

---

1. **Sweetmeats:** sweet food such as sugared cakes, pastry, or nuts.

2. **Distillations:** any beverage, particularly alcoholic, dependent upon separation of essential liquid by heat.

3. **Infusions:** steeped beverages, such as tea.

4. **loath…discover:** unwilling to reveal the truth.

At last our Fair One told her Lady, that she could not stay in the House with the young Gentleman; so once more beg'd her Ladyship to dismiss her. The Lady importun'd her to let her know the reason, and whether her Son was troublesome to her or not: She said, no; but her own Weakness was so. Then casting her self at her Lady's feet; beg'd pardon for having dar'd to cast her Eyes, on her Ladyship's Son, a Person so much above her: But alas; continued she, I am but a poor helpless Maid,[1] He a glorious Youth, whose Birth, Person, and Education, all combine to storm my Heart, guarded with nothing but Vertue and Innocence; wherefore, Madam, I beseech you to consent to my Departure, whilst I am innocent. The good Lady was greatly touch'd, and found a necessity to part with her; but withal resolv'd to provide for her, by putting her into some way suitable to her Merits. This she revealed to her Son, which he absolutely oppos'd, telling his Mother, that he was so far from parting with his Gypsie, that he was resolv'd to unite himself to her in the holy Bonds of Matrimony. The Lady was struck with Horrour and Amazement at this her Son's Declaration, much reproaching him for the Meanness[2] of his Thoughts, in divers sorts of Expressions suitable to the occasion. He, on the other side, defended himself with what Arguments he could, without breaking the bonds of Duty and Respect.

He alledged the Gypsie's Deserts both in Mind and Person, his own Affections, which he found impossible to conquer, or bring into any bounds of Reason; the Gypsie's vertuous and generous Deportment, in desiring to be dismissed, rather than blemish her Lady's Family with such an unworthy Alliance; With many other Arguments which he produced in favour of his beloved Gypsie; none of which his Mother could gainsay or disallow: But in fine, she was far unfit for his Quality or Fortune. Beside, said the Lady, your Father enjoyn'd me at his Death to promote a Marriage between you and Mr. *Truman's* Daughter, when you should return from your Travels. And now I have sent

---

1. **Maid:** maiden.
2. **Meanness:** lowness, inferiority.

my Steward[1] to make Proposals on that Subject, how can I absolve my
self of my Promise made to your dear Father deceas'd? I wonder not at
your loving the Gypsie; for 'tis certain, I love and esteem her in a great
degree; nevertheless Reason must be my Guide, and ought to be yours:
And though it be extreamly against my Inclination to part with her,
yet now your Folly compels me, Duty to my honourable dead Husband's Memory commands me, Respect to your Family obliges me,
and maternal Affection to you, finishes the Chain of all the indispen-
sible Reasons. Then calling for the Gypsie, told her, she had at last
resolv'd to comply with her Desires, of letting her go; therefore commanded her to dispose her self for her departure next Morning.

Hereupon our Gypsie cast her self at the Lady's Feet, assuring her
Ladyship that she had no ways contributed to any of this Disorder,
which had happened in her Family; Your Son, Madam, is here to testifie, that I never encourag'd his Passion, nor concealed any thing from
your Ladyship; but behav'd my self openly and above-board in all
things, except letting your Son know my Inclinations; but always refus'd
his Proposals, though never so honourable, being without and against
your Ladyship's Consent.

The young Gentleman was about to reply, by way of witness to her
Assertion, when behold the Steward (which the Lady had sent to her
Friend Mr. *Truman*) approached, and with him, Mr. *Truman's* Steward,
bringing a Letter containing the following words:

Madam,

*Heaven has justly punish'd me in the Loss of my Daughter, for the breach of
that Promise, I made to my worthy Friend your Husband in behalf of your
Son: When Riches tempted me I had no power to refuse; for a certain rich
neighbouring Gentleman gain'd so far upon me, that I lay'd my Commands
upon her to dispose her Person and Affections for him; which she receiv'd
with such Displeasure, that I have never seen her since, nor ever hope to see
her more; That I am now, Madam, as afflicted as guilty; one, implores your
Pity, the other, your Pardon, which I hope for from the abundance of that*

---

1. **Steward:** estate manager.

Goodness which made you at first comply with this propos'd Alliance with
your unworthy Friend and most obedient Servant,

J. Truman.

Whilst the Lady was perusing this Letter, *Truman's* Steward cast his
Eyes on the Gypsie, and knew her to be his Master's Daughter, and with
a suitable Obeisance,[1] saluted her by her Name, withal reproaching her
for the many and great Afflictions she had caused her Father by this her
long Absence.

This Discovery was the most pleasing and agreeable Surprize that
could happen to a Family. The Lady and her Son were delighted beyond
expression; our young Lady Gypsie was lost in a pleasing Confusion; a
Mixture of Shame and Satisfaction appear'd in her; one for having committed such a ridiculous piece of Extravagance in leaving her Father's
House; the other, for being discover'd to her Lover,[2] and her good, after
such a long Concealment. The good Lady put a period to all, by order-
ring her Equipage to be made ready to carry them all to her Friend Mr.
Truman's; where they celebrated the Marriage, to the great Satisfaction
of all Parties.

Thus was this young Lady deliver'd out of that Ocean of Disgrace,
into which her Folly and Rashness had cast her; and for an Augmenta-
tion of Happiness, Mr. *Tangerine* and his Family came to make them a
Visit, he being reconciled to his Wife, and lived with her as his Brother's
Widow; it being convenient on all accounts to keep the rest secret. To
these two Families one may very well apply the Proverb,

Give Folks Luck, and throw 'em into the Sea.

The Company were very much diverted at this Story, tho' they
blamed the Young Lady for her strange unparallel'd Enterprize, saying,
that surely she had been reading some ridiculous *Romance,* or *Novel,*[3]
that inspired her with such a vile Undertaking, from whence she could

---

1. **Obeisance:** bow of respect.

2. **Lover:** suitor.

3. **Romance, or Novel:** fictional narratives, often turning on idealized or adventurous love,
commonly considered dangerous reading for young, impressionable females.

rationally expect nothing but Misery and Disgrace. But Heaven was gracious and merciful, in preserving her from sinking into the most odious Infamy.

Thus having pass'd the short Winter's Afternoon, in Tea and Chat, the approaching Evening called them to their respective Habitations.

Galesia was no sooner got to her Lodging, but a Gentleman, an Acquaintance she had at St. *Germain's*, came to make her a Visit; and being seated, she began to enquire what good fortune had attended him since she left him there, and since his Arrival in *England*. To which he answer'd, I have been too strict an Adherent to Honour and Honesty, to hope for good fortune on this side Heaven. However, since you enquire, I will tell you a Romantick Adventure which fell in my way a few Days ago.

The *History* of *Dorinda*[1]

You know, Madam, that our narrow Circumstances at St. *Germain's* taught us a regular Way of living; that our Evening Bottle did not prevent our Morning Breakfast, nor *Cynthia*[2] encroach upon *Phoebus*;[3] but an early *Couché*[4] caus'd an early *Levé*;[5] that we had full time enough in the Morning to pay our Duty to God in his Church, and the King in his Chamber. After this, a Walk on the *Terras*[6] got us a Friend and a Stomach,[7] to repair to the Coffee-house, and over a Dish of Tea hear or make News. My Person and my Pocket being accustomed to this way of living, I lik'd it so well, that I believe, I shall never desire to change, tho' I am now in a Country where another method is practised.

Thus, being got up early one Morning, I took a Walk in the *Park* near *Rosamond's* Pond; after which, I sat down a while, ruminating on

---

1. **Dorinda:** conventional name of romance heroine.
2. **Cynthia:** Greek goddess of the moon.
3. **Phoebus:** Greek god of the sun.
4. **Couché:** bedtime.
5. **Levé:** awakening, rising.
6. **Terras:** terrace.
7. **stomach:** appetite.

divers Occurrences in *Europe,* which will fill the History of future times with amazing Truths; and casting my Eyes towards the Pond, I saw a fine-shap'd Gentlewoman walking close by the Pond's side, very much dagled[1] with the frosty Dew of the Morning. She seemed very melancholy, sometimes sighing, sometimes weeping, now lifting up her Hands and Eyes to Heaven, then casting them towards the Pond; at last, all on a sudden, she leaped into the Water, and had certainly perished, had not I been there: For depending upon mine ability in swimming, I leap'd in, and truly, not without difficulty and danger, got her out. I then called to some Soldiers I saw at a distance, and by their help brought her to a Seat, where she came to her self; but would not be persuaded to tell who she was, or where she lived, or whither she would go: So I got a Chair,[2] and carried her to my Lodgings; where, with much ado, I prevailed with my Landlady to receive her. She put her into a warm Bed, got a Nurse to rub and chafe,[3] and a Surgeon to bleed[4] her, and use all other Applications suitable to her Condition. When the Hurry was a little over, I went into her Room to comfort, and to get out of her the Cause of this desperate Transaction. She being thoroughly come to her self, washed and dressed in clean dry Head-cloaths,[5] I thought I had seen her some where; and at last called to mind where; and asked her if her Name was not *Dorinda?* yes, yes, said she, it was by that sham Name you formerly picked me up at the Play; and tho' Time and Fatigue has altered you, yet I remember your Features perfectly well; It was such Romantick Whimsies that brought upon me the Ruin and Distress in which you behold me; I had read Plays, Novels, and Romances, till I began to think my self a Heroine of the first rate; and all Men that flatter'd, or ogled, me were Heroes; and that a pretty wellbehaved Foot-man or Page must needs be the Son of some Lord or great Gentleman.

---

1. **dagled:** dampened.

2. **Chair:** sedan chair, on a pole and carried by two men.

3. **chafe:** rub until warm.

4. **bleed:** draw quantities of blood, considered therapeutic since it would drain poisonous humors.

5. **Head-cloaths:** covering for the head.

I affected to seek Adventures of divers sorts; amongst the rest, I went mask'd and unaccompanied to the Play-house; where you pick'd me up carried me to a Tavern gave me a handsome Treat; and I pleas'd my self to think how you would be baulk'd, when you should pretend to any Favours out of the Road of common Honesty; as you know you were. After this I met you again in *Convent-Garden* Square;[1] then on *Tower-hill;*[2] And thus I rambled, hoping all the while you would court me for Marriage; which indeed, was great Folly in me to expect, in the midst of such Behaviour; But when it came out that you was a married Man, you may remember that I abandoned all Commerce with you; For amongst all my Freaks and romantick Frolicks, I preserved my self from the great Offence; But that is not enough; one must remember the common Saying,

> *Those that will no evil do,*
> *Must do nothing tends thereto.*

For such conduct as mine, was as dishonourable in the Eyes of the World, as if one was a downright Prostitute; and not only dishonourable, but ridiculous; for it is according to the saying of a Poet,

> *Dye with the Scandal of a Whore,*
> *And never know the Joy.*[3]

Now, though I broke of your Company, yet I could not on a sudden detatch my Heart from the thoughts of you; but the *Revolution* came on, and your Devoirs calling you to follow the King, Time and Absence help'd me to overcome my Folly; and I became more sedate, so as not to ramble alone to Plays, nor to be seen in Places unfit for a young Gentle-woman; nevertheless, a Romantick Humour hung long upon me, that if any worthy Country-Gentleman made his Addresses to me, I set him in

---

1. **Convent-Garden Square:** celebrated London marketplace; site of houses designed by Inigo Jones, as well as taverns and theatres.

2. **Tower-hill:** principal place of execution by beheading of prisoners held in the Tower of London.

3. **Poet . . . Joy:** John Wilmot, second earl of Rochester (1647–80), "Song," lines 15–16 (ca. September 1680).

the rank of Justice *Clod-pate*,[1] or Justice *Calf*[2] in those Comedies, and
fancy'd their spruce young Footman some Prince or Hero in disguise,
like *Dorus* in Sir *Philip Sidney's Arcadia*.[3] But notwithstanding my having blotted my Reputation, and render'd my self ridiculous, by these
foolish Whims; I say, notwithstanding all this, a neighbouring Gentleman of an Estate made his Addresses to me; to which I consented, and
Writings were to be drawn. I told him, that such a Footman of mine
must be provided for, by my Father's order at his Death; to which he
readily consented, and said, he should be put to some honest Trade
whereby to get his Living. But I told him no; for Trades might fail, and
therefore I resolved to have an hundred Pounds a Year settled on him.
The Gentleman was disgusted at this Proposal (as very well he might)
and for the future visited me no more. After this, my Favourite Footman lighting me one Evening up Stairs, in a Freak caught him by the
Arm, and said, *Jack*,[4] I am in love with you; and in a gigling way, said, I
will marry you, thinking *Jack* would have been out of countenance,
scratched his Head, grin'd and looked like an Idiot; But truly, quite the
contrary; He brisked up, and kissed me, saying, he liked me so well,
that I should not need to ask twice. I was shock'd at this Boldness,
though my self had been the Cause, and so went into my Dressing-
room; a place that excludes all but my Maids, and some few Female
Friends; but he had the boldness to follow me thither, and briskly sat
him down by my Toilet.[5] My Woman hearing me gone into my Dress-
ing-room, came to me according to Custom, and seeing *Jack* sit there,
began to chide him with rough Words, and bad him get him gone out
of the Room, lest a Fire shovel forc'd him out with Blood about his Ears.
I, foolishly, was exasparated against her, as supposing (I believe) that she

---

1. **Justice Clod-pate:** loutish country fool in *Epsom-Wells,* a play by Thomas Shadwell (1640–92); also a nickname for Oliver Cromwell.

2. **Justice Calf:** a character in Thomas Baker's play, *Hampstead Heath* (1706). "Calf" is slang for dolt, fool.

3. **Dorus in Sir Philip Sidney's Arcadia:** shepherd in the prose romance (1590) by poet and diplomat, Sidney (1554-86).

4. **Jack:** an actual name and slang for common, ill-bred man.

5. **Toilet:** dressing table.

encroach'd on my Prerogative, in forbidding whom she thought fit; or what other Notion my ill Genius inspir'd, I know not; but so it was, that I espoused *Jack's* Cause, bidding her be patient, and she should know farther. In short, some Words of dispute passed; I still took *Jack's* part; at last, she said, if you have made *Jack* your Companion, or your Master, he shall never be mine; and so forthwith departed. I must own, this gave me some Uneasiness, or rather Confusion, and out of which he endeavour'd to recover me, with many fair Words, mix'd with Sighs and Tears, the Rhetorick the Sex has always ready wherewith to betray us; kneeling and kissing my Hands, begged me not to abate of that Goodness, which had inspir'd him with a Passion, on which his Life depended; for he having been bred up in my Father's Service, and reading many pretty Books, could speak well enough. However, I oblig'd him to depart for that time; and send my Chamber-maid to me. The poor Girl having been inform'd by my Woman, what had pass'd, entered in Tears, and found me in the same Condition. I bad her look in my Closet, and bring me some little Cordial,[1] that was there, and put me to bed; which accordingly she did; but not to rest: For I slept not that Night; but tossed and touz'd,[2] my thoughts being agitated with the utmost Vexation; not knowing how to undo what my Folly, or rather Whimsie had begun: For 'tis certain he was indifferent to me; but having thus far exposed my self to him, and my Servants, and in them to every body, I knew not what to do; I was like one on horse-back, plung'd in the midst of a violent deep Torrent, fearing to go forward, lest it shou'd be deeper; not daring to turn, lest that Motion should empower the rapid Stream to bear him down.

In this state were my Thoughts; I had no body to consult; shame forbidding me to tell my Story to any body wiser than my self: sometimes I pleas'd my thoughts, that if I married him, I should always be Mistress,[3] and not be under the Government and Correction of an imperious and surly Master; not reflecting that the whole Sex, of what degree soever, will always exert the Authority that God gave their great Grand-

---

1. **Cordial:** alcoholic beverage to stimulate the heart.
2. **touz'd:** tousled; messed up the bed linen.
3. **Mistress:** female in charge of the household.

father *Adam.* Then again, my romantick Brain would make me imagine, that he was of an Origin;[1] (if known) above what he appeared: for he had been a Beggar-boy, taken up at my Father's Gate, and was bred up in our House, as I have told you, nor would he ever be persuaded to tell his Name, nor from whence he came.

Then again, I would draw that Curtain from before the Eyes of my Reason, and behold him as the poor Beggar-boy *Jack*, whose business it had been to clean the Dog kennels, and at last, for a reward of his well-doing he was advanced to put on a Livery.[2] This Reflection grated my proud Heart: Then it was I wish'd there had been Protestant Nunneries, where I might have shelter'd my Disgrace, under a holy Veil, or at least, a pretended, if not a real Devotion.

Then again my Thoughts would roll the other way, and consider *Jack* made a Gentleman by me; resolving that if I married him, to buy him a Commission, and let him try to make his Fortune in *Flanders.* Thus my poor Head turn'd from Thought to Thought, without any Sleep in my Eyes, or Repose in my Heart.

In the Morning I heard a Bustle at my Chamber-door, which prov'd to be between *Jack* and my Maid; for she coming then to wait on me, according to custom, he follow'd her, and would go in with her; which she refus'd; with that he strugled with her, and at last got the Key; then pushing her away, came in and lock'd the Door fast, and shut her out. I was frighten'd at this; but he approaching the Bed side, on his Knees begged Pardon for this Action, making a thousand Protestations of Duty and Respect; adding the Violence of his Passion, which my Goddness[3] over night had kindled, in his Heart; at the same time he had the cunning to take hold on that Hand next my Bell, under a pretence of kissing it, launching out into many flattering Speeches not worth repeating; but the substance was, to press me to a Speedy Marriage, even that Morning. I suppose, he consider'd me as a kind of Romantick Humourist, (as I really was) and thought it best to make sure work, e'er I chang'd my mind.

---

1. **Origin:** of genteel birth.
2. **Livery:** uniform indicating the household he served.
3. **Goddness:** apparently a printer's error for *Goodness.*

Now I being thus shut up with him, knew that my Honour (as to outward appearance) was lost, and that I was more liable to Contempt than in being his Wife; so I e'en permitted him to go fetch a Parson; and was married that fatal Morning. At this the poor Creature (said the Gentleman) fell into a flood of Tears; but after a few Moments, drying her Eyes, she returned to her Story.

We passed this Day and the following Night in Jollity enough; but the next Morning my Steward came to Town, and was soon informed of this my Folly: When he approach'd my Presence, I was struck with Shame and Confusion, he being a Gentleman of a graceful Mien, and much respected in this Country. When he came in, my Husband, (for I must no longer call him *Jack*) kept his Seat, and without Ceremony call'd him by his Name, and bad[1] him welcome. The good Gentleman, though he knew the Case, pretended Ignorance, and bad *Jack* get out of his Presence, to prevent a good Kicking. Then with Tears in my Eyes, I told him what was done. At which he seem'd much troubled for my sake; and withal told me, that since I had made my Footman my Master, I must not have him longer for my Servant; and bidding me provide some body to receive his Accounts, turn'd short, and departed.

This Transaction, as well as that of my Woman before, were both very grievous to me; and did, as it were, take me down[2] in my Wedding-shoes; but soon after appear'd a business more mortifying for my Chamber-maid was found with child and lay'd it to my Husband, and produced a Promise of Marriage.

He opened my Cabinet, and before my Face took out Handfuls of Gold and Jewels, and gave her, without counting, bad her look out a decent House, and therewith furnish the same, make her self easie, for she should not be abandoned. He kept the Key of my Cabinet, and Scrutore;[3] in short of every thing, that I had not a Pair of Gloves or a Row of Pins but what he gave me out. Imagine now, how I began to see and feel my Indiscretion; but this was nothing to what follows.

---

1. **bad:** bade.

2. **take me down:** humiliate.

3. **Scrutore:** scrutoire; writing table.

He said, he would have me dispose my self to go into the Country, where he had a House of his own, and told me his Name, and the place of his Birth; at which I was a little pleased, hoping my Romantick Notion was come true, and that I should find something a little tolerable and decent, Suitable to his Person, which was truly handsome. But, good Heavens! When we came to the Place, how was I amazed, to find my self brought to a poor thatch'd Cottage! To say the truth, he had taken care to have it made as well as it would bear, against my coming; and had put decent Furniture therein, telling me, he did not intend my Stay should be long there; only till he could get his business done amongst some Friends and Acquaintance he had in that Country; So away he went, leaving me and my Maid, and wherewithal to live in that mean way. But instead of travelling the Country as he pretended, he went directly to *London,* made off my House, and Goods, Plate, Linnen, and Jewels, *&c.* in short, all. He gam'd, drank, whored, kept the Slut my Chamber-maid Lady-like: Thus, he soon ran through my personal Estate I left behind me, though it was of considerable Value. He came to me again e'er I was delivered of my first Child, and did not let me know how near he had spent all; but brought with him a handsom Supply, to sustain the Charges of my approaching Childbed.

Now it was that he propos'd to me the selling of a Lordship[1] I had lying far distant, and to buy one nearer *London,* where Rents were better paid, and less Charge and Trouble, in gathering and receiving the said Rents; and withal propos'd to spare something over, (that he had in View being less in Extent than the other) wherewith to buy him a Place in the Army, Court, Custom-house, or the like; all which I approved and so consented to the selling my Lordship.

But alas, I had soon Cause to repent, when I found there was nothing done, no Lordship purchas'd, no Place nor Post bought; but the Money squandered away, I knew not how; but I suppose, in Riot, Gaming, and Lewdness. However, I wanted nothing in that little Station in which he had plac'd me; and I began to be very well pleas'd, being out of the Hurry and Reproaches of the great World, and my Friends in particular.

---

1. **Lordship:** an estate under the protection of a lord.

He visited me sometimes; and always pretended great Business, Projects and Undertakings. I became with Child a second time; but it was about two Years after the first.

At this Juncture he pretended it was extreamly advisable to sell my other Lordship, to which at first I was very averse; but he alledging how great the Taxes on Land were, and like to continue, and that the Banks and Funds made a much better Return; which he pretended to know by Experience, as if he had put the Money of that other Lordship there; with another plausible Pretence he made, that in that Village where he had placed me, there was a good Farm or two to be sold with a handsom House on them, which he would buy, and sit up for my Habitation: All which look'd well; and made me hope, and flatter my self that things were better than I imagined: Whereupon, after many Difficulties and Disputes with my self, and him, I consented; thinking that his Pretences, of the Funds, and Banks might be in some degree true.

Moreover, I thought, that he, as well as others, lov'd to have things in their own Name. And thro' several other such Fancies, together with his Protestations, I deluded my self thoroughly to my undoing.

However, he was so far just to his Word in buying the said Farms, made the House very handsome both within and without, and there plac'd me, brought me a very handsome Chariot from *London,* and in it a young Gentlewoman, for my Companion, and Waiting-woman; all this look'd kind, and the Child was pleas'd with its Bauble.[1]

But alas, the Scale soon turn'd; and my waiting-Gentlewoman became Mother of a brave[2] Boy, which the false Wretch my Husband endeavour'd to shuffle off, telling me she was a Kinswoman of his unhappily married, and desired me to be kind to her; but she soon found the way to be kind to her self, and cruel to me; and as her Children grew up, (for she had more) she grew insolent to me and mine; and the Tables turn'd: For instead of her being my Waiting-woman, I was partly hers; for she ruled and governed my House and Servants; and I suppose, they had Orders under-hand to obey her rather than me; and

---

1. **Bauble:** small, showy ornament of little value.
2. **brave:** fine or strong.

my Husband when at home, abetted the same, shewing more respect to her than me; so that I plainly saw that all this House, handsome Furniture, and Chariot was all provided upon her account, not mine; and she commanded all as if really her own.

By this time my Son began to grow up fit for some sort of Education beyond that of a Country-School, and for which I press'd his Father to provide: At last he adher'd to my Importunities, and bought a little Horse on purpose to carry him to *London* with him: But I could never get him to tell me where, or about what Business he had placed him: For whenever I asked, I receiv'd nothing but a churlish[1] Answer: And if I complain'd of the Insolence of his insulting Mistress he had placed with me, I had no Redress; but all her Words and Actions approv'd, and mine disdain'd.

This Usage at last tired me out, together with an Ardent Desire of seeing my Son, or endeavouring to find him out. In all this a good neighbouring Lady assisted me, and lent me Money to convey me to *London,* advising me to go to my Friends, and humble my self to them, and thus endeavour to extricate my self out of these Vexations. This good Lady took my Daughter into her care, which was my second Child; and thus to *London* I came; I address'd my self to my Friends, from whom I found few Comforts, but many Reproaches.

Thus, having neither Friends nor Money, nor being able to find out my Son or Husband, nor knowing how to get my Living in the midst of these Afflictions, I did that wicked Action, of throwing my self into the Pond, from which you have been my Deliverer, and are a Witness of this last Act of Despair, as you was of my first Act of Folly. And, I think, the whole Sequel of my Husband's Behaviour, does most exactly fulfil the Proverb,

> *Set a Beggar on Horse-back,*
> *And he'll ride to the Devil.*

Dorinda had just finish'd her Story (said the Gentleman) when my Foot-Boy came to know whether I would dine at the Tavern, or have my

---

1. **churlish:** ill-tempered.

Dinner brought home; but hoping she might eat a Bit, I order'd it to be brought to my Lodging. The Landlady accommodated *Dorinda* with all Necessaries: For she had so well recover'd her self, that she came into the Dining-Room with a good Appetite: But whilst we sate attending the coming of Dinner, *Dorinda* fell a sighing, as if troubled with the Vapours, which I took to be the effect of her deep reflecting on things past, and in which I endeavour'd to consolate her, bidding her forget what was past, and hope for better to come. But she said, it was not Reflection that caus'd her Sighs, but the Sight of my Boy put her in mind of that Child her Husband had carried away. At which the Boy fell a-crying, and said, *Mamma, Mamma, Indeed, you are my Mamma.* This was a surprizing Discovery; wherefore we made the Boy tell us all he could remember since he left his Mother, which is as follows.

The *Story* of Young *Jack Mechant.*

I was mightily pleas'd (said the Boy) to go along with my Father, on the little Horse he had bought for me, especially, being to go to *London,* a Place I so much longed to see, as most Boys do of my Age. We travell'd till I was very weary, and I was glad when we got to a Town, which we did a pretty while before Night. We came to an Inn, where there happened to be some Persons pretending to be Pressmasters[1] raising Men to go to Sea. They scrap'd acquaintance[2] with me, and I with them; they told me such fine Stories of the Sea, and of Foreign Countries, such strange things, that I wish'd to go along with them. I pass'd the Evening with them, they continuing to amuse me with their Stories, Flatteries and Cajoleries,[3] till such time as Drowsiness call'd my Father and me to Bed, where my Day's Weariness caused me to sleep very sound, insomuch that in the Morning I never heard, or felt my Father when he rose: For he got up pretty early, and went away, leaving word with the Host, that I should come along with those Gentlemen, *i.e.* the pre-

---

1. **Pressmasters:** officers, often brutal or wily, in charge of enlisting men and boys into naval service.

2. **scrap'd acquaintance:** became acquainted by careful means.

3. **Cajoleries:** false, flattering words.

tended Press-Gang, and meet him at *London,* he pretending he had Business there which required Haste; so he left me to travel with those Gentlemen at leisure. I mistrusted nothing, but kept along with them very well satisfied.

When we came to *London,* and I did not see my Father, I began to cry; but they wheedled[1] me, and told me, he was busie on Ship-board, so they would carry me to him, and there I should see the Sea, and Ships, the most wonderful things in the World. I then went with them in a Boat, where there were several Boys and Girls, and so came amongst many Ships; at last we got to one, into which we mounted: They shew'd me the Ropes, and Tackling[2] of all sorts, amusing me, with telling the Use of them: At last, we were to go down to eat some Sweet meats, and drink some Punch; and very merry we all were.

Here I staid with my Companions, playing, and fooling with one another, till all on a sudden, we were lock'd down in this Place. Then our Mirth turned into Sighs and Tears, being doubly frighted, when we were told, we were sailing to the *Indies.* However, they wheedled us all, according to our respective Circumstances; in particular, they told me, I should meet my Father there, he being gone in another Ship, which they pretended was thro' Mistake: But I had now learn'd to believe nothing they said; but found we were, what they call'd *kid-knap'd.*

Thus, we all sate in Grief, till the Sea began to turn our Sorrow into Sickness; and a Storm arising, added Fright to the rest. The Cries amongst us were grievous; one crying, he should never again see his Father, and another, his Mother, this or that Play-fellow, and so on. But, amongst the rest, a Girl of about a dozen or fourteen Years old, with whom I had made a particular acquaintance, wept grievously, because she should never see *Jackey Mechant* any more. I wonder'd to hear her name my Name; so I ask'd her, who *Jackey Mechant* was? She said, he was a very pretty Boy, that lived next House to her Father and Mother, and was her Playfellow, and used to lie with her, till his Mother began to think her with Child; then it was that his Father and he together,

---

1. **wheedled:** manipulated, lied to.
2. **Tackling:** general term for a ship's equipment.

brought her to this Captain; to whom they sold her, and *Jackey* was to have the mony for himself. He promised me, continued she, that he would be sure to come to me on board, and go along with me to the *Indies;* but he is not come according to his word.

While we were in this Discourse, the Captain came into the Hold, bringing with him another Passenger, which he had bought just before he set sail; and promis'd to keep him in his Cabbin, and teach him *Navigation;* but in the storm his Cries and Fears were troublesome to the Mariners, so he told that Boy, he being so Hen-hearted, must e'en go amongst the other Slaves; the Girl looking up, and wiping her blubbered Face, soon found our new Passenger to be *Jackey Mechant;* we asked him why he was put to Sea, he said, that his Father had sold him to that Captain, for Faults he was forbid to tell till he got into the *Indies;* but with much persuasion, he told us, that it was for calling his Mother, *Whore;* for, said he, one of my Play-fellows, call'd me *Bastard* and *Son of a Whore,* for which we quarrelled, and I got him down; and in my Fury hurt his Eye so, that he is like to lose it, and I had like to be hang'd for it, if taken; but one of them bigger and older than the rest, told me, that my Mother was not Squire *Mechant's* Wife; but one that had been his Wife's Chamber-maid; and much more to this purpose.

Dorinda hearing all this, knew, that this Boy, her Son spake of, must needs have been her Husband's Bastard; she said, he was alike cruel to one as to the other; she then bid him go on, and tell how he got out of the Ship; the Storm was great (added he) and a cross Wind continued, which drove us on the Coast of *Portugal,* where the Captain cast Anchor for a little time; there he let us out of the Hold, to come on the Deck for Air, having been very Sick during the Storm. I seeing my self at liberty, and pretty near the Land, knowing I could swim very well, having practis'd the same among the Boys in the Country, I leaped into the Sea, and so got to Land; here I found some difficulty, having no Language but *English.*

At last I met with this *English* Gentleman who took me into his Service, and I attended him faithfully in divers places of his Travels, till I am arrived at the Feet of you, my dear Mother. She embraced him most tenderly; and many Tears were shed on both sides, till dinner came, which caus'd a Cessation of these Endearments; the poor *Dorinda*, not only din'd heartily, but the good Meal she made, was attended with great satisfaction, or rather Transport.[1]

As we sat at Dinner, reflecting on divers of these Occurrences, we heard a Hawker cry in the Streets, *The Tryal, Condemnation, and Execution, of* John Mechant *at Tyburn,*[2] *for having barbarously murdered a Woman by whom he had a Child; and because she ask'd him for Money to maintain it, he most inhumanly stab'd her.*

We listened to the Repetition of the Cry, and *Dorinda* plainly found it was the Name of her Husband, as indeed, it prov'd to be the same Person.

You may imagine, that great was her Surprize, Horrour, and Amazement. She retired to her Chamber; and I went to find out the bottom, whether it was so; and what could be made out for her support, which I hope will be pretty well; there being something considerable in the State-funds, besides those Farms in the Country; in all which I will be as helpful to her as I can.

You will do extreamly well said *Galecia;* and since your Wife is dead, when you have brought things to a Period, e'en take the Widow for your pains. The whole Story has been a Romantick Chain, of very odd Contingencies; so make that the last Link. Very well contriv'd, said the Gentleman. I will go home and

Take Counsel of my Pillow.

The Gentleman being gone, *Galecia* reflected on his Discourse, as also on those other Stories she had heard amongst the Ladies: She began to think the World was made up with Extravagant Adventures. Amongst the Old *Romances,* said she to her self, we find strange and improbable Performances, very surprizing Turns and Rencounters; yet still all tended to vertuous Ends, and the Abhorrence of Vice; But here is the Quintessence[3] of Wickedness design'd and practiced, in a special manner, in the story of *Jack Mechant,* who sold both his lawful and nat-

---

1. **Transport:** extreme pleasure.

2. **Tyburn:** principal place of public execution by hanging since 1388.

3. **Quintessence:** the ultimate; most essential part of any substance.

ural Son, and murdered his Concubine because she did not starve her Child.

Those honourable Romances of old *Arcadia, Cleopatra, Cassandra,*[1] &c. discover a Genius of Vertue and Honour, which reign'd in the time of those Heroes, and Heroines, as well as in the Authors that report them; but the Stories of our Times are so black, that the Authors, can hardly escape being smutted, or defil'd in touching such Pitch.

As she was in these Reflections, she heard a Noise in the Street; and looking out, she saw every body gazing up at a strange Light in the Sky: Good God! said our *Galecia* sure the general Conflagration[2] is begun, when the Almighty will purge the World from its Dross,[3] by Fire as heretofore he did from its Filth by Water.[4]

As *Galecia* was in these Thoughts, her Friend *Miranda*[5] came up into her Appartment, being frighted with that Light. She said, she durst go no farther; but beg'd House-room that Night; I can sit in a Chair by the Fire, said she, and not trouble you with a Bed-fellow: But *Galecia* readily offered her part of her Bed; telling her, they would take a Walk together in the Morning over the *Park,* to visit their old Friend *Amarantha.* They had some Confabulation[6] together, *Miranda* telling *Galecia,* how ill her Husband us'd her, how he had left her with Child, and went away with a Mistress; I will not say a Whore, said she, because the Creature is a Gentlewoman; otherwise she deserves no other Name. What is become of him, I know not. When he was landed in *Flanders,* he writ to me to Inform me he was got safe over Sea, but was soon to remove from thence; so bid me not write to him till I heard from him again: For he said, he was going home into his own Country, he having quitted his

---

1. **Cleopatra, Cassandra:** ten-volume heroic romances (1647–56, 1644–50), by Gauthier de Costes de la Calprenède (1614–63), which influenced English Restoration drama and romance.

2. **Conflagration:** fire.

3. **Dross:** impure matter.

4. **Fire . . . Water:** referring to God's punishments for humanity's wickedness. **Fire:** See Mal. 4:1. **Water:** the cataclysmic Flood; see Gen. 6–8.

5. **Miranda:** name typical of a romance heroine, and a possible reference to Prospero's daughter in Shakespeare's *The Tempest.*

6. **Confabulation:** familiar conversation or chat.

Post in the Army; whether he took this Lady with him as a Wife; or what else was the Mystery, I know not; but I have never heard from him since.

My Child dyed in few Weeks after it was born; which was an Addition to my Grief; However, it is happy; for the Count, his Father left me in such narrow Circumstances, I should have had much difficulty to have supported my self and him.

The Men of all Qualities, Countries, and Stations, said *Galecia,* are alike; there is no such thing as Vertue and Honour left amongst 'em, at least, in regard of their Wives; from the Lady to the Porter's Wife; I hear, all Womankind complain of the Unkindness of their Husbands. All which, said *Miranda,* proceeds from the Multitude of lewd Strumpets; who reign amongst us with Impunity. You are happy *Galecia,* continu'd she, that amongst your many Tribulations, you have not had the Affliction of an ill Husband to torment you; nor a good one, said *Galecia,* to consolate and protect me; But all these things are in the hands of Providence; in whose Protection let us recommend our selves this dreadful Night; for behold, the Sky seems more and more inflam'd; that, God only knows who shall live to see the Morning-Sun; or, perhaps, his bright Lamp may be quite put out.

Thus, our two Friends retired to their Rest, as if they were to rise to Immortality: to which we may apply the Proverb,

A good Conscience, is a continual Feast.

Vertue and Innocence are always safeguards; and screen'd our two Friends from fear that dreadful Night, so that they slept sound, and wak'd in the morning in due time to take a walk over the *Park,* to breakfast with their Friend *Amarantha,* who received them with all the marks of sincere Kindness and Friendship, as far as her melancholy circumstance would permit; for she had buried her Husband, since she had seen them, and tho' she had been a Widow some Years, yet the sight of these old Friends renew'd her Grief, and, spight of all Endeavours, made her shed a flood of Tears.

They endeavour'd to consolate each other with what Arguments they could on such an occasion. Ah me, said she, I could not be just to his memory, if I should cease to lament him as long as I live, his Loss being irreparable: He was the best of Husbands, best of Friends, best of Masters, a true Lover of his King, and the Laws of his Country, facetious amongst Friends, grave amongst Strangers, pleasant amongst the Young, and a Pattern to his Elders. In fine, his Deportment was instructive, and agreeable to all; but above all, to me, whom he most tenderly lov'd, and accordingly, was in every thing entirely obliging. In all which, replied *Galecia,* he did but render Justice to your Merit. But there are so few Husbands who do so in these Days, that one ought to prize that Man very much, who treats his Wife with common Civility, and does not place his Prostitute in competition with, or rather above her, not only in Affection, but even in external Behaviour; of which, this our beautiful Friend *Miranda* is an Example. To which *Miranda* replied, That she was not worthy to be an Example in Discourse; so beg'd them to call another Cause: In particular, said she to *Amarantha,* tell us, if you can, what is become of our old Friend and Play-fellow *Bellemien?*[1] Alas, said *Amarantha,* that poor Girl has been very unfortunate in her Marriage, as I shall relate to you, when Breakfast is over.

The *Story* of *Bellemien,*
Related by *Amarantha.*

There was a Widow-Gentlewoman somewhat decayed[2] in the World, who had but one only Child, a beautiful Daughter. This Gentlewoman apply'd her self, by Industry, to salve[3] those Sores which hard Fortune had made in her Circumstances, thereby to enable her to educate this her Daughter a little suitable to her Birth, without being dependant on her Relations. This caused her to let her House to Lodgers, but chiefly to Men, as being supposed the least Trouble: She likewise took their Linen to mend and starch; or any sowing-work,[4] whereby she could honestly get a Penny. Amongst these Gentlemen that lodged at, or frequented her House, there was one who became extreamly enamour'd

---

1. **Bellemien:** a name suggesting handsome appearance.
2. **decayed:** reduced in prosperity and health.
3. **salve:** treat with a healing ointment.
4. **sowing-work:** sewing.

with *Favorella* (for that is the Name of her beautiful Daughter;) which, as soon as the Mother perceiv'd, she took all possible care to prevent any dangerous Correspondence,[1] and the Daughter was no less circumspect. All which so inflam'd the young Gentleman, that sometimes he resolved to marry her: For though Riches were wanting, (which in these days is counted the main Article) yet where Beauty, Vertue, and Prudence, are united there is reason to hope for a happy Espousal; those three Ingredients being of force to draw in that other, to wit Riches. Nevertheless, though his Inclinations were strong, and the young Creature's Affections correspondent; yet they fear'd to marry, he having only a younger Brother's Fortune to depend upon, of which he should be depriv'd if he married without the Consent of his Mother, which he knew would be in vain to ask, when a suitable Fortune did not accompany his Request. Nevertheless, such were the Charms of the young *Favorella,* that maugre[2] all the oppositions of Reason and Interest, he was forced to comply with his Passion, in the Espousing her. However, they were so discreet, as to take care to keep their Marriage absolutely a Secret, till time should help them through the Difficulty. But as these clandestine Marriages seldom prove happy, so this between *Palemon*[3] and *Favorella* was wholly unfortunate.

Now thus it hapned, *Palemon's* elder Brother being married some time, and having no prospect of Children he began to joyn his Importunities with those of his Mother and other Friends, to make *Palemon* betake himself to a Wife, whereby to provide Heirs for the Family; and to further their Design, pitcht upon our Friend *Bellemien,* who, you know, is the only Child of her Mother, and has a Fortune suitable to his Family; and indeed, such was her Fortune, that her Mother would not have accepted a younger Brother, but that the way to the paternal Estate lay open, by the Defect of Heirs on the Elder Brother's side. At the same time, *Palemon* and *Favorella,* began to find their Circumstances too nar-

---

1. **Correspondence:** communication.

2. **maugre:** in spite of.

3. **Palemon:** heroic figure of romance, including Dryden's *Palemon and Arcite* (1700) and d'Urfés four-part *L'Astrée* (1607, 1610, 1619, 1624).

row for a decent Subsistance, which began to call loud on them to change the Measures of their living. His Friends knowing he had a sufficient Allowance from his Family, wonder'd that he could not live within compass; and thought he surely kept Company with lewd Women; therefore they pressed him the more to marry. The poor *Favorella,* told him, she was willing to ease him of the Burden of maintaining her, and so would go to Service, work to the *Exchange,* or any thing to make him easie.

At this time there was a Clerk just out of his time, who had a pretty paternal Estate, which he offered to settle upon her a Joynture, as not knowing of her prior Marriage.

Things being on this footing on both sides, truly, *Palemon* and *Favorella* agreed between themselves, that both of them should try to enlarge their Circumstances, by the way which seem'd chalk'd out by Fortune, and so each of them to marry the respective Persons thus provided; promising to continue a mutual Affection for each other, and if Fortune should ever turn things about, so as to have it proper for them to come together again, then to remember their first conjugal Vows, and live no longer asunder; in the mean time, endeavour to bear their Yoke in Patience in these their new Espousals, which courted their acceptance.

Thus the unhappy Couple dispensed each with other to an absolute Separation: He married our Friend *Bellemien,* and she married the young Lawyer, who honestly setled his Estate upon her: and they both lived in these their new Espousals well enough: Whether they held any secret correspondence, is unknown, we are bound to hope the best, and conclude they did not, (if one may call that the best;) but it is a moot point, which is best, or rather, which is worst, every way in such a Station, being bad, even to a great Degree of Wickedness. In due time *Palemon* had a Child; by this his new Wife, and all things went on in pretty good Order and Harmony amongst them; the Relations on both sides were pleas'd to see an Heir to inherit the Riches of both Families.

This Tranquillity held till the Death of our young Lawyer, *Favorella's* Husband; for he lived but few Years with her, and then *Palemon's* Flame began to revive, and burn with Violence. Then he began to have Gripes in Conscience, or at least, his Passion was disguis'd in that dress;

Favorella's Beauty dazled him, *Favorella's* Wrongs stung him; *Favorella* was his first Love, his first Wife, and ought to be the Object of his Affection; she ought to be righted, his Conscience quieted; But chiefly, (as one may suppose) his Inclinations gratified; which was no way to be done, but by quitting his latter Spouse, and cleaving to the former. We will suppose, that his Thoughts met with great Obstacles on the other side, to think how he should ruine a vertuous young Gentlewoman, expose the Child he had by her, arm all her Relations with Revenge, and disoblige his own Family.

Thus was this unhappy Gentleman become miserable through his own Folly. His Days he pass'd in Anxiety, and his Nights in Despair; his Bed was no place of Rest, nor his Table of Refreshment; his House was a Den of Horror, and abroad a Wilderness of Woe: his Wife's Kindness was disagreeable, and her very Caresses nauceous. He betook himself to Devotion, and reading good Books; all which served but to augment his Grief, by setting his Crimes in a just light, before the Eyes of his Understanding. He had no third Person to whom he could or durst to communicate this his Affliction, thereby to receive Counsel or Consolation; but was forced to feed this gnawing Worm of an ill Conscience secretly, till it devoured his whole internal Quiet.

Thus, after many Debates with himself, he at last comply'd with Inclination, and resolv'd secretly to leave his House, Wife, and Family, and go live in private Lodgings with *Favorella*, whom he thought was his true and lawful Wife. This he put in Execution, and writ the following Billet[1] to his latter Wife, our friend *Bellemien:*

Madam,

I have taken a resolution to live from you; I desire you, as you favour your own Quiet, not to inquire after me; I have very good reason for what I do; be kind to the poor Babe you have by me, for its sake and your own; for, I confess there is nothing due to it for my sake, its wretched Father,

Palemon.

---

1. **Billet:** short letter.

Having writ this Letter, he step'd into the Nursery, where the innocent Babe lay smiling in its Cradle.

At his approach, it sliggar'd[1] and stretch'd out his little Hands to catch hold of him, as if with dumb Shews, it would have said, *Pappa, will you leave me to the risque of Fortune? Will you leave me, your only Child, whom God has given you to support your Name and Family, by whom your Race must be continued? Ah, unkind Pappa!* And then its little face drew into a form of crying. He look'd on the innocent Babe with tenderness; and bowing down to kiss it, the poor innocent clasp'd its little Fingers in his Wig, as loth to part with its Father. This brought Tears from the Eyes of the unhappy *Palemon.* Oh, Wretch that I am, said he to himself, thus to leave this lovely Innocent, the Pledge of his Mother's tender Love! and thus to part from a faithful vertuous Woman; to leave her to the Censure of this World, as if guilty of some heinous Crime; or at least, as if she was of some ill Temper or froward[2] Humour, unfit to cohabit withal! Whereas she is sweet, vertuous, and mild, as Summer-dew, or the Vernal Sun. Her Family and Fortune have enrich'd and honoured thee, brought thee to be esteem'd and respected, above thy Merit! *Palemon,* to what exigence have thy Crimes and Follies reduced thee!

Thus sighing, thus weeping, thus regarding the Child with Tenderness, he heard the Nurse coming up stairs; upon which he hastily step'd into his Closet, where he made up the foresaid Billet; and then left his House, never more to return.

When his Lady arose, and saw his Closet-door open, she thought to run to him with open Arms, and wonted kind Caresses; but instead of her dear *Palemon,* she found the said surprizing Letter. At which her Grief and Wonder was such, as I cannot describe; therefore leave you (good Ladies) to guess. Her Mother and all her Relations, soon became Co-partners of her Grief and Disgrace. Which way to turn themselves in it, they knew not; where to enquire, or what measures to take, they were wholly ignorant. But length of time and much Enquiry, brought

---

1. **sliggar'd:** roused.
2. **froward:** perverse.

them to the Knowledge of his Habitation, and how he lived with *Favorella*, as Man and Wife. But when they came to the Knowledge hereof, they were at a loss where to begin, or at which End of this ill-spun Thread to take hold; some advis'd 'em to the spiritual Court,[1] there to prosecute him as an Adulterer; others, on the contrary, saying, that was playing the Game for them, just as they had dealt the Cards, and the way to bring on a Divorce; which was most useful to them of all things; Others advised differently, no body knowing how the affair was, touching his former Marriage with *Favorella*. Amongst many Enquiries, and Consultations, *Bellemien* chanc'd to be at a Friend's House, where she was relating her Griefs, and telling the differing sorts of Advice given her by several Friends; some for the Spiritual Court, some for Common Law, others for bringing the Case into Parliament.

Amongst these Gentlewomen, there was one (an absolute Stranger) who told her that she believed she could give her better Counsel than any Lawyer in the three Inns of Court, if she would go privately with her into the next Room; which accordingly she did; and there she told *Bellemien* the whole Story of his first Marriage, the Cause and manner of the Separation, all that had pass'd in his second Espousals; the manner of leaving his House, and the Grief he underwent in parting with his Child; insomuch that *Bellemien* was greatly surpriz'd, and thought this Gentleman at least, a *Scotch*-Seer,[2] if not a She-Conjurer;[3] or else that she had feign'd a Story.

Now, Madam, said the unknown Person, that you are inform'd of the true state of the Case, consider well how to act. Suppose you could get proof of this first Marriage, which will be difficult, what will it avail? 'Twill only make the Man you once lov'd affectionately, appear a great Villain, your self Mother of an illegitimate Child, and deprive it too of the Right of Inheritance, by proving it a Bastard; and his first Wife of a comfortable Subsistance, which she enjoys now in right of her second

---

1. **spiritual Court:** ecclesiastical court.

2. **Scotch-Seer:** probably a reference to Duncan Campbell (1680?–1730), celebrated soothsayer and subject of a 1720 life history by Daniel Defoe (1660–1731).

3. **She-Conjurer:** witch, sorcerer.

Husband, the young Lawyer, she married afterwards: For if a prior Marriage be proved, that Joynture[1] reverts to his Family.

Now, Madam, though this Women enjoys your Husband, she lies under the scandal of a kept-Mistress, a Prostitute, a Concubine, a Strumpit, *&c.* despised by all vertuous People; whilst you enjoy your Honour, your Reputation, the Compassion of all the World, who esteem you for your Patience, and your Child is Heir to its Family on both sides. Now, if you please, take the Counsel of the unhappy *Favorella,* your Rival: I say, take this Counsel from me, who am *Palemon's* first and lawful Wife; and remember, that, with the Proverb,

'Tis better, to sit still, than rise up, and fall.

At these Words, *Bellemien* swoon'd in her Chair, whilst *Favorella* fled out at a Backdoor, resolving for the future eternally to avoid her Presence.

This Story being ended, *Galecia* and *Miranda* took their Leaves, in hopes to get to Prayers, in their Way home: But they came too late, for the People were just coming out of Church, as they got thither.

Returning back, they found a Mob gathering, which almost obstructed their Passage; one crying out, *You Rogue, you detain my Wife from me; but I will make you produce her, or* Newgate *shall hold you.* Then another cry'd aloud, *Out upon thee, Villain, I am thy Wife.* Our two Friends thought, this was a feign'd Noise, design'd only to gather a Crowd, for the conveniency of picking Pockets; so they hastned by as fast as they could, each to their respective Lodgings.

By such time as *Galecia* had rested and dined, there came a Gentleman to visit her, bringing with him a young Gentlewoman, whom he presented to *Galecia,* telling her, that he took the Liberty to bring this Stranger to her, that she might receive a little Consolation, by discoursing in a Language she understood; because *English* was utterly unknown to her: For though she was the King of *England's* Subject,[2] yet being born at *Paris,* and always educated in a *French* Convent, she knew no

---

1. **Joynture:** property promised in marriage settlement to support a woman if she were widowed.

2. **Subject:** born abroad of English parents, she had the right to English citizenship.

other Language. *Galecia* received her with a civil Decency, bidding her welcome into *England,* and wishing her Happiness, in the Country which ought to have been the Place of her Nativity, as it is now (and I hope, said she will continue to be) the Place of your Abode.

No indeed, reply'd the Gentleman, such is her Misfortune, as deprives her of that Happiness, the Particulars of which I shall leave her to relate, and wait upon you again. O good Sir, said the young Stranger, do you inform this Gentlewoman of my unhappy Adventures; and do it in *English*, lest I sink with Confusion to hear my Follies related in a Language I understand. Hereupon the Gentleman began the story as follows.

The *History* of *Malhurissa,*[1]
Related by her *Friend.*

This Gentlewoman, said he, had the misfortune to lose her Parents when very young, who left her to the Care of her Uncle, a worthy Gentleman; but his Duty calling him to the Army, she was educated in a *Convent*, according to the Custom of those Countries, where they grow up under a constant Instruction and Practice of Vertue and Piety, in which she made a Proficiency suitable to the Endeavours of those holy Votaries. Her Uncle being to go to the Army to make his Campagne, thought it convenient to remove her to a *Convent* of a less rigorous Order, where she might learn the more polite Parts of Education; as Dancing, Singing, Musick, and the like; get acquainted with young Ladies of Quality, and be permitted to dress, something more according to the Mode of the World, than what was us'd in the other.

This Removal he committed to the Care of one, whom her Mother had brought out of *England* with her at the *Revolution,*[2] and had always attended this young Creature. He left with this young Niece her Mother's Rings, Watch, Necklace, and divers Suits of Apparel, with fine Linnen, rich Laces, and the like; and that she might want nothing for

---

1. **Malhurissa:** a name suggesting unhappy or unfortunate.

2. **Revolution:** Revolution of 1688, when James II fled from England and set up his court-in-exile at St. Germain-en-Laye, France.

that Year, he left an hundred *Louis' D'ors*[1] for her Pension and other necessary Occasions. Having thus disposs'd this Affair, he together with other Officers, went away to the Army.

Now it was, that this wicked Wretch the foresaid Attendant, had the Opportunity to betray the poor young Creature. When they were come out of the *Convent,* and in the Coach, in order to go to the other, together with their Trunks, and other Necessaries, her Attendant ask'd her, if she had not a Fancy to go to St. *Germain's,* which had been the Court of their *English* Sovereign; for, said she, now we are got in the Coach, we can go thither, and divert you for a Day or two, e'er you enter your Enclosure. The young Lady, who had never seen any thing but her Cloyster, was eager to embrace this Proposal; so to St. *Germain's* they went; and stayed some days, viewing the Castle, and all the Appartments, where the King, Queen, and Prince kept their respective Courts, the Garden, Walks in the Wood and Park, the Churches of the Fryers,[2] both in the Town and Forest.

Going to the Parish-Church to Prayers they met a Gentleman that claim'd acquaintance with Mrs. *Vileman* (for that was the name of our Attendant.) He told her, that he was going directly to *Paris,* to enquire for her, to let her know that her Father in *England* was dead, and had left her very considerable Effects, and shew'd them a Letter which he pretended to have receiv'd to this Purpose. Mrs. *Vileman* seem'd struck with Affliction, Confusion and Hurry, in which the Gentleman pretended to comfort her; particularly in reference to the good Fortune left her, for which it was necessary to go to *England,* as soon as possible.

Then the Question arose, whether she should go by *Callis* or *Diepe;*[3] but the Gentleman advis'd her, by *Diepe;* for being got so far towards *Rohan,*[4] it was easie and cheap getting, to *Diepe,* and so cross over to *Rye;*[5] But Mrs *Vileman* reply'd, she could not go directly thence; because she must carry that young Gentlewoman to the *Convent* assign'd for her

---

1. **Louis' D'ors:** golden French coins.

2. **Fryers:** friars.

3. **Callis or Diepe:** Calais and Dieppe; ports on the northern coast of France.

4. **Rohan:** town in northern France.

5. **Rye:** port in Sussex, southern England.

Reception. Ah me, said the young Lady, it breaks my heart to think of parting with you; Methinks, I wish I was to go along with you to *England:* For beside the Unwillingness of being *separated* from you, I long to see *England,* and in particular, *London,* with all its Pomp and Riches; they say, it is much beyond *Paris.*

Thus this poor young Thing nibbled at the Bait they had lay'd for her; and they reply'd in delusive Words very fit to excite and improve her Curiosity. At last, the Gentleman said, it would be but a Frolick suitable to her Youth, to make use of this Opportunity; and being with the Person into whose Hands she was committed, no body would have great reason to blame the Enterprize; but on the contrary, applaud her Endeavours to improve her Knowledge of the World, when she had so fair an Opportunity. In short, the poor young Creature fell into the Trap they had lay'd for her, and consented to go with them to *England:* so they made their Coach carry them to *Poisey,*[1] where they took Water, and away they went to *Rohan;* the Gentleman making Love to[2] our young Lady all the way. They stay'd at *Rohan* some time, under colour of buying Goods to freight the Ship; For he pretended to be a great *London*-Merchant, Son to a Country-Gentleman of an Estate, in which *Vileman* joyn'd her Attestation; whilst he assur'd her of his everlasting Love and earnestly press'd her to be married. The poor young Girl was soon catch'd in the Ambuscade of *Cupid,*[3] this being the first Onset she ever made in the Field of Love. She consented to a Marriage, but he put it off with one Shuffle[4] or another. However, having gained her Consent to Marry, the next thing was, to advise her to let him lay out her Money in Merchandize, which would be so advantageous to her, that one hundred Pistoles[5] would be at least two hundred in *England;* to which she agreed, and accordingly parted with her Money, with satisfaction, to the Man she thought her Husband, or at least, to be such very soon; so next Morning they were to be married.

---

1. **Poisey:** Poissy; town near St. Germain-en-Laye.

2. **making Love to:** attempting to seduce.

3. **Ambuscade of Cupid:** ambush by the Greek god of love.

4. **Shuffle:** evasion.

5. **Pistoles:** golden coins, especially those from Spain, France, or Scotland.

I need not tell you what Arguments he used to persuade her to be his Bedfellow that Night, we will suppose they were such as is common on those occasions; as, that their promise to each other was the true and substantial Marriage; that the Parson was only as a Witness to that Promise; that if she refus'd him, he had very little reason to depend upon her Affection, or else that she doubted of his, and took him to be the worst of Miscreants and a thousand such idle Stories, wherewith innocent Maids are betray'd to Ruin, as was this young Gentlewoman.

In short, she consented to lye with him upon promise of Marriage next Morning. But, behold, when Morning came, he had so lay'd the Business, that the Sailors came with Noise and Hurry, saying that the Wind serv'd, and they were ready to set sail, so they arose in great haste to get to the Ship, and so away they came for *England;* she all the while believing her self his Wife; and that she had a great Cargo of Merchandize in the Ship. They got safe to *London,* and plac'd themselves in a Lodging among their own Gang of Villains. Here he pretended to great Business at the *Exchange,*[1] *Custom-House,*[2] and *Post-Office,* always in a hurry, and full of Employment. At last, he told her, that he wanted Money to discharge the Duties of his Merchandize at the *Custom-House;* so begs her to lend him some of her Rings and Jewels to raise it for that use: She believing her self his Wife, parted with every thing he requir'd; and as soon as the Goods should be discharg'd, they were to make a glorious publick Wedding.

On the other hand, Mrs. *Vileman* was hurried in looking after the Effects of her dead Father; so she borrow'd the young Gentlewoman's Cloaths, thereby to appear genteel amongst her Relations, as she pretended, till she could get her self equip'd in Mourning; tho' in reality, she had no Relations, being only a Bastard of an Officer in the Army, who never own'd her by reason of her Mother's insatiable Lewdness.

---

1. **Exchange:** Royal Exchange; principal site of merchants' transactions.

2. **Custom-House:** governmental building where customs taxes were collected and ships regulated for departure and arrival.

Thus was this poor young Creature strip'd of all she had, by one Sham or another. Nevertheless, they liv'd very well, both in Meat, Drink, and Lodging.

When they had got all from her, (then, according as it was concerted amongst 'em) the Landlady arrested them for Board and Lodging; only by a Sham-Officer; and so pretended to carry *Vileman* and the Rogue to Prison; whereas it was only a Shuffle, to get them away, and drop, her, when they had got all: For she being the supposed Wife, was not to be taken to Prison with them.

This poor Creature being thus strip'd of all, debauch'd, disgrac'd, deluded, and abandon'd, helpless, friendless, pennyless, in a Country where she understood not a Word of the Language; she knew not what to do. In the midst of this her Distress, she bethought her self to go to the Chapel of an Embassador, where she hop'd to find some body that could speak *French:* She addressing her self to the Porter,[1] he immediately call'd me to her, (said the Gentleman) and she soon made me understand her Business; so I recommended her to go into the Chapel, and there offer her self to God, at his holy Altar, and then I promis'd to come to her again; which accordingly I did, and took her into a little Room, where she repeated to me all this lamentable Story. After I had heard her out, I knew she was the Person on whose account I had receiv'd a letter from *France;* which, if you please to peruse, you are welcome.

The *Letter.*

Sir,

I am so well assured of your Readiness to do any good Office, that I address my self to you with the utmost Freedom, begging you, if possible, to find out a poor lost Sheep, my Niece, and to send her home to her Friends, particularly to me: For thus it is, Sir, The only Child of my dear deceas'd Sister, has been deluded away into England *by a wicked Fellow, who has abandon'd his Wife here in* Paris, *a very honest industrious Woman; but he an idle Villain. My Enquiry reach'd after them to* Rohan, *where it is said, they lived*

---

1. **Porter:** one who has charge of the entrance of a building.

together as Man and Wife; after which, they went for England. *I hope, there is a Possibility of finding her, because she cannot speak one Word of* English. *She is young, and tolerably handsome. Sir, if you can find her, be pleased to send her to me: Assure her, that I will receive, and forgive her, even tho' she should be with Child by the Villain; and shall own my self extreamly oblig'd to you, who am, Sir,*

> Your Obedient Humble Servant,
> *Goodman.*

Having thus found her (continu'd the Gentleman) I was about to take her to a House, where I might give her something to eat (for she was faint,) when, just at the Chapel-Door, I met her pretended Husband; who immediately took hold of her, calling her *Wife.* Vile Wretch, said I, thou knowest, she is none of thy Wife; therefore touch her not. How! (reply'd he) will you dare to say, she is not my Wife? I have sought her three or four Days, and now I find who has debauch'd and detained her from me, for which I shall make you pay dearly. (He not dreaming I had any Letter from her Uncle;) and, I believe, he would have had the impudence to have enter'd a Process against me, in hopes to have squeez'd Money from me, supposing, no doubt, that I would give something to be quiet, and not be expos'd in the Face of the Church, and my Lord Embassador. This made him very clamorous, audacious and insolent; insomuch that a Mob gather'd about us, and there was no passing; he striving to get her from me, I holding her fast, and the People were clamorous, according to their several sentiments, so that I was going to call a Constable both for her security and my own.

But Providence sent us a better Officer of Justice, than any other in the King's Dominions: For at this juncture, his real Wife appear'd, crying out to him, Vile Wretch, how dar'st thou call any body Wife, but me. She had a Constable with her, who seiz'd him, in order to carry him before a Magistrate; for which reason the Mob dispers'd; so that we got out of the Crowd; and after I had refreshed her and my self at an Eating House, I conducted her hither, and now beg you to entertain her in *French,* whilst I go seek a safe Lodging for her, till I can convey her to her Uncle.

The Gentleman being gone, *Galecia* amus'd the young Lady as well as she could, by giving her Consolation, and blaming the Wickedness of *Vileman*, her Governante,[1] excusing her Folly, imputing it to her want of knowing the World; but chiefly applauding the extream Goodness of her Uncle, who verify'd our *English* Proverb,

A Friend in Need, is a Friend indeed.

Moreover, *Galecia,* the better to divert *Malhurissa* from the Thoughts of her Misfortunes, ask'd her, if she had no diverting Story or Rencounter that had hapned in her *Convent* amongst the Novices, or young Ladies the Pensioners.[2] To which *Malhurissa* reply'd, No; saying, nothing remarkable had appeared there, but extraordinary Vertue and Piety, the Religious performing their Devotions in exact Regularity, and the Seculars as perfect in their Respect and Obedience; so that all things went on in a constant Harmony, without the least Discord; which I am bound to acknowledge, though with Shame and Confusion of Face, for having so ill practis'd those excellent Precepts and Examples.

'Tis true, indeed, the wicked *Vileman* my Governante, for her abominable Behaviour, is extreamly blameable; but that would not excuse me, Madam, in the Thoughts of any less charitable Person than your self, who is pleased to disguise my Crimes in the Robes of Youth and Ignorance, and hide them under the Umbrage[3] of unthinking Innocence: Yet they appear to me in too true a Light, for my inward Repose; which brings to my Thoughts a Story I heard at *Rohan,* of a Vile Governante, who is a kind of Parallel with my Wicked *Vileman;* only her Crime exceeds, if possible, that of *Vileman's:* And it is a dreadful Truth, being recorded in the Courts of Justice at *Rohan;* as hereafter related.

---

1. **Governante:** governess.

2. **Pensioners:** students who board at the covent.

3. **Umbrage:** excuse.

The *Story* of *Succubella*,[1]
Related by *Malhurissa*.

There was a rich Merchant at *Rohan,* who had but one Child, a Daughter; whose Mother being dead, the good Father endeavour'd to find out a fit Person to attend her in the Quality of a Governess. This Woman seem'd very prudent, vertuous and just in all her Actions, and educated the young Gentlewoman accordingly, that she appear'd a fine well behav'd Creature, dutiful to her Father, respectful to her Betters, obliging to her Equals, civil to her Inferiours, charitable and compassionate to the Poor: She was assiduous in her Devotions to Heaven, and regular in all her Actions; in particular, she had a great Tendency towards the *Capuchins*[2] Order, and their extream Mortifications[3] took with her; so that her Father's House being pretty near their Cloyster, she went thither daily to Prayers, and the Superiour, of the House was her Ghostly Father.[4]

Thus had the *Governante* form'd this young Gentlewoman towards God and the World; by which she gain'd the Esteem and Commendations of every body: But now, behold, what a Snake lay hid in the Grass.

The *Governante* having one night got her Pupil to Bed, as usual; she did not immediately fall asleep; but lay quiet, and observed the *Governante,* who instead of undressing her self, in order to come to bed, seem'd to accommodate her Person, as if she was going a visiting; which the Girl wondered at, but said nothing: At length she saw her take something out of her Cabinet, and with it smear'd her self; and then immediately ran up the Chimney, The Girl was greatly amaz'd hereat, it being to her an unconceivable Mystery. However, between Thoughtfulness and Sleep, she pass'd the Night; and when she wak'd in the Morning found her *Governante* in Bed with her, according to Custom. She was amaz'd, remembring what she had seen over Night, and ask'd her,

---

1. **Succubella:** from succubi, female demons who have intercourse with the devil.

2. **Capuchins:** monastic order of St. Francis.

3. **Mortifications:** austere living, including self-inflicted bodily pain to direct one's attention to spirituality.

4. **Ghostly Father:** spiritual advisor.

whether she went, and what made her go up the Chimney; She shuffled and fumbled at first, but her young Mistress pressing the thing home, she said, Hush, Miss; this is a Secret to Girls; but when you are a Woman I will let you know.

Miss was forced to be satisfied with this Answer for a while; but afterwards began to press her about this Secret; still she put her off from time to time with divers Evasions. At last, the Girl being impatient, told her *Governante* that she should not pretend to keep her a Child always; therefore she would know this Secret. The *Governante,* perhaps, thinking that if she did not gratifie her, she would tell her Father, or ask some body else: Wherefore, she told her, if she would promise to be very secret, she would let her know all, and she should go with her to a Place where she would meet with good Company, Mirth, Feasting, Musick, and Dancing, *&c.* So the Girl promis'd Secrecy, and the next Night agreed to go together; which accordingly they did; the *Governante* and she, anointing themselves, utter'd some Words, and so both went up the Chimney; but flying over the *Capuchins* Cloyster, the Clock struck Twelve; and then Miss, according to custom, made the sign of the Cross in the Name of the Trinity, and down she fell in the midst of the Cloyster. The Religious getting up at that Hour, going through the Cloyster to their Church to chaunt *Mattins,*[1] they found this young Gentlewoman sprawling in the midst of the Cloyster, almost dead with the Fall: They took her up, and put her into a warm Bed, let her blood,[2] and apply'd all other Necessaries on such an occasion; so that she came to her self, though greatly bruised.

In the Morning the Superiour came to the Merchant's House, where he was kindly received by him; but the good Father told him, that he came that morning to visit Miss, his young Penitent.[3] The Merchant knowing nothing of what had happened, told him merrily, that his Daughter was so ill an Huswife,[4] that she was not up yet; so he sent to the *Governante* to tell his Daughter, that the Father Superiour was come

---

1. **Mattins:** matins; prayers recited at midnight.
2. **let her blood:** bled her to remove impurities.
3. **Penitent:** under the guidance of a confessor, one who expresses remorse for sins.
4. **so ill an Huswife:** worthless girl.

to visit her this mornning; the *Governante* sent word, that Miss had not rested well in the Night, so was asleep this morning, and she was loth to awake her yet. In the mean time, the Wicked *Succubella,* the *Governante,* was preparing for her escape: But the Father Superiour hearing this Answer, ask'd the Merchant, if he was sure his Daughter was in his House that Night. Which put him to a stand; the good Father added, that he was sure she was not, and desired the Merchant to go up with him into his Daughter's Chamber and assure himself of the Truth he told him; for said he, your Daughter is in our Cloyster at this time: whereupon they both went up into the young Gentlewoman's Chamber; where missing her, they immediately seiz'd on *Succubella,* the wicked *Governante,* committed her into the Hands of Justice, upon which her Process[1] was made, and she confess'd the whole Fact, succinctly, just as as the young Gentlewoman had told the *Capuchins;* so she had the Reward of her Sorcery, at a Stake where she was burnt alive; and is upon record, a miserable Example, of the extreamest Wickedness.

This Story, said *Galecia,* is very extraordinary, and seems, to oppose those who will not allow any possibility of Mortals having Commerce with Spirits, so as to give them power to move them at their pleasure; to make 'em run up a Chimney, fly into the Air, enabled to do mischief, and the like; the truth is, I am not Philosopher enough, to argue the point; I can only refer my opinion, to an old Proverb,

> *Needs must, when the Devil drives.*

'Tis true, indeed, said *Malhurissa,* when I was at *Rohan,* there arose a Dispute amongst the Company, of the Impossibility of the Devil's having power to raise Spirits; and from one thing to another, the Case of the Witch of *Endor*[2] was cited; which caused great Disputes to arise, which would, I think, have been almost endless, but that a Gentlewoman produc'd a few Verses of her own Composing, which the Company lik'd; and tho' I did not understand *English,* I beg'd a Copy, in hopes I should learn, being just coming for *England:* They are as follows,

---

1. **Process:** legal inquiry, trial.

2. **Witch of Endor:** sorceress who counseled Saul before battle; see 1 Sam 28:7.

The *Inchantment.*

In guilty Night, and hid in false Disguise,
Forsaken Saul *to* Endor *comes, and cries,*
Woman, arise, call pow'rful Arts together,
And raise the Soul that I shall name, up hither.
WITCH. *Whom shall I raise, or call? I'll make him hear.*
SAUL. Samuel *alone, let him to me appear.*
Methinks, thou'rt frighted[1]*: Tell, what dost thou fear?*
WITCH.————*Nothing I fear but thee:*
For thou art Saul, *and hast beguiled me.*
SAUL. *Peace, and go on; what thou seest let me know.*
WITCH. *I see the Gods ascending from below.*
SAUL. *Who's that, that comes?————*
WITCH.————*An old Man mantled o'er.*
SAUL. *O, that is he, let me his Ghost adore.*
SAMUEL. *Why hast thou rob'd me of my Rest, to see*
That which I hate, this wicked World, and Thee?
SAUL. *O, I am much distrest, and vexed sore;*
God hath me left, and answers me no more.
Opprest with War, and inward Terrors too,
For Pity sake, tell me what I shall do.
SAMUEL. *Art thou forlorn of God, and com'st to me?*
What can I shew thee then, but Misery?
Thy Kingdom's gone, into thy Neighbour's Race;
Thy Host shall fall by Sword before thy Face.
Farewel, and think upon these Words with sorrow:
Thou, and thy Sons shall be with me to Morrow.[2]

They had just finish'd reading the Verses, when the Gentleman, *Malhurissa's* Friend, came to call her away to the Lodging he had hired for her. They had no sooner taken their leave, but *Galecia* casting her Eye

---

1. The Witch trembles. [Author's note.]
2. **In guilty…Morrow:** This poem paraphrases 1 Sam 28:7–19.

on the Window, saw there a Book, which a little Miss of her acquaintance had left; and found it to be written by the ingenious Mr. *Dyke:*[1] In it she read the following *Considerations.*[2]

Considerations out of Mr. *Dyche's Book.*

What is Man! Originally Dust, ingender'd in Sin, brought forth in Sorrow, helpless in his Infancy, giddy in his Youth, extravagant in his Manhood, and decrepit in his Age. His first Voice moves Pity, his last, Sorrow.

He is at his first coming into the World, the most helpless of all Creatures: For Nature cloaths the Beasts with Hair, the Birds with Feathers, the Fish with Scales: But Man is born naked; his Hands cannot handle, his Feet cannot walk, his Tongue cannot speak, his Eyes cannot see, nor his Ears hear, to any Use. The Beasts come into the World without Noise, and go to their Dug without help: Man, as soon as born, extends his little Voice, and crys for assistance; afterwards, he is simple in his Thoughts, vain in his Desires, and Toys are his Delight. He no sooner puts on his distinguishing Character Reason, but he burns it with the Wildfire of Passion, and disguises it with Pride, tears it with Revenge, sullies it with Avarice, and stains it with Debauchery.

His next Station, is a State of Misery; Fears torment him, Hopes distract him, Cares perplex him, Enemies assault him, Friends betray, Thieves rob, Wrongs oppress, Dangers way lay him.

His last Scene deplorable; his Eyes dim, his Ears deaf, his Hands feeble, Feet lame, Sinews shrunk, Bones dry, his Days full of Sorrow, his Nights of Pain, his Life miserable, his Death terrible.

Again,

Man is a Tennis-Ball of Fortune, a Shuttle-cock of Folly, a Mark for

---

1. **Mr. Dyke:** Oswald Dykes (1670?–1728), one of the most prominent compilers of ancient and modern proverbs, accompanied by illutrative tales or fables. Barker appears to have drawn on his explications in *Good Manners for Schools* (1700), *Moral Reflections upon Select English Proverbs* (1708), and *The Royal Marriage* (1722). She also appears to have consulted *The Fables of Aesop* (1692), compiled by Sir Roger L'Estrange (1616–1704) and Dykes, his assistant at Oxford.

2. **Considerations:** Dykes's reflections upon the human condition and contemporary moral problems begin with a paraphrase of Psalm 8 and continue with allusions to Sophocles (ca.496–450 B.C.), *Oedipus at Colonus* and the *Ajax.*

Malice. If poor, despis'd; if rich, flatter'd; if prudent, not trusted; if simple, derided. He is born crying, lives laughing, dies groaning.

Ah me, said *Galecia* to her self, how many melancholy Truths, this Learned Man has set down; yet all but common to our Nature. How many more are there extraordinary, and particular to each Person, caus'd by their Passions, Follies, or Misfortune, such as would render Life insupportable, were it not for the Hopes of a Happy Futurity. Then, O gracious Heaven, let that Hope abide, support, and increase in me, till, Fruition crown this my Expectation: For here is no Happiness to be found; for whether we look behind or before us, on the right hand or on the left, or round about us, we find nothing but Distress, Distractions, Quarrels, Broils,[1] Debts, Duels, Law-suits, Tricks, Cheats, Taxes, Tumults, Mobs, Riots, Mutinies, Rebellions, Battels, *&c.* where thousands are slain; nay, we make Slaughter a Study, and War an Art. Are we not then more irrational than Brutes, who endeavour to preserve their own kind, and protect their own Species? For that poor dirty Creature a Swine, a Beast which seems extreamly careless, with its Head always prone to the Earth; yet if any of its Kind cry, the whole Herd, run grunting to it, as if it were to assist the distressed, or at least, to compassionate their Fellow-Creature in its Sufferings. But, if two Boys quarrel, and fight, the Men will stand by and abett the Quarrel, till Blood and broken Bones succeed; and amongst the Gentry,[2] Quarrels arise of much worse consequence.

In these Cogitations[3] our *Galecia* sate, till *Morpheus*[4] accosted her, and with his leaden Rod, stretch'd over her Temples, she leaned back in her Chair, and sleeping, had the following Dream.

Galecia's Dream;

She dream'd that she was walking somewhere, in a very rough bad Way, full of great Stones, and sharp Flints, which hurt, and cut her Feet, and

---

1. **Broils:** quarrels.

2. **Gentry:** men and women of good birth, just below the rank of nobility.

3. **Cogitations:** reflections.

4. **Morpheus:** god of dreams.

almost threw her down; in some places Coaches and Carts overturn'd; in other places, Horse-men thrown, Limbs broken, Robbers rifling, Ladies affronted, Maids deluded by false Lovers, insolvent Debtors drag'd to Jayls by rude surly Bayliffs,[1] Wives mis-used, Husbands abused, Whores slanting,[2] honest Women despised, Girls trappan'd[3] by Bawds,[4] Boys mis-led by Drunkards, Jilts and Thieves; In short, she dream'd of nothing good or happy; which we will suppose, proceeded from her serious reflecting on Mr. *Dyke's* Considerations.

Then she thought her self on the Sea, amongst Fleets, in danger of being cast away; and sometimes of being seiz'd by Pyrates; a Noise of Wars, Towns bombarded, Cannonaded, taken and retaken; at which she very often started in her sleep.

After many of these frightful Visions were past, she imagin'd she came into a pleasant Valley, fertile of Corn, Fruits and Pasturage; pleasant Brooks, Rills and Springs, such as are rarely to be found; for they never froze in Winter, nor abated of their Water in Summer. Woods replete with singing Birds, Shoals of Pigeons in the Dove-House, which cooed about the Yard, in amorous Addresses to their innocent constant Mates. Sure, said *Galecia* to her self, this is the *Eden*[5] of old, or at least, the Land of Promise, flowing with more delicious Streams than those of Milk and Honey.[6] She was extreamly delighted with this Valley, thought it almost a terrestrial Paradice, excelling in fact, whatsoever the Fancies of Poets or Romances could represent: Here she thought she walk'd secure from Wolf, Bear or wild Boar, to fright or molest her Walks by Day; or carking[7] Cares to disturb her Sleep by Night; not being so divided from Neighbours, as to render it a Desart; nor so near, as to have their Houses intercept either the rising or the setting Sun.

---

1. **Bayliffs:** officers of the court.

2. **slanting:** prone.

3. **trappan'd:** entrapped; tricked.

4. **Bawds:** women who procure prostitutes for customers.

5. **Eden:** Paradise; see Gen. 2–3.

6. **Milk and Honey:** symbols of peace and plenty in the Promised Land; see Exod. 3:17.

7. **carking:** burdensome.

Thus she thought her self very happy: But it fell out, as she was one day walking beyond her usual bounds, towards a little rising Hill, a strange and hideous Giant came out of his Den, where he liv'd upon Rapin, Malice and Mischief; he studied the Black Art,[1] and with the Claws of his Hands, or rather his Fore-feet he wrote strange Figures and Cyphers, wherewith he conjur'd up Spirits, and inchanted People, and so got 'em into his Den: For he could not run fast enough to catch any body, his Toes being rotted, or broken off, which was the reason he often miss'd of his Prey; and by this means *Galecia* escaped his Clutches. At the sight of him she ran down the Hill with the utmost speed; and at the bottom she met with a good Philosopher, who study'd the Stars, and had a place in *Astrea's* Court:[2] He took her into his Cave, and so secured her from the Attempt of *Omrison*,[3] for that was the Name of the Giant.

After this Fright, she thought, a pretty young Man took her by the hand, telling her, he was her good *Genius*,[4] and would conduct her to some Diversion after her Surprize; so he led her up a Hill, which he told her, was *Parnassus*;[5] and said he would introduce her, to see some of the Diversions of the Annual Coronation of *Orinda*.[6] They came somewhat late; so that the grand Ceremonies were over: But they were time enough for the Singing and the Dancing.

Thus, all things being placed in perfect Order, and *Orinda* seated on a Throne, as Queen of Female Writers, with a Golden Pen in her Hand for a Scepter, a Crown of Laurel on her Head; *Galecia's Genius* plac'd her in a Corner, where she might see and hear all that pass'd; when lo, a

---

1. **Black Art:** sorcery, conjuring.

2. **Astrea's Court:** Astrea; in Greek mythology, goddess of innocence, purity and justice. The most likely literary associations are with the immensely popular four-part French romance *L'Astrée* (1607, 1610, 1619, 1624) by Honoré d'Urfé. Barker drew upon this work in *Exilius; or, The Banish'd Roman.*

3. **Omrison:** a name suggesting laughing or mocking (Latin).

4. **good Genius:** protective Spirit.

5. **Parnassus:** a mountain in Greece, sacred to the Muses. One of its peaks was sacred to Apollo, god of poetry.

6. Our Celebrated English Poetess, Mrs. Philips. [Author's note.] Katherine Philips (1632–64), "the Matchless Orinda," poet, translator and writer of letters. Barker and many others admired Philips' poetry and moral excellence.

Band of Bards[1] came, and cast themselves at *Orinda's* Feet, and there offer'd their Crowns, Wreaths, and Branches of Laurel, every one making a Speech in Verse, in praise of her Wit and Vertue; which she most graciously accepted, and bid them rise; when ranging themselves on each side her Throne, one[2] began to sing as follows.

The *Bard* sings.

> *We allow'd you Beauty, and we did submit*
> *To all the Tyrannies of it.*
> *Cruel Sex, will you depose us too in Wit?*[3]

Hereupon there were a Choir of pretty Creatures in form of Grasshoppers, with Golden Wings, but as large as new born Babes: And these answer'd the *Bard* in Chorus, *twit, twit, twit, twit, twit,* and this they repeated with an harmonious Melody, charming one's Senses into an absolute Transport. After this, the *Bard* proceeded; and when he came to these Words,

> *As in Angels, we*
> *Do in thy Verses see,*
> *Both improv'd Sexes eminently meet,*
> *They are than Man more strong, and more than*
> *Woman sweet,*[4]

A great Flock of Nightingales (glorious like Angels) joyn'd with the Grasshoppers, which again repeated their *Chorus,* as if Echoes to the *Bard,* whensoever his Cadence suited to their Voices; singing in an admirable Consort, with strange Turnings Flights and Strains, *Sweet, Sweet, Sweet, Sweet, Sweet,* &c.

---

1. **Bards:** poets.

2. **one:** Abraham Cowley (1618–67), celebrated playwright and lyric poet.

3. **We . . . Wit:** Cowley, "Upon Mrs. K. Phillips her Poems," *Poems by the most deservedly Admired Mrs. Katherine Philips* (1667), lines 1–3.

4. **As . . . sweet:** Cowley, "Upon Mrs. K. Phillips her Poems," lines 51–55.

In this manner, the *Bard*, the Grasshoppers and the Nightingales finish'd their Song. Then another *Bard*[1] began his Song in praise of this Queen: To which the Choir of Nightingales sung the *Chorus*: But his Song not being in *English, Galecia* did not rightly understand it, so as here to repeat the Words; but the Musick was extreamly fine.

After this, there came in a Band of *Fairies,* following their Queen, dressed in her Royal Robes, with a Crown on her Head, singing an old Song, as follows.

The *Queen* of *Fairies* sings.

Come, follow, follow me,
You Fairy Nymphs, with Glee,
Come, trip it on this Green,
And follow me, your Queen;
Hand in Hand we'll dance around,
In praise of Queen Orinda, *crown'd.*
Hither, ye chirping Crickets come,
And Beetles, with your drousie Hum;
And if with none of you we meet,
We'll dance to th' Echoes of our Feet.

Hereupon they struck up a Dance, whilst a Multitude of Crickets, and Beetles, sung the Measures, such as made incomparable Musick; quite otherwise than what they make in our Chimneys, or such as we hear the Beetles hum in a Summer-Evening.

Whilst they were thus Dancing, the Fairy Queen spy'd *Galecia,* as she was in a Corner: And whether she was angry to see a Mortal in that Assembly; or that she was excited by Charity, is unknown; but she took a Handful of Gold out of her Pocket, and gave to one of her Gentlemen-waiters, bidding him carry it to that Mortal, and command her away from thence.

---

1. Monsieur Corneille. [Author's note.] Pierre Corneille (1606–84), French neoclassical dramatist. Philips received high praise for her translation of Corneille's *La Mort de Pompée* (1643; trans. as *Pompey,* 1663).

Jane Barker

Galecia was very attentive to the Musick and Dancing; when lo, an hasty Knocking at her Chamber-door awak'd her out of her pleasant Dream: The Person that knock'd, was a Gentleman, very well dress'd, who ask'd for *Galecia,* and she answered him respectfully, that she was the Person: He presented her with a Purse of Gold, and, instantly turning short, would not, by any means, be persuaded, either to stay, to tell his Name, or who sent him.

Galecia was greatly pleas'd with the Receit of this unexpected Treasure; and after having counted it over and over, she lay'd it by, and went to Bed; But, to shew that Money does not always make us happy, she was very uneasie and restless all the Night, being disturb'd with the Thoughts how, or in what manner she should dispose of it to the best Advantage, whether in the Funds, Lotteries, in Building, Traffick,[1] &c.

Thus she lay tumbling and tossing full of Inquietude; according to the following old Story of a Cobler,[2] who sate daily in his Stall, working hard, and singing merrily, any thing that came in his head. Now, it hapned, that a rich Usurer,[3] whose Lodging was just over this poor Man, wonder'd very much at his being continually so very merry, who had nothing to support him, or to depend upon, but this his daily Labour; whilst the Usurer underwent perpetual Thoughtfulness, sleepless Nights, and anxious Days, how to dispose of this Sum, how to recover that; how to enter this Process, and how to pursue that: His Head and Hands were incumber'd with Bills, Bonds, Mortgages, Buildings, Dilapidations, Forfeitures, and a thousand other the like Vexations. In the mean time the poor Cobler was always merry and unconcern'd: He resolv'd at last to try whether Money would discompose him; so watch'd an Opportunity when the Man was out of his Stall, and privately convey'd there a Bag of Money amongst the Rubbish: Which, as soon as the Cobler found, he was seiz'd with a great Consternation, not knowing how it should come there. Various Conjectures and Apprehensions appear'd to his View, not worth repeating; he was unwilling to discover,

---

1. **Traffick:** commerce.
2. **Cobler:** cobbler; shoemaker.
3. **Usurer:** moneylender.

but afraid to conceal it, lest it should be found upon him, and by some Mark or other, on the Bag, or some of the Pieces therein, he might be seiz'd for a Felon; or, if none of these hapned, then, what he should do with it, either to secure, or turn it to Profit. In short, a thousand things revolv'd in his Thoughts, which disappointed him of his ordinary mirth; so that his wonted[1] Chearfulness was turned into a dull pensive Melancholy, and his Singing quite ceas'd.

The Usurer took notice hereof, and ask'd him what was the reason he was not so jovial as heretofore? The poor Man frankly told him his Case, and the cause of his Inquietude. What succeeded between them, matters not; We are to apply the Story to our *Galecia;* who, as before-said, had tost about all night, till weariness brought her into a gentle Sleep, which held her to her Pillow till the Morning was pretty far advanced, when she was waked, by the coming of a Sea-Captain from the *Indies,* who was her very good Friend; and whose safe Arrival was great satisfaction to her.

After the usual Salutations, and Congratulations on such an occasion, She ask'd him what sorts of Goods he had brought from the *Indies* that Voyage? He told her, that the greatest of his Cargo was *Female Vertues;* which he hop'd would sell well in this Country, where there was so great a Scarcity. Of this *Galecia,* considered a little; and immediately resolv'd to lay out her *Fairie*-Treasure in this Merchandize, and so engaged the Captain, her Friend, to send her some Parcels of his Cargo. He perform'd with all convenient speed; sending her the choicest, and nicest of the *Female Vertues.*

She thought it her Duty and Interest to send to the Court in the first place: Accordingly, she put up a large Quantity of *Sincerity,* and sent it thither; The Factor or Agent offer'd it to Sale, with good Grace and due Recommendation; insomuch that the Ladies all commended the Goods; saying they were curiously wrought, and safely brought over; but 'twas pity they did not come sooner; for now that kind of Merchandize, was quite out of fashion. Nevertheless, she went from Appartment to Appartment, from Lodging to Lodging, traced the Galleries over and

---

1. **wonted:** customary.

over, every where offering her Traffick, till the Guards, Centinels, and Waiters almost took her for a Spectre; so she was forced to return without disposing of any.

The next Venture *Galecia* sent out, was a parcel of *Chastity;* which she sent into the Hundreds of *Drury,*[1] not doubting but to make a good return from thence: Here it was greatly lik'd, and highly prais'd, and gladly they would have bought, but had not wherewith to purchase so rich an Imbellishment. The Factor offered to give them credit, if they had any Friend that would pass their word for payment; but that was not to be found: For their Friends were lost, and Credit broken to that degree, that they had not Cloaths to cover them (even upon occasion of Profit) but what they either hired or borrowed;

Amongst this Crew, there was one, that looking over the Parcels of divers[2] of the Dealers, who had help'd to Stow the Ship, found thereon the Mark of two or three of her Acquaintance who had lived with her in the same Court, *viz. Betty Bilk; Sarah Shuffle, Polly Picklock,* &c. Ah, said she, is it possible that these Girls are grown such great Dealers in this kind of Ware? They were my intimate Friends; I narrowly escaped being carry'd with them to *Newgate;* and I wish I had gone, since they have had such luck by means of their Transportation:[3] But alas, it is too late to repent now, not being able to do any thing; for I have been so far from gaining by my Profession here, that I have lost Health, Wealth, Credit, Friends, and am become a poor abandon'd rotten Skeleton, which is not only my Fate; but the Fate of most of those who deal in this way of Trade.

The Factor could not forbear asking her how she came at first to be deluded? Alas, said she, it is a great difficulty to have so much Foresight to avoid all the Traps lay'd in this Town, to ensnare and catch our Innocence: But my Ruin was by a young Girl, my Play-fellow, whose Brother cast a wicked Eye on me; and under pretence of courting me for

---

1. **Hundreds of Drury:** London district noted for its theatres and prostitutes or "Drury-Lane Virgins." The "Drury-Lane Ague" was slang for venereal disease.

2. **divers:** sundry goods.

3. **Transportation:** relocation of criminals such as prostitutes and thieves to the North American colonies or Ireland.

a Wife, deluded me into Wickedness: The Subtilties, and methods he used, are too tedious to tell you at this time; but whenever you are more at leisure, if you will take the trouble to come, I will give you such a Catalogue of the Mis-adventures, as would make the brightest *Vertue* burn blue and ready to go out, at such relations.

The Factor finding her time elasp'd, and that she was not like to sell any of her Parcel, told her, she would come another time, hear some of their Adventures; and bring with her some other sorts of *Vertues,* as that of *Penance, Piety* or the like. So the poor Factor, was forced to return, with her Merchandize, but no Mony.

Having such bad luck at Court and Places adjacent, *Galecia* was resolv'd to try the City; which being accustomed to Traffick, she hoped there for better Success: Wherefore she put up a good Parcel of *Humility,* and sent amongst those rich and haughty Dames: Knowing, this sort of Goods was scarce amongst them, she doubted not of a good Market. But alas, it prov'd quite otherwise: for they would not so much as look on the Ware, nor permit the Factor to open her Parcel, telling her, they had greater store thereof in the City, than they needed; which appears daily (said they) by giving your Ladies place every where, by following their Fashions at all times; Whereas our Riches give us a right to be fantastical, and setters-up of new Modes; But 'tis our *Humility* that pervails with us, and makes us their Apes, at the same time; many of them being but meanly descended, they often run in our Debt, for their gaudy Trappings; and their Husbands borrow of ours, to support their Equipage, on the credit of their Acres.

To which the Factor reply'd, that the *Humility* they boasted of was only Home-made, whereas, that she offered, was right *Indian.* Away, reply'd they, you know, *Indian* Goods[1] are prohibited; had you brought some from *France* or *Spain,* from the Battel of *Bleinheim,*[2] or from *Madrid,* when King *Philip*[3] fled from thence; nay, if it had been but

---

1. **Indian Goods:** calicos and chintzes from India that deluged the English market after 1660.

2. **Battel of Bleinheim:** English troops, led by the Duke of Marlborough (1650–1722), defeated Franco-Bavarian troops on 2 August 1704 in the War of Spanish Succession.

3. **King Philip:** Philip V of Spain (1683–1746), driven from Madrid on several occasions by the English and Portuguese allies, who wanted to put Charles of Austria on the Spanish throne.

English Humility from *Preston*,[1] it had been something like: But to come into the City with your prohibited Ware, is Insolence in a high degree; Therefore be gone, before my Lord Mayor's Officers catch you, and punish you according to your Deserts. Hereupon our poor Factor was forced to hasten away, and glad when she had got safe through *Temple-Bar.*[2]

This was but a sorrowful Return to our *Galecia,* who had lay'd out her whole *Fairy*-Present in these *Indian* Goods: She began to despair of making any Advantage: but her Factors, who had been up and down the Hundreds of *Drury;* beg'd her to try there once more, not with the Vertue of *Chastity,* for it was to no purpose; but they had great hopes that *Repentance* and *Piety* might take. So *Galecia* sent away a good Parcel of each of those Vertues.

The Agent, or Factor carry'd them to the same House, where she had before promised to come, *viz.* to one Mrs. *Rottenbone's,* who receiv'd, her kindly and look'd carefully into her Parcels; fitted her self with divers Suits, both of *Piety* and *Repentance;* and sent to several of her Neighbours to come and do the same.

The first who came, was one Mrs. *Castoff,* who took of each a pretty Quantity: After her, came three or four more; and when they had fitted themselves, Mrs. *Rottenbones,* desir'd Mrs. *Castoff* to tell our Agent how things happen'd, that she came to esteem these Vertues, so as to dress her self therein; which she related briefly, as follows.

The *Story* of Mrs. *Castoff.*

I was Daughter of an honest Country-Gentleman tho' but of a small Estate, who had many Children. Now, there was a good Gentlewoman in our Neighbourhood, whose Husband died, leaving her no Child: She took me from my Mother, I suppose, to provide for me; which was esteemed a very great Kindness.

This Gentlewoman, some time after, mov'd from her Country-Residence, and took me with her to *London,* where we liv'd happily

---

1. **English Humility from Preston:** English and Scottish Jacobite rebels succeeded in taking Preston, Lancashire, in the uprising of 1715.

2. **Temple-Bar:** gate which marked original western limits of London, rebuilt in 1670 by Christopher Wren.

together, I being then about fourteen Years old: I waited on her in the nature of a Chamber-maid, thereby to initiate me into a religious and dutiful Behaviour: For she being a Widow, valued but little of Dress, except that of her Mind; her Devotions, Retirements and Instructions to me and her Servants, being the greatest part of her Employment; which, I doubt, was not so agreeable to my giddy Youth as it ought to have been; young People, too often having an Opinion of themselves, as if Instructions were needless, and themselves capable of being Teachers, instead of Learners.

How far this was my fault, I know not; but instead of keeping with her in her Chamber, I was perpetually making Errands, and pretences to be in the Shop where we lodged; and here my young Face call'd many young Fellows to cheapen Goods, and many to buy; For our Landlady kept a Millener's Shop.[1] These would often address themselves to me with some Question or other, as is usual among Youth, which had no other consequence, than making me grow pert, and think too well of my self: But my Ruin proceeded from one of my own Sex.

There was a certain comely genteel Woman, who frequented that Shop, and by degrees made an acquaintance with me, asking me if I was a Servant to that Gentlewoman, or related to her? I told her that I was neither; but let her know how it was. Upon which, she told me she could help me to a very good Place, where I should have not only very good Wages, but other considerable Advantages, and be in a Way for Preferment; but advised me to say nothing to any one, especially the Gentlewoman I then liv'd with, till she had spoken with the Lady for whom she intended me.

This pass'd on a while, she still giving me Encouragement and Assurance of her Diligence in this Affair. At last, she bid me dress my self the next *Sunday,* as if I was going to Church, but come to her, and she would go with me to a Lady, who had spoken to her to get her a pretty Girl to wait in the Nursery; but that it was best not to acquaint any body with it, till she saw how the Lady lik'd me.

In this Prospect I greatly rejoyc'd; and accordingly dress'd my self as if

---

1. **Millener's Shop:** milliner's shop for women's fancy apparel, including ribbons and bonnets.

going to Church, and so I went to this Woman's House; which prov'd to me the Den of Deceit, the Devil's Dungeon, which in some Degree I deserved for my Hypocrisie to Heaven, and my Ingratitude to the good Gentlewoman my Patroness, for thus forming an Intrigue of any kind without her Knowledge.

I got to my Deceiver in due time, who readily went with me to present me to the Lady. We came to a large magnificent House, and went up a Noble Stair-Case, into a stately Dining-Room, where, instead of a Lady, was a Gentleman, who immediately stood up; and speaking very friendly, told my Conducter,[1] he suppos'd, that this Young Gentlewoman was the Person she brought to offer to his Wife; and then addressing himself to me, Come, pretty Maid, said he, I will direct you to her: So he took my by the hand, led me into a Back-Room, and lock'd the Door; in the mean time my Betrayer departed.

I will not trouble you with the Repetition of the fine Speeches he made to recover me from my Surprize, and suppress my Tears; for he was a Man of Wit, and an engaging Mien; he promis'd me a thousand Fineries, gave me an handful of Gold, told me I should have a fine House of my own, a Coach and Servants, with all manner of Imbellishments to grace and adorn my Beauty; which Beauty (continu'd he) has chain'd my Heart, ever since the moment I beheld it in the Milliner's Shop, where I was (*incog*)[2] buying some things, on purpose to see you; for you were recommended to me by Mrs. *Wheedle,* the Woman that brought you hither.

In short, my Eyes were not blind to his Noble Person, nor my Ears deaf to his alluring Speeches, nor was my Heart made of a Stick or a Stone; but young and tender, susceptible of the Impressions of Love: For I will do his Lordship that Justice, he used no manner of Violence against my Youth and Innocence: But ——with that she wept, which stopt her proceeding for a while, but she soon recover'd her self.

I was placed (continu'd she) in a sumptuous Lodging, with Servants, and Fineries of all sorts about me; my Lord frequently came, and enter-

---

1. **Conducter:** guide.
2. **incog:** colloquial for incognito.

tain'd me with his Wit and Gallantry; he carry'd me abroad from time to time in his Coach to take the Air, and treated me at all Places of Diversion and Entertainment; in the Evenings we went to Plays, Balls and *Opera's*; I perk'd up in the Face of Quality,[1] and was a Companion for my Betters: Thus I liv'd in Lewdness and Profaness.

By this barefac'd Wickedness, my good Patroness found me out: For she was in great Affliction in consideration of what became of me. As soon as she knew, she sent one to me to enquire into the matter; which shew'd it self so foul, that she proceeded no farther in her Enquiry; only sent me word *she cast me off* for ever; This Menace I very little valued, thinking my self much above her Favour.

At last, the News of my lewd Life came to the Ears of my Father and Mother in the Country; who, good People, were sorely griev'd; and sent to me, desiring I would abandon the way I was in, and resolve to live vertuously and modestly for the future, and their House should be open for my Reception, and their Arms for my Pardon: But, alas, these Offers were, I thought, much below my acceptance; I scorn'd an old-fashion'd Country-Seat, with Bow-windows, low Roofs, long dark Passages, a slight Thread-Sattin Gown, Worsted-Stockins, plain Shoes, and such like Cloathing; or to have Swine and Poultry for my Companions; perhaps, on *Sunday* in the Afternoon some of the Farmers Wives: So I refus'd this offer'd Favour and Forgiveness.

Hereupon my good pious Parents sent me word, they *cast me off* for ever, bidding me think of them no more.

This, indeed, was some Grief at first; but the next Visit from my Lord with his courtly Behaviour soon asswaged it.

Thus I walk'd on in the open Path of Pleasure, and ascended the highest Pinacle of Pride; my Vanity being daily soothed with Praises of my Beauty; and the World solliciting me for Places and Preferments by my Lord's Interest. All which gratified my Vanity, and made me believe my self a great Lady; because I was Courted and Visited by my Superiours, and respected by my Equals.

---

1. **Quality:** people of wealth and influence.

Thus had the Devil raised me upon a high Pinacle, to make my Fall the greater; For all on a sudden, my Lord sent one of his Gentlemen, to bid me not dare to see his Face any more. I was earnest with the Gentleman to tell me the reason of this great Change; but, he could not, or would not; only he inform'd me, that my Lord was not very well. At the same time he told the People of the House, that they must look to me for payment of the Lodgings.

Thus was I *cast off* by my Keeper; and for an Addition to my Grief, they turn'd me out that very Day, and seiz'd all my Furniture, I not having Money at that time to discharge the Rent; my Profuseness, having always anticipated my Lord's Liberality.

In this Condition I went to Mrs. *Wheedle,* thinking to borrow a little of her, to release my things; and to have taken a Lodging with her, at least, that Night: But, alas, far from that, she not only refus'd me all Favour, but loaded me with Reproaches; and chiefly, for having so far abus'd my Lord's Bounty, and like an impudent Strumpet, I had depriv'd him of his Health.[1]

Thus was she a perfect Devil, leading People into Damnation, and then becoming their Tormentors. I was amazed to find my self charg'd with being the Cause of my Lord's Illness; of which I knew my self truly innocent; but Words of Justification were to no more purpose, than to fight with the North-Wind. Thus was I *Cast off,* not only by my Lord, but by this vile Wretch my first Seducer.

In the midst of this great Distress I got into a private poor Lodging, not knowing what to do, nor to whom to address. I was reduced to great Misery, being helpless, friendless, destitute, and abandon'd; and, what was worst of all, I began to find a great Alteration in my Health. I had only one Ring on my Finger when I was driven out of my Lodging. This enhanced my present Necessity.

Sitting in this deplorable Condition, a Gentlewoman came up Stairs; and entring my Room, I soon discover'd she was Waiting Woman to my Lord's Lady; and was come from her to assist me in my Sufferings. She went with me to my former Lodging; from whence we recovered my

---

1. **depriv'd him of his Health:** probably a reference to venereal disease.

things, sold 'em as well as we could, therewith paid all my Debts, and had Money left, for my Assistance. I thank'd, and on my Knees pray'd for this kind Lady, who is a Mirrour of Goodness; not only to forgive, but to seek me out, and relieve me.

Thus I pass'd on a while; But finding my Distemper[1] increase, I was forced to put my self under Cure; which so far devour'd the little Substance I had, that by such time as I was thoroughly well, I was in a manner pennyless: However, I having recover'd my Health, and not quite exhausted my youth, (for I was still young) I knew, I was able to go to Service; but the difficulty was, I had led so evil a Life, it was impossible to hope for a Recommendation from any body: This came to the Ears of my Lord's good Lady, who again sent her Woman, to consult with me; who advised me from my Lady to put my self under a Manteau-maker; which I approv'd, and resolv'd to be vertuous and modest, and she promis'd to be at the Charge. This greatly rejoyced me; and accordingly I was placed with a Person of that Employment.

Here I went on very well, learnt my Business in perfection, and in due time set up for my self, and began to have good Encouragement. But my unhappy Beauty was again my Ruin.

There came a glorious young Gentleman of Quality to lodge in the same House where I liv'd; his unhappy Person and Mien were extreamly engaging, and his broken *English,* (for he was a Foreigner) was with such a pretty Accent, that his Conversation was Charming; at least, it was so to me; he would often condescend to come and sit with me and my Workwomen, under pretence of improving himself in the *English* Language. Thus, Deceit on his side, and Weakness on mine, composed an Amour, to destroy my whole Life's Happiness.

I will not repeat to you, his Sighs, Tears, Vows, Presents, Treats,[2] and divers sorts of Gallantries, and lastly, his Promise of Marriage, if I should be with Child; and this on his Knees he swore; in these very Words, *If you prove with Child, I swear to marry you:* But for my sake, may no young Woman take Mens Words, nor believe the Oaths till the

---

1. **Distemper:** illness.
2. **Treats:** entreaties.

Parson puts the Hoop[1] on their Finger, that Circle which conjures the most notorious Rover into some decent Limits; if not of Constancy, at least, of Formality. I proving with Child, charged him with his Promise, which he answer'd in his broken *English;* Yes, Madam, *Me will marry you* to my Foot-man; if He be willing. But the Gentlemen in my Country do not marry vid de Whores; for dat is no good fashion; but go you gone Mistress; dere is Money for you; and so left me, and forthwith his Lodging likewise.

Thus was I *cast off* by this wicked Foreigner. But this was but one part of my Misfortune; for that most excelling of her Sex, my Lord's Lady, hearing of this my Misbehaviour, sent and took away those Cloaths I had of her's in making, and withal acquainted me, she *cast me off for ever,* and, by her Example, all other Ladies and Gentlewomen did the like. Thus I lost my Livelyhood; and with the Grief hereof, I had like to have miscarried; and having nothing, to do at my Manteau-making nor Strength, nor Credit to put my self into any other Business, I spent all I had, both Money and Cloaths; that when I was out of my Child-bed, I was like to starve; but the good Woman of the House, pittying me, and not knowing the whole of my Story (for I made her believe my Husband was an Officer, and gone into *Flanders;*) I say, this good Woman, got me to be a Wet Nurse[2] in a Lady's House. Here I was very happy for a while; but by some means or other my Lady heard of my Character, and so *cast me off,* getting another Nurse in my place.

Now was I reduced to greater Necessity than ever, having sold, pawn'd, and spent All, my Credit lost every where; and having my self and a Child to keep, Time and Poverty began to prey upon my Beauty; so that was not much to be depended upon; I had not Cloaths to grace me, nor Linen to keep me clean; that now I was forced to betake my self to the most scandalous and meanest sort of Lewdness, and became a Night-walker in *Fleet-street.*[3] Should I tell you all the Affronts, and

---

1. **Hoop:** wedding ring.

2. **Wet Nurse:** woman hired to suckle and nurse another woman's baby.

3. **Night-walker in Fleet-Street:** prostitute working the street whose name is still synonymous with the publishing trade.

Indignities I suffer'd here, 'twould make your Ears glow, being often beat, and made to expose my self stark-naked, for the brutal Diversion of those who pick'd up such distressed Creatures. By this time my Daughter began to grow up, and was very beautiful; and likely enough to fall into the same wicked Way; but that a good Gentlewoman, a Lawyer's Wife, taking pity of her Youth, took her into her House, giving her a vertuous honest Education; but upon condition that I should never come near her, nor she me.

Thus was I *a Cast off* from my own dear and only Child, which was very grievous to me; but was forced to bear it for her good; and the better to secure, and accomplish this Prohibition, I resolv'd to remove my self to the Hundreds of *Drury;* for I began to be too well known, to be acceptable any where else.

Thither I came, and there I lived in great Misery and Contempt; such as I would not wish to the greatest Enemy that ever was. However, it has so far opened the Eyes of my Understanding, as to know that nothing but a sincere Repentance will attone for my Transgressions. Hereupon she lookt into the Factor's Box, and took a large Parcel of these Vertues, wherewith she adorn'd her self, and according to the proverb,

Cast off Vice, when Vice cast off her.

The rest of the Company ask'd our Factor, if she had no good Books to put them also into a State of Repentance; so she produced a Book call'd the *Imitation of Christ*,[1] bidding them strictly peruse the Contents of that invaluable Treatise, and therein they would find *Rest for their Souls.*

The Factor, seeing she was like to dispose of no more of her *Vertues* at that time, put up her Goods, and went home.

Galecia perceiving, she made no better return of her Merchandize in *London*, resolved to try the Country, in hopes the Women of all Ranks and Stations would be better Customers. As she was busie in putting up

---

1. **Imitation of Christ:** *De Imitatione Christi,* mystical work by German Augustinian monk, Thomas à Kempis (1380–1471), that recounts the gradual progress of the soul to Christian perfection.

her things for this Journey, she heard a Chariot stop at the Door, and a Gentlewoman come up her Stairs; at whose Appearance she was ravished[1] with Joy, it proving to be the good Lady's Waiting-Woman; who by her Lady's Order, came to see if *Galecia* had done her business in Town; and if she was dispos'd to go into the Country: For, said she, my Lady very very earnestly desires your Company, now the Spring comes on. Therefore, dear *Galecia,* dispose your self to go with me.

This Invitation was an inexpressible Joy to our *Galecia;* so she hastned to put up every thing; the Gentlewoman lending her helping hand; soon finished and took her away in the Chariot to her Inn that night, in order to prosecute[2] their Journey early the next Morning.

FINIS.

---

1. **ravished:** consumed.
2. **prosecute:** begin.

SELECTED POEMS
from part two of the
MAGDALEN MANUSCRIPT:

"the greatest part of which were
writ since the author was in
France"

To His Royal Highness
the Prince of Wales, on
His birth day 1689: or 99:

The author having presented him
a Calvary set in a vinyard

Forgive me sr that on this happy day
On which all vertuous minds ought to be gay
I here appear in non-conformity,
Presenting you with a sad Calvary,
Yet sad as it seems, no present I cou'd give,   5
Wou'd more befit yr Highness to receive,
It being loves purest representative.
It allso represents, the frutfull state,
O'th' vinyard which you'r born to cultivate,
By purging out the sowr and fruitless race   10
And reimplanting true vines in their place
In which your Royal Highness shall out shine,
All Heav'ns fermers of your Royal line
For though cross accidents your merits wrong,
Tis but like weight to make the arch more strong   15
As usualy we have the brightest day

Title. **His Royal Highness:** James Francis Edward Stuart (1688–1766), the Old Pretender, son of James II (1633–1701) and Mary Beatrice of Modena (1658–1718). **birth day:** 10 June. The intention of the dual years is unclear. **Calvary set:** representation of Calvary or Golgotha, site of Christ's execution and death; see Mark 15:22–47. **vinyard:** vineyard; Biblical term frequently describing the Holy Land. Also actual vineyards near St. Germain-en-Laye, site of James II's court-in-exile.

Line 3. **non-conformity:** both inconsistent with the joyous occasion and as a Nonconformist or member of other than the Church of England.

Line 10. **sowr:** sour. William III (1650–1702) was a taciturn and obstinate man. **fruitless race:** William and Mary (1669–94) bore no children. Anne (1665–1714), second daughter of James II and Anne Hyde (1637–71), became queen at William's death.

Line 13. **fermers:** farmers, agricultural caretakers.

When the suns morning gown is sadest gray
But why do I, thus Sibillize to you?
Since all the world knows what you'r born to do,
To teach yr Highness this, I may as well,   20
Teach France obedience, England to rebell,
Or Heav'n in every goodness to excell.

  Then let's rejoyce, sing, love, and with you smile
Forgeting friends, estates, or native soyle,
For having you we'r here in full content,   25
Tis they in England suffer banishment.

  Hale then bright star of our north hemisphere
Whome all the wise and good love and revere,
And for your service have a glorious strife
Whilst Hell and Herods, seek your Royal life,   30
Young Prince, the life, and joy of all the court,
Whose tender hands, your fathers crowns support
And all your Royall mothers griefs deceive,
She in yr smiles and kisses seemes to live,
Tis you sweet Prince, aleviate all our cares,   35
And stop the sorce, of maids and widdows tears.
They mourn their faithfull dead, with little pain
When they consider tis for you they'r slain,
All who this day, approach this happy place,
Receive from you their ornaments and grace,   40
And their perfumes, take sweetness from your face.
You tune their songs, and teach their feet to move,

Line 18. **Sibillize:** to prophesy, from Sibyl, general term for Greek and Roman prophetesses.

Line 30. **Herods:** ruthless monarchs of Israel. At the time of Christ's birth, Herod the Great (73–4 B.C.) sent soldiers to kill male infants when told of the prophecy that a baby boy would become King of the Jews; see Matt. 2:1–16. As an adult, Jesus heard from certain Pharisees that Herod Antipus would seek to kill him; see Luke 13:31.

Line 37. this was writ, at the time of the first battell in Irland. [Author's note.] March 1689. Supported by money, arms, and troops from Louis XIV, James II attempted to regain his throne by a series of military campaigns in Ireland.

And dance the mesures, of their joy and love,
Even the cloyster'd convent pentioners,
Who nothing know, but how to say their prayrs   45
No sooner have your Royal Highness seen,
But love gives them a courtiers gentle meen.
That Adam left not his lov'd paradise,
With more regret than they this place of bliss.
Had Alexander, had a look like you,   50
The famouse Cynick, had turn'd courtier too,
Of this your sweetness enemys partake,
Heav'n sparing England for your Royal sake,
For they deserve to suffer Corahs fate,
Who in his crimes, themselves precipitate   55

    Mad people, to be managed with a shamm,
And think their game secure for having Pamm
And on that card stake honour wealth and lives
Their somptious houses, and their beautious wives
Whilst to the good oth' board they loudly call   60
Ne'er think of flush, but Pamm they still extole
Till for the good oth' board your Highness Loose them all.

Line 44. **pentioners:** residents.

Line 48. **paradise:** referring to Adam's expulsion with Eve from the Garden of Eden; see Gen. 2–3.

Line 50. **Alexander:** known as the Great (356–323 B.C.), conquered an empire that stretched from Greece to India.

Line 51. **famouse Cynick:** Diogenes (ca. 400–325 B.C.) led an austere life. In a reported meeting with Alexander the Great, the philosopher was apparently unimpressed by his power. **Famouse** has been regularized from Barker's famōse in the original.

Line 54. **Corahs fate:** Korah and his followers were punished for their rebellion against Moses; see Numb. 16. John Dryden (1631–1700) used Corah in his allegorical *Absalom and Achitophel* (1681) to represent Titus Oates (1649–1705), perjuror who ignited anti-Catholic hysteria by accusing the Pope, Jesuits, Queen Catherine, and the duke of York, later James II, of the "Popish Plot" (1678–79) to set fire to London, massacre Protestants, murder Charles II (1630–85) and the King's Council in order to install the duke of York on the throne.

Line 57. **Pamm:** knave or jack of clubs, highest trump in game of five-card loo; likely reference to William III.

Line 59. **somptious:** sumptuous, costly and elaborate.

Line 61. flush, the king of france being alone against all the confederates, so is justly call'd flush, or all of a sute. [Author's note.] **sute:** suit, such as hearts or spades.

To
Her Majesty the Queen, on
the Kings going to Callis
this carnival 1696:

Madame

It was not want of zeal, but want of sight,
That I did neither come, nor speak nor write,
To testify my joys, my hopes, and fears,
And to assure the king of my poor prairs,
If not in words, at least in silent tears.   5
My eys bound down, I heard the peopl say
The King, the King's for England gone away.
Such joys and fears, did then my heart o'erflow,
As saints shall at the resurection know.
This glimps of heaven, god gives in recompence   10
Oth' deprivation of my seeing sence.
Such vast distractions, all your subjects have
Compar'd to which the Bachanals were grave
Our minds strike up, our hearts dance in this ball
And Heav'n too seems to keep its carnival.   15
Nature methinks, is dress'd in masquerade,
As if in frolick England she'd invade.
The sun in greatest splendor does appear
Three months before the usual time oth' year.
The earth is mantl'd in her verdant dress,   20
So soon, one must conclude by Heav'n express,

Title. **Queen:** Mary of Modena.   **Callis:** Calais, France, where James II joined his troops for a joint excursion by Jacobites and the French to invade England.   **carnival:** Shrove Tuesday, preceding the fasting period of Lent.

Line 1. **want of sight:** lack of sight. Barker suffered near-blindness because of cataracts.

Line 6. her cataract was then couched. [Author's note.] **couched:** surgically removed by inserting a needle and lifting off the cataract.

Line 13. **Bachanals:** from Bacchanalia or rites of the god Dionysus, referring to the excesses of carnival behavior.

This cloth of sate is layd for Royal James,
To walk upon towards his silver Thames,
The leaves peep out, to see the King go by
Whilst birds huzza him with their warbling cry,   25
And little insects hum, vivez le Roy.
All things conspire, his foot steps to advance
Whilst gentle windes are pipers to the dance.
Nor heav'n nor earth can better musick hear,
Except yr Majestys all powerfull praier,   30
Such vows and praiers as yours, take Heav'n by force
And stop and turn even nature in her course.
The sun was once commanded to go back
But now is bid go forward for your sake
'Tis for your sake the elements have fought,   35
And on the statlyest fleets destruction brought,
'Tis for your sake the armes of france are bless'd,
And for your sake the Rebells are depress'd,
'Tis for your sake, god made France be our friend,
And for your sake, he'll peace on Europ send.   40
    Not good to be alone, th'Almighty said,
And forthwith He for man a help-meet made,
Such you have truly been, and such shall be,
Not only to the King but christianity,
In vertues perfect natural and acquir'd,   45

Line 22. **sate:** likely *state.*

Line 23. **Thames:** river that runs through London, seat of the rightful King of England.

Line 25. **huzza:** cheer, cry hurrah.

Line 26. **vivez le Roy:** Vive le Roi; Long live the King (French).

Line 33. **sun . . . back:** See Joshua 10:12–14.

Line 38. **Rebells:** English supporters of William III.

Lines 41–42. **Not . . . made:** referring to the creation of Eve out of Adam's rib; see Gen. 2:18.

Line 45. **vertues . . . natural and acquir'd:** according to Italian friar and theologian, Saint Thomas Aquinas (1225–74), the natural or cardinal virtues were fortitude, prudence, justice, and temperance. Acquired or theological virtues—faith, hope and charity—came about only by God's grace.

Less to be immitated than admir'd,
No saint so good, no Heroin so great
No wit so perfect, beauty so compleat,
So good a friend, and mother ne'er was seen,
So good a wife a mistress, and a Queen, 50
By your warm rays, starv'd vertue shall bud forth,
And Englands eyes, shall open to your worth,
No country so obscure or place so far,
Which shall not of your matchless merits hear,
And those who never heard of god before, 55
Shall now the god of Englands Queen addore.

To
Madam Fitz James, on the
day of her profession, at Pontoise,
she taking the name of
St. Ignace.

When Madam you were at the altar lay'd
And your whole self to heav'n an offring made,
Methought the wanton Cupids all did run,
Weeping away, crying undone, undone,
Fitz James, the fair Fitz James, is made a nun. 5
Whilst holy Angells did about you play,
For you made then, in Heaven a Holy-day,
And all the business, angells had to do,
Was to rejoyce that day, and weight on you.
    It was a moving sight to see a dame, 10
Who justly might all sorts of honours claim

Line 47. **Heroin:** heroine.

Title. **Madam Fitz James:** Arabella FitzJames (d. 1762), illegitimate daughter of the Duke of York, later James II, and Arabella Churchill (1648–1730).　**day of her profession:** the taking of vows as a nun, 30 April 1690.　**Pontoise:** an English Benedictine convent founded 1658 near St. Germain.　**St. Ignace:** French form of St. Ignatius (of Loyola, ca. 1491–1556), founder of the order of the Society of Jesus (Jesuits).

Line 3. **Cupids:** gods of love.

Abandon all, and make that humble change,
Betwixt the meek bando, and high fontange.
So pious, and so noble was the choice,
That France ev'n glorys that it has Pontoise,   15
And that alone, cause madame you are there,
Whose vertues brightens, your illustrious sphere.
If English Protestants your beautys saw,
They'd add new fury, to their furious law,
To keep out Popery with just excuse,   20
Cause fair Fitz James, has made her self recluse
Had you been pleas'd to shew your self abrod,
With how much transport had you been addor'd
Nought in the world had sounded but your fame
Your beauty by each man, your vertue by each dame   25
But you bless'd maid, have chose a better place
Your name in time, our Kallanders shall grace,
Where none shall be rever'd more than the chast Ignace.

To
Dame —Augustin nun
on her curious gum-work

Oft have I strove t'asscend that lofty ground,
Where th'immortal raritys are found,
But all in vain, Parnassus is too high,

Line 13. **meek bando:** public declaration.   **fontange:** tall headdress of ribbons, named after Mme de Fontanges, mistress of Louis XIV, who set the fashion.

Line 19. **law:** The first and second Test Acts (1673, 1678) prevented Catholics from holding most public offices. The Toleration Act of 1689 excluded Catholics from freedom of public worship. The Act of 1695 forbade priests to practice and Catholics to inherit or purchase property without abjuring their religion.

Line 20. **Popery:** Many feared that the Pope would rule England if a Catholic were on the throne.

Line 27. **Kallanders:** calendars.

Title. **Augustin:** the Catholic religious order named for early church leader, Saint Augustine (345–430).   **curious:** ingenious, clever.   **gum-work:** artwork formed of materials stiffened with dried tree or plant gum.

Line 3. **Parnassus:** a mountain in Greece, sacred to the Muses. One of its mounts was sacred to Apollo, god of poetry.

And I to weak either to climb or fly.
Then pardon madam that I bring to you, 5
Such flowers as I cou'd scramble up below,
Which so insippid are, compar'd to yours,
As dayses, amongst finest gilliflowers,
But whosoe'er pretends to immitate,
Your works, and not live in your holy state 10
Deserves to suffer proud Arachnas fate.
For those who will pretend to work like you,
Must do the work of saints and Angells too
For every Alaluja you repeat,
And every hym, or antiphon you set, 15
Makes either Rose, pink, lilly, violet.
Which holy Angells fresh in water keep,
(That water which ofor others sins you weep)
To dress heav'ns altars up, on propper days
When Augustin saints sing Alalujas. 20
And when in Rapture you are carryed there,
Thence in your minds the beautious figgures bear,
And like an other wonderous Moses you,
Transcribe heavens work, and natures far outdo,
Or like those painter who best pictures make 25
Who for a pattern their own children take.
We need not to Italion villas go,

Line 8. **dayses:** daisies. **gilliflowers:** gillyflowers, clove-scented flowers.

Line 11. **Arachnas fate:** In Greek myth, Arachne, a mortal weaver and embroiderer, challenged the goddess Athena to a contest to see whose art was best. Infuriated by the excellence of her challenger's tapestry, Athena turned Arachne into a spider, condemned to spin eternally; see Ovid, *Metamorphoses* 1:1–142.

Line 14. **Alaluja:** Alleluia, from the Latin "praise be to God."

Line 15. **hym:** hymn. **antiphon:** phrase sung by a choir in response to a phrase sung by another choir.

Line 21. **Rapture:** the state of being transported out of the ordinary world by heavenly bliss.

Line 23. **Moses:** received the Torah and Ten Commandments from God and communicated them to the Israelites; see Exod. 19:3–6, 34:29–35.

Nor yet versails, the Toileries st. Cloud,
T'admire the works of nature or of art,
Since you excell em all in every part,   30
Thus the great world, byth' little world's outdone,
Not' only so, but by the heart alone,
For the vast universe can never show,
So fine a structure, such a motion too,
Now though this member's small, and cloyster'd lives,   35
Yet to the whole, it animation gives,
So you bless'd Dames, insensibly dispence,
On all your sex, your vertuous influence,
Whilst you your selves, gain what this world can't give
A perfect life, heav'ns representative.   40

To
My dear cosen Coll — at his
return out of Irland into france.

Since Irlands loss, has brought you on our coast
Methinks I wish, it had long since been lost,
I then had been exempt from thousand fears,
T' original of many sighs, and tears,
Which nothing but your safty cou'd appeas,   5
Your hard won conquests, cou'd not conquer these,
Alas, I drew no pleasure from that pride,   ⎫
To hear you nam'd, as one half diefy'd,   ⎬
How you'd defended this, or that town fortifi'd.   ⎭
How the bold Rebells, did at Limerick fall   10
By Connocks battery, rais'd within the wall,

Line 28. **versails, the Toileries st. Cloud:** elegant French palaces, elaborately furnished and landscaped, in striking contrast with the simple beauty of the nun's handwork. **versails:** Versailles. **Toileries:** the Tuileries.

Line 31. man, the little world. [Author's note.]

Title. **cosen Coll—:** Barker's cousin, Colonel William Connock (d. 1738), served in the Irish campaigns and was named a Jacobite baronet in 1732.

Line 10: **Limerick:** site of early Jacobite victory over William's troops and ultimate defeat of James II's Irish-French army in the Irish campaigns of 1689–91.

Line 11. **battery:** weapons, attacks.

With many other brunts by land and sea,
Which fill'd fames mouth, with talk which pleas'd not me
For of this glory, I was still affraid,
And not for it, but for your safty prayd,   15
For which I to all howers of prair have gone,
Mass, vespers, mattins, prime, teirs, sex, and none.
No crucifix, I needed in my cell,
Nor yet the sounding of our convent bell,
T'excite my thoughts, or call me up to pray,   20
Whilst there were Limerick, Athlone, Galloway,
But when (good god) I heard that you were slain, ⎫
My sighs and tears, made then a hurricane,   ⎬
To wreck my heart, and overset my brain.   ⎭
And thinking praiers, for you all useless were, ⎫   25
I to you as my saint address'd my prayr,   ⎬
For such must they be who fall in this war.   ⎭
Your little son and I, then mix'd our tears,
As we before had done our hopes and fears,
The little knave, still play'd the gentle thief,   30
And spight of me, rob'd me of half my grief,
I dayly saw your figure in his face,
And in him springing my dear mothers race
Which carfully I cherish'd as I cou'd,
As the last little stream of Connocks blood,   35
For I ne'er thought to see his brother more, ⎫
Thinking him lay'd with you in deadly goar,   ⎬
But heav' for us, had better things in store. ⎭

Line 12. **brunts:** attacks.

Line 16. **howers of prair:** hours of prayer.

Line 17. **Mass, vespers, mattins:** three holy services. **prime . . . none:** denoting four times that prayers began.

Line 21. **Athlone, Galloway:** battle sites in Ireland.

Line 28. **son:** probably Timon Connock (d. before 1732), who was to serve as Aide de Camp to Philip V of Spain (1683–1746) and be knighted by James III.

Line 33. **mothers race:** Barker's mother was Anne Connock from Cornwall.

Now he and I, with humble joynt consent
To you our welcoms, and our joys present,   40
Whose absence caus'd us double banishment.
For, be assur'd, of all your suffrings,
Wounds, hunger, nakedness, and other things,
We bore a part, though seas did us divide
Such is loves force, when like ours rarifi'd,   45
Then think not strange, that now we'r overjoy'd.
Your safe arival, gives us joy compleat,
We are incapable, to feell regret,
For our own losses, or the general,
Or which side's up'most of this tumbling ball,   50
Who fortunes favorits in camp or court,
Or who from her cou'd never smile extort,
Nay I'm ariv'd to such indiffrency,
That I scarce long my native land to see,
For my friends safty, all things is to me.   55

The
Miseries of St. Germains, writ
at the time of the pestilence and famin,
which reign'd in the years, 1694 et 95

Preachers no more, you need your people tell,
Of curses, judgments, or the pains of Hell:
Bid em but to st Germains come and see,
Cains curss at large, Hell in epitomy,
The plague of Athens, Can'ans want of food   5

Title. **pestilence and famin:** Over one million people died of famine and plague in France, 1694–95.

Line 4. **Cains curss:** the curse upon Cain for having slain his brother Abel; see Gen. 4:5–12.

Line 5. **plague of Athens:** probably the plague with which the misanthrope Timon cursed Athenians in Shakespeare's *Timon of Athens,* based on various classical sources, and adapted in 1678 by Thomas Shadwell (1642?–92); or the calamitous 430 B.C. plague, survived and reported by Thucydides (ca. 460–ca. 400 B.C.). **Can'ans want of food:** the famine that brought Jacob and his sons into Egypt; see Gen. 42:1.

Israells murmuring, by th' bitter flood,
The pride of London, scotlands poverty,
Hollands Religion, young monks biggotry,
In all much Pharisaicall hipocrisie.
In fine, those judgments, which deverted were,   10
Byth' ninnivits humility and prayer,
Were hoorded up, and executed here.

    The people howling in the streets for bread,
Envy their camerades which by them ly dead,
Friends follow friends, lamenting to the toomb,   15
But greater cause of grief they find at home,
Children with hunger, to their mothers cry,
Mothers with hunger, and with pitty dy,
The husbands are ith' field of battell slain,
The wives at home expire with greater pain,   20
One to the grave by pestilence is borne
The other is at home by famin torne
Some search the ditches, and on carrion feast,
Whilst others, like that mighty king oth' East
Take their repast, amongst th'admiring beasts.   25
Then to accomplish all their misery,
Curss god, themselves, fate, orange, and so dy.

Line 6. **Israells . . . flood:** the Israelites' constant complaints while wandering in the desert before arriving at the Promised Land; see Exod. 15.

Line 8. **Hollands Religion:** Calvinism.

Line 9. **Pharisaicall hipocrisie:** pertaining to the Pharisees, known for their external show of faith without the spirit of piety and for their opposition to Jesus and the early Christian movement; see Mark 3:6, 7:1, and 10:2; Matt. 23; John 11:47.

Line 11. **ninnivits:** Ninevites, who turned away from evil and violence when Jonah, God's messenger, prophesied that their city would be destroyed; see Jon. 3:2–4:11 and Matt. 12:41.

Line 14. **ly:** lie.

Line 18. **dy:** die.

Line 24. Nebuchdnezor who eat grass [Author's note.] **Nebuchdnezor:** Babylonian king (605–562 B.C.), who, in his madness, ate grass as oxen did, until he acknowledged the dominion of heaven; see Dan. 4:9–37.

Line 27. **orange:** William of Orange, by this time William III.

Thus curssess, passing bells, and dying groans,
Ring hells carrillion in the worst of tones:
Whilst howling doggs, the scriech-owl, yalling cat,   30
The croaking raven, night-crow, sulling batt,
In their dire prophesies, to th' rest proclaim,
They must prepare, with speed to do the same,
By what instinct they know, we cannot tell,
Whether they do the deadly atomes smell,   35
Or the firce destroying angell see,
Or mans ill genius, or hear Destiny,
Tell Time his glass is run, and bid him grind,
His syth, with which he mows down human kind
Is all uncertain, only this we know,   40
By dire events, what these dread signes foreshow,
As lightning does before the thunder go,
At least our sences tell us it does so.
But to return, and to the castle stear,
We finde the miseries are no less there,   45
For as ith' gallery one goes along,
Instead of meeting there a courtly throng,
Of pouder'd heads lace'd coats, cravats rich plumes,
Fine stenkerks, falbellas, paint and perfumes
One sees poor widows, with their wretched train,   50
Crying their parents, were at Achrim slain,
My husband was at Limerick kill'd says one,
And mine in prison dy'd at lost Athlone
My father rais'd a troop, and so lost all,

Line 29. **carillion:** set of bells.

Line 31. **sulling:** sullying, soiling.

Line 39. **syth:** scythe.

Line 48. **pouder'd heads:** powdered wigs. **cravats:** cravates, elaborate neckware.

Line 49. **stenkerks:** Steinkirks, neckcloths of fine lace intentionally in disarray, worn by women and men, in imitation of the disorderly lace cravates of gentlemen going hastily into battle at Steinkirk (1692). **falbellas:** flounces on women's clothing.

Lines 51–57. **Achrim . . . Athlone . . . Flanders . . . Savoy:** sites of Jacobite defeats.

And I have prisoner been e'er since the fall 55
Of my unhappy friends, and now am come,
To seek in Flanders, or Savoy a tomb,
Or else some mony to conveigh me home.
Some with lost armes, and some with leggs of wood,
Crying they lost those limbs because they stood, 60
When others fled, at Boyn's unluckey flood.
All with petitions drawn, and ready cry,
To charge the King and Queen as they pas by.
But above all poor virgins suffer most,
Who have their fortunes and their lovers lost, 65
And though both for the King were lost or slain,
Still modesty forbids them to complain.
        But to return with King and Queen up stairs,
We find no miserie can eaqual theirs,
They run the gantlet, 'twixt the pittious noyse, 70
Of ladys sighs, and wretched colonells crys.
Now though ones heart below did less relent,
Or that one charity was less intent,
Cause misery partly, is their element.
But who can see the beautyfull and brave 75
Shed tears, and not a true compassion have:
Than what compassion must our Royal pair,
Have for the sufferings oth' brave and fair,
Whose very souls compos'd of pitty are.
And as the smallest member never akes, 80
But presently the head therof partakes,
With what regret, none but themselves can know,
They say they've nought but pitty to bestow.
How hard it is, to souls sublime and great,
When heart and fortune's disproportionate, 85

Line 61. **Boyn's unluckey flood:** in 1690, the troops of James II lost a major battle near the Boyne River, Ireland.

This is a mighty misery indeed,
When Royal hearts, do for their subjects bleed,
Because they can't assist them in their need.
The suppliants seeing they have nought to give,
Not for their own, but their Lords griefs they grieve,　90
And for his sake wish they cou'd cease to live.
Thus mutual kindness, mutual griefs create,
As lovers who love most, are most unfortunate.
　　Now let's consider, shall we follow yet
Toth' toilett, bedchamber, or cabbinet:　　　　95
And hear the ladys represent with tears,
The case of such, or such petitioners,
In stead of deckings, put the Queen on grief
How to accomplish this or that relief,
Or on the other side, the just and good,　　　100
King, preaching up some Ninth beatitude,
No, let's begone, for here we can't supply,
Our selves with meat, or loaves that multiply.
People by poor instructers, ne'er are mov'd,
But the rich preacher's, follow'd, prais'd and lov'd　105
For so deprav'd, fraternal love is grown,
We love none for their own sakes, but our own,
　　Then let us to the garden go and there,
Instead of dinner take some tarras air
With thred-bare officers, whose ragged cloathes,　110
Capp'd shoos, no shirts, black cravats, tatter'd hoase,
Appear like Luxembourgs old beaten drums,
Or Diepe with its two thousand English bombs,

Line 89. **suppliants:** humble petitioners for aid.

Line 95. **toilett:** dressing table. **cabbinet:** small, private room.

Line 101. **Ninth beatitude:** Jesus said: "Blessed are ye when men shall revile you and persecute you, and shall say all manner of evil against you falsely, for my sake"; see Matt. 5:11.

Line 103. **loaves that multiply:** Jesus' blessing turned five loaves of bread and two fishes into enough to feed 5,000 people; see Mark 6:38–44.

Line 109. **tarras:** terrace.

Line 111. **Capp'd shoos:** repaired shoes.　　**hoase:** hose, stockings.

And what's more irksome than this poor aray,
They'r allways dun'd, but ne'er have ought to pay.   115
   Instead of lovers meetings, assignations,
Ogling, laughing, talking of new fassions,
Whether this Borgoin lookss best plain or lace'd,
Which patch the pocket-glass says is best place'd
Which periwigg does which face best befit,   120
The cavalier, the bobb, Hispaniolet,
The only study is, where one shou'd dine,
At least to get a crust, or glass of wine.
Thus are we more contemptible by far,
Then old wives tale, old maid, old cavalier.   125

To
my friends who prais'd my Poems,
and at the begining of the little
printed book placed this motto.

——pulcherrima virgo
Incedit, magnâ juvenum stipante catervâ. (Virg.

I doubt not to come safe to glories port,
Since I have such a troop for my escort,
This band of gallant youths, bear me along,

Lines 112–13. **Luxembourgs . . . bombs:** French military leader, François-Henri de Montmorency, Duke of Luxembourg (1628–95), defeated English and Dutch troops at Fleurus (1690) and Neerwinden (1693).   **Dieppe:** town on the northern coast of France, virtually destroyed in attacks by English and Dutch allies (1694).

Line 117. **fassions:** fashions.

Line 118. **Borgoin:** Bourgoigne; section of the jacket at the neck.

Line 120. **periwigg:** wig.

Line 121. **cavalier, the bobb, Hispaniolet:** styles of wigs.

Title. **my friends:** Cambridge University students with whom Barker published *Poetical Recreations* (1688).

Epigraph. **pulcherrima...catervâ:** based on Virgil (70–19 B.C.), *Aeneid* I:496–97, "the most beauteous virgin goes [to the temple] with a vast company of youths thronging around her." This epigraph substituted "virgin" for the queen "Dido" in honor of the unmarried Barker.

Who teach me how to sing, then praise my song,
Such wreaths and branches, they've bestow'd on me, 5
I look like Daphne turn'd into a tree,
Whilst these young sons of Phoebus dance around
And sing the praise of her themselves have crown'd.
Not like those Idole-makers heretofore
Who had no right to praise, much less adore, 10
No justly I a poets honour claim,
'Cause they have powers to make me what I am.
    Ye learned youths, most learned of your time;
Of all your Reverend mothers sons the prime,
Ye gayest, sweetest, gentlest, youths on earth 15
Tell me what constellation rul'd my birth,?
That I'm become copartner of your bays,
And what's more glorious, subject of your praise,
'Twas not for beauty, learning, eloquence,
No, 'twas your vertue, lov'd my innocence, 20
My Rural muse, which never higher aimes,
Than to discourse, of shepherds and their lambs,
Of groves, obscure retreats, and to dispise,
What I deserve not, wealth and dignitys
Your good ness make, these humble fances please, 25
And your own worth supply defects in these.

Line 5. **wreaths and branches:** laurel wreaths to crown the celebrated poet.

Line 6. **Daphne:** in Greek mythology, maiden who was turned into a laurel tree in order to escape the unwanted amorous advances of Apollo.

Line 7. **Phoebus:** Apollo, god of poetry.

Line 17. **bays:** laurel wreath.

Lines 21–23: **Rural Muse . . . retreats:** writing pastorals.

Line 25. **fances:** fancies; notions.

On the death of the
Right honourable the Earl of Exiter.
1700

What Alien is there, ha'n't a pious tear,
To wet the herse of this illustrious Peer,
Then how much more, are we bound to lament,
Our countrys darling, and its ornament.
No less than we, the muses ought to mourn,   5
Whose early wit their science did addorne.
He his ripe years, in greater things imploy'd,
He studyed man, and mankind edify'd
To learn, in divers countrys, he thought fit,
And tought each place, more than he learnt of it.   10
In him abroad, the English worth was known,
And made each foreign excellence his own,
Italian prudence, French civility,
Mix'd with the English magnanimity.
All vertues in his mien, seem'd to unite,   15
And in this union, each one shin'd more bright.
He study'd bookes, but was himself the best,
All learning was concenter'd in his brest:
That who read him, a liberary read,
From Aristotle, to the christian Bede.   20
Riches and honours, he injoy'd such store,
Ambition cou'd not ask of fortune more:

Title. **Earl of Exiter:** John Cecil, fifth earl of Exeter. The Barkers leased agricultural property from the Cecil family, supporters of the House of Stuart, as early as 1662.

Line 2. **herse:** hearse.

Line 6. **wit:** intelligence. **science:** knowledge.

Line 9. **divers:** diverse; numerous.

Line 15. **mien:** manner, appearance.

Line 18. **brest:** breast.

Line 20. **Aristotle:** Greek philosopher (384–322 B.C.).   **Bede:** historian, writer of biblical commentaries, and scholar of Latin and Greek (673–735)

Which wisely he imploy'd to noble ends,
To serve his god, his country, and his friends.
Patron toth' poor, and the unfortunate, 25
Councell toth' rich, example to the great,
An hospitable friend, a generous Lord,
A chearfull welcome, waited his full board.
Two seeming opposits he made agree
The patriots care, the subjects Loyalty. 30
I name him not, as husband, father, son,
Cause each deserves, an elegy alone,
His life was to the world a true receit,
How to live happy, vertuous, wise and great,
　　Then weep mankind, tis just you shou'd do so, 35
　　And with his mourning countess mix your woe.

At the sight of the body
of
Our late gracious sovereign Lord King James 2d
As it lys at the English Monks.

Hic jacet, oft hic jacet poets sing,
Of such who acted many a glorious thing,
But ne'er Hic Jacet Hero, saint, and King.
　　But here lys one, whome all the world must grant,
　　Was prince, and Hero, King, and glorious saint. 5

Line 26. **Councell:** counsel, advisor.

Line 28. **full board:** generous table.

Line 33. **receit:** recipe.

Line 36. **countess:** Anne (ca. 1648–1703), widow of the earl of Exeter.

Title. **English Monks:** the body of James II (d. 16 September 1701) lay in state at the priory church of the English Benedictine monks in Paris.

Line 1. **Hic jacet:** Here lies (Latin).

Line 3. **saint:** self-sacrificing defender of Roman Catholicism, whose blood was thought to have healing powers. Barker wrote that her cancerous growth (probably a cyst) had miraculously detached itself from her body after being touched by a rag that had been dipped in James's blood.

By sacred right, the Diadem he wore,
By right of conquest victors lawrells bore;
Lawrells so verdant, Diadems so bright,
One cou'd not say, which most oblig'd the sight,
Each crown, was by each other, so well grac'd,   10
That each or both, upon his temples place'd,
None cou'd distinguish, which became him best.
So perfectly with Kingly gifts indow'd,
As if cast in the mold, oth' publick good.
Prefer'd the peoples good, in every thing,   15
Himself though king, their patron to the King.
He had strong baises, to support the weight,
Both of the populer, and kingly state,
His well turn'd genius, knew the just extent,
Of Regal power, and rights of Parliment,   20
He knew when to conced, when to controle
How to make all things in their channell role,
He to the body politick was soul.
As King, or Prince, or noble general
Or mearly man, or Englands Admiral,   25
All was exceeding great, brave and august,
In every station, allways James the just.
For though to every vertue he inclin'd,
Yet justice was the minion of his mind,
And in his truth a pattern to mankind,   30
Though glory was the idol of his youth,

Line 6. **sacred right:** divine right of kings.   **Diadem:** both an earthly and heavenly crown.
Line 7. **lawrells:** laurels.
Line 13. **indow'd:** endowed.
Line 17. **baises:** biases; beliefs.
Line 19. **genius:** intelligence.
Line 20. **Parliment:** Many in the English Parliament had opposed the king's power.
Line 25. **mearly:** merely.
Line 26. **august:** lofty.
Line 29. **minion:** dearest friend, favored child.

Yet to this idol he ne'er bow'd his truth,
No courtly intrest or the peoples crys,
Cou'd ever make his truth do sacrifice.
For these and other things, fame ran on score,   35
He was her creditor, and lent her more,
Than all her lowest praises can restore.

    Three kings we read of travail'd from a far,
Conducted by a new form'd glorious star,
But to find one, we shou'd be at a loss,   40
Who left three Kingdoms, guided by a cross,
This was his scepter, and his crown the same,
And thus equip'd a pilgrim he became.
This mighty missioner by heav'n was sent,
For others good his peoples punishment.   45
The peoples sins, and Royal martyrs blood,
For punishment to heav'n cry'd oft and lowd,
But nothing cou'd by heav'ns just hands be done,
Till this our Royal Righteous Lot was gone.
(This righteous prince was to this people giv'n   50
As if it was a stratagem of Heav'n,
T'inhance their crimes, and leave em no excuse,
Who of such mercy, made so ill an use.)
Beside, he cou'd not be at home confin'd
He being made to reign ore all mankind,   55

Lines 31–32. always own'd his Religion [Author's note.]

Line 35. **ran on score:** accumulated debts.

Line 38. **Three kings:** Magi or wise men who followed a star to the birth site of Christ; see Matt. 2:1–12.

Line 41. **three Kingdoms:** England, Scotland, and Ireland. **cross:** the symbol of Christianity, especially Roman Catholicism.

Line 43. **pilgrim:** one who journeys for a holy purpose.

Line 44. **missioner:** missionary.

Line 46. **martyrs blood:** the blood shed by one who has suffered for Christianity.

Line 47. **lowd:** loud.

For when he from his native land was gone,
In every foreign heart, he found a throne,
And mighty Lewis, shar'd with him his own.
This Royal host, receiv'd this Royal gest,
For which all former glories were increas'd,   60
As AEgypts court, was for the patriarch bless'd.
Of his lives travells, this was the last stage,
And now in Heav'n he ends his pilgrimage,
Great in his life, but greater in his death,
In both a true defender of the faith,   65
His vertues future ages shall admire,
Himself a saint, a Martyr was his sire.

A dialogue between
Fidelia and her little nephew,
Martius,
as they walk in Luxembourg.
disguis'd as a shepherdess or country maid

Fidelia
    Why weeps my child, why weeps my dearest boy,
Martius.
    To see you weep, dear aunt, it is I cry,
    Dry but your eyes, mine of themselves will dry,
    Wipe, wipe away those tears, then hugg and buss,
    As you are wont, your little Martius.   5

Line 58. **Lewis:** Louis XIV (1638–1715).

Line 59. **gest:** guest.

Line 61. **patriarch:** Joseph; see Gen. 39:1–6 and 41:38–43.

Line 67. **sire:** Charles I, beheaded in 1649.

Title. **Fidelia:** Barker's literary persona as reflective Catholic. **nephew:** Timon Connock. **Martius:** from *martial,* referring to the Connocks' several generations of military service. **Luxembourg:** gardens in Paris. **shepherdess:** conventional figure of pastoral.

Line 4. **buss:** kiss.

Line 5. **wont:** accustomed to doing.

Then tell me why you left your native land,
And when you took ill fortune by the hand,
For I remember you in better state,
Then tell me how you came unfortunate,
Methinks you've not a shepperdess's mien,   10
Sure you amongst the Rural maids were Queen.
Fid To vertue I too nearly was aly'd
   To have good fortune ever on my side.
   But though we suffer, by hard fortunes froun, ⎫
   A vertuous mind, can never be cast doun,   ⎬   15
   And that I allways shall depend upon.   ⎭
   Now since you ask my fate of former years,
   And what's the cause of present griefs and tears,
   Come sit thee doun, I'll tell thee how ith' fenn,
   We fed our flocks upon the banks of the **Glenn**.   20

        My father and his brother **Cavaliers**,
   Stuck to their king as did their ancestors,
   Wives portions, and paternal means they spent,
   To serve the King against the Parliment,
   Thus for their Loyalty being both undone,   25
   Were force'd to quit the court, the camp, and town,
   They sold their swords and other warlike things,
   As did their wives, their petycotes and rings,
   And therwithall, bought equipage for plows,
   Betook themselves, to mannage sheep and cows,   30

Line 7. **native land:** England.

Line 19. **fenn:** fen; swampy marsh.

Line 20. **Glenn:** river in Lincolnshire, near Barker's home.

Line 21. **Cavaliers:** Royalists, supporters of Charles I (1600–49) and Charles II (1630–85) against Puritan Parliamentarian leaders in the English Civil Wars (1642–49).

Line 23. **wives portions:** dowries. **paternal means:** property inherited from their fathers.

Line 26. **court:** positions at court, including Thomas Barker's reported position as "Secretary to the Great Seal." **camp:** military service.

Line 29. **equipage:** outfittings, including harnesses.

Instead of scarlet, Russet now they wore,
And sheep-hooks were the leading staves they bore,
Free from court factions, and the discontents,
Which dayly rise in Rebell Parliments,
Free from ambitious plotings how to get,   35
This prise amongst the rich, that place amongst the great,
And for their Loyal losses, never felt regrett.
They acted peacefully their homly scean,
And lookers on, thought with a gracefull mien.
Where fortune wou'd not with their wish comply,   40
They made their wish bear fortune company,
Here we as in a little Can'an liv'd,
And for our former manna never griv'd.
Here milk and hony, did not only flow,
But we'd a little kind of Eden too,   45
Well furnish'd with good fruit, fresh herbs, gay flowers,
Fountains and grass-plats, walks, and shady bowers,
Yet more by nature, than by art was dress'd
And our content made of its fruits a feast.

    A good old tippling swain, was gardner here,   50
He'd been my unkles corporal ith' war,
This good old man, wou'd wond'rous storys tell,
Of what at Nasby, and Edge-hill befell,

Line 31. **Russet:** coarse, homespun woollen cloth of reddish-brown color, associated with peasants and rural folk.

Line 32. **staves:** lances.

Line 36. **prise:** prize.

Line 38. **scean:** scene.

Line 42. **Can'an:** Canaan or Promised Land, where Moses and his followers arrived after 40 years of wandering in the wilderness; see Gen. 15:18, Exod. 6:5–8.

Line 43. **manna:** bread that God rained from heaven, sustaining the Israelites in the wilderness; see Exod. 16:15, 18:31–35.

Line 44. **milk and hony:** milk and honey, symbolic of peace and plenty in the Promised Land; see Exod. 3:17.

Line 45. **Eden:** Paradise; see Gen. 2–3.

Line 50. **tippling:** tending toward excessive consumption of alcohol. **swain:** rustic.

At York and Woster, and I know not where,
At this place wounded, that a prisoner.   55
Then with a pack of cards, he wou'd make out,
This siege, that fight, and which side had the rout,
This made us children, all such Cavaliers,
We took the Parliments, for mear Bugg-bears,
The solemn festival of Chrismass day,   60
Fell short of his dear twenty ninth of may.
He'd skipt'd about the Bon-fire like a boy,
And spight of bald-pate burn his cap for joy:
Then out He'd pull his pipe, and play theron,
(Whilst we all danc'd) **The King injoys his own**.   65
Thus we pass'd on our days in harmless mirth,
Till time and fate, gave my misfortunes birth,
But therwithall I will not discompose,
Thy tender mind, which yet no sorrow knows.
Martius,
    Your tale's so pleasing, I cou'd wish to be,   70
    Nothing but ears, and you all mouth to me,
    Then pray tell on. ———
Fidelia
    My brother dy'd, ———   she weeps
    ———That clebrated man,
    A gallant youth, philosopher and swain,   75

Lines 53–54: **Nasby...Woster:** battles in the Civil Wars. **Nasby:** 14 June 1645, defeat of Royalist troops by Parliament. **Edge-hill:** 23 October 1642, first major battle and Royalist victory. **York:** April–June 1644, beseiged site where Charles I had set up his court. **Woster:** Worcester; garrison city and site of heavy Royalist losses in 1651.

Line 57. **rout:** victory.

Line 59. **mear:** mere. **Bugg-bears:** hobgoblins, imaginary beings invoked to frighten people.

Lines 61–63. the day of the Restauration [Author's note.] Charles II assumed the throne on 29 May 1660, thereby marking the restoration of the monarchy. **spight of bald-pate:** in spite of being bald.

Line 64. **pipe:** musical wind instrument.

Line 65. **The King injoys his own:** a Royalist tune.

Line 73. **brother:** Edward Barker (1650–75?).

Such depth of learning, grac'd his natural parts
That Aristotle might of him learn'd arts,
Nought but his vertue, cou'd his wit exceed,
In fine, he no accomplishment did need.
His vast fraternal love, one cannot tell,   80
Only on earth, none ever lov'd so well,
That vertue which beyond example drives,
Can only be describ'd by negatives,
Then wonder not, that I again repeat,
No love was e'er so true, pure, perfect, great.   85
Him in my thoughts I plac'd as my defence,
'Gainst course of nature took my parents hence,
'Gainst their lives clue was spun, then by his thred,
Through this worlds labrinth, I thought to be led,
But Heav'n depriv'd me of his needfull aid.   90
My parents for his death, so much did grieve,
That long they cou'd not this great loss survive.
Now did my life, a different manner role,
Since Heav'n gave this new byas to the bowl,
My flocks decay'd, my barns and houses fell,   95
My lands grew barran, in fine nought went well,
Thus helpless, friendless, destitute forlorn,
'Twixt debters, creditors, and lawyers torn,
I wander'd on, in hopes of better chance,
Till curssed orange drive us all to France,   100
And here we wander vagabons alone,
Not knowing any, or to any known,
And all methinks do our acquaintance shun.

Line 77. **Aristotle:** Greek philosopher.

Lines 88–89: **thred . . . labrinth:** in Greek myth, referring to the thread that Ariadne used as a guide to lead Theseus out of the treacherous maze of Minos at Crete.

Line 94. **byas to the bowl:** term at lawn bowling, referring to the path of the ball.

Line 96. **barran:** barren. **nought:** nothing.

Line 100. **curssed orange:** William of Orange.

But honour, conscience, vertue brought us here,
We cannot sink, since they the vessell steer.   105

    In this discourse, little Martius
    falls asleep in her lap

Hah fast asleep-that leaden footed god,
Has o'er his temples stretched his heavy rod;
They say that sleep's, death representative,
In him's so lovely who wou'd wish to live,
Tis true, his glittering eyes, and noble grace,   110
Are hidden, by sleeps curtains o'er his face,
But innocence is seat'd in their place.
His moving lips more sweet and beautious are,
Than roses wafted by a western air,
What is't those pritty lips talk in thy sleep,   115
Tis somthing sad, because it makes thee weep,
Martius asleep
    'Twere happiness to be a shepherds-boy,
    If prid did not that happines distroy.
Fidelia
    This truth thou'st found, in sleeps obscure recess,
    That pride imbitters all our happiness.   120
'Tis not true want, that this or that we crave,
But pride makes us think we too little have.
For human nature's by few things supply d,
If we'd lay superfluitys asside.
This truth, some power does to this child reveal   125
As he lys dreaming on the griefs we feell.
The bright rays of thy soul peirce the dark cloud
of thy low fortune, which its glories shroud,

Line 106. **leaden-footed god:** god of sleep.

Line 118. **prid:** pride.

Line 124. **superfluitys:** that which is unnecessary.

So a fair plant in its small seed remains,
Till proper time, its beautious leavs expands   130
Thy noble race, has not a fairer sprout,
If fortune do but shine to bring it out,
Yet I'd not have thy honour grow too fast,
Lest it obnoxious be, to envys blast.
Wake, wake my sweet, and dry each trickling tear,   135
Thy worth methinks proclaimes good fortune near.

On the great cares,
And small injoyments of parents.

How short and transient joys of parents are,
And those too, mix'd, with anxius pains and care,
No sooner is the infant from the pap
Teeth, slabbering-bib, the nursses armes and lap,
The cradle, going-stool, and all the noys   5
That rise from needfull, and from needless crys,
But from its parents armes it must be took
And put where it may learn to hate its book.
Sent here and there to colledges and schools,
To learn to be irreguler by rules.   10
From thence to travail, or to serve ith war,
All which, serves but t'augment the parents care,
Lo every step, and station of their lives,
Whether in making fortunes geting wives,
What's troublesome, toth' parents still arives.   15
Their hopes are doubtfull, but their cares are sure,
Their joys are passant, but their griefs indure.

Line 2. **anxius:** Barker's original had a bar over the u.

Line 3. **pap:** a nursing nipple or soft food for infants.

Line 11. **travail:** work.

Reflection on dreams

A dream to me seems a misterious thing,
Whate'er the naturalists for causes bring,
Whilst sleeps dull fetters, our frail bodys ty,
Th'enlarged soul finds plesant company,
With fellow spirits, midnight revells make,   5
Where things forgot they see, and things to come forespeak,
Some times in figures, and in dances they,
Present to us th events, oth' coming day,
Dull things, by th' grave currant, brisk ones byth' minoet.
Sometimes they mount, allmost toth' place of bliss,   10
Then doun again into the deep abys,
With such agillity and ease they go,
Compar'd to which the lightning moves but slow,
Yet as they pass, all things they see and know.
But as a country lady after all,   15
The pleasures of th' exchange, plays court an mall,
Force'd to return, to her old country seat,
T''instruct her hinds, and make em earn their meat,
So comes the soul home to her course retreat.

The lovers Elesium,
Or fools Paradice: a dream.

Sleeping byth' river Glen, methought I found,
My self into a pleasant labrinth wound,

Line 2. **naturalists:** natural philosophers, who seek rational reasons for all phenomena.

Line 3. **fetters:** bindings, restrictions.

Line 9. **grave currant:** slow pace. **minoet:** minute and minuet, a dance.

Line 16. **exchange:** New Exchange, London, popular site of many shops, including specialty clothing shops. **mall:** The Mall, fashionable promenade near St. James's Park.

Line 18. **hinds:** agricultural workers.

Title. **Elesium:** Elysium; in Greek myth, home of the blessed after death.

Line 1. **Glen:** river in Lincolnshire, near Barker's home.

Line 2. **labrinth:** labyrinth, after the palace designed by Daedalus for King Minos of Crete; a complex and confusing maze.

Whether the pritty windings of the stream,
Or love or youth, presented me this dream,
Or my good genius shew'd me here my fate,   5
How my lives steps, shou'd be all introcate.
Or what original it matters not,
But for a while, I all my griefs forgot.
    These turnings all were strew'd with flaming darts,
Knots, chains, devices, verses, bleeding hearts   10
Lo here one meets, all sorts of company,
Old, young, gay, sad, wise, mad, reserv'd and free.
A gentle youth I found amongst the rest,
Whom I thought mortal, and to him addres'd,
Asking him divers questions of this place,   15
To which he answer'd, he a stranger was,
Having but latly left mortality,
Alas (said I) what envi'ous malady,
Brought you so soon - - - - - -
(Ah me) said he) it was a hapless fate,   20
I lov'd but lov'd a shee false and ingrate:
Who having promis'd me her faith and love,
Like all her sex, did most unconstant prove,
Then to devert my griefs, I took the field,
And at Sedge-more deservedly was kill'd: 25
But e'er I dy'd, I did in mercy trust,
I saw my guilt, and pray'd for **James the Just**,

Line 5. **good genius:** good spirit.

Line 6. **introcate:** intricate.

Line 9. **darts:** darts of Cupid that cause one to fall in love.

Line 10. **devices:** intricate designs.

Line 15. **divers:** diverse; numerous.

Line 25. **Sedge-more:** Sedgemoor, site of the July 1685 military defeat of James, duke of Monmouth (1649–85), illegitimate son of Charles II, who attempted to wrest the throne from James II.

Line 27. **James the Just:** James II.

Mor'over did forgive, that faitless she,
Who made me actor, in this tragidy.
This my **Repentance** God receiv'd so well,   30
That with the others, I went not to Hell.

    In this discourse we many turnings pass'd
And to a statly bower ariv'd at last.
With entrys turns, and doors of strange device, ⎫
And lest one shou'd the propper entrance miss,   ⎬   35
Upon the gate was writ fools paradice.   ⎭
All who live here, are given up to folly,
Some mad with mirth, and some with melancholy
Some read Romances, some love-letters writ,
Some curss'd their chain, and some were fond of it.   40
Some ly'd and swore, with such audacious mien,
One wou'd have thought they'd Salamancas been,
Generaly in talk they were profuse,
As the french tongue, in letters of no use,
But of all things that place their humer hits,   45
Who spight of sence will needs set up for wits.
Lord Majors and aldermen in weighty chains,
The emblems of their riches, and their brains,
Thought to link their mistresses theirby,
But little mrs Prudence was too sly,   50
She took their glittering presents in good part,
Mean while to Jobe the 'prentice gave her heart.
The men of titles, hop'd thereby to gain,

Line 33. **statly bower:** distinguished habitation.

Lines 42–44. oats was a dr of salamance [Author's note.] **oats:** Titus Oates, conceiver of the "Popish Plot." **salamance:** referring to Salamanca, Spain, where Oates falsely claimed to have earned a degree of Doctor of Divinity.

Line 45. **humer:** humor; mood.

Line 46. **spight of sence:** lacking in good sense. **wits:** men of intelligence.

Line 47. **aldermen:** representatives of sections of the city.

Line 48. **link:** impress. **theirby:** thereby.

Line 52. **'prentice:** apprentice.

The Cyty heireses, but hope'd in vain.
For now a days, few vallew Ladyship.   55
Since in th' Exchange it is so very cheap.
A *Style* is but a mere impertinence,
To which belongs no hedge or other fence.
Balk'd maids, their habbits, hair, and faces tore,
Some sigh'd and wept, and some dire vengance swore,   60
All was confusion here, they'd but one rule,   ⎫
That none must enter, but must play the fooll: ⎬
That justly one might call it follys school.   ⎭
I ask'd em, what Religion they had there,
And if there any priests, or altars were,   65
'Twas answer'd; lovers, to each other pray'd,
The brightest altar, was the fairest maid.
For consecrated persons, ne'er come there,
Nor such who place their happiness in prair,
To heav'n they go, who use those tallants well,   70
Or for th' abuse, directly into Hell.
Then here me thought, I wou'd no longer stay,
And streight an angry power snatch'd me away.
He made me a stupendious mountain climb,
Where I beheld ith' retrospect of time,   75
That very place, that seat, that pleasant shade,
Where I a contract, with the muses made,
Renouncing allthings, for their frutless bough,
And on a smooth bark'd ash, writ this my vow,
And though some years were past, since, it was writ, ⎫ 80
Yet time had not obliterated it.   ⎬
And still methinks I can the words repeat.   ⎭

Line 55. **vallew:** value.

Line 56. **Exchange:** London site of commercial transactions.

Line 59. **Balk'd:** discarded. **habbits:** clothing.

Line 70. **tallants:** talents.

Line 74. **stupendious mountain:** Parnassus, sacred to the Muses.

The contract with the muses
writ on the bark of a shady ash-tree,

Methinks these shades, strange thoughts suggest,   85
Which heat my head, and cool my brest,
And mind me of a lawrell crest.

Methinks I hear the muses sing,
And see em all dance in a ring,
And call upon me to take wing.   90

We will say they assist thy flight,
Till thou reach fair Orindas height,
If thou canst this worlds follys slight.

We'll bring this to our bright aboads,
Amongst the Heroes, and the Gods   95
If thou and wealth, can be at odds,

Then gentle maid, cast off thy chain,
Which links thee to thy faithless swain,
And vow a virgin to remain.

Write, write, thy vow upon this tree,   100
By us it shall recorded be,
And thou fam'd to eternity.

When I these harmless lines had read,
Methought my uncouth guardian said,
                 - - - - - - unluckey maid,   105
    Since, since thou has the muses chose,

Line 87. **lawrell crest:** laurel crown, symbol of poetry.

Line 92. **Orindas height:** the moral and artistic excellence of Katherine Philips (1632–64), the "matchless Orinda," celebrated poet and translator.

Hymen and fortune are thy foes,
  Thou shalt have Cassandras fate,
  In all thou sayst unfortunate,
  The god of wit, gave her this curss   110
  And Fortune gives thee, that and worse,
  In all thou doest, though ne'er so good,
  By all the world misunderstood.
  In best of actions, be dispis'd,
  And fooles and knaves, above thee pris'd. 115
  Foes like serpents his and bite thee,
  All thy friends agree to slight thee.
  Love and lovers, give thee pain.
  For they and thou shallt love in vain,
  Either death shall from thee take em, 120
  Or they thee, or thou forsake em,
  Thy youth and fortune, vainly spend,
  And in thy age, have not a friend,
  Thy whole life pass in discontent,
  In want, and wo, and banishment. 125
  Be broken under fortunes wheell,
  As proverb goes, lead Apes in Hell.
At this harangue, my grief was so extream,
That I awak'd and glad it prov'd a dream.

Line 107. **Hymen:** Greek god of marriage.

Line 108. **Cassandra's fate:** in Greek myth, condemned by Apollo to have the gift of prophecy but never to be believed.

Line 110. **god of wit:** Apollo.

Line 116. **his:** hiss.

Line 127. **lead Apes in Hell:** suggesting that women who do not marry will inevitably go to hell and that they will precede even the brutish apes. "'Tis an old proverb, and you know it well,/That women dying maids lead apes in hell." Author unknown, *The London Prodigal* 1.2 (1605).

The Virgins paradise
a dream.

As I upon a bank of lillys lay,
With thoughts as pure, and innocent as they: }
To gentle slumbers, we became a prey.

    I dream't that I'd a pair of wings to fly.
Which carryed me above th' Etherial sky,   5
Above the spheres, above the poles,
Allmost to th' region, of the blessed souls.
Each planet to its house invited me,
But chiefly venus, Sol, and mercury.
But I to them excus'd my self so well,   10
By what instinct push'd on, I cannot tell, }
But I pass'd safe where thousand others fell.
Thus having pass'd each planet sphere and zoan,
And all which one day, shall be melted doune,
Methought I wander'd in a Region vast,   15
And to a statly palace came at last,
But to discribe, the wonders of this place,
Is quite beyond the reach of human race
Unless, they'r tought, by cherubins to sing,
Or have a pen, drop'd from an angells wing.   20
But what Ideas in my thoughts remain,
I'll tell in such a method as I can.

    Before this palace, was a statly gate,
But e'er that one, cou'd enter in therat,
One must pass through sev'n porches on a row,   25
The first of which, is arch'd so very low, }
That to get in, one very much must bow.

Line 7. **region . . . souls:** Elysium, home of the blessed in Greek myth.

Line 9. **venus, Sol, and mercury:** three deities in Roman mythology. Venus: goddess of love. Sol: the sun. Mercury: the messenger god.

Line 25. the seven vertues [Author's note.] **seven vertues:** faith, hope, charity, fortitude, prudence, justice, and temperance.

Line 26. faith [Author's note.]

No sooner, I assay'd to enter here,
But and old portress to me did appear.
Of looks devine, in wond'rous garments dress'd,   30
Crowns on her head, and crosses on her brest.
She told me if I'd not be veil'd by her,
Nothing so certain but I'd grossly err.
Not only so, but I shou'd swallow'd be,
In that three corner'd gulph I there might see,   35
Then looking in, I saw the gulph turn round,
And saw withall I cou'd not scape be'ing drownd,
Then I resing'd me to her as I ought,
And through the porches, and the gate was brought.
When I was in, good God, what wond'rous joys!   40
What pleasures all my sences did surprise,
All was vast raptures, and strong extasies.
Nor is it strange, where Angells in full quires,
Sing Alalujas to celestial Lyers.
The musick of the sphers compar'd to this,   45
Are but like huzzas of rude prentices.
The ground, (I mean) the place whereon they tread,
Is of soft clou'ds with stars imbrodered,
The curling lambent flames, appear above
Pure and asspiring as celestial love,   50
From hence the Angells take immortall fire,
When with gods love, they mortall hearts inspire.
Perfum'd the air, which stifles not but chears,

Line 29. the church [Author's note.]

Line 32. **be veil'd:** take the vows of a nun.

Line 35. the trinity [Author's note.] **trinity:** Father, Son, Holy Ghost.

Line 38. **resing'd:** resigned.

Line 43. **quires:** choirs.

Line 44. **Allalujas:** Aleluias; Latin for "praise be to God." **Lyers:** lyres.

Line 46. **huzzas:** noisy greetings. **prentices:** apprentices.

Line 48. **imbrodered:** embroidered.

Line 49. **lambent:** passing delicately.

And all the water, made of virgins tears,
For all the tears, which are by virgins wept,   55
With resignation here are choicely kept,
Which make clear fountains, and immortal springs,
Where angells bath their fatigated wings,
And in this court, were many a curious one,
Cut out of rubys, pearl, and jasper stone.   60
Storys carv'd, with many a rare conceit,
To represent the fate of those who wept,
Some for dead parents, some for cruell ones,
Amongst whome, Jepthas daughter makes her moans,
And many who in monesterys dy'd,   65
Not for devotion, but their mothers pride.
Who hide their daughters to hide their own age,
Mean time spend what shou'd make their marriage.
Large were the streams, which helpless orphans mourn,
Betwixt false guardians, and fals Lawyers torne,   70
But that stream was the greatest of them all
Which from balk'd lovers, took original.
I thousand other raritys saw there,
Which were too tedious, for me to declare.
If my capacity cou'd reach so far.   75
What languages there they spake I cannot tell,
But there I thought, I understood it well,
What e'er it was, I'm sure it was but one
For Babells sotish jargon; there's not known,
Foolls that we are, nay mad, or somthing worse,   80
To pride our selves in what's mankinds great, curss.
For pride of Languages, and cloaths, the same,
Is being proud of punishment and shame,

Line 58. **fatigated:** fatigued.

Line 61. **conceit:** notion.

Line 64. **Jeptha:** a judge of Israel who sacrificed his daughter to keep a rash vow; see Judg. 11–12.

Line 79. **Babells sotish jargon:** confused, inarticulate speech, God's punishment of the citizens of Babel for presuming to build a tower reaching Heaven; see Gen. 11:1–11.

For diffrent tongs our Babell folly tell,
And Cloaths shew forth the cause for which we fell.   85
But to return; I march'd up to the gate,
Which opens to the virgins Room of state,
Before this gate, were two large banners spread ⎫
On which heavn's conquest were imbrodered, ⎬
For which those maids their due thanksgiving paid. ⎭   90
And those who were the banners for that day,
Were Sedge-more fight, and how Gray ran away.
How the Kings guards, made there the Rebells bleed,
One wou'd have thought the blood ran down indeed.
And all the rest which at that place befell,   95
Which I not minded 'cause I knew it well,
And now was with an eager longing frought,
Of seeing what can't enter human thought,
They briskly shut the door against my face,
Saying that mortals there cou'd have no place,   100
At this repulse, dispite so fill'd my brest,
That I awak'd, and so lost all the rest.

Reflections on mr. Cowleys words,
The Muses fleece lys dry.

Tis that unluckey sentance which has lost ⎫
More hearts than wou'd have conquer'd Ceasors host ⎬
It is to buding Loyalty a frost, ⎭
And what's yet worse, it ever must remain,
unkindness to a poet's dy'd in grain,   5
If poets neither drink nor porrige have,

Line 92. **Sedge-more:** Sedgemoor, site of the July 1685 defeat of James, duke of Monmouth.
Gray: Lord Grey of Warke, notorious for political intrigues and an affair with his sister-in-law,
was a good friend and advisor to Monmouth; his troops were easily routed at Sedgemoor.

Title. **Cowley:** Abraham Cowley (1618–67), playwright and lyric poet. **The Muses fleece lys
dry:** "And upon the quickened Ground, / The fruitful seed of Heaven did brooding lye, / And
nothing but the muses fleece was dry," "The Complaint," lines 72–74. Cowley's Muse accuses
the melancholy and aged poet of not having met his artistic potential because he has pursued
worldly matters.

Line 2. **Ceasor:** the Roman emperor, Julius Caesar.

Line 6. **porridge:** a thick soup.

They will not cough, but they'll talk in their grave,
Tis ominous to treat a poet ill,
As tis our merry chimny guests to kill
A poet like a cricket where he comes,   10
Bodes good or ill, as he findes warmth or crums.
Perhaps one cause, of mischief to mankind,
Poets and saints, till dead no kindness find,
The world admir'd, this mighty Cowleys wit
But more admir'd, he had not bread to eat,   15
Not only his, but Hudibras's name,
Serves to immortalize mans crying shame,
In true necessity his days he pass'd,
And by the parish, was inter'd at last.

A song

When poor Galaecia aged grew,
   Young Strephon in his prime,
The nosgay which to her was due,
   Poor nymph she gave to him,

Which coldly he receiv'd and sed,   5
   Alas I her bemoan,
This nosgay's like her maiden-head
   The roses are o'er blown.

Line 9. swallows and crickets, are not to be kill'd [Author's note.]

Line 16. **Hudibras's:** referring to Samuel Butler (1613–80), author of the satire, *Hudibras* (1663, 1664, 1678).

Line 19. **parish:** the parish was responsible for burying paupers.

Line 2. **Strephon:** Bosvil, the lover who caused Galesia such apprehension in *Love Intrigues.*

Line 3. **nosgay:** nosegay; bouquet of flowers.

Line 5. **sed:** said.

Line 7. **maiden-head:** virginity.

Line 8. **o'er blown:** old, with petals fallen off.

Index of First Lines of Poems

This index lists poems and poem fragments by Barker or presumed to be by her in the Galesia novels and poems printed from part two of the Magdalen manuscript.

331